Research Methods *in* Crime, Justice, *and* Social Problems

Research Methods *in* Crime, Justice, *and* Social Problems

A Mixed Methods Approach

Second Edition

Mark M. Lanier
University of Alabama

Lisa T. Briggs
Western Carolina University

New York Oxford
OXFORD UNIVERSITY PRESS

Oxford University Press is a department of the University of Oxford. It furthers the University's objective of excellence in research, scholarship, and education by publishing worldwide. Oxford is a registered trade mark of Oxford University Press in the UK and certain other countries.

Published in the United States of America by Oxford University Press
198 Madison Avenue, New York, NY 10016, United States of America.

For titles covered by Section 112 of the US Higher Education Opportunity Act, please visit www.oup.com/us/he for the latest information about pricing and alternate formats.

Library of Congress Cataloging-in-Publication Data

Names: Lanier, Mark, author. | Briggs, Lisa T., author.
Title: Research methods in crime, justice, and social problems : a mixed methods approach/Mark M. Lanier, University of Alabama, Lisa T. Briggs, Western Carolina University.
Other titles: Research methods in criminal justice and criminology
Description: Second edition. | New York : Oxford University Press, [2019] | Includes bibliographical references and index.
Identifiers: LCCN 2018005877 (print) | LCCN 2018006667 (ebook) | ISBN 9780190694487 (ebook) | ISBN 9780190694432 (pbk.)
Subjects: LCSH: Criminal justice, Administration of–Research. | Criminology–Research.
Classification: LCC HV7419.5 (ebook) | LCC HV7419.5 .L36 2019 (print) | DDC 364.072/1–dc23
LC record available at https://lccn.loc.gov/2018005877

Contents

Inserts vii
Preface viii

Chapter 1
Why Research at All? 1
The History of Research 6
Good, Yet Critical, Science 10
Research Distinctions 12
Critical Thinking Exercises 26

Chapter 2
The Stages of Research: A General Overview 27
Step One: Selecting a Research Topic 28
Step Two: Identifying a Testable Research Question 32
Step Three: Finding Research 35
Step Four: The Literature Review 41
Step Five: Research Design 43
Step Six: Data Collection and Variable Coding 49
Step Seven: Data Analysis 51
Step Eight: Reporting of Results 52
Step Nine: Conclusion and Limitations 52
Final Suggestions 53
Critical Thinking Exercises 54

Chapter 3
Research Ethics 56
The Quest for a Perfect Study 57
Common Ethical Principles 58
Human Research Protection Program 59
Institutional Review Boards 60
Ethical Guidelines 64
Other Ethical Notes 76
The (Ever-Increasing) Role of the IRB 76
Ethically Questionable Studies 78
Final Thoughts 87
Critical Thinking Exercises 88

Chapter 4
Validity and Reliability: Threats to Research Integrity 89
Validity and Reliability 91
Types of Validity 97
Other Research Threats 119
Critical Thinking Exercises 121

Chapter 5
Qualitative Research Strategies 122
Historical Synopsis of Qualitative Research 123
Requisite Qualitative Research Tools 126
Field Research 127
Other Types of Qualitative Research 129
Factors Influencing the Qualitative Data Collection Process 152
Summary 157
Critical Thinking Exercises 158

Chapter 6
Research Designs and Survey Research 159
Operationalization and Coding 163
Composite Measures 165
Choosing a Research Design 166
Experimental Research 168

Experimental, Quasi-Experimental, and Pre-Experimental Designs 175
Other Research Strategies 184
Survey Research 189
Summary 199
Critical Thinking Exercises 200

Chapter 7
Mixed Methods 201
Illustrations of Mixed Methods 212
Mixed Methods for Program Evaluation 220
Steps to Mixed Methods Research 222
Critical Summary of the Mixed Methods Approach 224
Summary 225
Critical Thinking Exercises 226

Chapter 8
Sampling Strategies 227
Probability or Nonprobability Samples? 231
Critical Thinking Exercises 252

Chapter 9
Elementary and Intermediate Quantitative Data Analysis 253
Basic Quantitative Analysis 255
Univariate and Descriptive Statistics 260
Intermediate Data Handling: Bivariate and Multivariate Statistical Analysis 266
Bivariate Statistics 266
Frequency Distributions 267
Multivariate Statistics 277
Summary 280
Critical Thinking Exercises 281

Chapter 10
Qualitative Data Analysis 282
Critique of Causality 283
Traditional Qualitative Analysis 293
Contemporary Statistical Qualitative Analysis 299
Mixed Methods Analysis 300
Critical Thinking Exercises 301

Chapter 11
Beyond Research: An Aid to Writing Success 302
Plagiarism 303
Publication Manual of the American Psychological Association (APA) 305
Effective Writing Practices 307
Becoming a More Professional Writer 309
Writing Tip Summation 320
Critical Thinking Exercises 322

Glossary 324
References 334
Index 337

Inserts

4.1 History and Other Threats to Research: The Stage Is Set Wendy L. Hicks, PhD 99
4.2 Regression to the Mean and Owning Some Chumps William R. Smith, PhD 109
5.1 Interviewing "Role Play" Doreen Morici 136
5.2 Reimagining and Remapping the Gendered Geography of Human Trafficking: Surveying Documentary and Fictional Films Christine Ivie, MS 142
6.1 Formulating Hypotheses Christiaan Bezuidenhout, PhD 170
7.1 A Practical Lesson from the Assessing Police Use of Force Policies and Outcomes Project Eugene A. Paoline III, PhD and University of Central Florida Orlando, Florida and William Terrill, PhD Michigan State University 207
7.2 Werther Effect in School Shooter Events? Examining Potential Copycat Behavior D. R. Hughes D. J. Griffin, & M. J. Egnoto 215
8.1 How Institutional Review Board (IRB) Standards Vary between Types of Universities Amber Perenzin, MS 238
10.1 The (Insurmountable?) Divide between Qualitative and Quantitative Methodologies David Polizzi, PhD, MA, LCAC 286

Preface

This is the second edition of the original mixed methods book published in 2014. Our original objective was for a short, simple to read, yet comprehensive, book about research methods. Based on reviews we successfully met that goal; however there is always room for improvement and primarily based on student and faculty feedback we have made several significant changes: we have broadened the appeal to include additional academic disciplines, we have added color to the text to enhance visual appeal, we have enhanced the critical thinking skills exercises and improved the free, open access website.

Importantly we have retained the original features that made the book unique and successful. The original text was written primarily for students in the social sciences who examine crime and deviance, generally students of criminal justice and criminology. Therefore, most of the original examples and illustrations were from those disciplines. However, many of the faculty who adopted, reviewed and assigned the original book were from disciplines outside criminal justice and criminology. Consequently, the primary change, and improvement, is the inclusion of numerous illustrations and examples from other disciplines. Furthermore, increasingly academic boundaries are blurred and quite often researchers from different disciplines collaborate with one another, so this multidisciplinary approach is beneficial for the advancement of science and solving social problems. This is particularly relevant with mixed methods research since interdisciplinary research teams are often employed. Furthermore, research methods vary very little between the social sciences; students of sociology, public health, psychology, interdisciplinary studies, political science, emergency and disaster management, and many others will find it useful.

As we argue throughout this book, the use of rigorous research methods is critically important for individuals, institutions, society, and the planet itself. For example, the often illegal overfishing of certain species may lead to depletion of ocean fisheries which will have global consequences. While illegal fishing appears just as a criminal justice issue, it is very interdisciplinary. The sciences, which research methods are based on, greatly contributed to humans' ability to fish wide areas for long periods of time, albeit with disastrous long-term results. Yet at the individual level you may enjoy fishing and have "scientifically" determined the best bait, time, and location to pursue your hobby. Crime, environmental health, law, political science, geography, and criminology are all at the heart of the example—since who controls the world's resources? How are the resources protected? Who should protect them? Who has jurisdiction? How will the depletion of fish affect human health, ocean resources, and the overall food chain? How can fishing, far from any shore or national border be policed? Is preservation of natural resources the responsibility of self-appointed groups like Greenpeace in the absence of effective government intervention? Or, are groups like Greenpeace criminal for interfering with commerce? The research questions to be asked and addressed from this one example are vast and can be targeted from many different academic disciplines. Science can be at the individual level, such as how a person who enjoys fishing has "scientifically" determined the best bait, time, and location to pursue the hobby. They have determined the best way to preserve the fish, clean the fish, and perhaps cook the fish. At the same time, science can be at the macro or societal level and must be studied from a multidisciplinary approach. International law and agreement may specify amounts of specific species that can be harvested. The example also introduces issues of personal and societal ethics. Our vegan friends question if we should fish at all.

The ethics involved in overfishing remind us of the importance of critical thinking and ethical discussions in each chapter of this book. In this second version of the text, we have enhanced and challenged readers to consider ethical issues in society and ethical issues between scientist and researchers. For example, if laws are created to benefit society as a whole, then ethical individuals will conform to these rules and regulations. Even in offshore or in remote fishing areas where little chance of government intervention exists, ethical individuals would conform to the regulations for the greater good. Likewise researchers are obligated to adhere to accepted, codified social science research ethics and methodological practice. Future researchers, for example students, may need to be reminded (or taught) what research ethics are. Thorough and accurate research skills, as will be delineated in this text, are relevant and vital. Critical thinking skills are equally important. Critical thinking entails questioning everything, and accepting "facts" after careful, rigorous scientific investigation. This text will show that even the research methods employed need critical contemplation.

We are cognizant of student apprehension. Despite the critical importance of research methods, students often fear it. In conducting the research necessary to write this book alone, more than 50 texts on research methods were reviewed. It was disconcerting to discover how many actually started with a discussion of students who "fear," "dread," "delay," and so forth, a course in research methods. Quite often, students will delay taking this course until their final semester, which necessarily inhibits their ability to perform well in other classes absent the important research skills and critical thinking ability. Part of this apprehension to research methods is due to the subject matter being perceived by the student as outside his or her particular field of study in the social sciences.

Unfortunately, the authors of many of the textbooks may also unwillingly create part of the apprehension. This apprehension is unwarranted. Using this text to obtain a basic understanding of research methods should allay your anxieties and bolster your confidence while enhancing your researching and thinking skills. The majority of students will greatly benefit from this course and some will even enjoy the subject. Bear in mind, however, that this course does differ from other courses. Virtually everyone in society has some concept of what social problems exist, they just do not know how to address the problems. For example, one problem unique to "police, courts, and corrections" involves the influence of television programs, movies, and the news media. The addition of internet-based media to the old standbys of broadcast and print media has made it virtually impossible for anyone outside of undeveloped countries to escape a basic knowledge of "police, courts, and corrections." However, with the recent exception of shows like "CSI" and "Dexter," most mass media formats rarely discuss research—and fewer, including "CSI" and "Dexter", do it accurately. Further, do not assume the mass media accurately reflect actual criminal justice practice (Surrette, 1999) any more than the media unbiasedly represents political campaigns. Through our critical thinking exercises, we challenge students to acknowledge these problems and incorporate relevant research methods techniques to address them.

The easy-to-understand, conversational style of writing employed in this book should relieve some of student apprehension. It is intended to provide useful skills as well as explaining the ethical and critical theoretical basis underlying research methods. Also, the students who take research methods sooner, rather than later, will derive more benefit from the course by being able to apply this knowledge to other classes. It is perhaps the most important, vibrant and invigorating subject addressed by university curricula.

While we cover both qualitative and quantitative research methods in this text, we also advocate mixed methods research. Thus, further discussion of the scope of this book is warranted. Prior to the 1960s, qualitative methods (ethno methodology, participant observation, unobtrusive methods, etc.) dominated the social sciences. Two factors changed this focus. One was the desire of many social scientists to have their research taken more seriously, like the conception of the "physical sciences" which used experimental research designs and statistical analysis. The second factor was the advent of personal computers, which made it much easier and faster to manipulate large data sets. Consequently, the research emphasis in the social sciences shifted towards quantitative methods (statistics and large-scale survey research). Despite this shift, qualitative methods remain the preference for some fields of study, and for some researchers, despite often being given second-rate treatment in research methods textbooks and journal publications. The fact existed, and sometimes still does, that journals were more likely to publish quantitative studies.

This disparity needs to be addressed for several reasons. First, the research topic itself should dictate which research method is employed, not the researcher's training or available software. Second, different theoretical paradigms prefer, and often demand, different research methods. Positivists often rely on quantitative methods while postmodernists and critical researchers may lean toward qualitative methods. Often the theoretical perspective of the author dictates which research method is utilized. In this text neither quantitative nor qualitative methods are given preferential coverage; it is hoped each are covered adequately enough to enable students to utilize each method.

Consequently, like the first edition, this book presents what has been termed *mixed methods research*. We move beyond that, however, to include what we term *fluid research*. This is explained in great detail in subsequent chapters, but for now just be aware that research methods are as much an art as a science. In other words, if it were a "science" the same rules would apply to every researcher, in every study, at all times and, therefore, all researchers would be equally dependent on a cookbook formula, or recipe for designing studies. This would lead to little variation, stifle creativity, and generally inhibit research breakthroughs and scientific progress. The reality is that some researchers are brilliant, others are average, and some are poor. What differentiates researchers is intuition and the artistic application of varied research methods (just as some fisherpersons are more accomplished and successful than others). You, even as students, must learn all of these methods to become proficient researchers. Equally important you must be flexible, or FLUID. Fluid research coupled with a mixed methods strategy allows and encourages a variety of decisions to be made at every stage of the research process. This is something that has been missing from most other research methods textbooks.

The whole point of this book is to help you *do* research effectively. The best way to learn something is to actually do it. You can watch mixed martial arts (MMA) or soccer for years, but until you participate in the sport you will only be a spectator, never really appreciate it, and certainly not master the necessary skills. Have you ever watched a televised football game with a former player? If so, you are probably aware that they can turn the volume down and provide better commentary and explanation than most TV announcers (except for those announcers who are former players as well). Research is the same. You will learn more by actually *doing* research projects. This book shows you how.

A NOTE TO STUDENTS

It has been our mutual experience that Research Methods is a course that many students are not overly excited about taking, or have an appreciation for the true value of. It is our hope that with the right textbook (which of course must be read), students will begin to see the significance of the subject matter and can begin to conceptualize research methods as beneficial tools. The basics learned from this book can assist in ALL of your course work, as well as provide career benefits later.

This book is written in a conversational style that should help students disarm anxieties, move beyond simple regurgitation of information, and think critically about science and the research methods used to produce it. Some new terms specific to the subject are introduced, but the book, as much as possible, is devoid of overly technical or verbose language. Learning these new terms will be important to your success, and most students should already appreciate that utilizing a single word to represent an entire process is a convenient way to communicate. For example, consider how people communicate via text messaging: you probably recognize "lol" immediately as "laugh out loud," and soon you will understand words like "operationalization" with similar ease. Just embrace the terms as they come your way, instead of making them more complicated than they are.

Overall, the right attitude will enhance the experience you have in research methods. Use this book to empower yourself. We have considered the factors that our own students have struggled with and have tried to address them in this book. In the next several paragraphs those issues are addressed more specifically.

WHY WE WROTE THE BOOK

There are several reasons we wrote this book. First, student apprehension can be lowered, interest can be increased, math anxiety can be reduced, and critical thinking skills can be enhanced with the right approach in the text (and supplemental materials). We also think it is important to present *each* of the various types of research (qualitative, quantitative and mixed methods) in a single book. Typically, the authors of research methods books predominately align either with one or the other, but do not expose readers sufficiently to all approaches to research. In fact, "mixed methods" is a newer term (although the concept has been used for years) and typically absent in the many existing research methods textbooks, as is fluid research. Third, we believe a restructuring of the order in which the material is presented will be beneficial to students. For example, in this book, unlike many others, the sampling discussion comes after research designs because the type of sample selected is dependent on which research design is utilized. Also, a focus on ethics needs to come earlier rather than later in the book because such standards serve as a guide to all other decisions made.

Through the experiences of teaching research methods we find some students come into the course absent some basic, but important, skills that most books on the topic do not address. For example, not all students are on the same writing level. A solid writing foundation is critical. The inability of students to present their research in a professionally written form is a large barrier to success in a research methods course (or any course, for that matter), so a chapter dedicated to that purpose is included. Neither of us claims to be an English professor, but most students could use some help and confidence building in how to write and, importantly how to *cite* others' work, so we have provided such resources in this text.

Similarly, students are typically not trained in *how* to locate existing research and how to identify quality work from lesser quality. Too often students rely on the internet and fail to note the difference between the more common resources. This text includes a section on the procedures and resources for identifying and locating peer-reviewed research.

Again, part of the motivation in this book's approach is to address obstacles that have existed in our classes (we will continue to discuss those more specifically in the next section). As a result of addressing those barriers through the years, we have developed techniques and material for our own classes that we believe will assist our colleagues in their own courses. We hope that this book and the supplemental materials that accompany it will make the Research Methods course more effective, more productive, less feared, and even fun!

THE APPROACH AND PRIMARY FEATURES

Many reasons exist for students' apprehension of research methods, including their **D**isinterest, **R**elevance **A**rgumentation (viewing statistical skills as detached from the "real world") and **M**ath **A**nxiety (aka ***D.RA.MA.***; Briggs, Brown, Gardner & Davidson, 2009). This **D.RA.MA.** focus is a key differentiating feature of this book. Many college students majoring in the social sciences are *disinterested* in research methods, because often students perceive their degree as not requiring math-based, scientific, research, or quantitative skills. Dealing with disinterest is a related, but different, challenge from dealing with *math anxiety*. While dealing with math anxiety is difficult enough, another potential obstacle arises when students do not appreciate the value or "relevance" of the course they have been forced to take in order to fulfill degree requirements. It is not uncommon for professors teaching research methods or statistics to find themselves addressing complaints from students as to why they have to take the course to begin with, or what research methods have to do with their specific disciplines anyway. This type of obstacle is best understood as *relevance argumentation* (Briggs et. al, 2009).

We will focus on relevance argumentation throughout this book. The very first chapter of this book attempts to help establish for students "why research at all?" As argued throughout this book, the use of rigorous research methods is critically important for individuals, institutions, society, and the planet itself. A goal of this book is to reveal the science associated with many things that are taken for granted. Through detailed examples (e.g., the fishing example above), students can begin to make the connection between social phenomena and ethical, even criminal issues, and see that the intersections with social phenomena, science, ethics, and legal issues are complex, fascinating, and important to understand.

In this book, we attempt to address student relevance argumentation by providing simple (yet often socially complex) examples that students should be able to relate to, such as the ability through research to develop ways to treat and even cure cancer and other disease; we then get students thinking about the benefits of research to all social disciplines. Keeping with the critical aspect, we also challenge students to consider how some of the research advances have also caused problems.

One hallmark of advanced education is the ability to think critically and so, rather than presenting the research methods and concepts in an unquestioned manner, they are offered alongside alternative, critical views for consideration. One of the defining features of an educated individual is the ability to critique, that is, to critically analyze something, rather than simply accepting what one is told or has read. As Aristotle noted, it is the mark of an educated mind to be able to entertain a thought without accepting it. As thinking individuals, students must decide which is "correct," "best," or of "most" value; however, students should recognize that the "best" decision is based on situational, political, and contextual contingencies and will inevitably change. These are value judgments and require flexibility and fluidity. As students (and even instructors) progress as researchers and scholars, the choices they make and the positions they hold may change. This is acceptable, understandable, and inevitable. We encourage students to allow the research problem to dictate the research methods employed rather than letting a certain type of training, the quickest or easiest method, or the opinions of others provide the rationale for choosing a research strategy. A background in research methods that fosters intuition and artistic style, as well as adhering to "science," will provide the most solid research. Ultimately, the answers scholars seek through research may be best ascertained through qualitative methods, quantitative methods, a combination of both, or neither.

It is typical in research methods texts to focus on either quantitative *or* qualitative methodology. Our goal is to develop a text that avoids that segregated approach. It is important that students be equipped with an appreciation of both types of methodology. For example, most current research methods texts allocate only one chapter to qualitative research approaches, and few (to none) acknowledge the possibility of combining both types of methods into one study, often termed *mixed methods*. In this book, focused attention is given to *each* type of methods of research; both the positive and negative aspects of the various approaches are presented with an ultimate goal of fostering students' ability to be critical consumers of information themselves.

Because we include qualitative analysis, some instructors may categorize this as a *qualitative* research methods book. It is not. It is a book that is simply trying to avoid aligning with only one "camp." For example; we dedicate chapters to quantitative data analysis (statistics). Some universities have a two-part course offering: research methods and statistics. In those cases, a two-part process is effective; cover research methods in one and quantitative data analysis in the other. Some programs, however, may only offer the research methods course. Therefore, we believe it is beneficial to at least provide cursory exposure to data analysis for both qualitative and quantitative methods. An overview of statistics does not detract from the equally valuable qualitative methods (qualitative researchers may also rely on statistics). Rather than just a description of the math and equations the statistics chapter is focused more on reading and understanding what the statistics mean. This addition is important in pulling all of the pieces of the puzzle together and will help prepare students for understanding the entire process of research methods and data analysis. This basic understanding of statistics should also help bolster confidence when students read empirical research of others.

Quite often, students will delay taking research methods until their final semester, which inhibits their ability to perform well in other classes because they may be lacking in important research skills and critical thinking abilities. Part of many students' apprehension to research methods is due to the subject matter being outside the customary and widely understood academic disciplines. Some research methods textbooks may unwittingly be creating part of the student apprehension by the *way* the material is presented. With the right text and pedagogical approach, perhaps students will take a methods course sooner in their academic careers. Then, the knowledge base can be applied to other classes, making for a more successful academic experience. It is perhaps the most important, vibrant, and invigorating subject addressed by university curricula.

ORGANIZATION

In order to provide a variety of perspectives, several prominent researchers and colleagues wrote short sections, or inserts, for this book. All the inserts are original and are provided by the best researchers on each subject. Each of these authors has a different *voice* and perspective, which allows for readers to experience variety in research methods. The astute reader will note differences between how qualitative and quantitative researchers write. We purposefully did not edit their work since we desire students to recognize the importance of *voice* and tone.

The book is organized in a logical and, with a few exceptions, traditional manner. The first chapter provides an overview of the history of research methods and introduces why science is important at all. It also presents the various types of research and the changing role of science. It includes examples of how research has improved (and in some cases harmed) social and physical conditions.

The second chapter presents the usual stages associated with conducting a typical research project. The chapter is designed to aid students through these stages and enable them to have a better understanding for conducting research on their own. This chapter provides readers with a basic "map," or conceptualization, of research methods before subsequent chapters diverge into more specific details regarding components of research processes. We believe this overview will empower students by providing a typical approach that is followed when conducting research.

The third chapter focuses on research ethics. Surprisingly, research ethics have not been a formalized part of research for very many years. This chapter begins with a general discussion of ethics, follows with ethics specific to research, and concludes with examples of studies having ethical problems. The role and problems associated with Institutional Review Boards (IRBs) are also articulated.

Chapter 4 examines issues related to validity and reliability. Regardless of the methodology employed, threats to validity and reliability will always be present. This chapter provides a comprehensive discussion of the internal and external validity including subsections of each type (history, maturation, testing, instrumentation, statistical regression, selection, mortality, etc.). Special attention is given to how issues of validity and reliability vary between qualitative and quantitative methods.

Qualitative research strategies are covered in chapter 5, and chapter 6 presents the more common experimental designs and includes a large section on survey research. Strengths and weaknesses of each design are illustrated. This chapter examines topics such as questionnaire development, how to create and apply survey instruments (questionnaires and interviews), and problems with each.

Chapter 7 begins with a synthesis of chapters 5 and 6 by presenting a detailed discussion of mixed methods research. While this chapter presents the benefits of combining the best of qualitative and the best of quantitative approaches into one study, it reminds readers that not all studies are conducive to a mixed methods approach and it describes other factors that serve as barriers to a mixed methods research project.

Chapter 8 deals with sampling strategies. Sampling is of critical importance and depending on the research subject, different strategies are preferred. This chapter shows the strengths and weaknesses of each strategy and provides examples of their use and misuse from actual research. Again in this chapter, both quantitative and qualitative sampling strategies are covered, although it features a greater emphasis on quantitative methods, since sampling is often a larger component of this type of research. Some texts present sampling *prior* to introducing research designs; however, since the type of sample drawn is dependent on the specific research design employed we contend that a more logical placement is to first introduce the different types of research designs before providing a discussion on how samples are selected.

The best and more commonly used analytical strategies for making sense of and presenting data are discussed in chapter 9. This chapter covers very basic descriptive and inferential statistics at the univariate and qualitative level and includes a discussion on how to present data through the use of tables, charts and graphs. Unlike the wide acceptance of statistical techniques there is no consensus on the best way to analyze and present qualitative data. Some researchers prefer to "quantify" qualitative data and other researchers argue that this detracts from the rich, narrative understanding provided by the data. These, and other debates, are presented. The development of themes and theory is included along with the best methods of presenting the qualitative findings. The companion discussion of quantitative analysis also appears in the chapter. Chapter 9 presents elementary data analysis typically associated with bivariate and multivariate analysis. This chapter also touches on a few more advanced (actually intermediate) statistical techniques that are commonly used by social science researchers. Chapter 10 is a brand new chapter on qualitative data analysis. While qualitative analysis predates quantitative analysis new software (and hardware) have dramatically altered how this type data is collected and analyzed. We try to present a brief overview of these changes.

The final and eleventh chapter covers, in great detail, how to improve writing abilities so that research projects can be presented in a professional manner. It has been our experience that not all students are equally equipped with the foundation that enables them to be effective writers. We have taken great pains to provide a chapter that will assist in their writing success.

Please do not hesitate to contact either of us with concerns, suggestions or questions. It was this type of correspondence from the first edition that led us to revise the original book.

ACKNOWLEDGMENTS

Never is a book the product of only one or two writers; rather, it reflects an accumulation of a lifetime of experiences and influential people. For Mark those influences include Robert "Bob" Langworthy at the University of Central Florida (UCF) and Doug Klutz at the University of Alabama (UA). Other influences came from unlikely places, mostly my blue collar biker and surfing companions, whose intellect often surpasses that of those more formally educated, some are Jim Santore (IMC), Dennis Harrison, Ken Morris, Greg Ashcraft (Skinworx), Brad Talley (BFMC) and Cody Wood (BFMC). My Graduate Assistant, Conner Birdsong was a help, as were several undergraduates who are passionate about research, including Neisha Riley.

For Lisa, she continues to remain indebted to Steve Brown (WCU), for fostering a more acceptable work schedule to facilitate academic writing, and to her students who remind her everyday why it is all worth it.

We would also like to thank Steve Helba, editor; Larissa Albright and Katlin Kocher, editorial assistant; Hannah Whitcher, project manager; Holly Haydash, production editor; Stephanie Castello, cover designer and Farzana Razak, text designer, at Oxford University Press, for their support and exceptional guidance on this project. We are forever in the debt of those anonymous reviewers who took the time to give important feedback. All these individuals, and many others not listed, have our gratitude.

For their very helpful suggestions throughout the writing process, we would like to thank the following reviewers, as well as those who chose to remain anonymous:

Second Edition

Francisco J. Alatorre—New Mexico State University
Thomas S. Alexander—University of Maryland
Christian L. Bolden—Loyola University New Orleans
Tarika Daftary-Kapur—Fairleigh Dickinson University
Thomas Dearden—High Point University
Camille Gibson—Prairie View A&M University
Brian Hill—Central Connecticut State University
Judith Kirwan Kelley—Curry College
Thomas C. Laughner—American International College
Mary Ellen Mastrorilli—Boston University
Shelly A. McGrath—University of Alabama at Birmingham
Amy Smoyer—Southern Connecticut State University
Shanna R. Van Slyke—Utica College
Kento Yasuhara—University of New Haven

First Edition

Stephanie L. Albertson—Neumann University
Gaylene S. Armstrong—Sam Houston University
Jeb A. Booth—Salem State University
Peggy Bowen-Hartung—Alvernia University
Kenneth Clontz—Western Illinois University
Dorinda L. Dowis—Columbus State
Sheila J. Foley—Bay Path College
Amy Smoyer—Southern Connecticut State University
Tina Freiburger—University of Wisconsin-Milwaukee
Aviva Twersky Glasner—Bridgewater State University
Kyung Yon Jhi—University of Nebraska at Kearney
Jerry W. Joplin—Guilford College
Linda Keena—University of Mississippi
David A. Kessler—Kent State University
Dae-Hoon Kwak—Illinois State University
Sean Maddan—University of Tampa
Jerome McKean—Ball State University
E. Britt Patterson—Shippensburg University
Rebecca Paynich—Curry College
Thomas D. Stucky—Indiana University Purdue University—Indianapolis
Christopher Sullivan—University of Cincinnati
John Tahiliani—Worcester State University
Mary Ann Zager—Florida Gulf Coast University

DEDICATIONS

My part is dedicated to the Murfee legacy as best exemplified by Ann Murfee Sullivan.

Mark M. Lanier, February 13, 2018

This one is dedicated to Kent, thanks for so many exciting, adventurous experiences through the years, and for trying to let me be me.

Lisa T. Briggs, February 13, 2018

CHAPTER 1

Why Research at All?

CHAPTER OBJECTIVES

After reading this chapter, students should:

- Be able to better comprehend the utility of science and the research methods associated with it.
- Have a better understanding of common terms such as positivism, inductive reasoning, and deductive reasoning.
- Distinguish the primary differences between qualitative and quantitative research.
- Be knowledgeable about the mixed methods approach to research.
- Understand the different research designs and components common with qualitative, quantitative, and mixed methods.
- Have an increased awareness of the evolution of science, as well as the challenges facing early scientists.
- Realize there are positive and negative outcomes associated with the advancement of science.
- Be reassured in knowing it is beneficial to critically analyze scientific information, how it is gathered, and who gathers it.
- Understand what causality is and the necessary conditions associated with it.
- Be able to defend a fluid research strategy.

"*I love Brian Piccolo and I want you to love him too*" is a famous line spoken by National Football League (NFL) legend Gale Sayers to honor his Chicago Bears teammate Brian Piccolo. Sayers gave the emotional speech when he was awarded the NFL's George Halas Most Courageous Player Award in 1969. Most who have watched the classic movie *Brian's Song* (the story of a teammate who contracted cancer) would agree that it resonates the appreciation one person can have for another. If a similar sentiment can be conveyed regarding research methods presented through this book, then the text will have been a success. We hope that likewise research methods are something students come to appreciate and, yes, maybe even love! Even if students do not experience "love at first sight" for science, research methods, or statistics, it is our hope that they will have an epiphany when realizing how relevant and important these are to our daily lives.

While learning effective research methods can be a challenging endeavor for some, we hope that the process and outcome of good research can be greatly valued by all. Even if students do not experience "love" for science, research methods, or statistics, we hope they will recognize how relevant and important research is to peoples' daily lives and professional careers.

For many, after the initial trepidation and perhaps even fear, research methods will become a favorite course. The authors' intent is for students to have a clear, concise, engaging, and useful book, rather than one that is intimidating. Although no one expects for all students to "love" research, the goal is that this text will make research less intimidating by providing criminal justice, criminology, sociology, social work, interdisciplinary studies, political science, psychology, and public health (and many other disciplines) students a practical, easy-to-understand, comprehensive, and yet *critical* coverage of traditional, and some nontraditional, research methods.

Regardless of the academic discipline, the methods of good research in the social sciences are virtually the same. Denzin and Lincoln note that in the last 40 years in the social sciences, there has been a "methodological revolution" (2008, p. viii) in large part because there has been a blurring of disciplinary borders. While psychologists may rely more on scales and inventories, lawyers on document analysis, criminologists on questionnaires, and sociologists on participant observation, the methods are interchangeable among disciplines. The topic under examination (e.g., mental stability, legal statutes, crime) is what varies. Most of the illustrations in this book focus on crime, justice, and related social problems, but regardless of the topic, the research methods employed can, and should, be utilized by any and every academic discipline. Further, it is often advantageous to develop research teams comprised of people from different disciplines. This cross-fertilization between disciplines can have many positive effects. The probability of scientific breakthroughs is enhanced when the autonomy among disciples is reduced and problem solving and contributing to the advancement of science is a multidisciplinary endeavor. This text intends to demonstrate the interconnectedness of social problems and to demonstrate how similar research methods are across disciplines, and how they can be used to address societal issues and advance science.

When NFL player Brian Piccolo died from embryonal cell carcinoma on July 16, 1970, that form of cancer was 100% fatal; today it is 95% curable. Why the dramatic improvement in chances of surviving this once-deadly cancer? This is because of science and the research methods that accompany it. Every person reading this book probably knows of someone with an illness such as cancer and is thankful scientific methods exist to find cures and prolong the lives of loved ones. However, it is not just medical (hard sciences) advances that help cancer patients. Studies have found that a positive attitude and healthy outlook (social sciences) have a profound impact on a patient's recovery and rehabilitation (as shown by Gale Sawyers in the movie *Brian's Song* during his strenuous and multiple knee surgeries). There are many examples of research influencing our lives, and as time passes, students' appreciation for research methods should increase. As students develop and conduct their own research projects, many will realize this process can actually be very enjoyable and rewarding. Research methods should prove to be among the most helpful of academic subjects, providing benefit to careers, education, and even quality of life.

Research allows the quest for knowledge and information to be fulfilled in the most rigorous manner. Answers, knowledge, edification (teaching and learning), and perhaps even enlightenment can come from numerous sources, including religious, artistic, drug-induced, spiritual, or other personal "moments of clarity." For example, long-distance runners, after experiencing a "runner's high" (technically a rush of endorphins), report clearer thinking and a euphoric-like state of heightened awareness. Great ideas, or answers to questions, can occur during a long run. Some people have knowledge conveyed to them through dreams. Intense spiritual moments, meditation, and prayer may reveal insights not previously grasped. Many doctoral candidates have prayed for clarity while writing or defending their dissertations. (A dissertation is a piece of original, hopefully significant, research required to earn the doctor of philosophy [PhD] degree.) Other people rely on meditation and self-induced states of awareness for ideas and intellectual clarity. All these methods, as well as others, may provide help, insight, guidance, and assurance in the quest for answers.

A field of study called epistemology examines all these sources of knowledge. **Epistemology** examines the means of determining *how* it is we know what we know. In other words, epistemology seeks to determine what the legitimate sources of knowledge are. Although there are many "methods" of acquiring knowledge, only one means of creating and verifying knowledge is widely accepted among business, academic, government, and social organizations: science and the tools employed by scientists, *research methods*.

Epistemology: A branch of philosophy that focuses on understanding how we know what we know.

The most reliable and most widely accepted source for acquiring and validating knowledge is by using the time-tested principles associated with science. It is by creating quality studies, which can be replicated by others, that we arrive at answers with a sound scientific basis. Keller and Casadevall-Keller, in a nicely titled book, *The Tao of Research*, note the following:

> Research—the word itself puts us on the path to understanding its mission and its methods. Say it slowly . . . re-search. Research is looking again, trying once more to find something that was not found before. At a fundamental level, it is a search for truth, and nothing is harder to find or more tenuous to hold.
>
> *(2010, p. viii)*

The term *methodology* is derived from three Greek words: *meta* (along which), *hodos* (path), and *logos* (knowledge). Literally, in this context, methodology means "the path along which knowledge is gained." Thus, research methods are the procedures used to gain knowledge in order to contribute to science.

It is important to learn some vocabulary associated with research methods. Throughout this text, some new terms will be introduced; some are more important to understand and remember than others, but they will all serve to provide a deeper understanding about the field of research methods. For some, the terms may be intimidating, but this is likely due to the fact that the words are just unfamiliar. Comfort will come as the words are used more frequently. The great thing about research methods verbiage is that one or two words can be used to describe complete processes. For example, the novice researcher will be able to utilize the word *operationalization* instead of having to define the process of taking abstract concepts and putting them into forms that can be measured quantitatively and qualitatively.

Positivism: Knowledge acquired through direct observation or experimental observation.

Deductive reasoning: Logic that begins with a theory and then tests that theory.

Social sciences: The study of human behavior, including the fields of criminology, sociology, political science, psychology, and others.

The basis for knowledge derived from the use of science is called *positivism*. Positivism is thus simply the theoretical basis for science. **Positivism** is a method for using precise empirical (scientific) observations to confirm or deny rules that can predict human (or other) behavior. As such, positivism is generally a **deductive reasoning** process (meaning it starts with an idea but seeks verification through scientific means of study). The basic principles are derived from natural, or "hard," science research, which often takes place in a laboratory setting and involves experiments. Some scholars think that the procedures used in the natural sciences can and should be replicated in the **social sciences** (to explain human interaction and social problems). Other scholars completely reject positivism and, consequently, advocate alternative methods of inquiry in the social sciences. In other words, some contend we can inform, or create, knowledge by means other than following scientific formulas or experimentation.

Science is not a "cookbook"; otherwise, all researchers would be equal in their capabilities. In reality there are very good, marginal, poor, and everything in between in regards to the quality of research studies and researchers themselves. One difference that exists between researchers is that some argue science should operate in a circular manner. Researchers can start at different points (e.g., theory testing or observation) and still arrive at valid conclusions. Some traditionalists may argue that science must start at a specific point, with a predetermined process.

Fluid Research: An acceptance that research methods and focus may be altered during the course of a study to take advantage of new situations.

In a further contrast to a predetermined process, some researchers also advocate for what is termed "**fluid research.**" A research strategy is not "set in stone" but can be altered as needs and circumstances dictate. A quick example will illustrate this guiding principle. Early in a research career (in fact, while completing a Master of Science [MS]

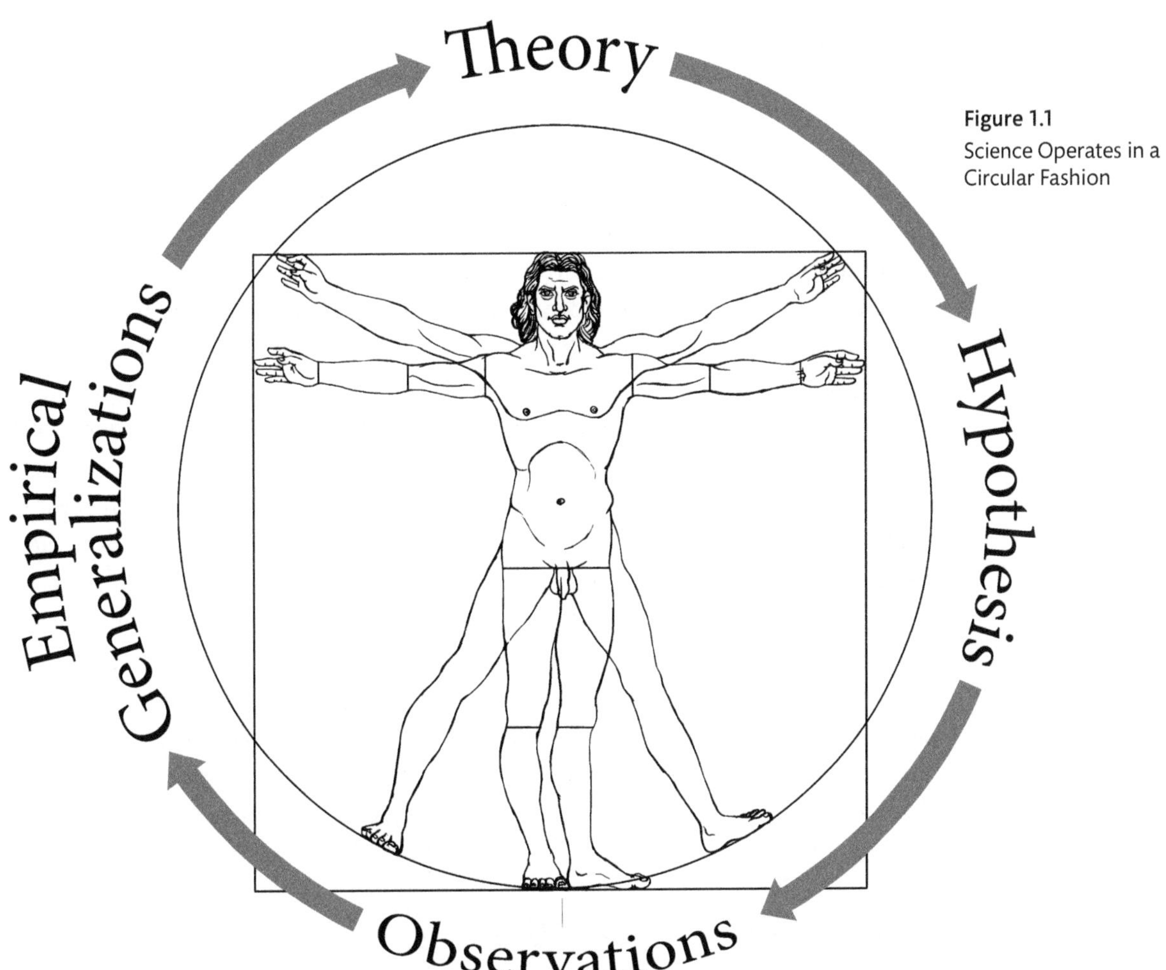

Figure 1.1
Science Operates in a Circular Fashion

thesis) a study was undertaken to examine the knowledge, attitudes, and behaviors of all incarcerated juvenile delinquents in the state of Alabama (DiClemente, Lanier, Horan, & Lodico, 1991). The research was scheduled to take place over one year in 13 different locations. Unbeknown to the researchers, the Alabama Department of Youth Services quickly provided an AIDS education program to all the juveniles. This was an obvious contaminant to the study and would have biased the research outcome as originally conceived. However, the study was quickly altered since fluid research allows change and modification to take advantage of new opportunities. Approximately one third of the juveniles received the entire 5 days of AIDS education, another third received 3 days, and the remaining juveniles received no AIDS education. By a slight change in focus, the "new" study now examined the impact of AIDS education on juvenile delinquents (Lanier & McCarthy, 1989) and became the first study ever to identify this population as being at high risk for HIV/AIDS. One problem with fluid research revolves around IRB approval (which is discussed in a later chapter). There are still other areas of variation between researchers.

Researchers who do not accept positivism as being the only method, or even the best method, for acquiring scientific knowledge typically adhere to underlying philosophical arguments most visibly reflected in the research methodologies employed by qualitative research. In other words, qualitative methods have a different underlying theoretical or philosophical basis (this is discussed later) compared to quantitative methods. A theme of this book is to expose the novice researcher to *both* of these methods, and each method is discussed in every chapter. Many researchers prefer one method to the other; however, it is important to become familiar with each methodology, since the research question should actually determine which is the best research methodology for a particular study. Over time, the *best practices of research* have evolved, which guide efforts in our pursuit of knowledge and understanding, but a more recent approach uses both qualitative and quantitative methods in the same study. Each of these approaches—qualitative, quantitative, and mixed methods—is presented in this text. Professors and students will likely favor one method over the other; however, it is our objective to initially provide a review of each so that researchers will be better informed to choose a method and to illustrate that it is the particular research question that should determine which research approach is employed.

THE HISTORY OF RESEARCH

Historically, or at least since humankind began recording its progression, knowledge advanced very slowly until about two hundred years ago—when positivism and scientific principles (research methods) were first introduced. Initially, since science refuted many religious ideas of the time, scientists were persecuted and even killed for their beliefs. One of the most notable examples is Galileo Galilei, typically referred to as "Galileo," who is often touted as being the father of modern science. Galileo was forced to stand trial before the Catholic Church on suspicion of heresy (questioning established religious beliefs) and was condemned for his heliocentric hypothesis, which merely observed (hypothesized) that the *sun* is the center of the universe, and the earth and planets revolve around it. Galileo was originally summoned to Rome to defend his hypothesis that Earth is not the center of the universe (completely radical thinking for the time and against religious indoctrination). When Galileo refused to comply with the Inquisition's sentence requiring him to denounce his findings, he was ordered imprisoned, a sentence that was later commuted to house arrest. His *Dialogue Concerning the Two Chief World Systems* (Galileo, 1632) was banned, and publication of any of his prior or future writings was forbidden as well. Although Galileo died in 1642 while still confined under house arrest, it was not until 1718 that the Inquisition's ban on publishing any of his writings was lifted, and not until 1758 that the general ban on publication of writings advocating the heliocentric viewpoint was lifted. Even though the Pope and the Catholic Church ultimately acknowledged their error in the handling of the Galileo controversy, it was almost three hundred years after his death before the blemish on his contribution to science was completely removed by the Catholic Church. In 1939, Pope Pius XII, in his first speech to the Pontifical Academy of Sciences, within a few months of his election to the papacy, described Galileo as being among the "most audacious heroes of research . . . not afraid of the stumbling blocks and the risks on the way, nor fearful of the funereal monuments" (1939, p. 34).

Throughout history, many religious leaders have denied the validity of science and have persecuted scientists. The various inquisitions (Medieval Inquisition, Spanish Inquisition, Portuguese Inquisition, Roman Inquisition, etc.) during the Enlightenment, Renaissance, and Reformation, as well as a number of witch trials, are prime examples. Religious resistance to science, it should be noted, was not limited to Catholicism or to any specific scientific discipline or specific geographic region. The reasons for this resistance are abundant and include fear, panic, rigid adherence to personal and traditional belief systems, economic concerns, and apprehension of what could cause the "powers that be" to lose control of the masses or their followers, whose actions were governed by the existing belief system.

Historically, scholars and critical, forward thinkers have been doubted, persecuted, or sometimes killed for their willingness to promote scientific methodology, especially when it conflicted with established religious principles. Today, failure to acknowledge and use scientific principles is considered primitive (yet the science supporting phenomena such as global warming is still critiqued by some, as it should be). Over time, humankind has begun to rely on scientific principles rather than superstition, religion, or tradition as the means of understanding human behavior and social problems. Along with this growing body of knowledge came the "technology explosion" (e.g., electronic advances and developments) and a "data explosion" (e.g., the abundance and ease of data recording and analysis) that further increased knowledge founded on science and the scientific method (Bezuidenhout, 2006).

Many of the classical theorists laid the groundwork for varied social science research methodologies that are still in use today. Men (we refer to "men" here because, with a few notable exceptions such as Oberlin College in 1833, Antioch College in 1853, and Bates College in 1955, most major institutions of higher education did not admit women until the mid-1900s) such as Auguste Comte, Émile Durkheim, Karl Marx, and Max Weber all presented theoretical paradigms that led to different types of research strategies. Each was also very influential in establishing separate academic disciplines. More recently, other contemporary "great thinkers" such as Michel Foucault and Jürgen Habermas have questioned some of the previously held, and widely accepted, premises on which science is based. A goal of this book is to emphasize that science "happens" because we question and build on previous paradigms and thoughts of others. As mentioned previously, it is helpful to remember *research* means just that: "re-search." Replication of studies over time is a key to the development of scientific foundations.

In the 19th century, it took about fifty years to double the world's knowledge. Today, however, the base of knowledge doubles in less than a year (Emory University, Commission on Teaching, 1997), and some argue that knowledge now doubles every 12 hours (Schilling, 2013). Contrast this with the stagnant state of knowledge that existed for thousands of years.

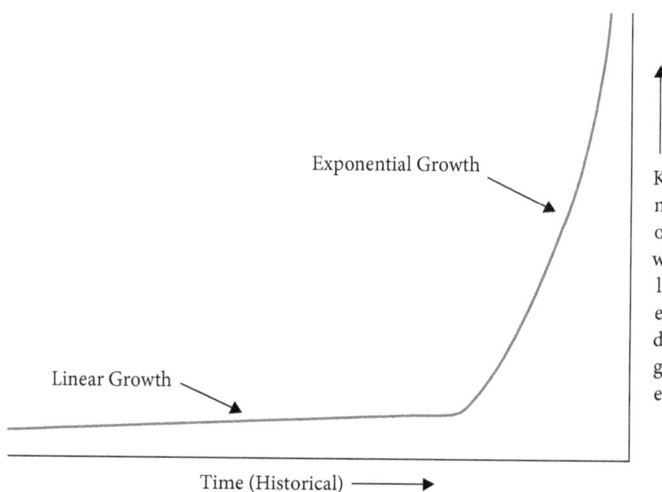

Figure 1.2
The Knowledge Doubling Curve
http://www.futuristgerd.com/bing.com

Some common examples of this change illustrate the difference that science has made in contemporary life. Consider that many elderly people alive today did not have televisions, cars, or even telephones in their youth. Middle-aged people today grew up with only a few television stations when they were young, and most did not have access to computers or ATMs, Facebook, or cell phones. The youth of today have available hundreds of television stations, as well as other forms of visual stimulation, information, and resources on their cell phones. In fact, parts of this text were written from an iPhone. Certainly, technology contributes to science, but science is what developed the technology.

With the vast development and growth in technology also came more and varied types of crime. Brown, Esbensen, and Geis (2004) affirm that technological changes have resulted in more valuable and more portable items that are easier to steal, such as personal computers, cell phones, and media devices. Routine activities theory in the 1970s started noting that as technology changed, so did crime. The technology explosion also has led to the proliferation of new types of crime such as identity theft, and science is needed in order to understand and reduce the negative consequences of technology. There is an abundance of topics to study (criminal events) that have been fueled by technology. For example, Sameer Hinduja has had a stellar career examining "cyberbullying"—a newer type of crime based on technological changes (Hinduja & Patchin, 2015; Patchin & Hinduja, 2016).

Technological advancements, brought about by science, present fresh challenges and raise new questions, which translate into new research endeavors, including the examination of technological crimes; it will be scientific methods that will help address new social problems created by technology. Because there is widespread agreement on the importance of science, it is surprising there is no single agreed-upon definition for the term *science*. Some even argue that a social science (such as criminology, which is applicable to the study of human behavior) is not even really possible; however, we put those arguments aside and proceed under the (sometimes-contested) assumption that science does exist and can be used in the social sciences (just as in the physical sciences). **Science** simply reflects a way to go about obtaining knowledge that provides some confidence that standards are met before conclusions are drawn. Science helps us understand the world we live in and helps solve some of society's problems, although science and the advancement of technology can be the very cause of some societal and human woes. While the authors of this text are willing to promote the idea that scientific methods can be used to help understand *human behavior*, importantly, we want students to be *critical* of science and its methods. Part of our duty as researchers is to question everything and to be critical thinkers—and yes, it is indeed acceptable—even desirable—to be critical of science.

Science: A rigorous process used to provide a reliable method or means of knowing things.

GOOD, YET CRITICAL, SCIENCE

Do not assume that society's reliance on science is all "good"; science itself is neither good nor evil. It is a tool that, like any other tool, has the potential for producing a good product or a bad product. With that being said, how *people* might use science *can* be evil or good. It is dependent upon "whose hands the tools are in" and how that individual or group (or sometimes an entire subculture, culture, or nation) chooses to use, or abuse, the possibilities of science. Some of the consequences of science are in fact horrific. For example, science allows greater mechanical fishing, and now our oceans are rapidly being depleted of fish, turtles, and other marine life. Coral reefs are dying at an alarming rate due to the advancement of science. Science and its contribution to the use and abuse of fossil fuels have led to major ecological disasters worldwide.

After 25 years, the *Exxon Valdez* oil tanker accident is still harming Alaska. A more recent event, the horrific British Petroleum (BP) Deepwater Horizon oil well disaster in the Gulf of Mexico, will likely cause harm for many decades. The future impact is still uncertain, but it is assured that fish exports and sea life were damaged, and some species such as the yellowfin tuna may actually face extinction as a direct result of this massive oil spill. We do not yet know what the ramifications will be, and science is currently being used to ascertain them. Science provided the means for humans to drill for oil a mile deep under the ocean's surface, but the science has not yet been developed to stem the flow quickly or successfully when an accident occurs.

Solutions to this type of problem are not without controversy; some even appear bizarre. For example, it was argued that the leak might have been contained very

Source: curraheeshutter

rapidly if BP and the U.S. federal government were willing to "bomb" the pipeline and seal it forever. The former Soviet Union has successfully used this strategy since 1966, when a test in sealing an underground gas well in southern Uzbekistan was successful. The Russians have used nuclear bombs four more times since then for capping runaway wells (Hsu, 2010). With this strategy, however, the well could no longer be used, companies would lose their financial investment, and certainly public sentiment would be heightened about the use of nuclear devices. These reasons contribute to a capitalistic company like BP instead looking for alternative methods. This example underscores how effective science had *not* been developed to deal with potential problems. Recall the mass request for ideas or solutions to be submitted over the Internet (by anyone), which resulted in a plumber from Tampa, Florida, submitting a crude drawing of a "cap" founded on the same principles as a fire hydrant.

A strikingly similar cap was ultimately built, tested, and used to abate the flow of oil into the Gulf. It is not likely that this plumber considered himself a scientist, yet it was his idea that put things in motion to fix a significant problem.

Like the plumber, students of research methods (yes, you) are able to arrive at accurate, verifiable, and useful solutions to many social problems. It is through the process of formulating (testing and retesting) ideas that knowledge is advanced. For example, consider how forms of communication have been altered over time. Text messages now outnumber "traditional" phone conversations by four to one. In earlier periods, scientifically created technology, letters to replace smoke signals, telegraphs to replace letters, telephones to replace telegraphs, , and so on. While these technological advances are useful, many argue that texting and e-mailing have replaced face-to-face interaction, and that this change could come with its own social consequences. In addition, while some studies have been conducted, the physical or medical consequences of such advanced technology are still unknown. It will be important to continue to utilize science to determine the connection between new technology and health problems.

Because of science, Brian Piccolo in all likelihood would have survived his cancer today (and perhaps some of our own loved ones have survived what were once fatal illnesses). Scientific medical breakthroughs have alleviated much pain and suffering. Science has even helped reduce crime, but we must remember that science has also created harm (we explore this further in the chapter on ethics). For students of research methods, it is important to acknowledge that science has contributed to the well-being and greater understanding of society, but it is also important to be critical thinkers. Be aware that science has contributed and will continue to contribute its own unique problems; the hope is that science will also find a solution to these human-made, scientifically enabled problems.

RESEARCH DISTINCTIONS

A review of science and the research methods scientists employ will show that science is multifaceted and the methods employed are varied. Several distinctions are used to classify types of research. The main ones are discussed next.

Inductive or Deductive Reasoning?

Inductive reasoning: Logic that begins with data (a problem) and then tries to develop a theory or explanation.

The first scientific distinction to be made is in how a problem is viewed. Some methods first look at a problem or situation and then try to develop a theory or explanation. This is called inductive reasoning. **Inductive reasoning** moves from the narrow to the broad, from the specific to the general, from the problem to the theory. For example, the police may have data demonstrating a particular problem in their jurisdiction. Then, as information is shared about their data (numerical account of a problem), a pattern is identified (consider a spike in a particular type of crime). Inductive research would consider the data provided and then develop a theory to explain the increase in crime. If there is an increase in burglaries (data), is it occurring because the local factory has closed due to economic pressures and more people are unemployed (theory)?

Conversely, one may first have a grand idea or theory and subsequently apply it to a specific case, problem, or situation. For example, one person may have a notion that security systems will reduce burglaries. This is an argument based on a theory of deterrence (potential offenders will be deterred and avoid homes with security systems). This theory could be tested. Research that begins with a theory and then tests that theory is called deductive reasoning.

Deductive reasoning goes from the general to the specific. It can be difficult to distinguish between *in*ductive and *de*ductive reasoning. Think of it in a simplistic form: *in*ductive as *in*venting, *in*vestigating solutions to deal with *i*dentified problems (the data exist first). *De*ductive is *de*veloping, *de*ciding intellectual reasoning first (theory), which then can be tested with data. Scholars and philosophers throughout time have advocated different methods for arriving at knowledge or truth. In examining the various schools of thought, students will be better equipped to determine the best method, or combination of methods, that can be used to increase knowledge.

Quantitative research: Provides *a numerical or statistical analysis* of social issues in order to contribute to science.

Quantitative, Qualitative, or Mixed Method?

The second major distinction is based on research type: quantitative, qualitative, or mixed method. **Quantitative research** deals with data and numbers and relies on statistics to address research problems. **Qualitative research** methods provide an in-depth personal experience or understanding of something to contribute to knowledge. An easy way to remember the difference is by noting the *n* in qua*n*titative and the *l* in qua*l*itative. *Quantitative* is derived from the word *quantity*, so to quantify something it is necessary to take counts, measures, numbers, and statistics. Thus quantitative is *numerically* based (hence the *n* in the middle of the word). *Qualitative* is derived from the word *quality*; researchers are better able to understand the quality of something when it has been personally experienced (either by themselves or by the person they are researching). Quality, then, provides an in-depth, personal experience, or a *lived* experience; hence the letter *l* in the middle of the word. One can also look for the *quan* and *qual* and use the terms literally. Think about analyzing existing letters or diaries of someone's life or talking to the person directly to have a better understanding of his or her experience. The research goal would not necessarily be to conduct statistical analysis but to garner a richer understanding of the lived experience. Qualitative research is aimed at providing the researcher an in-depth, comprehensive understanding of the research topic by reliance on all empirical sources, including but not limited to sight, hearing, scent, and feeling. Qualitative methods are essentially and generally non-numerical, and they focus on an actual experience to provide knowledge and insight (although "themes" in the research can be counted). The intent of qualitative research includes understanding processes and how things are, and how they came to be that way.

Qualitative research: Provides an *in-depth personal experience* or understanding of social issues in order to contribute to science.

If large amounts of data are collected with numerical representations (e.g., a group of students' grade point averages (GPAs), the number of burglaries in a neighborhood, the statistical association between gender and criminal behavior), then the methods employed are quantitative. The researcher can also try to establish the relationship between variables (e.g., whether the number of burglaries and the closing of the neighborhood factory are statistically associated). Thus, specific numerical measurements are necessary for quantitative research. This approach provides the fundamental connection between empirical observation and the mathematical demonstration of quantitative relationships between variables (Bezuidenhout, 2011).

To contrast qualitative with quantitative research, consider the following example. As part of a class project, a student may go to the county jail and give a questionnaire to the last 1,000 people arrested for the criminal offense of driving under the influence (DUI). The survey may ask the respondent to answer questions about what happened, what it cost, how it feels to be arrested or incarcerated, and so forth. Typically, for quantitative research, the options to the questions are provided, and the respondent selects the answer that best identifies with his or her situation (i.e., close-ended questions). For example, a closed-ended question might read,

"How many DUIs have you had? 0, 1, 2, 3, etc." Basically, a numerical measurement of the DUI arrest experience would be gathered from each of the 1,000 participants in a quantitative analysis.

Alternatively, if the student was actually arrested for a DUI, experienced a strip or body cavity search, had his or her car towed, had no way to contact someone for assistance because the cell phone (with the numbers needed to summon help) was in the towed car or was confiscated, heard the bars clanging shut, smelled the body odor of jail mates, or feared what the other inmates may do, he or she has had a qualitative experience and a better understanding of what a DUI arrest experience really *means*. A qualitative research process would be an attempt to capture the true essence of the experience. Qualitative researchers may also use a questionnaire or interview to assess the experience, but the process would be more "free-flowing." Respondents would typically be asked "open-ended" questions that allow the researcher to gain a deeper understanding of the research participant, such as this: "Please describe what a typical night in jail is like." *Survey research*, which we present later, is common with either a qualitative or a quantitative approach; however, the way the survey is constructed and the type of information desired distinguish the two.

Table 1.1 is a synopsis of the major features differentiating the basic research elements of qualitative and quantitative strategies. Some of the items will make more sense as the book is read. Use this table as a resource throughout the course. It is also important to note that new approaches to research are being developed to combine the traditional methods of qualitative and quantitative methods in a process called **mixed methods research.** For example, certainly a survey could include both qualitative- and quantitative-based analysis. Much more on mixed methods is discussed later in the text.

Mixed methods research: Combines research practices from both qualitative and quantitative analysis of social issues in order to contribute to science.

As shown in Table 1.1, the intent, purpose, or reason for conducting the study is one difference between qualitative and quantitative research. Qualitative researchers are seeking an in-depth understanding of one particular phenomenon or group, and so they often rely on inductive methods. Quantitative researchers more often seek to test a theory and want their results to apply to a broad group. This is achieved most often by relying on deductive methods.

At this early stage in the course and in the text, Table 1.1 might be useful for guiding students through the steps necessary to complete research-related projects. For example, an important element of a research project is the literature review (greater detail on this is provided in the next chapter). Generally, however, the reason that quantitative researchers conduct a literature review is to identify similar studies, provide the rationale or reasons for the study they are conducting, and help develop

TABLE 1.1 *Mixed Methods Research Matrix*

Elements of Qualitative Research Tend Toward...	Process of Research	Elements of Quantitative Research Tend Toward...
• Understand meaning individuals give to a phenomenon inductively	**Intent of the research**	• Test a theory deductively to support or refute it
• Minor role • Justifies problem	**How literature is used**	• Major role • Justifies problem • Identifies questions and hypotheses
• Ask open-ended questions • Understand the complexity of a single idea (or phenomenon)	**How intent is focused**	• Ask closed-ended questions • Test specific variables that form hypotheses or questions
• Words and images • From a few participants at a few research sites • Studying participants at their location	**How data are collected**	• Numbers • From many participants at many research sites • Sending or administering instrument to participants
• Text or image analysis • Themes • Larger patterns or generalizations	**How data are analyzed**	• Numerical statistical analysis • Rejecting hypotheses or determining effect sizes
• Identifies personal stance • Report bias	**Role of the researcher**	• Remains in background • Takes steps to remove bias
• Using validity procedures that rely on the participants, the researcher, or the reader	**How data are validated**	• Using validity procedures based on external standards, such as judges, past research, statistics

Adapted from *Designing and Conducting Mixed Methods Research*, by J. W. Creswell and V. L. Plano Clark (Thousand Oaks, CA: Sage, 2007), p. 29.

study questions and the hypothesis that will be tested. Consequently, the literature review is of great importance to quantitative researchers. The literature review actually "sets up" and justifies the entire project.

This is not necessarily true for qualitative researchers. Qualitative researchers may use the literature on the topic to help them articulate the need for the study and may reference other studies at the conclusion of their project. More often, the literature in a qualitative study is scattered throughout the final paper or report in contrast to a quantitative study, where it is generally placed at the beginning of the paper. For either case, conducting a literature review is very important in order to determine what has already been reviewed or established on the subject. There is very little that has not been studied in some form already, so good researchers find out all they can about their topics before they undertake their own studies to avoid "reinventing the wheel" or omitting important information. Gathering information is therefore an important aspect of the research process regardless of the research approach.

As mentioned earlier, a major difference in research methods is *how intent is focused*, which simply means how issues or questions are approached. Qualitative researchers would be more likely to ask "open-ended" questions and normally examine one situation, or a single location, in great detail. For example, qualitative researchers would ask inmates to convey the details of their experiences and let the incarcerated persons dictate their own responses. The researcher may then compare the responses of several inmates to look for common themes or patterns of experience that might contribute to a greater understanding of the overall experience of being incarcerated. Another qualitative researcher may actually subject himself or herself to the entire process of being arrested, booked, and incarcerated to gain a better, or richer, understanding; this researcher would contribute to knowledge by sharing this personal experience. By contrast, a quantitative researcher seeks to test the hypothesis and variables that were predetermined prior to collecting the data, thus more often relying on close-ended measures. The objective of quantitative researchers in the fields of criminology and criminal justice is to study social issues by assigning numerical values, which can then be analyzed through the use of statistics. These values allow the application of statistical techniques in order to create formulas that are used to verify or refute hypotheses. Because we have not yet defined what hypotheses are, simply think of them as "educated guesses" about the relationship between variables; variables are simply social phenomena or abstract concepts that have been expressed in forms that can be statistically measured.

A quantitative researcher examining incarceration as a research topic will prepare in advance a questionnaire that addresses incarceration issues and will usually provide responses from which the respondents select the most appropriate answers. An example of a survey question of this sort would be to ask an inmate his or her marital status; the response categories could be single, married, separated, divorced, or widowed. The respondent would simply select from the options provided.

There are valid reasons for providing predetermined responses as opposed to asking open-ended questions in quantitatively designed studies, but primarily it assists in the data entry and data analysis stages. It basically aids in researchers' ability to analyze the survey results statistically. We address this process of coding and entering data later in the text, but it is important to raise this issue here because it helps provide clarity on the difference between qualitative and quantitative survey research. We also dedicate an entire chapter to validity and reliability, but for now we emphasize that in quantitative research, it is important that all respondents be given the exact same questions and the exact same answer choices. This helps one trust the statistical outcomes of the data a bit more.

The next major difference between qualitative- and quantitative-based research is the means by which data are collected. Qualitative researchers examine a very limited number of study participants in a specific location at one point, although perhaps for an extended period of time (sometimes years). By contrast, quantitative researchers want to gather as much numerical data as possible and therefore rely on many participants, multiple locations, and less lengthy time frames. That is one reason survey instruments are so popular. They can be given to large numbers of people, in a relatively short period of time, at relatively low cost.

Obviously, the type of data collected will also have a huge bearing on the analytical tools used. Quantitative researchers rely heavily on statistics and statistical analysis packages such as Statistical Package for the Social Sciences (SPSS), Stata, or Statistical Analysis Software (SAS), whereas qualitative researchers look for themes or patterns of action that can be identified in the data. Increasingly, qualitative researchers employ software and other forms of technology to help synthesize the data (e.g., NVivo, MAXQDA, Quirkos). Mixed methods research relies on both approaches. These analytical strategies are examined in greater detail in later chapters.

The type of study to be conducted also determines the role "played" by the researcher. Qualitative researchers generally acknowledge that their mere physical presence influences the study and research participants and will often have a biasing effect on the outcome of the study. This issue and subjectivity are acknowledged and addressed, but they are included as an accepted, though perhaps unfortunate, part of research. Some qualitative researchers remain committed to minimizing biasing influences of their presence by taking precautions to limit their involvement in the study. Quantitative researchers, in contrast, take *every* precaution possible to limit their influencing the study and take rigorous steps to remain objective and eliminate or reduce any type of bias. While some people question whether this can ever really be achieved, it is an optimal goal of quantitative-based researchers to make all attempts possible. With either approach, it is important for the researcher to remember his or her role in the study; certainly, research is more likely to be trusted by others if the researcher is able to remain objective, neutral, and committed to avoiding any behavior that could influence the study's outcome.

The final major difference is the means used to confirm, or validate, the data collected. The quantitative researcher will compare his or her study results with those of similar studies, with the use of impartial "peer" reviewers or through the application of rigorous statistical procedures. The qualitative researcher, however, must rely on his or her own judgment and on the opinions of the study participants.

While this method has more potential for researcher bias, as well as participant bias and/or misleading responses from participants (whether intentional or unintentional), qualitative work is praised for collecting "richer" data.

The biggest difference, which is not reflected in Table 1.1, is based on the underlying *theoretical* basis of the study. Quantitative researchers rely on positivism and the scientific method. As discussed earlier, positivism is the notion that if proper scientific methods are followed, there are universal truths about human behavior that can be identified. Some qualitative researchers, by contrast, argue that there is no one, or universal, truth and that each person may have his or her own version of reality. Chapter 5 examines this inherent conflict in greater detail, but the theoretical approach of research designs distinguishes them from each other. For example, some (in fact, many) qualitative researchers reject the principles of positivism (Denzin & Lincoln, 2008), which serve as the foundation for quantitative methods. In the social sciences, positivism infers acceptance of the validity of the natural sciences research model. This gives rise to a scientific view based on the premise that universal laws determine human behavior. This research approach is therefore based on objective (controlled) observation and measurement. On the other hand, some qualitative researchers, and many antipositivists, insist that human behavior cannot be investigated in the same way as the natural sciences (e.g., biology and chemistry), which study things such as plant growth and cell development. Philosophical debates persist concerning the nature of social sciences and which research approach should be used. While this debate will never be resolved, there are coping mechanisms.

In general, the nature of the social problem or question should determine which method or combination of methods should be used; many times in reality, however, researchers prefer a specific method. Sometimes this is simply based on what they *have* or *have not* been exposed to. Certain academic programs evolve to specialize in one methods or another. For example, in the doctoral-level field of criminal justice, the University of Maryland is known as a quantitative program, while Florida State University was traditionally considered more qualitative, and Michigan State University stresses each method. To highlight the contrast between the two paradigms, qualitative researchers acknowledge that the human experience is *socially constructed* and not necessarily designed in a way to be experimentally, statistically measured in terms of "quantity, amount, intensity or frequency" (Denzin & Lincoln, 2008, p. 14). This is in direct contrast to the logic of quantitative studies, which emphasize the quantification of the human experience and analysis of causal relationships between variables. Qualitative researchers acknowledge biases and value judgments in research; quantitative researchers promote the idea that scientific investigation of human behavior can, in fact, be value-free.

Even though there are areas where qualitative and quantitative researchers seem to diverge on philosophical grounds, the two approaches can be combined to make a study stronger. This is often referred to as "mixed methods." By joining qualitative methods with quantitative methods—in the same study—much can be gained. In fact, some argue that mixed methods research is emerging as the third major methodological approach in crime studies (Kraska & Neuman, 2011, p. 269). Chapter 7 covers the strategy of mixed methods in greater detail, but we discuss the approach in nearly every chapter. Mixed methods are increasingly being employed, and some scholarly journals are now devoted to examination of the methodology.

Recall from the preface that not all researchers are equal in ability, intellect, or *agreement on best approaches*. Different techniques are used to address research questions, solve problems, and contribute to science. It is our opinion that it is a "good problem to have" that not all researchers agree on *one*, single best approach. This is what science is all about because it causes us to continue to critically analyze methods more completely. If researchers agreed on only *one* way of gaining knowledge, science could become too routinized and mundane. If all knowledge were actually determined by only one type of researcher, this could be more problematic than disagreeing on best approaches. A beginning researcher may find it difficult to ascertain which method of research has more merit. Again, it is worth repeating that the subject or topic of interest should dictate which method or combination of methods is actually best; as a researcher gains more experience and confidence in research methods, this will become more evident.

Applied or Pure?

Another distinction of research is based on the underlying motivation, or reason for the study. This distinction is between what is termed pure/basic research and applied research. The type of research depends on the purpose the researcher has and the practical application thereof. **Applied research** is defined as the "scientific planning of induced change in a troublesome situation" (Fouché & De Vos, 2005, p. 105) with the focus on a specific problem (Neuman & Wiegand, 2000, p. 22). For example, a researcher may assist the local sheriff with determining the best means of preventing home invasions.

Applied research: A type of research with a specific goal in mind, typically directed at program evaluation or policy analysis.

Basic research is defined as research that is concerned with "extending the knowledge base" (Fouché & De Vos, 2005, p. 105) and can focus on disproving, or supporting, theories that explain social problems (Neuman & Wiegand, 2000, p. 21). Basic research is often conducted without the researcher having a specific problem or application in mind, and also, often with no idea of what the ultimate

Basic research: A type of research driven by the curiosity of the researcher, typically designed to expand knowledge in general, often with no specific goal in mind.

outcome will be. When the National Aeronautics and Space Administration (NASA) developed Velcro, the scientists involved had no idea it would have such widespread and practical usage.

Other aspects of pure and applied research also need consideration. Much more common than pure research is applied research, in which a specific problem exists (e.g., crime) and solutions are sought. Most corporations and government agencies that fund research will not provide funding without first having a clearly defined problem to be addressed. Increasingly, government is involved in research. The role played by government is largely financial, and the studies that are most often funded are quantitative. For example, during the Bush administration, embryonic stem cell research encountered a ban on federal funding, in large part due to pressure from the religious "right wing" (Pittman, 2006). Pittman interjected:

> The federal government funds most scientific and medical research in this country. Without federal financing, there would not be enough money for such research, nor would there be the type of quality control and federal regulation that some believe is necessary to ensure that the research adheres to acceptable standards.
>
> *(2006, p. 133)*

In-house research: Research conducted by someone *within* the organization seeking the information.

Hired-hand research: Research conducted by someone *outside* the organization seeking the information but hired directly by that organization.

Third-party research: Research conducted by an *outside* researcher not paid by the organization seeking the information.

Yamamoto provided further affirmation of the increasing role government plays in research: "The only possible source for adequate support of our medical schools and medical research is the taxing power of the Federal Government" (2004, cited in Pittman, 2006, p. 1712). Whether the funding is being requested from the federal government or another agency, it is necessary for most research projects to obtain money to finance the study. As an aside, being able to write a comprehensive and effective grant proposal is another important skill for researchers to master because such funding is often necessary.

In-House, Hired Hand, or Third Party?

Fitzgerald and Cox (1994) have also argued for a fourth distinction between research types founded on "who" conducts the research: in-house, hired hand, or third party. **In-house research** is conducted by a person within the organization, whereas **hired-hand research** is conducted by someone external to the organization but paid by the organization. **Third-party research** is conducted by a person external to the organization and paid for by means outside the organization. This categorization of who conducts the research is not as commonly referenced as the first three, but it does merit consideration primarily because it has serious implications. For example, it would be difficult to trust the police to research their own use of excessive force, right? Even though they would have better access to data on police use of excess force than would outside agencies or independent researchers, the results are less likely to be taken seriously or trusted if such a study was conducted internally.

The distinction of who conducts the research seems simplistic and noncontroversial, but it is not. Consider this: large institutions and governments have trained researchers on staff and have sufficient resources to employ the very best researchers. Why, then, are most researchers located in universities and working as professors (for much lower pay)? The answer is to provide either objectivity or the *illusion* of objectivity. **Objectivity** means the conclusions are founded on careful observation rather than personal bias. Objectivity may be hard to achieve, however. Quantitative researchers attempt to achieve objectivity (or the illusion of it), whereas qualitative researchers are more likely to just acknowledge its elusive nature.

Objectivity: Means that conclusions are founded on careful observation rather than personal bias.

Exploration, Description, Evaluation, or Explanation?

Another distinction of research is based on its purpose. Most textbooks in the field acknowledge exploration, description, or explanation as the basis of research, and more recently evaluative research has been favored. Avoid feeling any anxiety over what these terms mean because the basic goal or purpose is actually embedded in the word itself. Just think about what the word means. Exploration is designed to explore or to investigate; description is to simply describe; explanation is to explain or tell why; and evaluative is to evaluate.

Let's begin with **exploratory research.** This approach to understanding a social phenomenon is very common—at least in crime and justice. For example, the neighborhood crime problem of burglaries mentioned earlier could entail exploratory research as an initial step to determining the extent of the perceived problem. How many, if any, burglaries are actually occurring? It is necessary to determine if there is an *actual* spike in burglary or if there just seems to be an increase because of media hype or sensationalism. The problem would need to be *explored* by a researcher to determine the scope of the situation. The same can be said of another social problem such as the spread of sexually transmitted disease among the prison population. One may think this problem is confined to the field of criminology, but in fact it is a far-reaching problem that transposes many disciplines including the medical and health care profession, economics, the fields of psychology, sociology, and social work just to name a few. In exploratory research, a first step will be to determine the scope of sexually transmitted disease among this segment of the population. Is it a problem? Has a spike in sexually transmitted disease occurred? Does it vary by type of prison or level of custody?

Exploratory research: "Explore"; a method of research used when a problem is not yet clearly defined; involves developing an initial understanding of the issue under consideration.

Descriptive research: "Describe"; a method of research focused on describing (counting or documenting) the details of the social issue under consideration.

The second and related distinction is **descriptive research** and is conducted to describe a problem, policy, or program. A researcher would need to document enough information to be able to effectively describe the problem, policy, or program to another. The synthesis of information allows others to have more clarity. An example would be describing how community policing works in a particular neighborhood. A researcher could describe the agency's approach to this type of police work, how many officers participate, whether the officers like or dislike the method, how the public perceives the policing style, and so forth. Descriptive research is also very common for criminal justice and criminology researchers, but is equally important in all methods of inquiry. For example, oftentimes K9s are used to assist in the location of missing persons. One can analyze and describe the various types of breeds used and techniques used to train the dogs can be descriptive and important in contributing to knowledge.

Evaluation research: "Evaluate"; a method of research focused on assessing a program, problem, or policy.

Evaluation research, or "program evaluation," involves evaluating an actual program, policy, or initiative. Evaluation research, which is becoming increasingly common, uses the same skills, techniques, and methodologies common to all forms of research. The fundamental difference is that this takes place in a political or organizational context. In other words, evaluation research is conducted within an organization (e.g., a police department) to see if the agency's practices are effective. This is becoming more common in all disciplines because it is important to determine whether "attempts" of addressing social problems are successful. Because costs (typically taxpayers' dollars) are involved in supporting programs and initiatives, it is important to determine if such attempts are really effective. Evaluation research is designed with that goal in mind. Think about any rehabilitative, correctional, or preventative program that has been discussed in a typical criminal justice course. Or think about whether an awareness campaign in the health care field to reduce the spread of the swine flu or Zika virus is effective. Think about the millions of dollars elected officials spend on commercials; is it truly cost-effective? From a business investment model, does the use of cameras really reduce the probability of theft or violent crime? Think about the importance of evaluating whether the efforts are really beneficial. One justification for the death penalty is based on a theory of deterrence. When killers are executed, other would-be killers should be deterred from committing murder themselves; however, evaluative research on the deterrent effects of capital punishment suggests otherwise. Also consider, for example, recidivism rates (the probability an inmate will return to prison). A controversial topic related to both controlling the inmate population and reducing recidivism rates is conjugal visits (allowing inmates to have intimate relations with their spouses while the inmate is incarcerated). Some may be appalled by the idea, but what if helping facilitate "intact" relationships reduces the likelihood of inmates returning to prison? If evaluative research determines the utility of conjugal visits, taxpayers could save a lot of money by avoiding the cost of housing and caring for the same inmates over and over again.

Explanatory research is a type of study where causes, motivations, and reasons are revealed and explained. This type of research examines why some people chronically abuse drugs while others abstain or are only causal or occasional users. Why do some college students binge drink while others do not drink at all? Why is it that some individuals are racist or sexist when others are not? Why do some officers use excessive force while others employ de-escalating techniques in the line of duty? Why is it that some individuals are extremely successful in their jobs or in obtaining their education, but others fail at such attempts? Why is it that some babies are born with mental or physical disabilities? What are the specific explanations for why the behavior of males and females may vary under certain situations? Explanatory research is one of the more challenging methods because it is difficult to state with certainty *why* people do the things they do. If we can confidently list the reasons for human behavior, then we should be able to *predict* the behavior of others. Having this predictive ability would greatly benefit policy makers, criminal justice professionals, and people in their everyday lives. One tenet of positivism is this idea, or elusive goal, of prediction. For prediction or predictive hypotheses to be reliable, the researcher must be able to ascertain causal factors, or determine causality. Statistical analysis is important in determining causality and is the reason that positivism and quantitative research are closely associated.

Explanatory research: "Explain"; a method of research focused on explaining *why* the specific social issue or problem exists.

In light of the "critical" and thus questioning tone of this text, the astute reader may well wonder if these steps to establishing causality are valid. Qualitative researchers in particular may reject these steps (see chapter 10), whereas quantitative researchers will champion their necessity. To that avail, another area where there is a divide among the two research approaches is identified; let's examine the criteria of causality because it is very important in quantitative research.

From a positivistic research perspective, **causality** means being able to ascertain the effect that one variable has on another. It can be extended to making deductions from other propositions and assumptions; causality is also needed to show what an intervention has accomplished. In other words, causal explanation means that the researcher is confident that the variable or variables being examined are the actual source of any change in the study. In order to have confidence in these predictions, the researcher must be able to establish a causal relationship. There are three necessary steps, or requirements, to being able to determine a "cause-and-effect" relationship. These are concomitant variation, temporal sequencing, and the elimination

Causality: Specifying the cause for why things occur. In order to have confidence that one thing really *causes* another, three criteria have to be met: (1) the two variables must "covary" (as one variable changes, so does the other), (2) the cause must *precede* the effect, and (3) no other variable may be affecting the relationship between the independent and dependent variables.

Concomitant variation: A way to say there is a true relationship between variables: as one variable changes, so does another.

of rival casual factors. **Concomitant variation** is simply a scientific term that means covariance or a relationship must exist between variables. In even simpler terms: when one variable changes, the other changes with it. For example, the more one eats high-fat foods, the more weight one will gain. The more one associates with binge drinkers, the more likely it is that one will also binge drink. Basically, concomitant variation means that when there is an increase or decrease in one variable, there is also an increase or decrease in the other variable. As the amount of time spent studying for an exam increases, the score on the exam also increases.

The *direction* of change does not play a role in establishing causality. It can be a positive relationship, as when one variable increases (caloric intake) and the other also increases (weight gain), or the relationship can be "inverse," meaning when one variable changes, the other variable changes in the opposite direction. As physical activity *increases*, body fat *decreases*. Or, the more alcohol a student drinks, the worse his or her grades become. Concomitant variation simply establishes that there is a relationship, or association, between the variables. It is just a fancy word that means the variables are statistically associated.

Temporal sequencing: One of the fundamental requirements for determining causality; it means the cause must precede the effect.

Temporal sequencing means the *cause* must precede the *effect*. A person must increase calories *prior* to gaining weight. Increased physical activity precedes a reduction in body fat. This seems elementary, but temporal sequencing can be difficult to establish. In an earlier example, we mentioned an association between increased alcohol use and reduced grades; suppose, however, the school failure came *before* the alcohol use. Suppose a heroin addict ordered by the court to participate in a drug rehabilitation program successfully quits using heroin before the program even begins. Could the researcher say with any certainty that the drug program caused the addict to stop using heroin? In this case, the answer is no (based on the information that we have). The reason is that some other unknown factor(s) may have accounted for the motivation to stop using drugs. We don't know what came before or during the participation in the program. Was someone hurt as a result of the addict's drug use? What were the family pressures on the addict? Did the addict have a spiritual awakening? Was the addict at risk of losing his or her job? These other factor(s) could account for, or be responsible for, the discontinuation of heroin use. The drug rehabilitation program could be the cause, or it could also be a consequence of one or more other, unknown causal factors. This leads to another important distinction in determining causality.

Rival causal factors: Determines if all the factors influencing the relationship between independent and dependent variables are considered.

The third criterion needed to establish causality is the elimination of other **rival causal factors,** or accounting for factors that may have influenced the change. What other variables might have accounted for the addict quitting heroin use? Perhaps the addict's arrest itself motivated him or her to stop; perhaps the addict was diagnosed with a disease prior to appearing before the judge.

Fortunately, there are ways to help identify these important issues. If the study was set up properly, the researcher can use statistical techniques to determine the "weight," or influence, of these other possible factors. The issue of considering whether some other variable is the actual cause of the observed change is referred to as spuriousness. **Spuriousness** occurs when an apparent causal relationship between variables is actually due to some alternative, unrecognized variable. Maybe the heroin addict had a bad physical reaction to the drug, and thus was motivated to discontinue its use (and the discontinuation of heroin had nothing to do with the court-ordered drug rehabilitation program). The bottom line is that, for a researcher, it is important to think through and "control" for all influencing variables. It is essential to be a critical thinker!

Spuriousness: When the relationship between dependent and independent variables is really due to some variable that is not known or accounted for in the study.

We hope that, after reading this chapter, the student has a better understanding of *why* science is so important. Science can improve the quality of life and inform many social problems. Consider the effort people had to go through to store their food before the invention of refrigeration. Imagine how difficult it was to travel before the invention of motorized transportation. Think about how challenging it was to conduct research and write papers before the invention of computers. Remember that people once died from smallpox, and now vaccines prevent it. Finally, specifically related to criminal justice, think about the importance of finding ways to reduce pain and suffering, reduce crime, have a more efficiently functioning criminal justice system, and have programs and policies that meet the goals they are intended for and not waste taxpayers' money or make situations worse. As a researcher, be a critical thinker. Embrace research methods, be a scientist, because it is students of research methods who will soon be the ones using science to contribute knowledge and solve problems.

KEY TERMS

Applied research
Basic research
Causality
Concomitant variation
Deductive reasoning
Descriptive research
Epistemology
Evaluation research
Exploratory research
Explanatory research
Fluid research
Hired-hand research
Inductive reasoning
In-house research
Mixed methods research
Objectivity
Positivism
Qualitative research
Quantitative research
Rival causal factors
Science
Social sciences
Spuriousness
Temporal sequencing
Third-party research

CRITICAL THINKING EXERCISES

1. Identify the difference between qualitative and quantitative research. Discuss at least four distinctions.
2. From a historical standpoint, what challenges did early scientists have to endure? Has this changed?
3. Draft a statement regarding why research is important. How has science contributed to social development? Provide examples.
4. Has science created any negative consequences for society? Provide examples.
5. What is the underlying theoretical or philosophical basis for each research method? Does this create a problem for mixed methods research?
6. What determines which research methods should be used? Why?
7. Why might fluid research be controversial? Discuss the pros and cons of fluid research. Develop a scenario that would demonstrate the benefits of fluid research. Develop a scenario whereby a fluid approach would not be beneficial.
8. Review the following link and provide a critical discussion on how and why knowledge is changing so rapidly. What are the benefits and risks associated? http://www.industrytap.com/knowledge-doubling-every-12-months-soon-to-be-every-12-hours/3950

CHAPTER 2

The Stages of Research: A General Overview

CHAPTER OBJECTIVES

After reading this chapter students should:

- Have more confidence in picking a research topic and be more aware of the reasons to avoid a topic that is too broad.
- Understand the importance of theory development and know the difference between a philosophy and a theory.
- Distinguish the difference between independent, dependent, and exogenous variables.
- Understand what research replication is and why it is important.
- Be more confident in locating quality research and understand the benefits of using "peer-reviewed" work.
- Be able to develop a literature review and avoid simply summarizing one article after another.
- Understand the process of operationalizing variables.
- Know how to code variables and understand why this process is important for data analysis.
- Be able to identify the level of measurement of variables and what can be done statistically with each level.
- Identify the different types of research designs.
- Know the difference between univariate, bivariate, and multivariate analysis.
- Know what a sample of the population is, and why certain sampling strategies are superior to others.
- Know and understand why response rates are important.
- Formulate the "steps" associated with a research project.

Before getting further into the specifics of research methods, this chapter provides an *overview* of the typical research process; however, it should be noted that each study is different, so no true "typical study" exists; this is a survey of the common sequence of steps. It is helpful to have a broad overview of the research process before addressing the specific issues surrounding the science, ethics, and politics associated with conducting research. Most of the issues addressed in this chapter are developed more fully in the remainder of the text. Also be aware that even the ideal research design will often be altered as the study progresses, as first mentioned in chapter 1, this is called **fluid research.** We do not intend to present research as a concrete formula, but for beginning researchers this step-by-step approach can be helpful until more confidence is gained. Conducting research studies can be fun and, as mentioned in chapter 1, beneficial to society. After reading this chapter, it is our hope that novice researchers will have a better comprehension of the complete process.

Fluid research: A research approach providing flexibility (not viewing the process of research as a set concrete formula) and the ability to adapt to changing circumstances, including taking advantage of new research opportunities that may present themselves during a study.

STEP ONE: SELECTING A RESEARCH TOPIC

The first research step is to select a topic, or identify a researchable problem. As easy as this sounds, it is often very difficult. There are so many interesting things to study that it can seem overwhelming. Often students have not thought about problems from the position of how to best study and eventually help solve them. It is important when selecting possible topics to pick things of interest, and these will vary among individuals. Become conscious of what is most important and most interesting. A good habit to start in college (the earlier the better, of course) is questioning everything. In other words, think *critically*. Why do things happen the way they do? Why do certain things exist? Do programs and policies actually work? Why do people act the way they do? What are the sources of problems? What are possible solutions to problems? Notice the issues that spark the most classroom discussion, and become aware of topics that are personally motivating. In addition, notice that problems and issues are usually multifaceted. There are multiple directions that can be taken with *any* problem, and issues are often embedded in other issues. When a topic is chosen, consider the many different ways it can be studied. By first reading the literature, one can determine what has already been done and then perhaps develop a plan of action that will provide an even better method of analyzing the problem, or simply replicate an earlier study (discussed later in this chapter) to determine if the findings are still true in a different location and time. Many students are apprehensive about literature reviews, but reviewing what studies have already been conducted on a topic is a rewarding, crucial, and necessary process. Furthermore, reviewing existing studies is also intellectually empowering, and will guide research questions, hypothesis development, and theoretical orientations, and it will advance research designs.

Events in one's life might also help determine a research topic to select. For example, some students' parents divorce, some students are raised in foster homes, very strict religious homes, or very lenient homes, some experience physical or verbal abuse, some have changed schools often, some have medical problems, some have family members who are addicted to drugs, or perhaps have been arrested, and maybe some have witnessed a serious crime or the death of a loved one. A person's life experiences can motivate interest and academic inquiry; however, it is very important to be careful that a personal experience does not interfere with the ability to be neutral and **objective** in conducting research. Some experts question the ability of a researcher to remain truly neutral; others question whether objectivity is really as important as once thought. Lacey (2016) explains that his research reveals that he has not been able to identify any scientist or philosopher who has been able to adequately defend that science should be responsive to the concept of values being absent in science. What he proposes to those who argue for completely value-free science is instead rehabilitating the notion of neutrality. He argues for democratic oversight committed to the ideal of *impartiality* and suggests that values might even promote better science by developing more "robust methodological pluralism." By forgoing the ideal of "value-free" science, by not trying to *deny* the role of values, better science can actually occur. He believes in setting the priorities of science so that social life benefits from its development through the commitment to "inclusiveness and evenhandedness" (p. 83), not to the commitment of complete neutrality.

Objectivity: The ability of the researcher to remain "neutral" and avoid allowing any influencing factors to taint or bias the study or the conclusions reached.

Regardless of one's position about values and neutrality in science, researchers should be careful that their biases do not influence the *outcome* of the research. It is acceptable to allow personal experiences to motivate research interest, it is acceptable that researchers desire to affect positive social change, but researchers need to remain aware of the potential problems associated with letting that passion jeopardize ethical standards. Make sure that perceived opinions or biasness are not influencing the study. It is also advisable to make any known biases explicit and to discuss steps taken to counteract potential concerns with biases. Being willing to accept the data even if it does not support your preconceived notions is an obligation in science. In other words, the data should always speak for itself. Agent Daniel McKenzie of the U.S. Immigration and Customs Enforcement (ICE) agency was the regional supervisor on a multistate human trafficking task force. He conducted his master's thesis on the actual number of human trafficking cases that occur. Due to his occupation and experience, he anticipated a high number of human trafficking cases. The data, however, showed a relatively small number of cases (McKenzie, 2017; Lanier and McKenzie, 2017). His research reported the actual smaller number even though it counteracted his hypothesis and personal expectations.

Sometimes the World Wide Web (www), social media, current events, newspapers, historical occurrences, or the library can help provide research possibilities. Reading academic literature is a great way to get ideas for potential research projects. The limitations of existing research and suggestions for future studies are helpful; this can often (and should) be found in the concluding section of published research articles. It is also common and beneficial in the field of social science to replicate other studies. As mentioned in chapter 1, *research* means to search again ("re-search"). **Replication** is conducting the same study again to determine if the same results will be found. In other words, do not be worried about choosing topics that have already been studied (most everything has); doing so can actually be very beneficial to science (just be sure to cite the original study). It is through reproducing research, and coming to the same conclusions over time, that true knowledge is actually established. Also, if future replications (similar studies) find dissimilar results, this must be explained, and further research is warranted when inconsistencies are found. Making slight modifications can be a worthy contribution to science, however; remember that replication does not always mean the study has to be an exact copy (a different sample could be used or new variables can be introduced, for example). It is unlikely that a student's research project will involve novel, never previously researched subject matter. Most studies deal with research topics that have already been examined. The key is to be able to locate what has been done and *advance* the knowledge in some meaningful way. This is what science is all about.

Replication: The practice of duplicating existing studies in order to validate or refute previous research findings.

The review of the literature on a topic is not only crucial in the development of a study, research questions, and a hypothesis, it can also help guide the theoretical orientation used to explain social science phenomena being examined.

Theories, or ideas, about human behavior, group action, or how agencies operate are a vital part of research. A **theory** is basically a *logical proposition* to help make sense of reality. Students who have already completed theory courses (e.g., criminology, political science, public health, sociology, environmental science) may thus be at an advantage in research methods. For those who have not had exposure to theory, the process of reviewing the literature becomes even more important. The connection between discipline-specific theory and research methods is strong. One very fruitful strategy is to take a theory from one discipline and apply that theory in a different context to another social problem. For example, Lanier, Pack, and Akers (2010) took a public health theory about how disease spreads and applied it to how gang-related drug use spreads. This is often done in interdisciplinary studies.

Theory: A proposition developed to help make sense of reality. The researcher would need to ask, "Are the propositions [logical guesses about reality] testable?" If logical explanations about reality cannot be tested (i.e., are not falsifiable), then they are not recognized as legitimate theories.

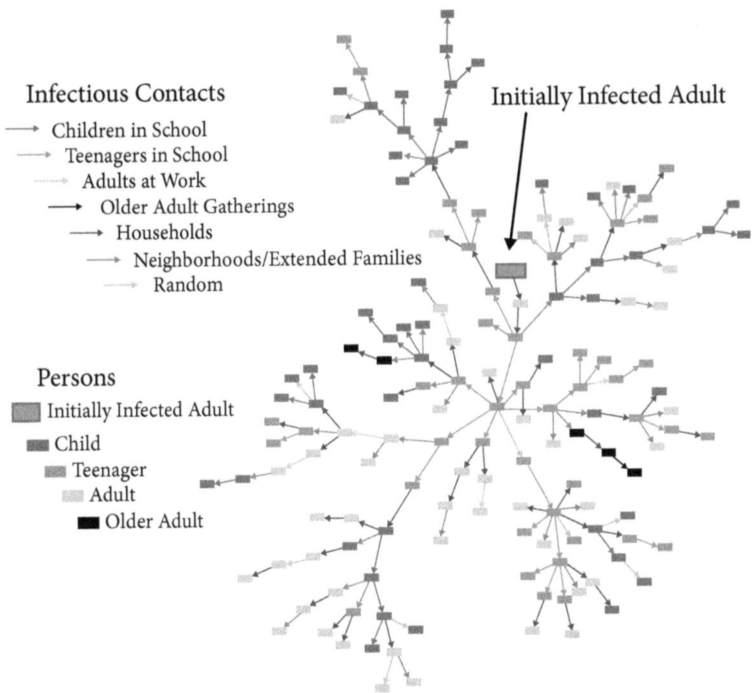

Figure 2.1
Can the visual below be used to explain crime as well?

For illustrative purposes, consider how the chart shown in Figure 2.1 shows how a disease might spread. Replace the term "disease" with a specific type of crime and see if it works as well. For example, some female students are increasingly engaging in the "Sugar Daddy" means of support. There are even websites specifically devoted to the practice (e.g., www.sugardaddyforme.com; www.honeydaddy.com/a/honey-daddy). As this practice grows in popularity it spreads much the same as the disease vectors shown in Figure 2.1. Can the chart be used to explain gang-related drug use or another type of crime of interest?

Theories are a great source of research ideas and questions. In turn, research findings can stimulate theory development. One often fosters the other. This was suggested in chapter 1 when deductive and inductive reasoning were presented. Theories suggest testable hypotheses about issues, and research evaluates whether those theoretical hypotheses have heuristic value. Typically, one of the most important requirements of a good theory is that its propositions are testable (falsifiable). A good way to think of theory is to remember that if the logical propositions cannot be verified (and some suggest they have to be *empirically* verified, which means using statistical data analysis), then it cannot be considered a credible theory. Those things that cannot be verified might be considered philosophies instead, because according to the principles of the Scientific Method theories should be scientifically and statistically verified.

Developing practical theories, and then empirically evaluating them, is one of the most important functions of the sciences (both physical and social). Good researchers want to know why things happen the way they do and have confidence that it can be scientifically validated. While that is often challenging, especially in the social sciences, research methods and the tools employed are the necessary processes to advance science.

It is a good idea when choosing a topic to keep it *narrow*. A common barrier to a successful project is that the focus is too large. Some students who choose a very broad topic may find 250,000 related articles (internet "hits"). For example, a search for "mental illness and pedophilia" will yield too many hits to be useful. It is difficult to begin to review the literature when the amount is so overwhelmingly large. Doing so can create a situation in which the student's work is disorganized and incoherent, and frustrating both for the student and for the advising professor. The key is to keep the topic as specific as possible at first, and then widen the scope later, if necessary. For example, instead of taking on the grand project of researching pedophiles, narrow the focus to the recidivism of pedophiles, correctional programs for pedophiles, causes of pedophilia, or victims of pedophiles. When conducting the research, select only those trustworthy and credible articles that are directly connected to the specific topic. For example, if the topic is the *victims of pedophiles*, do not include reference material on the different treatment programs available for sex offenders. Keep all research reviewed focused on the *victims* of sexual predators for this particular study. Approaching the topic this way will help reduce the probability that the student's research is disorganized and thus confusing.

Hypothesis: Is based on an informed, educated guess about the relationship between variables in a study.

Null hypothesis: Is based on the logic that there is *no* relationship between the variables in a study.

STEP TWO: IDENTIFYING A TESTABLE RESEARCH QUESTION

Part of the researcher's task is not just selecting a researchable topic but developing a testable research question (or multiple questions). The approach to addressing a specific research question will vary depending on whether the investigation is qualitative or quantitative. In a quantitative design, the research question is generally framed as a **hypothesis**, which is a testable proposition about the relationship between two or more variables. Basically, a hypothesis is an informed, educated guess about the relationship between variables. A **null hypothesis** means there is no expected relationship between the variables and is actually what is tested statistically in quantitative analysis (more on this later). It is necessary to rule out that there is no true statistical relationship between the variables of interest. Much like the brief examples in chapter 1 on the relationship between alcohol use and grades, one can hypothesize that as the use of alcohol increases, the grade point average (GPA) of a college student may decrease. Researchers are just guessing (although educated and guided by the literature review) about the relationship between the two variables. Statistical formulas are useful to aid in determining if these "guesses" are valid. The *dependent* variable (Y) is what the researcher is trying to explain (the social phenomenon of interest), and *independent* variables (X) are what the researcher expects will explain or influence the dependent variable. For example, GPA could be the dependent variable. In this case, the researcher is trying to determine what is causing variation in GPAs among students in her class; could it be due to alcohol use, study habits, class attendance, etc.? The independent variables *influence* the dependent variable, and in this case the researcher is questioning whether alcohol consumption could have anything to do with the change in GPA. It is worth repeating: the dependent variable is what the researcher is trying to explain (determine), and the independent variables are what are thought to explain or *influence* the dependent variable. Remember: *d*ependent variable (*d*etermine), and *i*ndependent variable (*i*nfluence). If one increases or decreases the independent variable, if there is a true statistical relationship between the variables, it has an influence on the dependent variable. If alcohol consumption is increased or decreased, does the subject's GPA change? There are also other variables, called exogenous or intervening variables (Z), that can be expected to influence study findings. For example, a chronic drinker might be able to function and maintain grades,, whereas a binge drinker might experience difficulty. Weight, age, and gender are other potential exogenous variables that could impact findings. A good research project will "control" for these influences when designing the research project. The following is an example of a research problem stated in the form of research questions, with hypotheses and theoretical propositions provided.

Research problem: Binge drinking of alcoholic beverages among college students.

Research questions: What are the causes of binge drinking? Who is more likely to binge drink? Are university programs designed to reduce binge-drinking working? Is binge drinking harmful to individuals? Is binge drinking more of a problem at urban or rural universities? Is binge drinking more common among student-athletes or general students? Is binge drinking more common among college freshmen or college seniors? Are students with an alcoholic parent or guardian more likely to

binge drink? Does binge drinking influence one's grades? Is binge drinking more common among males or females?
Note: A research question can take many forms. For now, just focus on one question.

Null hypothesis: There is no difference between the likelihood of binge drinking between males and females.
Note: A null hypothesis is what is typically "tested" in quantitative studies.

Research hypothesis: Males are more likely to be involved in binge drinking than are females.
Note: We simply made an educated guess about the relationships between variables.

Now let's think about *why* we would make such a guess.

Theoretical assumption: Hegemonic masculinity, opportunity theory, peer pressure, male bonding, and self-control theory are theories that can be used to inform the hypothesis that *males* are more likely to binge drink.
Note: See why it is so important to turn to the literature? Quality information already exists!

Justification of research attention: By identifying who is more likely to binge drink, university education campaigns can be geared accordingly. Perhaps student safety and academic success can be increased?

Dependent variable: Binge drinking (this is what is trying to be better understood).

Independent variable: Gender (this is one variable that is thought to influence the rate of binge drinking). Note that there are many other independent variables, such as year in school, student-athlete status, Greek affiliation, alcoholic parent/guardian, and so on. The possibilities are vast. That is what is interesting about research.

There are many positions that can be taken, and each may present different research possibilities. This is the case with most social issues. Besides hypothesis testing, program reviews also are worthy of a researcher's attention. For example, consider whether the university has already implemented educational programs regarding binge drinking. A researcher could evaluate the effectiveness of the program. Is it really making a difference? There are so many options to study that this is what often makes selecting a research topic and developing a research question difficult, but at the same time fun—it allows one to actually think! As mentioned earlier, if given a choice, pick an interesting topic and assess whether the study can actually contribute knowledge to the field. It is a good idea to develop a list of possibilities and then begin narrowing the possibilities by determining which research question is most feasible under the time and financial constraints, and which is conducive to the methodological and statistical skills of the researcher.

It is a good practice at this point in the research process to select the best option from the list and write out a few specific research questions (as done earlier). Next, write out a couple of specific hypotheses related to the overall questions (what do *you* expect the relationship to be between variables? The literature helps in this regard), and identify at least five (for now) worthy references (prior research) on the topic. Once some of the literature has been reviewed, write out at least one paragraph justifying why the topic is important and worth studying. What is the purpose of the research? Then, write out at least one paragraph on how the hypothesis will be assessed/tested. As the text is read, this part will become clearer. This will help narrow the scope of the study, help in developing a plan of action, and direct the focus of the advanced literature review. Locating existing quality research is a very important part of the research process. Once related research has been read, the hypothesis may need to be amended because of new information gleaned from the literature. It is acceptable at this stage to make changes; this is partially what fluid research is all about.

STEP THREE: FINDING RESEARCH

When trying to find previous research on a specific topic, refer to the statement indicating the purpose of the current research project. This will help ensure that the research focus is not taken in different directions. If it cannot be clearly articulated how the information *directly* relates to the current study, then do not include it. Avoid including research simply because it is available; make sure it directly informs the current research project. Once this habit is formed, it will help with the flow and organization of the writing and the focus of the research project. Also, avoid just selecting the first articles written on the topic, be critically selective!

A successful researcher becomes skillful at knowing what kinds of research to include in the literature review. Choose only those prior studies that are *specifically* relevant to study and only those that are *credible*. Learning where to get credible research is very important. With the invention of computer technology, the options are virtually endless. Quickly searching the internet and trusting the first available result is not accepted research practice. This is particularly important knowing that Google and other search engines filter topics based on their internal criterion. It is

Peer-reviewed article: Research that has been evaluated by selected experts (reviewers) before it is allowed to be published in an academic journal; normally the study authors are not identified, so it is often called a "blind peer-review process."

Refereed research: The same as "peer-reviewed." Reviewers evaluate the work before it is published.

important to reference only quality work, and **peer-reviewed articles (refereed research)** are preferable. Briefly, peer-reviewed research is work that has been reviewed and critiqued by others in the field before it is published. Typically, the manuscript "reviewers" are selected because they have some expertise in the subject, which adds credibility to the review process. Once feedback is given, the publisher will require necessary corrections from authors before publication is allowed. Most often, more quality research is also a blind peer-reviewed process, which means that the research authors' names are kept from the reviewers. This helps reduce bias in case the reviewers might like (or dislike), know, or otherwise have a relationship with the research authors.

If one simply does a World Wide Web (www) search on a topic, there is no assurance of reliability or credibility. It is much better to use research sources that have been academically peer reviewed and/or refereed. The panel of experts evaluates and approves the publication of the material, yet keep in mind this does not guarantee *excellent* work. It is, however, an *attempt* to hold researchers accountable.

Students have the luxury of access to vast amounts of literature through the university library, and this can often be acquired by computer technology. It is therefore worth the time to learn how to *navigate* this valuable resource. Trial and error (practice) can be an effective way to learn, but most university libraries make it relatively simple to locate quality literature, and a visit to the library will likely result in quicker learning. For example, starting on the university library home page, click on keywords that suggest a link to research, such as "research guides by subject." Once there, most libraries will be organized by subject, for example, "criminal justice" or "interdisciplinary studies," "psychology," or "political science." Once the discipline (field of study) has been located, the next link will likely be to an academic search engine, such as SOCINDEX, PSYCINFO, Educational Resource Information Center (ERIC), Masterfile Premier, National Criminal Justice Reference Service (NCJRS), Military and Government Collections, Criminal Justice Periodical Index, PUBMED, Criminal Justice Abstracts, Business Source Premier, Academic Search Premier, Applied Science and Technology Abstracts, LexisNexis Academic, and NetLibrary (and there are others). Pick one of the search engines (one should actually review *multiple* search engines) and begin entering keywords related to the research topic in the "subject" search. For example, if the topic is sexual victimization, begin the search with those words, but remember to have a *list* of keywords already developed (*molestation, rape, sexual abuse, victims of pedophiles, child molesters, victims of sex crimes*, etc.). The list of keywords is an important step because sometimes it takes different "triggers" to pull up related articles. If it is available, click the toggles that say "scholarly peer-reviewed journals" and "full text." There may be an important article that does not have full text available, but there are ways to obtain it. Just ask the librarian, or use interlibrary loan (see the following paragraph).

Professors who are older, and older students, will remember when literature could only be reviewed by going to the actual library and using the Dewey Decimal System to locate related information. That was step one. Step two involved walking through aisles of books until the specific reference was found. Because it has become so easy with computers to find research, it is understandable why some faculty members have little patience for students who are unwilling to search for and include quality references. It is so easy now! Be aware, though, when using the university library, that some items may not be available online, but the library has them in its printed collection. This may require an actual trip to the library. Also, most libraries use the word *holdings* to refer to the location of the reference. Some universities are in the same system, which allows materials to be sent from one library to another. In this case, **interlibrary loan** may be an option. The references may be borrowed from another university library. Just realize that actually getting the literature may take a little time, so do not wait until the last minute to try to locate it.

Interlibrary loan: The process of "borrowing" research studies or books that may not be available at one's own university library.

The search engines accessed through the library will likely review articles published in common journals in specific disciplines. Each area of social (and physical) science will have a core of academic journals. There are hundreds of journals devoted to just crime, criminal justice, deviance, and delinquency, for example. By going through the university library, many of the providers of these resources have already been purchased—consider it part of tuition—so utilizing the resources through the university library is a much wiser and more cost-effective way to conduct research.

Source: gnagel

While university libraries are the best sources of quality journals, the internet, if used correctly, also provides access to peer-reviewed research. It may be that the topic of interest is covered in a chapter of a book, and this might be available free online. Using sites such as Google Scholar is often preferable to just "surfing the net" because it is typically free and has tools available to limit the search to scholarly work. Be prepared that sites such as Amazon are "for-profit" book retailers, and some cost may be involved in securing the text. Some articles may be offered by online vendors such as Publist (www.publist.com), but usually for a fee. Again, this is another reason to utilize the "free" service of the university library, while at the same time providing access to more scholarly work than typical internet searches.

Yahoo also has a subject directory (http://dir.yahoo.com/social_science) that can, at times, be used to locate literature in the social sciences. It is not a search engine to the World Wide Web but does have a collection of articles, books, and related links within Yahoo. From the main page, links are provided to discipline-specific materials such as sociology and criminology. Another part of Yahoo's subject directory (see http://world.yahoo.com) has sites for other countries, which could be helpful if country-specific research is needed. Note that some of the articles and links may not be in English, depending on the country.

Many government documents, studies, reports, and statistics are made available to the public, often via the Web. Usually government reports do not go through the peer-review process, as do referred journal articles, and there is a possibility of biased results, so a researcher should be especially cautious. To reduce the possibility of including biased references in the work, it adds credibility when *more than one* source indicates the *same or very similar results*, so try to verify the information with multiple references.

It cannot be stressed enough that with any research, credibility is added when the article comes from a refereed, reputable journal. Many search engines offered by universities allow the ability to exclude articles that are not peer-reviewed. This is not as easy when selecting materials from the World Wide Web. If one is unsure whether work is credible, here is a tip to help decide. A possible method to determine credibility is by searching the actual name of the journal and determining whether it uses the peer-review process. Normally, the journal will include this information on its homepage in the section that describes the journal. Journals usually want to indicate that they use a referee process before accepting articles for publication because it makes them more prestigious and trustworthy; so, when in doubt, be sure to read about the actual journal's information. It is equally important to use a citation index to determine how good a particular journal might be. This is simply a numerical value that allows researchers to rank journals by prestige. Because not all material on the internet can be trusted, necessary steps must be taken to ensure that the resources being used are credible.

Students consistently want to use Wikipedia, maybe because it is the first site that often appears in a search on the internet. As an exercise, review Wikipedia's own disclaimer as printed on *its* webpage (http://en.wikipedia.org/wiki/Wikipedia:Disclaimers):

> Wikipedia is an online open-content collaborative encyclopedia. . . . The structure of the project allows anyone with an Internet connection to alter its content. . . . Please be advised that nothing found here has necessarily been reviewed by people with the expertise required to provide you with complete, accurate or reliable information.
>
> *(Retrieved October 24, 2012)*

Currently, absolutely anyone can post and change information on this site. Wikipedia has experienced controversy and legal ramifications regarding the reliability of its information, and while the site has begun a process of trying to be more professional and even trying to verify facts, the quality of the "verification" is questionable. Therefore, it is best to avoid the temptation to use Wikipedia and similar sites as academic references. At least minimize their use to assisting in the location of possible *scholarly* work. With its new format, Wikipedia sometimes will reference scholarly work, but it is still necessary to go to more credible sources. In addition, the internet can be used to locate conference papers, as conference programs are available *online*. Often, conference papers are difficult to obtain, and, although they are scholarly, most have not been reviewed by other experts in the field.

It is not difficult to find information by using the internet. What is difficult is determining if the information can be *trusted*. Remember, *anyone* can post information to the World Wide Web, and most can make their site *seem* credible. It is the responsibility of the researcher to verify that the sources used are trustworthy, accurate, and factual. If there is no journal, author, or contact information available, it is not likely to be a very good source. At a minimum, the name and location of the author where inquiries are welcome should be included. Start paying close attention to who is actually creating the web pages. Noticing the domain name may also be helpful. Always identify how the URL ends (the letters after the last dot). Here are some examples:

.edu (educational site, e.g., college or university)
.gov (government site)

.com (commercial business site)
.mil (U.S. military site)
.org (U.S. nonprofit organization)
.net (network service provider, organization)

Finally, consider some of the concerns with these sites. Why would some of the materials from these locations provide biased (one-sided) information? If it is a .org, .com, or .net promoting the legalization and sale of a specific drug, it is likely that not all the facts will be presented. What about a .gov? Will "damning" information about the government likely be presented? Could neutral research findings be omitted? Even .edu sites may have an *agenda*; but of the domains listed earlier, the .edu and .gov sites are likely to have *fewer* organizational agendas than the others. Because many websites have their own organizational (or even personal) agendas, additional verification of facts is needed (multiple verification is beneficial, anyway). Because of the lack of regulation of the internet, some commercial sites are developing their pages to appear scholarly, so be careful. Even medication vendors (a business) now appear to be scientifically based. Do they have an agenda? Do they want to market and profit from their drugs? Of course! Many internet sites are there to accomplish some personal goal of the page owner; therefore, the information is likely to be biased as well as non-credible. In short, be a critical consumer of information!

Another problem with using the internet is that what is there today may be gone tomorrow; therefore, it is important to keep a copy of the material, as well as exact URL information and to record (and reference) the date it was retrieved. Even the sites referenced in this chapter may be unavailable or altered by now.

As indicated at the beginning of this section, there is an endless amount of literature available; it is part of the researcher's job to distinguish between credible and non-credible resources. It is also important to know when the literature has been reviewed sufficiently. A lot of time can be consumed searching for research, and some novice researchers will have a hard time knowing when to stop and what is sufficient material (of course, there are those who will not gather enough—try to avoid being that person). One way to know when sufficient research on a subject has been gathered is when the same author or work reappears (is referenced) in the literature. Notice if the same themes are reappearing; notice if the same work or authors reappear. Think of this as finding out what the "granddaddy" or original work is regarding the particular subject. You will want to look for the main researchers on a topic. When those have been identified and similar work reappears, you can feel a little more confident that a sufficient search has been conducted.

A bibliographic-type index such as the **Social Sciences Citation Index (SSCI)** can be helpful in identifying credible references. The SSCI has a feature that shows how often an article has been cited in the literature. Finding out who the major contributors are on the specific social science subject is often necessary. Researchers do not want to overlook major works. Once it has become clear that these have been included, a researcher can be confident that an adequate job of identifying important, related research has been accomplished. If a citation index is not used, a general rule is to be mindful to include articles that are cited in multiple manuscripts. Look for repetitive patterns in the literature. As more literature is read, similar arguments, methodologies, and findings will start to appear; when new viewpoints are no longer being encountered, it can be reasonably assumed that that part of the literature has been sufficiently reviewed (Leedy & Ormrod, 2001). A good researcher will always periodically return to the literature, however. New research is constantly being published. It may be difficult to find a compromise between doing too much and not doing enough. It is better to be on the side of excessive coverage of a topic, rather than deficient coverage. A lot of words in this chapter have been devoted to finding existing, quality research; the point should be clear by now that it really is an important foundation of any research project. What happens once that research has been located is equally important. The literature review and how it is incorporated into the research project vary by the research design, but reviewing the literature is equally important regardless of whether it is a qualitative, quantitative, or mixed methods approach.

Social Sciences Citation Index (SSCI): A research tool showing how many times particular research has been referenced in the literature.

STEP FOUR: THE LITERATURE REVIEW

There is very little that has not already been studied in some form; good researchers find out all they can about their subject before they undertake their own study. Not only is it important to find out what is already known about the subject, but the literature is able to identify what is *not yet* known or well understood. By examining the existing literature, the researcher can verify what else needs to be done. A **literature review** is a great way to help set up a research project; by indicating what already exists, it helps provide ideas on what to do next regarding the research problem. Look at what has been done already, identify conflicting outcomes of studies, and what has been learned as well as what has not been learned from past studies. Consider what can be modified on past studies that will better inform the research question. A literature review is a great tool for providing ideas for changing some of the conditions or variables of previous studies, which may result in different

Literature review: The process of gathering and evaluating existing research that can help inform research projects.

outcomes. A literature review not only makes researchers more educated about a subject, but it can actually aid researchers in designing their own studies.

A literature review is an important aspect of *any* research project. The reasons may vary between quantitative and qualitative researchers, but reviewing the literature is equally important for both. The goal of a literature review for a quantitative researcher is to identify the progress of similar studies, which helps provide the rationale or reasons for the study being conducted; this can assist in the development of research questions and hypotheses that will be scientifically tested. The literature review actually "sets up" and justifies the entire project.

Qualitative researchers use the literature review to articulate the need for the study and may reference related studies throughout the project; however, the literature review usually does not "set up" the entire project. *Generally*, the literature review comes at the start of a quantitative research project and is scattered throughout in a qualitative one. In either event, it is beneficial to find out as much as possible on the topic of study. Reference material is helpful in identifying facts and in convincing the reader of the importance of the study to the discipline. A well-prepared literature review adds credibility.

The literature review will be lacking if it is no more than a summation of the articles found. The literature needs to be "intertwined" with and heavily connected to the research question of the current project. Avoid including an article in the review just because there is access to it. Let it be obvious that the articles are included because they *inform* the identified research question. Do not simply reproduce what has already been written; instead *integrate it*. As other writers in the field suggest, literature reviews should *never* be a chain of isolated summaries of the writings of others (Leedy & Ormrod, 2001). The goal is to *integrate* the work of others as it *informs* one's own research study.

Initially, assessing each article is important, but a good literature review moves beyond that. Again, one should avoid leaving the reader wondering why a specific study was included in the first place and why a variety of details about past studies were "thrown" into the current project. Some stuff is just not necessary to include. Include it only if it informs the current project. Some researchers (e.g., Bachman & Schutt, 2011) suggest that specific items are important to include, such as hypotheses, the dependent and independent variables, the theoretical orientations, the methods used, the sample and response rate, the ethical considerations or violations, and the overall findings of past studies. It is good to provide readers with a basic understanding of past work, but the unique contribution comes when those studies are *integrated* as they pertain to the current project. Demonstrate the *connectivity* of the studies included in an identifiable manner to the *current* research project. Considering whether things were identified in past studies that support the current project is important and worthy of a researcher's time. Identify how past studies help spark ideas about what new research angles need to be taken, or where the pitfalls are that need to be avoided. Consider critiquing the varying theoretical perspectives on the topic, or identify how the problem and the approaches to deal with the problem (or *study* the problem) have changed over time. One thing that makes a literature review strong is to explain how limitations and unanswered questions in previous work *justify* the current project. In other words, use the literature to make sense of the current project; do not just "string along" a bunch of studies!

Once a review of the literature is conducted, it should provide enough knowledge about the topic to allow a sensible introduction to be written. Some introductions are distinct from the literature review, and some are intertwined with the literature review. In either event, the introduction needs to place the research problem in context. Often an introduction will demonstrate the areas in which the subject remains problematic, which should help establish the justification and importance of the study. The first words written are often the most important in order to capture the reader's attention.

STEP FIVE: RESEARCH DESIGN

A researcher needs to decide how to best assess the research questions by determining a "blueprint" (research design) for how the research will be conducted. This is often referred to as the "methods" section. The research questions and how the variables are measured will often determine the type of research design to be used. Before presenting (albeit briefly in this chapter) the different types of research designs, a discussion on how concepts are measured is warranted. Measuring abstract concepts in a concrete way is especially important in empirical (quantitative) studies; it is referred to as operationalizing the variables. **Operationalization** refers to putting abstract concepts into a measurable form. In fact, since this part of research determines the overall quality of the study, the process of operationalizing variables is critical to learn. One of the most difficult things to do as researchers in the social sciences is to figure out how to put abstract concepts of interest into forms that can be assessed or measured (i.e., operationalization). A simple variable like "political party" should be relatively easy to be operationalized and measured, but even this variable can come with some confusion and some controversy, as some respondents may prefer to identify themselves as

Operationalization: The process of putting abstract concepts into forms that can be measured.

"voting for the candidate and not the party," for example. If political party affiliation is a really important variable to the study, gathering more information about a person's beliefs may be necessary. For now, consider that it is the respondent's choice which party (if any) to identify with; a researcher's job is to provide the exhaustive options from which the respondent can select. It could hypothesized that either Democrats or Republicans are more likely to be involved in violent street protest, for example; so in this case it would be important to include a measure of politics in the study. The independent variable of political party is operationalized into categories that the respondent will select. What about another social construct like "family environment"? Could the family in which a person is raised contribute to the likelihood of the person being involved in violent crime? Here, operationalizing the variable "family environment" becomes a bit more difficult. What is meant by "family environment"? It actually could mean a variety of things. If a researcher asks five people what it means, he or she will likely receive five different answers. Therefore, researchers need to be specific in defining concepts and variables. For example, if researchers want to measure how often a parent and child spend time together, they need to specifically assess that. Researchers could operationalize this variable by counting the number of activities a parent and child do together in a week. If family environment means growing up in a home with a biological mother and a biological father, then the researcher needs to ask that specifically. With an abstract social construct such as family environment, the options are many. It is the researchers' responsibility to actually measure what is intended (validity), so great care needs to be given to the wording. Sometimes it is best to compute a scale from a variety of related questions to measure a specific social construct (more on this later). For now, it just means using multiple related questions to help measure a construct.

Validity: In research methods, the ability to measure what is actually intended. Researchers must ask the question, "Am I really measuring what I think I am measuring?"

Reliability: In research methods, having confidence that similar results, responses, and conclusions would be reached if the study were repeated.

If one is studying criminal behavior and wants to know about a person's mental health and asks if the respondent has "ever skipped school," is the researcher actually measuring *mental illness*? The answer is no. One has to be sure to really measure what one intends (**validity**), and that the concepts are measured in a way that the same answers would likely be given today as tomorrow (**reliability**). Later in this chapter, and throughout the book, the issue of why validity and reliability are so important to research is discussed. Remember for now, however, a key to it all lies in how the concepts are operationalized, and decisions must be made how to *best* do this. Studies cannot even be replicated if the variables are not measured well. Two important decisions must be made: How will the research study be designed, and how will the variables of interest be assessed? This is referred to as the research design.

Research Designs

In this chapter all the different types of research designs are not discussed, but an overview of some of the more common ones is provided to give the reader an introduction to options.

With **field research,** a researcher will go out and gather the actual research themselves, through personal direct observation of behavior. If the researcher were interested in airport security, an example of field research would be to obtain approval from the Department of Homeland Security (DHS) and find out how many airports can be penetrated with prohibited devices. While field research can be either qualitative or quantitative, accuracy in noting the data as they actually exist in the natural setting is imperative for both. If a researcher is conducting a qualitative study, accurate and effective note-taking skills are very important. Another example would be if a researcher wants to know about the influence of the environment on a decomposing human body (as is done at the Body Farm at the University of Tennessee and the Forensic Osteology Research Station (FOReST) at Western Carolina University), the researcher will measure the effects and changes to the corpse as time progresses. Keeping accurate field notes is crucial. Paying attention to every environmental factor and every change noted in the decomposition process is key. Of course, comparing the influence of the variables is the main objective that contributes to science. This science is indeed multidisciplinary since anthropology, sociology, biology, chemistry, criminology, environmental health science, and so forth all benefit from the knowledge. For example, consider how important such knowledge is to solving crimes and prosecuting murders. Even the maggots which contribute to the decomposition process can be studied for clues—just as the DNA from the offenders can be left behind, and used as evidence.

Field research: Is where a researcher goes into the research setting to observe behavior, facts, or processes, and gathers original data.

Experimental research can be approached in many ways. Some researchers are very motivated to have representative samples and make use of a *random* sampling of the study population; others are not concerned with being able to generalize results to entire populations. Basically, with true experimental research, a stimulus, intervention, or independent variable is introduced to participants in a controlled environment in order to observe the effects. In experimental research the stimulus is introduced to one group, which is compared with another group not receiving the stimulus in an effort to determine its effects. For example, a researcher who is interested in recidivism and offender rehabilitation would need to gain the necessary consent and approvals and then divide the offenders into experimental and control groups. The **experimental group** receives the specific treatment of interest

Experimental research: A research approach designed to introduce a stimulus in order to test its influence on the dependent variable using randomly selected samples.

Experimental group: The portion of respondents in the sample who receive the stimulus (treatment) in order to compare with the control group.

Control group: The group in an experiment that does not receive any treatment (stimulus) and is compared with the group that does (experimental group).

(e.g., on-the-job training); the **control group** does not. The two groups would be compared to determine which has lower recidivism rates (with necessary controls in place, of course). This means the groups would be compared to see if those receiving "on-the-job training" while incarcerated are less likely to return to prison. In the previous example with human decomposition, an experimental study could be conducted to see if different chemicals change the outcome of the deterioration of human remains. Various forms of compost, for example, speed the decomposition process. This is important to know since murderers may be using chemical compounds, or natural compost, to dispose of their victims. Control groups of cadavers can be set up and observed to note the chemical or compost effects (see Urban Death Project).

It is important to note here that true experimental research is less common in some fields than others. In criminal justice and criminology, for example, it is less common as many studies choose *purposeful* populations and worry less about having true randomly selected samples due to the inherent realities of conducting research in actual physical and social environments such as neighborhoods as opposed to laboratories or human decomposition facilities. Chapter 6, where research designs are presented will help increase appreciation of this. This also supports the premise that a multidisciplinary research approach to science is important.

Secondary data: Data that have already been collected by others.

Another method, especially when time is limited, is to analyze existing data. There are many avenues for obtaining **secondary data**, and much of this material is free to those with educational motives. Researchers with quantitative designs and research approaches typically use secondary data sets, including government-collected data. Qualitative researchers often use existing options as well; case studies, life history studies, climate data, record studies, health records, voting trends, police reports, court records, demographic data, geographic factors, content analyses of diaries, memoirs, journals, or letters provide a form of existing information that can be analyzed for research purposes. For example, if one wanted to know how political decisions are made, reviewing a politician's email record would provide great insight, which is one reason why the law mandates that official correspondence of political figures be preserved.

Survey research: Research utilizing questionnaires or interviews to gather information.

One of the most common research designs in some areas of social science, such as criminology, sociology, and political science is **survey research** (utilizing questionnaires or interviews). How surveys are constructed is determined by what type of research is intended. A qualitative researcher would want a survey that is free-flowing to allow the respondent to share openly and to be unrestrained in providing responses. A quantitative researcher would want each respondent to be provided with responses to the questions because it assists in analyzing the data statistically.

The terms *open-ended* and *closed-ended* questions are used often in research. This is covered later in the text, but for now, know that survey research is very popular, because it is less expensive and more expedient than other designs. Also, because there is less likelihood of risk to participants with survey research than with experiments, it is sometimes easier to obtain institutional review board (IRB) approval (discussion forthcoming).

Research Sample

Another important aspect to research is deciding who to study; in other words, which potential research subjects should be included in the study? Is it going to be a true random selection or a purposeful sample? It is also important to reveal the response rate of the sample. **Response rates** indicate the number of subjects, out of the total sample, who *actually* participated in the full study. The higher the response rate, the better the study will be perceived. This is especially true in survey research, as there might be reasons that people would not participate in the study which could be important to note. For example, in survey research on academic integrity among university students, if the participation rate is very low among certain groups of the study population (say, freshmen or seniors), then this not only could influence the outcome of the study but also might suggest there is a specific reason that freshmen or seniors did not want to participate. This absence needs to be considered, evaluated, and discussed in the conclusion.

Response rate: The number of individuals who actually participated in the study out of the total number of participants desired. A researcher would divide the total that actually participated by the total number desired to determine the actual response rate.

A **sample** is a selection of the total population of interest; typically, samples are chosen in ways that best represent the entire unit of study. In reality, several methods can be used for selecting samples, which is discussed later in the book (e.g., simple random sample, cluster sample, purposive sample, snowball sample, etc.), but with any method it is always important to describe the sampling techniques that are used to select respondents for participation in the study. With qualitative research, the sample is typically both smaller and purposively chosen. Alternatively, if a researcher wants to make sure that the study is *representative* of the total population, then one would need to make sure the study could be generalized to everyone in the population. This technique requires detailed attention, but is doable and often time-worthy. If interested in a study of college students, a researcher would want a large representative sample where all schools or all respondents have an equal chance of being randomly selected for participation in the study. This type of sample, referred to as *probability sampling*, allows for larger inferences to be made regarding the findings of the study.

Sample: A subgroup of the total population.

As mentioned earlier, purposeful samples are being conducted in the social science fields and do not require the same criterion as in random selection of subjects. In other words, they are nonprobability samples. For example, perhaps researchers will study students at their own universities because these students are easily accessible; the resulting data are still informative, but there is less focus on the ability to suggest that the results reflect *all* college students everywhere. An entire chapter is devoted to this later, so do not worry too much now about the specific types of designs or how samples are selected—just know that these important decisions will have to be made.

In this book, as in most research methods texts, an entire chapter is devoted to ethical considerations. The importance of protecting subjects and maintaining integrity and professionalism throughout the study cannot be overstated. The demonstration of the steps taken to ensure this are usually presented in the methods section of a research manuscript. This includes things like how the respondents' permission is obtained, verifying that IRB approval is given, and demonstrating that the subjects' risks are minimized and their identities kept confidential. Basically, the more transparent the details of the research process, the more trust is added to the quality of the design. Also related to ethics is the issue of plagiarism. A whole chapter of this book is devoted to helping students become more successful writers and addresses the importance of referencing borrowed work appropriately. Great detail is given on how to avoid plagiarism and other ethical problems. For now, the actual process of collecting data is presented.

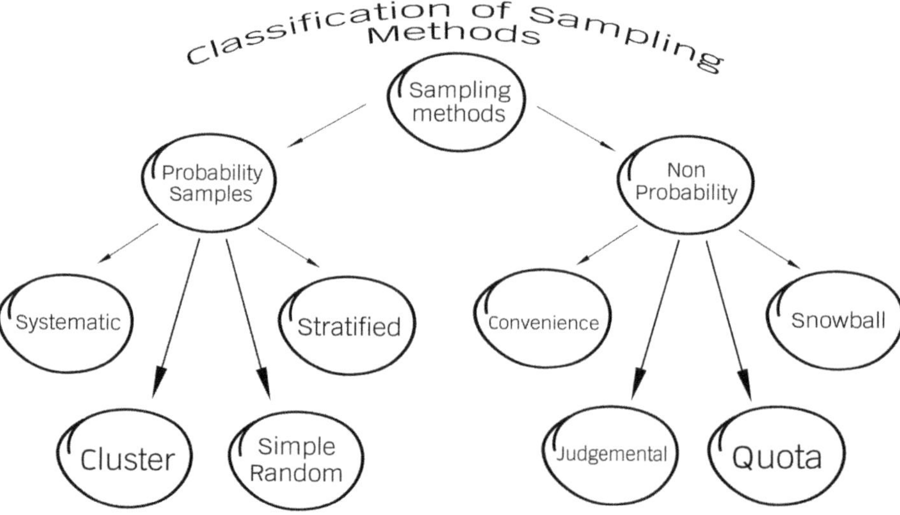

Figure 2.2
Samples Are Drawn From Populations And Can Vary in Method

STEP SIX: DATA COLLECTION AND VARIABLE CODING

Regardless of the research design and regardless of whether the method is qualitative or quantitative, and regardless of the field of study, data must be collected. This is true whether the method of choice is a mail survey, a telephone survey, an interview, an experiment, field research, or secondary data analysis. During the data-gathering phase, a considerable amount of time and attention will need to be given to the actual collection of the data. If the study is quantitative, the data will need to be translated into a form that can be recognized by a computer program such as SPSS, Stata, or SAS. Remember that statistical formulas analyze numbers and not words or abstract concepts, so an important phase of quantitative research is to code the data for statistical analysis. **Coding** the data simply means putting results in a form that statistical programs can understand. It means translating variables and their attributes into numbers. Then a statistical analysis on the numbers can be conducted. Here is a typical example. Gender is a common independent variable in many studies. *Typically*, individuals identify themselves as one of two attributes (categories): male or female. In order to generate statistics, the variable gender would need to be reflected by a numeric. The researcher could code "male" as 1 and "female" as 2 (or vice versa; it really does not matter much as long as there is consistency). Once the attributes have been coded, the statistical package will be able to generate statistics on the variable. For the variable of gender, for example, the statistical program can simply tabulate how many 2s (females) and 1s (males) there are. The researcher then gives a name and value label for the variable in the codebook of the data file to assist in identifying the variables and the actual attributes. It is also important to understand the different levels of measurement of variables because they determine what statistical analysis can be conducted on the variables. The following paragraphs will help clarify what "levels of measurement" means.

Coding: The process of transforming the attributes of a variable into representative numbers so that statistical analysis can be generated. It also involves giving names and labels to the social constructs (variables) in the study.

Level of Measurement of Variables

The way variables are operationalized results in those variables being on different levels of measurement, and this determines what statistical procedures can be conducted in an empirical analysis (most often in a quantitative study). There are four basic scales of measurement: nominal, ordinal, interval, and ratio (these are also covered in more detail in a later chapter). *Nominal scale measurement* simply means the variable represents a name of a category. The respondent is either in the group or not: Group A versus Group B, dog owner versus non-dog owner, yes versus no, and so forth. The respondent simply belongs to the category or does not. Because the attributes are just categories that cannot be ranked or the distance between them measured, the statistics for nominal level data are limited.

Ordinal scale measurement allows a researcher to rank order the data (the attributes of the variable). For example, the level of education can be measured on a rank-order scale. If someone has an elementary school, high school, or college education, there are different levels. With ordinal, there is rank order, but an *exact* distance between the attributes cannot be determined. A researcher knows one attribute is higher than another, but he or she cannot know by how much exactly. For example, a study could assess whether a person feels safe on campus at night. When attributes are ranked on a Likert scale, they are ordinal based. There is "rank order"; for example, a person responding, "strongly agree" has a higher weight than one who responds "agree" (to the fact that they he or she feels safe on campus, for example), but from a measurement standpoint, the precise weight cannot be ascertained.

Interval scale measurement is the third category. What characterizes interval level data is that the data have equal units of measurement and can have a *zero* point (but, note, the zero point is established arbitrarily—there is no set zero or exact starting point). In other words, there is an expected equal distance between the attributes (mathematically there is an equal distance between the categories of response). For example, there might be a 15-point difference between IQs of 135 and 150, and this is the same distance as between IQs of 150 and 165. One can measure the difference. But in regard to the zero, there is no true value of "nothing" because no one has an IQ of zero. In other words, if there is a zero in the scale and the zero has absolutely no value, then it would be a ratio-level variable; if the zero is just arbitrary, then it is interval. Remember, it is the meaning of the zero that distinguishes the two. *Ratio* data must have an exact starting point of zero (much like a ruler; hence, remember the *o* at the end of *ratio*).

Regardless, for both interval- and ratio-level data, there are equal levels of measurement between the data points within the operationalized variable, and the distance between the attributes can be explained (1.5 inches of yarn is 0.5 inch bigger than 1 inch of yarn). Interval and ratio levels allow any statistical procedures that rely on addition and subtraction (means, standard deviations, and statistical tests of correlations such as Pearson's correlations), which means that as the level of measurement of the variable increases, so does the ability to test relationships statistically.

"Cleaning the Data"

For a quantitative study, after the data are collected they need to be entered into a statistical software package. It is important to demonstrate that the data were "cleaned" before analysis (meticulously reviewed in order to demonstrate integrity and reliability). This is a process of "checks and balances." Researchers should conduct frequency analyses on all the variables to ensure accuracy. For example, if the attribute codes for a particular variable are 0 and 1, and the number 2 shows up when frequencies are generated, then one knows a problem occurred in the data entry stage. All issues like this need to be addressed before the data analysis stage begins.

STEP SEVEN: DATA ANALYSIS

Whether the research project is qualitative or quantitative, or mixed methods, the information discovered in the research process will need to be analyzed. If a researcher is going to advance his or her research ideas and move beyond literature reviews, one method is to evaluate research with analysis techniques; these can be qualitative or quantitative. For qualitative data analysis, looking for themes and stories that can be told from the data will be the focus of the analysis. For example, in a study conducted on inmates on death row, Briggs analyzed pen-pal letters written by inmates and found a number of themes. For example, the study (of letters from about 30 inmates) revealed that many had lost connections to friends and family on the outside, many still professed their innocence, and many had been on death row for a very long time.

In quantitative data analysis, trying to determine the statistical relationship between variables and determine causality is the goal. For example, a researcher could create a closed-ended questionnaire and send it to death row inmates about aspects of their lives that led to their criminal behavior. One might ask the respondent to select from the options asking about the presence of the father in the convicted inmates' lives. Recall that the research question drives the sample selection process. The attributes (answers that the respondent is allowed to pick from) can give some insight into the physical or psychological presence of the father figure. One would of course not simply measure this variable using one single question, as a series of questions about the *role* of the father figure is warranted to truly measure this variable. Once the data are returned, statistical analysis could help determine what factors contributed to their crimes.

In either event, once the data have been collected, they will need to be evaluated and analyzed. Because it is the statistical analysis aspect that might be new or intimidating, more attention will be given to quantitative analysis later in the text. First, it is important to recognize that data can be measured on the univariate, bivariate, or multivariate level. Simply put, **univariate analysis** describes a single variable

Univariate analysis: Provides a statistical summary of each individual variable in the study. Basically, it involves describing one variable at a time in order to illustrate the total variables in the analysis.

(e.g., how many inmates on death row are male versus female). A researcher could provide basic statistics on the mean, and mode of gender (percentages). In **bivariate analysis,** the researcher examines the statistical relationship between two variables (e.g., gender and violent crime; are more males more likely to be on death row?); in **multivariate analysis,** a basic goal is to determine the level of influence of the independent variables on the dependent variable (can knowing a person's gender or family structure help predict violent crime?). Begin to think about what univariate, bivariate, and multivariate analysis actually means.

Bivariate analysis: Demonstrates the relationship between two variables of interest. A researcher would ask, "As one variable changes, does the other variable change with it?"

Multivariate analysis: Involves examining the relationship between several variables. The goal is to "predict" the dependent variable by knowing the independent variables.

STEP EIGHT: REPORTING OF RESULTS

Findings are often described narratively and simplified into graphs, tables, or charts. This is true for qualitative, quantitative, and mixed methods research. The research results of the data analysis are usually kept separate from the interpretations of the findings, but this often varies by quantitative or qualitative approaches. In quantitative research, the findings section is simply for reporting of the facts and not elaborating on theoretical and analytical dialogue, which suggest the reasons for the various results or conclusions drawn from the data. The findings section should be very factual and neutral without interjections being made on why the researcher believes the data turned out the way they did. The reporting of the data results and the actual discussion of the data should be separated in a research manuscript. The actual results of the analysis are factual. The interpretation of what the results mean is more subjective, and someone may analyze the data and interpret what it all means and how it ties to theory in a different way from someone else. This is what science and theoretical development is all about. If the mission is to truly contribute to science, it is best to keep this section "clean" and straightforward. Simply report the facts.

STEP NINE: CONCLUSION AND LIMITATIONS

A good conclusion systematically presents a review of the major points and elaborates on the importance of the findings to the overall problem being considered. The conclusion needs to pull the whole project together and describe the implications for the future, as well as make a call for further research attention on the topic, if it is needed. Also, one may develop in the conclusion how the findings inform public policy. Importantly, because *no* research project is perfect, there are always limitations and areas for improvement. The conclusion is the appropriate place to present them. The work will be less likely to be criticized if the researcher identifies what these weaknesses are and suggests ways to make improvements for the next researcher who analyzes the problem. Often reviewers will skip to the conclusion of research projects in order to determine if the manuscript is worthy of their time to review in its entirety; therefore, the conclusion needs to be written in a way that keeps the reader's attention and provides sufficient details. Think of the conclusion as a mini project inside of the larger manuscript. If sufficient effort is not put forth in the conclusion, it leaves the entire project unfinished. Some writers have a tendency to "fizzle" at the conclusion; avoid this temptation.

Many researchers save writing the abstract until the very last step, and of course, thought should be dedicated to developing a parsimonious (concise) and descriptive title for the study. Depending on the project and the audience, an abstract may need to be included at the beginning of the manuscript. An **abstract** usually has word limits, typically 100 or 200 words. The goal of an abstract is to enable the reader to determine the relevance of the research study without having to read the entire manuscript; therefore, it includes statements regarding the topic, the methodology, and a summary of the major findings. Therefore, even though an abstract comes at the beginning of the manuscript, it will be one of the last sections to be written. Often an abstract is a condensed version of the conclusion; both provide similar goals to the reader.

Abstract: Typically a 100- to 200-word summation of the research project that comes at the beginning of the manuscript. A good abstract will explain each major part of the study (e.g., literature review, problem statement, methods, and findings).

FINAL SUGGESTIONS

With every research stage, it is important to self-impose a deadline and try to adhere to it. Completing a research project from start to finish is a time commitment, as much as it is an intellectual obligation. A researcher can make his or her life much easier, and the final product more successful and professional, by avoiding the common problem of procrastination. Be aware of the available time, resources, and skills needed to accomplish the study in its entirety. Most important, do not fail to allocate enough time to complete it. Anticipate that it will be necessary to write multiple drafts of the manuscript. Even for professors and professional authors, multiple drafts are a necessary part of the process of *any* manuscript (e.g., drafts of this book were read over 15 different people). Having another person edit the manuscript is a great idea. Typically, university writing centers are available and free; consider it a service that comes from tuition fees.

This chapter is an overview of what to expect in a typical research project or proposal. Emphasis has been placed on explaining both quantitative and qualitative processes, and more often studies are combining the two approaches: mixed methods. It is not likely that you understand all concepts at this point, but do not worry. Greater detail is provided in the forthcoming chapters and in classroom lectures; for now, try to visualize a "snapshot" of what to expect and try to *begin* to hone in on details related to each process.

KEY TERMS

Abstract
Bivariate analysis
Coding
Control group
Experimental group
Experimental research
Field research
Fluid research
Hypothesis
Interlibrary loan
Literature review
Multivariate analysis
Null hypothesis
Objectivity
Operationalization
Peer-reviewed article
Refereed research
Reliability
Replication
Response rate
Sample
Secondary data
Social Sciences Citation Index (SSCI)
Survey research
Theory
Univariate analysis
Validity

CRITICAL THINKING EXERCISES

1. What did you learn in a previous class, or through another experience, that you would like to know more about? In a few sentences, explain what you know about this topic, and what else you would like to know. Avoid replicating an example used in this chapter.
2. Frame the response to question 1 in terms of an identifiable research question, null hypothesis, and research hypothesis, and identify dependent and independent variables.
3. Identify key terms (search words) for the research problem identified in Question 2. Simply put the term into the search link of a browser like Internet Explorer. How many "hits" did you get on the topic? Now do the same process through your university library web pages (as discussed in this chapter). Describe the difference between credible and non-credible research. What are some ways to identify which resources are more credible?

4. Identify and define the four levels of measurement as discussed in this chapter. Provide an example of each based on the research problem identified in the response to Question 2. Avoid using examples provided in this chapter.
5. Describe the difference between univariate, bivariate, and multivariate analysis. Provide an example of each. How might you study your research question identified in Questions 1 through 4 based on these forms of statistical analysis?
6. After reading this chapter, outline the steps to a typical research project. For the things that you do not completely understand, write down the questions that you have. Brainstorm and try to figure out the answer yourself—use the book as a guide, talk to your fellow students, and have discussion with your friends; then finally ask your professor for an elaboration.
7. Take the chart on page 7 on disease spread and see how well it works with a specific type of crime that you are familiar with.

CHAPTER 3

Research Ethics

CHAPTER OBJECTIVES

After reading this chapter students should:

- Know all the required ethical standards that must be met.
- Understand why research ethics are important.
- Identify the role of the institutional review boards (IRB).
- Describe why IRBs are important.
- Describe why the IRB process may pose *obstacles* to research.
- Discuss examples of ethical violations in research.
- List what steps can be taken to prevent violating ethical standards.
- Articulate why the perfect study may not exist.
- Understand how different methodologies present unique challenges.
- Understand why even non-harmful studies must still be approved by Institutional Review Boards.

Imagine that you have unprotected sex and wake up the next morning with an undesirable burning sensation when urinating. Understandably, medical attention is desired; however, because you are a student with limited financial resources and no health insurance, you must go the county health department for free medical care. After blood work and a complete checkup, you are assured that nothing is wrong but are instructed to return to the clinic once a year just to "keep an eye on things." Years pass, and you graduate, marry, have children, and live a normal life. Suddenly you start to lose your eyesight! After rushing to your private doctor (since you are now an affluent working professional), you are shocked to learn that you have had untreated syphilis for 10 years, ever since that first unprotected sexual encounter in college. Obviously you are irate and very concerned.

How many other people have you infected? What about your newborn child? Your partner? As you start to investigate your original health department treatment, you are stunned to learn that you have been an unwilling participant in a United States Government study on syphilis, along with every other student in your school who visited the local health department during the years while you were in college. Once this information becomes public, the official government response is simply an "apology." Does this sound far-fetched and impossible to you? Keep reading this chapter, then!

THE QUEST FOR A PERFECT STUDY

A perfectly designed and flawlessly implemented study is certainly desirable; however, as novice researchers progress in their quest for creating and implementing the best research study possible, it will become increasingly clear that "perfect" research is an elusive goal. Babbie (1992) and many others have long noted that several factors conspire to prevent the perfect study. Some of these are financial or political realities that "come into play," others involve time constraints, and there are the common ones specifically related to research methods such as sample size, uniform application of an intervention, reluctance of study participants, survey construction issues, problems with analysis or interpretation of results, and many more. Even things like the weather can jeopardize the perfectly designed study. Many of these factors are discussed in greater detail later (e.g., specifically when we give attention to one of the most serious challenges to perfect research, called "threats" to validity and reliability), but first consider one of the most important and often unavoidable reasons for the inability to achieve a perfect study—**research ethics.** Certainly, high ethical standards in conducting research are desirable, but as more bureaucracy is implemented, it becomes more and more difficult to execute the *perfectly* designed research study while at the same time adhering to all ethical standards. Because it is crucial to maintain ethical standards, the result is often "watered-down" research designs, albeit less potentially harmful ones. Researchers must work within the established legal and ethical boundaries. Most research methods books present these boundaries and explain why ethics are important to maintain at all times; it is important to remember that being critical thinkers and being aware that necessary constraints are placed on research are a direct result of these standards. So the critical thinker will understand two sides of the issue. The need for researchers to adhere to ethical principles to protect human subjects may also impede lofty goals of research progress.

Research ethics: Principles designed to govern the practices of researchers and to assure accountability.

COMMON ETHICAL PRINCIPLES

Ethical standards: Guidelines developed to lead and direct research so that little or no harm occurs to research subjects (or to researchers).

Every organized group has ethical standards. Attorneys, accountants, doctors, bankers, and many more professionals have written **ethical standards** dictated by a governing body. Those students in the ROTC or in active military duty are also likely aware of ethical standards, since the U.S. military has some of the highest ethical requirements of any organized group. Many sports fans are aware of the long list of restrictions placed on coaches and student athletes by the National Collegiate Athletic Association (NCAA). Because most NCAA rules for student-athletes do not include *criminal* offenses, they can be considered *ethical* requirements. These include things like amount of time allowed to work at a job, amount of money allowed to be made above scholarship stipend, amount of time a coach is allowed to require practice, and so forth. The NCAA sets ethical guidelines for the high school athlete recruiting process as well. For example, the University of Central Florida (UCF) football program was placed on a 2-year probation term in 2010 because of coaches' text messaging high school recruits too frequently. While these guidelines are necessary and are designed to protect the student-athlete as well as the integrity of the sport, they are nevertheless constraining to those involved. Researchers are no different.

Researchers tied to state and federal agencies also have governing bodies or organizations that provide ethical guidance and requirements. Although many definitions exist for ethics (examples include the discipline dealing with what is good and bad and with moral duty and obligation; a set of moral principles or values; a theory or system of moral values; and the principles of conduct governing an individual or group), the definition that is most applicable and simplest for the purposes of research methods is found in Merriam-Webster's online dictionary (https://www.merriam-webster.com/, accessed in 2017), which defines ethics as "the principles of conduct governing an individual or a group." These groups are typically professional organizations.

For example, there are two large professional organizations to which many criminal justice and criminology researchers belong: the American Society of Criminology (ASC) and the Academy of Criminal Justice Sciences (ACJS). The ACJS publishes general ethical procedures for all members. At time of this writing, there are 22 standards for researchers to abide by. A couple of them are listed here:

> Members of the Academy should adhere to the highest possible technical standards in their research, and since individual members of the Academy vary in their research modes, skills, and experience, they should acknowledge the limitations that may affect the validity of their findings. In presenting their work, members

> of the Academy are obliged to fully report their findings. They should not misrepresent the findings of their research or omit significant data. Any and all omitted data should be noted and the reason(s) for exclusion stated clearly as part of the methodology. Details of their theories, methods, and research designs that might bear upon interpretations of research findings should be reported.
>
> *(http://www.acjs.org/page/Code_Of_Ethics accessed February 20, 2017).*

Historically, researchers simply self-imposed research standards and ethics; more recently, however, academic professional organizations have provided their own very specific guidelines. See, for example, the American Sociological Association (ASA), as well as the standards from the American Public Health Association (APHA; https://www.apha.org/~/media/files/pdf/membergroups/ethics_brochure.ashx).

Do a quick exercise and look up any social science discipline and compare the similarity to the commitment of members to adhere to high ethical standards.

HUMAN RESEARCH PROTECTION PROGRAM

If researchers are engaged in health- or medical-related research they will likely encounter a Human Research Protection Program (HRPP). The purpose of the HRPP is the "*protection of human subjects from mental or physical harm arising from participation in biomedical or behavioral research*" (Curry and Nunez-Smith, 2015, p. 282). Of course, if there is a multi-disciplinary research team or study this is also relevant. Mixed methods research, due to its qualitative component, faces unique challenges. Many of the reviewers on ethics panels are much less familiar with qualitative methods and so may minimize the risks. For example, "clinical researchers who are accustomed to considering the harm associated with clinical or biomedical research may underestimate risks and fail to safeguard against potential harm" (Curry and Nunez-Smith, 2015, p. 284) associated with mixed or qualitative methods. This problem is compounded if the study is conducted in multiple locations or involves multiple agencies—each of which will likely require that their specific ethics requirements be met. For example, universities must adhere to Family Educational Rights and Privacy Act (FERPA) guidelines, and jails must meet multiple ethics guidelines for inmates to participate in research. The onus is often on the local member of the research team to submit and receive research ethics approval. HRPP's are broadly inclusive and include other research protection mechanisms such as Institutional Review Boards (IRB) and research ethics committees. The policies, procedures, and guidelines can be cumbersome, especially when multi-disciplinary and multi-research approaches are combined, but it is the duty of the researcher to accomplish the challenges set forth to protect participants and attempt to ensure the integrity of the research. At the university level, the primary governing board to approving research studies is called the Institutional Review Board.

INSTITUTIONAL REVIEW BOARDS

Increasingly, primarily due to past abuses and excesses, research ethics have evolved and increasingly come to influence the research process. More recently, fear of litigation and the encroaching corporate business model have had a profound effect on modern research ethics. These developments have led to the creation of **institutional review boards (IRB)**, which, as discussed earlier, are groups of people who must approve planned research studies prior to being conducted, as well as monitor and review the studies, with a focus on protecting the rights, safety, and well-being of study participants—as well as researchers themselves.

Institutional review board (IRB): A bureaucracy, often in a university or government agency, created to ensure that ethical standards are met and necessary steps are taken to reduce risks to research participants.

This chapter includes standard and important ethical research principles, which are included in every basic research methods text. This discussion is followed by a summary of some studies that have historically been cited as being unethical or harmful. One important study, the Kansas City Preventive (Police) Patrol study, has not previously been listed as "unethical"; however, it is included because, in today's IRB-dominated research climate, it would not have gained research approval by many universities (reasons for this are presented later). Some researchers argue that, to some degree, "politics" penetrates all research, including everything from personal relations, cultures, and resources of research units and universities, to policies of government research departments, and powers of the state. Nastasi and Hitchcock (2016), for instance, examine just the role of culture and context. What is common in one culture may in fact be very abnormal in another. For example, in the grieving process after death, some cultures will moan loudly and may even collapse, while other cultures accept the death in a somber, stiff, and regal manner. The ethical researcher must recognize these, often pronounced but sometimes obscure, cultural nuances. All these factors influence the design, implementation, and outcomes of research (see Punch, 1986, p. 13).

Consider a more specific example. Part of the IRB approval process requires submitting the complete *intent* of the research prior to actually beginning the study. For example, if an interview or questionnaire is the method of data collection, the survey instrument itself (showing the individual questions) needs to be preapproved by IRB committee members. There is even a qualifier that stipulates that specific questions cannot be changed unless those changes are resubmitted and preapproved. In reality, if researchers (especially true with qualitative studies) knew in advance what questions to ask, they may not even need to conduct the study. Since qualitative researchers want respondents to dictate the flow of the interview (e.g., open-ended), IRB requirements can be especially troublesome for them. Many times the responses of the subject may steer the researcher into a different line of inquiry than the one originally anticipated. A criminal justice researcher was once interviewing Charity Keesee, one of the infamous, self-proclaimed "vampire" killers convicted of a double homicide in Eustis, Florida. During one of the interviews, Charity began to talk about "feeding circles." Having no idea what she was talking about, the researcher questioned her further on this topic (Lanier & Henry, 2010, pp. 158–161). How could the researcher have possibly received IRB ethics approval in advance for this unanticipated line of inquiry? Because he did not have ethics approval, should he have ignored her reference to feeding circles? Should he have terminated the interview until he could secure the necessary approval?

The IRB is intended to protect research subjects from being harmed and to ensure conformity with other ethical standards, presented later in this chapter. This is a laudable and vital function; however, as they have become increasingly bureaucratic and legalistic, IRBs have also stifled some types of research (as is discussed in the conclusion of this chapter). This is particularly true for qualitative research, and, understandably, qualitative researchers have expressed the most concern over the IRB approval and oversight requirement, which is often perceived as hindering scientific progress. Mixed methods researchers may face even greater challenges, as discussed later (Clark & Ivankova, 2016).

No doubt it is important to protect subjects and enforce ethical behavior among researchers; however, many times the bureaucracies created in the process become so confining that they limit the ability to conduct ideal studies. Students in the social sciences have likely heard of work from Max Weber and his concept of the "bureaucratic iron cage" that results when policies are created to accomplish a goal but cause other barriers in the process. Institutional review board policies could be considered one example. While challenges are imposed on today's researchers from modern-day bureaucratic processes, a review of history is a quick reminder of why it is vitally important to have ethical standards in place and enforced. A lot of people's rights have been violated, and people have even been physically, emotionally, and financially harmed in the name of science.

The necessity for IRBs was primarily brought to light by the egregious abuses of researchers in two infamous research studies, one being the experiments of Nazi doctors during the World War II era and the second being the Tuskegee syphilis study in Alabama, which is discussed in greater detail later. Most research abuses occurred in the health and medical research, but the hard lessons learned have been applied to social science research.

The most important ethical concerns for studies involving human subjects are outlined in the *Belmont Report: Ethical Principles and Guidelines for the Protection of Human Subjects of Research* (National Commission, 1979). The ***Belmont Report*** specifies three general ethical principles: (1) *respect for persons*: treating persons as autonomous agents and protecting those with diminished autonomy; (2) *beneficence*: minimizing possible harms while maximizing benefits; and (3) *justice*: distributing benefits and risks of research fairly. More specifically, the *Belmont Report* states that researchers should obtain the fully informed consent of participants, ensure that no harm is done to participants, provide truthful disclosure regarding the purpose of the study, and protect vulnerable populations such as the young and the incarcerated against exploitation during research.

Belmont Report: One of the first comprehensive guides and recommendations for protecting subjects of research.

IRBs were initially established to regulate biomedical and laboratory science methods (some experiments were unconscionable). Such controls are necessary for clinical trials involving the testing and approval of new drugs, for example, and the logic of protecting subjects is self-evident; however, that same standard of applicability to the field of social science has been widely contested, particularly by qualitative researchers. Should the same standards be applied in an open-ended questionnaire interview designed to gather information on a particular social issue? The overly burdensome requirements compared with the relative risk are often cited as an argument by critics who question whether review boards are even necessary in social science studies. While controversies exist, most researchers do comply with and respect the role played by IRBs.

The point being conveyed here is that while it is important to understand the *need* to ensure ethics through IRB procedures, at the same time, as a critical thinking student of research methods, it is important to appreciate the sometimes confining nature of IRB approval that has become increasingly political, bureaucratic, and legalistic. Punch, one of many qualitative researchers who objects to some IRB requirements states, "informed consent as the first of a long and even more tortuous series of bureaucratic attempts to destroy our freedom of truth seeking" (1986, p. 36). Recall that informed consent requires that the subject *know* he or she is being studied and also to be made aware of the goals of the study. Could this knowledge influence the integrity of the data collected? In the next chapter these "threats" will become even clearer.

Most researchers agree that the most important ethical consideration is that no harm should come to study participants. As simple as this seems, it is sometimes difficult to achieve. For example, merely asking a crime victim about his or her victimization may create additional mental or psychological trauma, since the victim is asked to describe, and consequently relive, a horrific event. The level of harm also varies by individual. What would be very disconcerting to one individual or jeopardize that person's home life, social life, or career might not even faze another. It is necessary, then, to balance the risk or potential harm to the participant with the potential benefit to society, and this is acknowledged by ethical standards. According to the Code of Federal Regulations, "The Institutional Review Board (IRB) should determine that the risks to subjects are reasonable in relation to anticipated benefits" (21 CFR 56.111(a) (2)). It is therefore important that review boards in the various fields of study appreciate the nature of specific disciplines and allow some potential risks to be taken. Researchers cannot appreciate and understand abused women if they do not learn more about victims' experiences, for example. Ellsberg and Heise (2002) have written extensively on ethical issues surrounding research on at-risk populations, such as abused women. Several lessons can be learned from their studies. First, researchers have a clear moral and ethical obligation to make research subjects aware of social services that may benefit them, such as counseling and medical care. According to Ellsberg and Heise, "The principle of distributive justice demands that individuals bearing the burden of research should receive an appropriate benefit, and those who stand to benefit most should bear a fair proportion of the risks and burdens of the study" (2002, p. 1603). One way this can be accomplished is by incorporating nongovernmental organizations (NGOs) and service agencies in the research, even as early as the research conceptualization stages. At the outset, advocacy and direct service groups could be included as advisers or even partners in the research (Ellsberg & Heise, 2002).

The study of crime and deviance present its own unique research challenges. When studying criminals, what is the researcher's obligation to society in the event he or she learns of crimes committed but not discovered or prosecuted? What about a planned crime? If, in the process of acquiring information for a study, the researcher is made aware of crimes previously committed or intended to be committed; should this information be reported to the authorities? Is it the responsibility of researchers, or are researchers even permitted to reveal confidential research data collected in an attempt to prevent future crimes? Or should researchers simply compile the data, proceed with the study, and not interfere with the course of events? These are just some of the dilemmas social scientists may face when conducting research studies. Hopefully, some of the complexities associated with research are becoming clear.

ETHICAL GUIDELINES

No Harm to Participants

No harm to participants: Researchers need to take necessary steps to reduce the possibility of harm to their research participants. While harm can come as a direct result of participation in research, the subject should be made aware of the potential risk and knowingly agree to participate in the research event.

The principle of **no harm to participants** is presented first, since it is probably the most obvious and important ethical consideration. As shown earlier, however, it is not simple. It is not "black or white," particularly for researchers interested in studying deviance and crime, there are many gray areas.

Harm can take many forms, some obvious and others hidden. As stated earlier, the scope of harm can vary by individual. One person may joke about being a crime victim, while another may be devastated by the same event. Harm from research can also come in many forms: physical, emotional, psychological, or financial (Zimbardo, 1973). Despite the wide range of possible harms, the ethical researcher should put the safety and well-being of the research subject *first*. This principle of no harm to participants is probably the biggest reason for the development and codification of research ethics. It was past harmful and intentionally negligent research that led to the creation of IRBs to begin with. We review some of the more horrific examples at the conclusion of this chapter. For now, let us continue to review some specific potential harms.

Emotional or psychological harm at times can be imperceptible, although it can be as devastating as other types of harm such as physical, fiscal, and legal. Particularly in the field of criminology, studies may ask questions regarding deviant or immoral behavior, the recollection of which may have a detrimental emotional impact on participants. Subjects who are asked to recall traumatic experiences and reveal them to researchers may consequently be at risk of emotional harm. The potential psychological effects, therefore, must be given weight, as well as physical, financial, or legal considerations.

The potential for physical harm can likewise often be difficult to measure. Seemingly innocuous questions to one person could put another individual, living under different circumstances, at great risk for harm. Victims of domestic violence (who may live with, or have regular contact with, a violent abuser) are but one example:

> Poorly designed research could put women in violent relationships at substantial risk. Main concerns include ensuring safety of respondents in a context in which many live with their abuser, protecting confidentiality when breaches could provoke an attack, and ensuring the interview process is affirming and does not cause distress.
>
> *(Ellsberg & Heise, 2002, p. 1603)*

Ellsberg and Heise continue their discussion of domestic violence research by bringing home another point, that of balancing risk with potential benefits:

> The inherent risks entailed in research can only be justified if the interview is used to provide information on available services and is a source of immediate referral when necessary, if high-quality data are obtained, and if findings are used to raise awareness of, and improve services for, women who experience domestic violence.
>
> *(p. 1603)*

Ultimately, potential risks may vary based on the research group. The potential benefit gained from the study will vary as well. In any event, the potential gains must be weighed against the potential risks.

Another consideration for researchers in applying the no-harm principle is the potential for financial harm. This can come in many forms, including the subject's employment being put at risk or the possibility of abandonment by a family member or an individual who is the subject's primary means of economic support. Consider, for example, a study on employee theft whereby an employer learned of a participant's (employee's) admittance of guilt. Is it likely that the employee would be terminated?

The final potential harm to be discussed here is the potential for legal harm. Will the disclosure of information regarding the subject expose him or her to possible legal action? Has the subject been involved in illegal activities that, absent participation in the study, might not have otherwise been uncovered? Consider the just-mentioned employee; in addition to losing employment, could legal ramifications ensue if that person's identity became known? Could the subject, through what was divulged in the study, be subpoenaed as a witness in another case? All these types of potential harm must be considered when conducting a research study. In attempting to ensure that ethical principles are applied, especially the principle of no harm, researchers must evaluate, and to the extent possible mitigate, minimize, or completely eliminate, the possibility of harming the subject.

It is not only research subjects that the ethical researcher must protect. Risk to staff, students, or any other partner in the research process must also be minimized. In addition, researchers should beware of placing themselves in dangerous situations. Ellsberg and Heise provide a related example:

> Although respondents may face the greatest risk of harm, researchers and field-staff are also at risk when doing research on violence against women. Risks include threats to physical safety, either from unplanned encounters with abusive

> individuals who object to the study, or as a result of female interviewers having to travel into dangerous neighbourhoods, or travel late at night.
>
> *(2002, p. 1601)*

Often commonsense precautions can alleviate, if not eliminate, many potential problems; diligent care should be put into every decision a researcher makes.

Informed Consent and Voluntary Participation

Informed consent: Informing potential subjects about research participation (benefits and risks) and securing consent before the study begins.

Voluntary participation: Means that every participant has the right to refuse to be a part of a research study. Participants must agree to participate.

The individuals who participate in research studies should provide their knowing and willing consent to do so. Most universities now require a signed, written consent form. This standard and increasingly prevalent IRB requirement is, however, not always possible, desirable, or feasible, as is shown in the chapter conclusion. **Informed consent** means that the research subject has knowledge of the study and gives permission to be researched. Title 21, Part 50, of the Code of Federal Regulations addresses the protection of human subjects: "The Institutional Review Board (IRB) should determine that . . . the consent document contains an adequate description of the study procedures" (21 CFR 50.25(a) (1)). It also specifies that no coercion can be used to acquire the research participants' informed consent; otherwise this "consent" would not constitute willing, **voluntary participation.** Specifically,

> Except as provided in Sec. 50.23, no investigator may involve a human being as a subject in research covered by these regulations unless the investigator has obtained the legally effective informed consent of the subject or the subject's legally authorized representative. An investigator shall seek such consent only under circumstances that provide the prospective subject or the representative sufficient opportunity to consider whether or not to participate and that minimize the possibility of coercion or undue influence.
>
> *(21 CFR 50.20)*

Coercion can take many forms. Will inmates perceive that they will receive better treatment from prison staff if they "voluntarily" participate in a request by officials? If a professor asks students to complete a survey in his or her class, will subjects feel pressure to comply, since grades are (at least partially) dependent on satisfying the instructor? If subjects are given the opportunity to receive a potentially lifesaving new experimental medicine, is that voluntary when the alternative is certain death? Is it coercion to offer a poor person an economic benefit to participate in a study?

When evaluating the possibility of coercion or undue influence, the *vulnerability* of the subject, not only the action that could be considered coercive, should be taken into consideration. Specifically vulnerable to exploitation are the poor, the homeless, the sick, the elderly, those who are incarcerated, and children. Historically, minority groups have been a vulnerable population; as is shown later in this chapter, vulnerable populations have been targets of research experiments and have not been protected in the past.

Participants must be able to choose freely, voluntarily, willingly, without duress, and without being subjected to threats or the promise of too great a reward. Juveniles are a particular concern for criminological researchers, since so much research is focused on delinquency. The issue is whether a juvenile can make informed consent. In general, if a person is under 18 years of age, parental consent is required, but typically juveniles' parents are not easily accessible.

Another common dilemma relates to financial "carrots" and the issue of coercion. Typically, because payment for participation can be coercive or exploitative, IRBs evaluate the *amount* and *method* of payment to subjects to ensure that subjects are not *unduly* influenced to participate in the study. Basically, ethical standards do allow for payment, but it has to be within reasonable limits, and it must be demonstrated to the IRB that the researcher has considered the effect of payment upon the subject and determined it is not coercive. The IRB must be made aware of the terms of payment, and the board's approval must be obtained prior to the start of the study and before the recipient receives any funds. Although the IRB will examine each research study independently, there are some expenses that are generally considered acceptable. Subjects typically can be reimbursed for time away from work, travel, and recruitment initiatives, especially when there is little direct benefit of participation otherwise. It is not uncommon for subjects to receive compensation, but the amount and schedule of payment must be evaluated by IRB members in an attempt to ensure payment is not coercive or unduly influential (21 CFR 50.20). The job of the IRB is to protect participants from potential harm, and financial compensation should not be a justification or allowance for placing subjects at excessive risk. IRBs have the daunting task of trying to identify and prevent a wide range of harms; the ultimate responsibility lies with the researcher.

The process a researcher might take in obtaining a participant's informed consent is outlined in Figure 3.1. As is shown, because much social science research is fluid, consent may be required at more than one point during a study. It is also important to remember that even if a participant consents to being involved in a study, and consents to being exposed to possible risks, those risks must still be minimized.

Qualitative research presents extra ethical challenges. Ethnography—where the researcher participates in varying degrees in the subject—presents particular

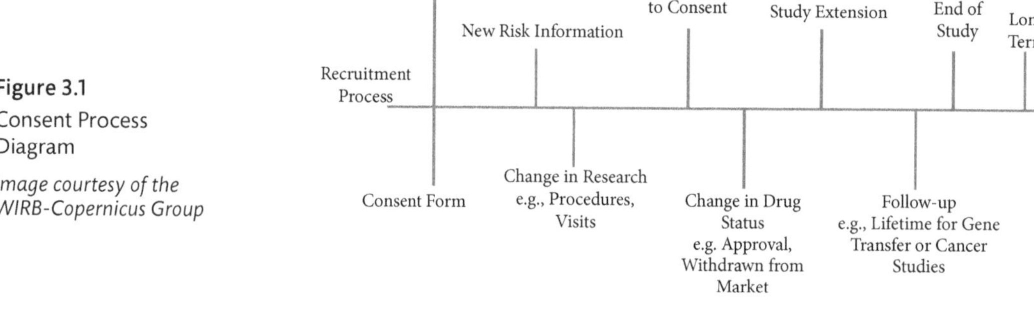

Figure 3.1 Consent Process Diagram

image courtesy of the WIRB-Copernicus Group

ethical challenges. The researcher often does not know in advance what situations might present themselves, so how can IRB approval be obtained in advance? In a widely cited study, Perrone (2009) conducted fieldwork on the club party scene and specifically examined the use of the club drug ecstasy. Could Perrone have asked every patron at the rave club she studied in New York City to sign an informed consent and voluntarily participation form? Could (or should) she have told each person she was examining about the harms associated with the use of ecstasy? Would she have been able to perform her important study if she had? Could she have obtained IRB approval? Cheek (2008) argued that some IRB requirements are not practical for qualitative research. In personal interviews or field research, the scope of the dialogue cannot be predicted. The requirement that each question be *preapproved* does not lend itself to the nature of *qualitative* exploration. Qualitative studies and researchers seem to be more problematic for IRBs, and vice versa.

Anonymity and Confidentiality

Anonymity: The status of not being identified. Research participants have the right for their identities not to be revealed.

Research subjects have a right to expect privacy with regard to what they reveal during the course of the study. This is relatively easy to accomplish with some types of quantitative research. Having a subject complete a questionnaire with no name, number, or other identifying mark provides anonymity to the research subject, for example. **Anonymity** means no one, including the researcher, can identify any specific research study participant.

What if the researcher, however, needs to track the same subject over an extended period? How will the research subject be located, especially if the researcher does not have identifying artifacts? In this situation the researcher must know who the subject is and how to contact him or her for follow-up research. By promising to ensure and keep the subject's identity a secret, the researcher can attain **confidentiality.** With qualitative research, such as personal interviews, anonymity is not feasible, but confidentiality is.

Confidentiality: The process of knowing the identity of a research subject but keeping it private. It involves taking necessary steps to protect participants' identities from others.

Instructors and professors must know the scores received by each student in their classes so that they can issue a grade; however, they will not tell the rest of the class anyone else's scores—this is confidentiality. Likewise, there may be situations where the researcher knows the identity of a participant but creates safeguards to prevent anyone else knowing it. This is particularly important for criminal justice and criminological research that examines crime and deviance. Punch (citing Reiss, 1979, p. 73) notes that the release of private information about a subject can be harmful. The "more deviant and secretive the activity," the greater the risk (1986, p. 47). In contemporary society, however, the line between public and private information is not always clear. As long ago as 1986, Punch recognized that

> there is no simple distinction between "public" and "private" while observation in many public and semi-public places is tolerable even when the subjects are not aware of being observed. . . . [G]etting into areas where people believe they are in private and free from observation—at home or in a brothel—becomes more risky and delicate.
>
> *(1986, p. 45)*

With the vast reliance on the World Wide Web in communication, determining what is private and what is public is increasingly problematic. People release information publicly now that was once considered very private; yet research into particularly deviant areas, even online, is not without risk of invading privacy and causing harm to study participants.

Ariane Prohaska and Jeannine Gailey (2010) examined deviant behavior in part by observing and monitoring chat rooms devoted to the topic of "feederism." Each time she enters this cyberspace research zone, she faces the ethical dilemma of whether to reveal herself to be a researcher or not. Would the patrons of these websites devoted to deviant sexual practices continue to participate if they became aware that they were under scientific scrutiny? Would their privacy be violated? Prohaska, to her credit, uniformly presents herself as a researcher due to ethical considerations, yet the timing and substance of this revelation are sometimes complicated, as are the steps taken to protect the identity of her research subjects.

Quite often, the steps required to achieve confidentiality are very complex. During a large, five-state, multi-year evaluation of inmates with AIDS (Lanier &

Potter, 2010), confidentially was required. Since the inmates had to be located and evaluated years after release from prison, however, considerable personal information was required, such as contact person, last known address, and so forth. The fact that all participants had either HIV or AIDS made confidentiality even more critical. The problem was addressed through the use of "unique identifiers" and computer-generated random numbers. Even prior to this, "personal identifiers" were compiled using initials and portions of birth dates. These were then entered into a computer program that generated the unique identifiers. In other words, numbers were substituted for names. These numbers were then scrambled. Confidentiality was thus assured, yet respondents could still be located for follow-up research or to complete the posttest. In the end, both approaches—anonymity and confidentiality—have the same goal: protecting the identity of the research participant.

Deceiving subjects: The practice of tricking or misleading a subject for the purpose of research.

Deceiving Subjects

Another ethical requirement researchers must observe is that subjects not be deceived. It is a simple, but crucial, requirement. Researchers must inform research subjects of the nature, purpose, and intent of the study. Easy, right? Yet this is an area of considerable controversy (Baumrind, 1985; Duncombe & Jessop, 2002; Korn, 1997), as the "feederism" research example cited earlier illustrates (Prohaska & Gailey, 2010). Does letting subjects know they are being studied, and for what purpose, potentially change their behavior or responses? Can this awareness influence reality and even jeopardize the study? Suppose a criminal justice researcher wants to examine local police use of excessive force. How many law enforcement chiefs and sheriffs are going to allow their agency and officers to participate in a study of excessive force by the police? Not very many. If the officers know they are being observed for occurrences of excessive force, is their typical behavior likely to be altered?

How do researchers resolve this problem in conducting important research in sensitive areas—ethically, that is? One solution might be to propose a study on police-community relations. Should information on excessive use of force be revealed, then researchers have met all IRB ethical requirements and are still able to collect sensitive, vital, and informative data. This is an important technique in reducing potential bias. For example, if researchers provide too much information about the details of the study to the respondents, it could bias their responses and jeopardize the credibility of the study. Excessive force is a component of police-community relations, and by being just a bit broader in study perspective (and minimizing information provided to the participants), some potential problems can be reduced.

The researcher has to be careful, however, that ethical principles prohibiting deception are not violated. There is a difference between being a "bit vague" in providing specifics regarding study intent and intentionally deceiving study participants. Some may even question whether this type of vagueness is unethically deceptive.

Police officers, especially in undercover roles, often will "fake" friendship to collect evidence against their "friends." This is standard and accepted, yet dubious, police practice (Manning, 1979). Should researchers be held to a higher standard than police officers? Should researchers "fake it" for the sake of gaining unbiased data (Duncombe & Jessop, 2002)? Researchers cannot deceive subjects, but they must also be aware of the consequences of revealing too much information about the purpose of the study because it not only could bias the data, but also could possibly put the researcher in jeopardy. Hunter S. Thompson was once beaten by members of the Hell's Angels Motorcycle Club (HAMC). The HAMC requested part of the proceeds from the profits generated by an ethnographic book Thompson wrote about the club. Thompson had been honest about his role and his intent during the course of his study (despite not being a legitimate social science researcher), yet the research subjects apparently changed their views during the course of his study. The honest approach placed the researcher in direct danger. Another ethical issue is: were the Angels correct in requesting a fair share of the profits?

At the risk of jeopardizing the reliability of the data or increasing potential risk to the researcher, some question whether the researcher should reveal the intended purpose of the study, or even the fact that they are researchers. Others argue that it must *always* be done, regardless. Kai Erikson (1967) made an eloquent, often cited

Source: Uncleroo

argument for full disclosure, suggesting that it is unethical "for a sociologist to deliberately misrepresent his [or her] identity for the purpose of entering a private domain to which he [or she] is not otherwise eligible" (p. 373). He further argued, "It is unethical for a sociologist to deliberately misrepresent the character of the research in which he [or she] is engaged" (p. 373). Erikson's four objections to disguised observation in social research were questioned by Goode (1996, p. 32), who argues that occasional deceptive prying is acceptable as long as no one's safety is jeopardized. Erikson mitigates his own objections and moderates his concern by advocating balance regarding the question of disguised observation:

> It would be absurd, then, to insist as a point of ethics that sociologists should always introduce themselves as investigators everywhere they go and should inform every person who figures in their thinking exactly what their research is about.
>
> *(1967, p. 368)*

This exchange illustrates just one of the differences of opinion regarding what constitutes ethical, as opposed to unethical, research practice—again, reinforcing that issues are not simple, clear-cut, or "black or white" and that correcting one issue often can cause others to emerge in the process.

Analysis and reporting: The process of making sense of the research data and reporting the findings to others.

Analysis and Reporting

If a research study is funded through a grant or contract, then the sponsoring agency will probably require the inclusion of both "raw" data and analyzed data in the final report. The researcher who collects and compiles the information has access to the raw data before the funding agency, however. It is considered very inappropriate and unethical to "massage," manipulate, alter, or delete any data (Best, 2001). Obviously, researchers need to take every precaution to assure that data are "clean" and error free, but researchers can never remove or change responses that do not fit their idea of what is right, moral, or correct. It is important to be objective and keep one's belief system or worldview from biasing the study. Let the data speak for themselves! That is why research is conducted—to try to get to the "real" truth. A researcher should never alter the data other than ensuring results are "cleaned" (i.e., that coding mistakes are corrected).

With quantitative survey research, ensuring accurate data is a relatively simple task. This is what is referred to as "clean" data. First, look through the surveys for obvious problems. For example, one subject (actually a student) drew a picture of a large ocean wave on the survey response form (knowing the professor liked to surf).

This survey was not counted or used, since the respondent did not take the study seriously. An initial review of the surveys for glaring problems such as this is always advisable before assembling data from subjects' responses. Before this stage, however, it is necessary to determine how the data were coded. Coding data will come up often in a research methods course, so let's clarify what coding means and how the process connects to ethical considerations.

Coding means converting words into numbers so that statistical analysis can occur (e.g., "1" represents a male and a "2" represents a female; a Catholic respondent might be coded "1," Protestant "2," Jewish "3," and so on). As is shown later in the text, the way in which one codes the data can impact, or harm, the findings, and it is unethical to code in a manner that is not neutral and objective. There are ways that recoding variable attributes can change the data outcome, for example. "Fishing around" to try to get desired results is unethical. We will bring up this issue again during an example of gun ownership research.

Coding: A process of assigning numerical values to a variable answer option (e.g., male = 1).

Ethical violations can occur at the data entry stage (intentionally or unintentionally) when data are entered into a statistical analysis package. In quantitative studies, the raw data are entered into some type of computer program. Many criminologists and others in the social sciences use Statistical Package for the Social Sciences (SPSS), but there are many other good statistical software programs. Because errors can happen in data entry, it is a good idea to have another person double-check each answer or response on every single survey item with what is in the statistical analysis raw data "file." Some diligent researchers actually go through this verification step three times. This process, called double data entry, helps ensure the data are accurate. It is time-consuming, but research ethics demand that every effort be made to have accurate data. These processes also lend credibility that the data were not unethically manipulated. Once this process is completed, analysis and sharing data with others can begin.

After the data are entered, by running frequencies on the data set, the "cleaning" process can be enhanced. Frequencies are described in the statistics chapter, but for now understand that they just show the baseline data. An example of baseline data would be how many females and males completed the survey. During this process, it is important to check for discrepancies. For example, the attribute codes may be "1" to represent male and "2" to represent female, so if a number "5" appears in the frequency column, it is a clear indication that there was a problem, or error, when the data were entered. This error will need to be resolved by rechecking the original responses on that particular questionnaire; a failure to do so would be unethical. Again, this can be a time-consuming process, especially when working with very large data sets, but research ethics mandate that the effort be made. Finally, a temptation may exist to include "bad" or inaccurate surveys to improve response rates, since response rates are one standard by which the quality of a study is determined (e.g., the higher the response rate, the better). Even if doing so adversely affects the response rate, ethics demand that surveys with issues (e.g., unclear or multiple responses) be excluded from the analysis. As mentioned earlier, these include things like inappropriate comments written on the survey instrument or if one respondent took the survey twice.

Compared with quantitative data, entering qualitative data is actually harder and more time-consuming. Entering field notes into a software program for later analysis has more potential for interpretive error than entering numbers in a quantitative analysis. Qualitative data are also more complex and multifaceted, and thus harder and more time-consuming to interpret; however, the same ethical principles need to be ensured, and double data entry can be used for qualitative studies as well.

After making sure that the data are entered honestly (ethically) and correctly, another possibility for unethical research will present itself. Which data are reported? Suppose the researcher has 10 measures of attitudes toward handgun ownership, and 8 of these measures support the research hypothesis, while 2 refute it. Does he or she report only the 8 measures (since there are more of them)? What if the 2 other measures support the researcher's own personal beliefs? Does he or she only report them? The answer is that researchers must report all the findings honestly, completely, and accurately.

Yet another possibility exists. Let us say one of the 10 measures is a scale that asks respondents to rank their feelings about gun ownership on a scale of 1 to 10, with 10 being "strongly disagree" with the right to own handguns. With quantitative studies and data, the researcher may find it helpful to "collapse" the data. For example, say the researcher asked about firearm ownership and had respondents rank the right to own guns on a scale of 1 to 10. Commonly, the data are then reduced so that 0–2 = "strongly agree," 3–5 = "agree," 5–7 = "disagree," and 8–10 = "strongly disagree." Now he or she runs the statistical test or analysis. Maybe the findings do not support the researcher's hypothesis and personal belief (or what the funding agency wants!). After much deliberation, the researcher decides to recode answers to reflect an "agree" versus "disagree" opinion from the survey respondents (basically collapsing the data further into fewer categories). Selections from 1–5 are recoded as "agree" and 6–10 as "disagree." Guess what? The findings apparently change. Now the researcher can present the data, and they *appear* to be less opposed to his or her own opinion on the topic. Is this ethical? Does this type of data manipulation happen often? Although it is considered unethical and should be avoided, it does happen and is referred to as "massaging" the data. This is an example of ethical considerations related to coding (fishing around). Hopefully, it is beginning to make sense to readers why "re-search" is important.

With qualitative data, the same problem exists but in a slightly different form. One criminal justice researcher conducted a large, qualitative study regarding community policing in 17 Midwestern cities, which lasted three years. During that time he became close to the officers he was studying and viewed them in a very positive, "glorified" way (despite beginning the study with negative to neutral feelings). As he began to sift through the data, he found himself biased toward conclusions and findings that reflected well on these officers. Would it be ethical if he omitted the data that reflected poorly on his new friends? Was it "human" to want to do so? How could bias be avoided? The solution was to put the data aside for a while and "regroup." He took a job at another university and was removed from the officers, then waited 12 months before beginning data analysis. After this self-imposed "cooling-off" period, the researcher found it much easier to be reflective and honest in his appraisal of what had occurred during the course of the study. Should time have not allowed such a process in order to regain neutrality and objectivity, it may have been beneficial to bring in an unbiased researcher to shadow the project. Examples such as this are commonplace if we are truly honest with each other. The potential for unethical behavior is always present. It is how we deal with the temptation that is important. When writing up the study, being as transparent as possible is also important.

In another study, an ethical researcher utilized students to interview 10 respondents each. The researcher was elated to discover that the data supported the hypothesis that was the catalyst for the study. The data were collected and analyzed and the publication process started; however, there was a problem with the study that she was unaware of until the reporting process was well under way. She later learned that some of the student researchers had provided the answers to the 10 interviews themselves. In other words, they faked (or falsified) the data. The researcher in charge of the study only became aware of the dishonest means of "gathering" data because one of the student researchers felt guilty and revealed the deception to her. Unfortunately, there was no option but to abandon the project and not publish the falsified results.

While chapter 11 on writing tips addresses plagiarism in detail, it is worth noting now that plagiarism (using others' research as one's own) and falsification of data (making up data to serve some agenda) are serious ethical, perhaps even criminal, violations. This is another reason why replication of studies is important. Oftentimes research outcomes determine action taken in the criminal justice system; therefore, poorly designed and unethical studies must be guarded against.

OTHER ETHICAL NOTES

The mere fact of the researcher's presence also has the potential for influencing data collection. The demographic characteristics and physical presence of the researcher may also impact the study, especially in qualitative research. Catania et al. (1996) find that demographic characteristics of the interviewer can impact participants' responses. Punch (1986) points out with regard to fieldwork for observational studies that the researcher is his or her own research instrument due to the nature of the relationship between himself or herself and the subject. This comes with its own unique considerations. The gender, race, cultural background, socioeconomic status, or personal characteristics of interviewers, and even those who are merely giving out questionnaires, can influence the study. For example, if a subject has a prejudice, the researcher may trigger reactions that jeopardize data results. It is impossible for researchers to alter their demographics, but if researcher characteristics are suspected of having a mitigating or aggravating effect on responses, it must be explicitly acknowledged in the limitations of the research section.

Mixed Methods Ethics

As mixed methods research increases in popularity, specific ethical considerations are becoming apparent. Clark and Ivankova go so far as to define ethics specifically for mixed methods as "a set of moral principles that are aimed at assisting researchers in conducting mixed methods research ethically and in compliance with existing standards for research involving humans" (2016: 222). They correctly argue that the "logistics" of mixed methods demand additional ethical consideration. One logistical concern is that collecting quantitative and qualitative data requires different degrees of "sensitivity—for example, using standardized instruments versus unstructured open-ended interview guides" (2016, p. 222) will predicate different explanations and descriptions be provided by the IRB. Furthermore, due to the preponderance of quantitative studies, an IRB is less likely to be familiar with the unique and flexible requirements of qualitative research—especially that involving ethnography. For a detailed discussion of acquiring mixed methods ethics approval from varied approving bodies, see Plowright, 2011.

THE (EVER-INCREASING) ROLE OF THE IRB

Protecting research subjects is praiseworthy, yet surprisingly it is a relatively recent development. The first recorded case of subjects being protected by legal statutes was the **Nuremberg Code** (1947), which addressed research ethical issues following the medical abuses committed by Nazi Germany in World War II in the name of "science" (Cheek, cited in Hesse-Biber, 2010). Subsequently, in 1966, the U.S. Surgeon General issued a decree addressing a study in which elderly patients (research subjects) were injected with live cancer cells. This mandate led to the formation of the first IRBs in 1966 (Ireland, Berg, & Mutchnick, 2010; Riesman, 2002, cited in Hesse-Biber, 2010). Consequently, the protection of human subjects, primarily due to biomedical research, was the motivation behind the establishment of the IRB. The next major change came when, after several revisions to research guidelines, in 1971 the Department of Health, Education, and Welfare (DHEW) published a booklet that became the guide for conducting ethical research. Among other things, all studies involving human subjects, even social science studies, became subject to institutional review.

Nuremberg Code: Evaluated the ethical issues of experiments in World War II and helped develop legal statutes to protect human subjects.

Increasingly, modern societies in general, and universities in particular, are guided by a legalistic, corporate style of management. This has permeated the classroom and has encroached on research as well. Funded research has taken priority over unfunded research. Concerns with litigation and "possible negative" effects have led to serious difficulties for certain types of research and researchers. Had these principles always been dominant, many of the major scientific breakthroughs of the 19th century would not have occurred.

In keeping with the analytical yet "critical" aspect of this text, it must be mentioned that the "funded research" concept itself might be problematic. Cheek (2008) has written an excellent essay on this topic in which she makes this astute observation:

> Derrida (1977) holds that any positive representation of a concept in language, such as "funded research" rests on the negative representation of its "opposite," in this case, unfunded research. In a binary opposition, there is always a dominant or prior term, and conversely there is always a subordinate or secondary term. For example, consider such common binary oppositions as masculine/feminine and reason/emotion. In each case, the first named term is given priority over the second, which is often defined in terms of "not" dominant.
>
> *(2008, p. 70)*

While some may correctly assume there should be no difference between "funded" and "unfunded" research if the real objective is to study the social world and learn what transpires, in the contemporary research domain, funding does matter.

Cheek cautions that the increasing emphasis on funded research due to its money-generating (profit) capacity for universities may undermine the research process itself. She argues as follows:

> A struggle is exacerbated by a trend in which the act of winning funding for research is itself viewed as a currency to be traded in the academic marketplace. For example, promotion and tenure committees (an employment review process that determines if faculty keep their jobs) in many universities are influenced by the amount of funding received as a measure of research success. This has the effect of maintaining the binary opposition of funded/unfunded research.
>
> *(2008, p. 71)*

The pressure to acquire funded research is real, especially in larger, research-focused institutions. Securing the approval of IRBs further complicates the research process, especially if the project is funded. This effect is compounded and research hampered when "ethics committees thus become another layer of decision making as to what research will be, and will not be, funded" (Cheek, 2008, p. 57). Hopefully what is becoming clear is the need to balance the ability to conduct research with the practice of ensuring ethical research and protection of subjects. This is not to say that IRBs will not approve questionable research or research with potential risk to participants. The potential benefits must be weighed against the potential risks. In some cases, as long as subjects willingly agree to participate, and understand that there may be associated risks involved, potential harmful research is still conducted. There is a difference between violating ethical research standards and executing studies with potential risks associated.

Ethical decisions need to be made *throughout* the study, and attempts need to be made to uphold those ethical standards. The next section presents some of the most famous, or infamous, studies that are widely cited for being ethically questionable. An additional study is added to this group—the Kansas City Preventive Patrol Study, as well as another research study involving a recent medical fraud at Duke University. Every academic discipline has questionably ethical research, and in every academic discipline it can be questioned if not only ethical violations occurred, but perhaps even criminal conduct. When reading the "Deception at Duke" example, consider both elements of ethical as well as criminal violations.

ETHICALLY QUESTIONABLE STUDIES

Deception at Duke (Public Health)

A more modern-day example happened at a prestigious university in North Carolina when Duke University was involved in unethical, even illegal, research practices. Comments included in this case are taken from a *60 Minutes* news report which can be viewed in its entirety at the *60 Minutes* website. In addition, a YouTube source can be located with the search words "Deception at Duke." The following are summary scripts from

"Deception at Duke"
which aired on Feb. 12, 2012.

Duke University announced, and the findings were published in prestigious medical journals, that it had uncovered the Holy Grail of cancer research. One researcher was primarily responsible for the medical breakthrough. Born in India, Anil Potti, M.D., was reportedly known as a hardworking, earnest Rhodes Scholar, who did research at the University of North Dakota before eventually being hired by Duke University in 2003. He conducted research in the renowned lab of Joseph Nevins, M.D., that had a reputation for producing important medical research. When Potti decoded the genetic makeup of hundreds of tumors, the research created enormous computer files of data. These data became proof of a huge medical advance, and results were published in top medical research journals under the names of Potti and Nevins.

Anil Potti had apparently discovered how to exactly match the perfect formula of chemotherapy to a patient's own genetic makeup. Matching the DNA of the patient's tumor to the exact chemotherapy treatment was a huge scientific breakthrough. A drug that kills a tumor in one person, for example, might not work in another, so this DNA match would transform medical treatment. Potti, his associate, Joseph Nevins, as well as Duke University stood to make *a lot* of money. It is reported that Potti and Nevins were securing patents and business models in order to personally benefit from the findings of the study.

Because Potti stated that he was 80% confident that he could find the perfect treatment for advanced cancer, participants were willing to be involved because for many they might have only one chance at effective treatment. A recording by Potti and the Jacobs family, who were participants in the drug trials, revealed that Potti stated "I will help you, trust me." So they did, as did many others.

As has been mentioned several times in this book, *research* is about searching again (*re-search*), and that is what, in this case, led to the conclusion that not only was the Duke University breakthrough treatment a failure but it may end up being one of the biggest medical research frauds ever.

At MD Anderson Cancer Center in Houston, Texas, Kevin Coombes and Keith Baggerly began analyzing Potti's data to verify his results (e.g., re-search). It was then that they starting noticing some serious problems with the data. They emailed their questions to Duke University, and Potti admitted a few clerical errors but argued that his continued research further confirmed his initial findings. Duke moved ahead with the trials and research and Drs. Nevins and Potti applied for patents and started a company to market the process. Coombes and Baggerly suspected Dr. Potti had somehow reversed some of the data, and that some of the patients could be getting not the best drug for their tumor but the worst.

The National Cancer Institute, which was trying to replicate the data, said they too had concerns. Duke eventually suspended the enrollment of patients and asked an outside review committee to analyze Potti's discovery. After three months, the review committee concluded that Potti was right; the study resumed and patients were again admitted into the promising treatment. In the meantime, Paul Goldberg, the editor of a small independent newsletter called "The Cancer Letter," got a tip from a confidential source that he should try to verify the Rhodes Scholarship that Potti had listed on his applications for federal grants. Once researched, it became clear that Potti was not, in fact, a Rhodes Scholar.

As more suspicion grew around Potti and his work, Nevins finally came to the conclusion that Potti had actually manipulated the data. Potti manipulated his credentials and people's trust. With apprehension, Nevins, in his interview with *60 Minutes*, admits that there was no explanation for the medical breakthrough other than the fact that the data had been manipulated to prove Potti's hypothesis. If the data were not manipulated in the way that they were, the hypothesis would not have been supported. As a result, Dr. Potti resigned from Duke. At time of this writing, an investigation into research misconduct is still underway. It does seem, however, that in the meantime Potti is working as a cancer doctor in South Carolina, with glowing remarks attached to his name and credentials.

https://www.youtube.com/watch?v=eV9dcAGaVU8

Tearoom Trade (Sociology)

When Laud Humphreys was working on his PhD in the mid-1960s, he became interested in a deviant and, at that time and location, illegal practice. He simply wanted to know who the patrons of homosexual activity in public bathrooms were. Humphrey's study, "Tearoom Trade" (1970), made history and is now mentioned in virtually every research methods text. Humphreys was awarded the American Sociological Association (ASA) Stuart Mills Award for the best study conducted that year. That is not, however, the reason it is so widely discussed. Quite the contrary, it is cited so often due to the ethical problems it created. The following account of Humphreys' study provides the best overview of the study and its problems; it comes from

> **http://web.missouri.edu/~bondesonw/Laud.html**
> *(accessed December 14, 2009).*

> Laud Humphreys, a sociologist, recognized that the public and the law-enforcement authorities hold highly simplistic stereotyped beliefs about men who commit impersonal sexual acts with one another in public restrooms. "Tearoom sex," as fellatio in public restrooms is called, accounts for the majority of homosexual arrests in the United States. Humphreys decided that it would be of considerable social importance for society to gain more objective understanding of who these men are and what motivates them to seek quick, impersonal sexual gratification.
>
> For his PhD dissertation at Washington University, Humphreys set out to answer this question by means of participant observation and structured interview. He stationed himself in "tearooms" and offered to serve as "watchqueen"—the individual who keeps watch and coughs when a police car stops nearby or a stranger approaches. He played that role faithfully while observing hundreds of acts of fellatio. He was able to gain the confidence of some of the men he observed, disclose his role as scientist, and persuade them to tell him about the rest of their lives and about their motives. Those who were willing to talk openly with him tended to be among the better-educated members of the "tearoom trade." To avoid bias, Humphreys secretly followed some of the other men he observed and recorded the license numbers of their cars. A year later and carefully disguised, Humphreys appeared at their homes claiming to be a health-service interviewer and interviewed them about their marital status, race, job, and so on.
>
> Humphreys' findings destroy many stereotypes. Fifty-four percent of his subjects were married and living with their wives, and superficial analysis would suggest that they were exemplary citizens who had exemplary marriages. Thirty-eight percent of Humphreys' subjects clearly were neither bisexual nor homosexual. They were men whose marriages were marked with tension; most of the 38% were Catholic or their wives were, and since the birth of their last child conjugal relations had been rare. Their alternative source of sex had to be quick, inexpensive, and impersonal. It could not entail any kind of involvement that would threaten their already shaky marriage and jeopardize their most important asset—their standing as father of their children. They wanted only some form of orgasm-producing action that was less lonely than masturbation and less involving than a love relationship. Of the other 62% of Humphreys' subjects, 24% were clearly bisexual, happily married, well educated, economically quite successful, and exemplary members of their community. Another

24% were single and were covert homosexuals. Only 14% of Humphreys' subjects corresponded to society's stereotype of homosexuality. That is, only 14% were members of the gay community and were interested in primarily homosexual relationships (Humphreys, 1970).

In the long run, Humphreys' research has helped persuade police departments to stop using their resources on arrest for this victimless crime. Many would count this as a social benefit.

There were also social costs. The research occurred in the mid-1960s before institutional review boards were in existence. The dissertation proposal was reviewed only by Humphreys' PhD committee. Only after the research had been completed did the other members of the Sociology Department learn of it. A furor arose when some of those other members of the department objected that Humphreys' research had unethically invaded the privacy and threatened the social standing of the subjects, and petitioned the president of Washington University to rescind Humphreys' PhD degree. The turmoil resulted in numerous other unfortunate events, including a fistfight among faculty members and the exodus of about half of the department members to positions at other universities.

There was considerable public outrage as well. Journalist Nicholas von Hoffman, who was given some details of the case by one of the angered members of the Sociology Department, wrote an article about Humphreys' research and offered the following condemnation of social scientists: "We're so preoccupied with defending our privacy against insurance investigators, dope sleuths, counterespionage men, divorce detectives and credit checkers, that we overlook the social scientists behind the hunting blinds who're also peeping into what we thought were our most private and secret lives. But there they are, studying us, taking notes, getting to know us, as indifferent as everybody else to the feeling that to be a complete human involves having an aspect of ourselves that's unknown" (Von Hoffman, 1970).

Prepared by Dr. Joan Sieber, visiting research scholar, Kennedy Institute, 1977–1978, and professor of psychology, California State University, Hayward.

Clearly, some harm occurred; however, much more harm was possible had the unwilling subjects' identities been inadvertently or accidentally revealed. Ultimately, more harm was perhaps inflicted on Humphreys than on any study participants. Faculty suffered (and tried to rescind his earned PhD), the reputation of the university suffered, and the reputation of social science research itself suffered damage. All this resulted from a seemingly innocuous curiosity Humphreys had that he turned into a research project. The positive result was much greater attention to ethics in social science research.

The next study presented is much worse and caused physical harm and even death. One may be surprised (or not) to learn the *U.S. federal government* conducted it, rather than a lone, curious researcher like Humphreys.

Tuskegee Syphilis Study (Public Health)

The most infamous study conducted in the United States was carried out in rural Alabama and lasted nearly five decades. If it were not well documented, it would be hard to believe that it actually happened. The following description was taken from the local university near where the study occurred.

http://www.tuskegee.edu/global/story.asp?s=1207598
(accessed December 14, 2009).

In 1928, the director of medical services for the Julius Rosendale Fund, a Chicago-based charity, approached the U.S. Public Health Service (PHS) to consider ways to improve the health of African Americans in the South. At the time, the PHS had just finished a study of the prevalence of syphilis among black employees of the Delta Pine and Land Company of Mississippi. About 25% of the sample of over 2,000 had tested positive for syphilis.

The PHS and the Rosendale Fund collaborated in treating these individuals. Subsequently, the treatment program was expanded to include five additional counties in the southern U.S.: Albemarle County, Virginia; Glynn County, Georgia; Macon County, Alabama; Pitt County, North Carolina; and Tipton County, Tennessee (Jones, 1981).

During the set-up phase of the treatment program, the Great Depression began. The Rosendale Fund was hit hard and had to withdraw its support. Without the Rosendale Fund, the PHS did not have the resources to implement treatment.

During this period, there was a debate occurring in health circles about possible racial variation in the effects of syphilis. Dr. Taliaferro Clark of the PHS suggested that the project could be partially "salvaged" by conducting a prospective study on the effects of untreated syphilis on living subjects. Clark's suggestion was adopted.

In the beginning stages of the project, the PHS enlisted the support of the Tuskegee Institute. Since the Tuskegee Institute had a history of service to local African Americans, its participation increased the likelihood of the "success" of the experiment. In return, the Tuskegee Institute received money, training for its interns, and employment for its nurses. In addition, the PHS recruited black church leaders, community leaders, and plantation owners to encourage participation.

At the time of the project, African Americans had almost no access to medical care. For many participants, the examination by the PHS physician was the first health examination they had ever received. Along with free health examinations, food and transportation were supplied to participants. Thus, it was not difficult to recruit African American men as participants in the study. Burial stipends were used to get permission from family members to perform autopsies on study participants (Jones, 1981).

While study participants received medical examinations, none were told that they were infected with syphilis. They were either not treated or were treated at a level that was judged to be insufficient to cure the disease.

Over the course of the project, PHS officials not only denied study participants treatment, but also prevented other agencies from supplying treatment.

During World War II, about 50 of the study subjects were ordered by their draft boards to undergo treatment for syphilis. The PHS requested that the draft boards exclude study subjects from the requirement for treatment. The draft boards agreed.

In 1943, the PHS began to administer penicillin to patients with syphilis. Study subjects were excluded.

Beginning in 1952, the PHS began utilizing local health departments to track study participants who had left Macon County. Until the end of the study in the 1970s, local health departments worked with the PHS to keep the study subjects from receiving treatment.

The project was finally brought to a stop 1972 when Peter Buxton told the story of the Tuskegee Study to an Associated Press reporter. Buxton was a venereal disease interviewer and investigator for the PHS who had been attempting to raise the issue within the PHS since 1966. Despite his protestations, the "experiment" was still being carried out when the story appeared on the front pages of newspapers around the country (Jones, 1981).

Congressional subcommittee meetings were held in early 1973 by Senator Edward Kennedy. These resulted in a complete rewrite of the Health, Education, and Welfare regulations on working with human subjects. In the same year a $1.8 billion class action suit was filed in U.S. District Court on behalf of the study subjects. In December of 1974, the U.S. government paid $10 million in an out of court settlement.

The Tuskegee Syphilis Study remains one of the most outrageous examples of disregard of basic ethical principles of conduct (not to mention violation of standards for ethical research). In 1976, historian James Jones (1981) interviewed John Heller, director of the Venereal Diseases unit of the PHS from 1943 to 1948. Among Heller's remarks were the following: "The men's status did not warrant ethical debate. They were subjects, not patients, clinical material, not sick people" (p. 179).

The suspicion and fear generated by the Tuskegee Syphilis Study are evident today. Community workers report mistrust of public health institutions within the African American community. Alpha Thomas of the Dallas Urban League testified before the National Commission on AIDS: "So many African American people I work with do not trust hospitals or any of the other community health care service providers because of that Tuskegee Experiment" (National Commission on AIDS, 1990).

Kansas City Preventive Patrol Experiment (Criminal Justice)

Perhaps the most famous research study on police practices was conducted in 1972 and was funded by the Police Foundation. This study influenced police practices worldwide and is among the most widely cited of any criminal justice study. Any study of this magnitude will receive critique, as it should; however, consider what ethical concerns can be identified—based on *today's* ethical standards for research. The following summary comes from an agency called the Police Foundation, responsible for conducting the study. The report can be viewed in its entirety at

http://www.policefoundation.org/docs/kansas.html
(accessed December 15, 2009).

Patrol is considered the backbone of police work. Billions of dollars are spent each year in the United States to maintain and operate uniformed and often superbly equipped patrol forces. The assumption underlying such deployment has been that the presence or potential presence of officers patrolling the streets in marked police cars deters people from committing crime.

But the validity of this assumption had never been scientifically tested. And so, in 1972, with funding and technical assistance from the Police Foundation, the Kansas City Police launched a comprehensive, scientifically rigorous experiment to test the effects of police patrol on crime.

The Experiment The experiment began in October 1972 and continued through 1973; it was administered by the Kansas City Police Department and evaluated by the Police Foundation.

Patrols were varied within 15 police beats. Routine preventive patrol was eliminated in five beats, labeled "reactive" beats (meaning officers entered these areas only in response to calls from residents). Normal, routine patrol was maintained in five "control" beats. In five "proactive" beats, patrol was intensified by two to three times the norm. The experiment asked the following questions:

- Would citizens notice changes in the level of police patrol?
- Would different levels of visible police patrol affect recorded crime or the outcome of victim surveys?
- Would citizen fear of crime and attendant behavior change as a result of differing patrol levels?
- Would their degree of satisfaction with police change?

Information was gathered from victimization surveys, reported crime rates, arrest data, a survey of local businesses, attitudinal surveys, and trained observers who monitored police-citizen interaction.

Major Findings interestingly, citizens did not notice the difference when the level of patrol was changed. What is more, increasing or decreasing the level of police patrol had no significant effect on resident and commercial burglaries, auto thefts, larcenies involving auto accessories, robberies, or vandalism—crimes traditionally considered to be prevented by random, highly visible police patrol.

The rate at which crimes were reported to the police did not differ in any important or consistent way across the experimental beats. Citizen fear of crime was not affected by different levels of patrol. Nor was citizen satisfaction with police.

"Ride-alongs" by observers during the experiment also revealed that 60 percent of the time spent by a Kansas City patrol officer typically was noncommitted. In other words, officers spent a considerable amount of time waiting to respond to calls for service. And they spent about as much time on non-police-related activities as they did on police-related mobile patrol.

Implications The findings do not prove per se that a highly visible police presence has no impact on crime in selected circumstances. What they do suggest, however, is that routine preventive patrol in marked police cars has little value in preventing crime or making citizens feel safe.

The overall implication is that resources ordinarily allocated to preventive patrol could safely be devoted to other, perhaps more productive, crime control strategies. More specifically, the results indicate that police deployment strategies could be based on targeted crime prevention and service goals rather than on routine preventive patrol.

The Kansas City Preventive Patrol Study was vital in many regards. Most obviously, it altered police tactics. It was also important because it showed that "experiments" could be conducted in criminal justice and "real-world" settings. It was creatively designed and rigorously implemented (though with some problems) and has provided tremendous benefit to society, social science research, police, and others. Presumably no one was harmed. Sadly, under current IRB standards, it is very doubtful the study could be conducted.

Under contemporary IRB standards, would the police be allowed to *withdraw* police patrol from crime-infested, inner-city areas? Are local political leaders brave enough to withdraw police patrol from their areas of responsibility? Is the sheriff or police chief concerned enough with research to permit this? Imagine the media frenzy if violent crime rates had spiked in these areas due to an "experiment" (the study found they did not). Would many universities accept this liability "for the sake of research"? Some stringent IRBs may not even permit researchers to conduct a "ride-along" with the police due to risk of harm. Other IRBs may insist on approving the exact questions researchers plan to ask officers and citizens during a ride-along. And do not forget the requirement to obtain written, signed, informed consent from every officer and citizen encountered during the study. The increasing roles of contemporary IRBs are defining science. This is a complicated yet simple truth.

FINAL THOUGHTS

In defense of IRBs, one of the anonymous reviewers of this text noted that the IRB process is serving its purpose quite well. While there are historical cases of direct harm coming to subjects, there are few recent social science research studies where there is evidence that someone was harmed. This perception helps point to the success of ethical guidelines, IRBs, and the greater emphasis that social science researchers are placing on ethical considerations that seem to be protecting subjects and increasing the integrity of research. However, recall from chapter 1 how the Catholic Church persecuted and even put to death early scientists. The Catholic Church was not acting out of malice but was doing what *it* felt was best for society. Today, IRBs are acting out of *good faith* and doing what *they* consider best for society. The question is, despite all their good intentions, are they stifling good research? The Kansas City Preventive Patrol Experiment would never get IRB approval today, yet no harm occurred, and considerable research knowledge was gained. Philip Hamburger in 2005 made an astute and scholarly legal argument that IRBs as they currently operate probably violate the First Amendment and have resulted in a new form of censorship. Alternatively, consider the recent "Deception at Duke" medical study that occurred, went through proper channels of approval, and nevertheless violated ethical standards and possibly directly harmed participants. The need for balance to protect participants from harm and maintain ethical studies while at the same time allowing research to be conducted is a noble and lofty goal that must continue to be sought.

As research projects are drafted, it is important to consider worst-case scenarios and take precautions as necessary. Keeping ethical considerations a top priority is warranted, as is trying to address problems in designing the perfect research study around the restrictions imposed by IRB guidelines. Overall, plan in advance and try to anticipate potential ethical problems that might arise. When and if ethical issues arise, deal with them quickly and openly, and document everything extensively so that there is transparency in the research.

KEY TERMS

Analysis and reporting
Anonymity
Belmont Report
Coding
Confidentiality
Deceiving subjects
Ethical standards
Informed consent
Institutional review board (IRB)
No harm to participants
Nuremberg Code
Research ethics
Voluntary participation

CRITICAL THINKING EXERCISES

1. Why did ethical standards for research develop?
2. Who is responsible for making sure research is ethical?
3. What are the different types of possible harm due to research?
4. Why are IRBs sometimes criticized?
5. What additional ethical challenges are faced by qualitative researchers?
6. Discuss which of the studies in this chapter caused the most harm, and why?
7. Why would a mixed methods study present unique and additional ethical concerns?
8. Choose a study from your academic discipline and identify discipline-specific potential ethical issues.

CHAPTER 4

Validity and Reliability: Threats to Research Integrity

CHAPTER OBJECTIVES

After reading this chapter students should:

- Understand the various barriers to a well-developed and rigorous research study.
- Comprehend the different forms of research *validity* and why each is important.
- Comprehend the different threats to research *reliability* and how to address each.
- Know what it means to operationalize variables and become more confident in being able to do so.
- Conceptualize scale development and appreciate how to test the quality of scales with statistical formulas.
- Demonstrate familiarity with the vocabulary of research methods as it pertains to threats to validity and reliability.
- Know what exogenous or intervening variables are.
- Understand research hypotheses and be able to identify exogenous variables that may be influencing the relationship between the independent and dependent variables.
- Design research projects that guard against common research threats.
- Summarize the meaning of the bell-shaped curve and why it is important for data analysis.
- Identify outliers and understand how they influence data results, and how their influence can be minimized.

This chapter is critically important for a number of reasons. Most of the potential problems that might occur during research studies are described; yet, rather than just presenting the problems, the chapter addresses some solutions to most of the problems. These problems are called **threats** in research terminology.

Threats: The challenges in research studies that jeopardize the validity, reliability, and integrity of the study.

Some parts of the research process allow more flexibility to make corrections or changes than do others. For example, initially a researcher may fail to do a sufficient job researching or summarizing prior studies for the literature review section (the portion of a research paper or proposal in which similar studies are evaluated and discussed). However, at any point after an initial review of the existing literature, the researcher can always go back and update and otherwise improve upon it. For example, relevant new research may be published on the topic that needs to be included. A good researcher constantly attempts to locate, update, and incorporate other relevant studies into the research report. Since new studies and findings may be available, it is important to reevaluate this part of the process. Fortunately, at any stage of the research process, the researcher can make changes to the literature review.

This type of flexibility is not afforded during every phase of the research process. For example, once a sample is selected for study, it is very problematic to alter that sample. Similarly, once a pretest (such as a questionnaire) has been given, one cannot alter the survey instrument prior to the posttest. In other words, if a researcher was going to introduce a stimulus to a group of participants (sample) and evaluate the influence of that stimulus on the dependent variable, he or she cannot change how the effects are measured, nor can he or she change the sample. Consider that if a researcher wants to know if this chapter is helping students understand possible threats to research. The students' knowledge of those threats could be gauged via a survey instrument and measured with a pretest. Then, those same students could be required to read and take notes on this chapter (stimuli), then the same students (sample) could be reevaluated with a posttest to determine the influence that the stimulus had on the dependent variable—which in this case is the knowledge base of the students regarding threats to research. The researcher could not add students to the sample that did not take the pretest, nor could the professor change the survey instrument used to evaluate student knowledge (pretest and posttest).

While fluid research (the ability to make change) is encouraged in many situations, there are times when a researcher must adhere to the research design and abide by it so that the validity, reliability, and integrity of the study are not weakened or jeopardized. One of the main issues for a researcher to consider early is how they intend to go about studying a research problem; then they need to develop a plan of action. In most situations, the plan can be edited and tweaked—up to a certain point. Once a study has officially begun, however, caution should be used in making changes. There are, of course, exceptions that will be discussed later, but they mostly deal with ways to address unexpected occurrences in the research process.

The issues presented in this chapter are intended to encourage students to think critically and analytically about their research projects, to anticipate possible problems/threats, and to determine methods to eliminate, or minimize, them from the study before they occur. Having carefully considered possible threats *early* in the conceptualization and planning stages of the study is important. Many of the threats to validity and reliability have to be addressed *prior* to starting the study or very soon after the study commences. Few of these issues can be *fixed* or addressed after the study has begun, and even fewer problems can be resolved after the study concludes (Campbell & Fiske, 1959).

Researchers typically find the process of addressing validity and reliability intellectually stimulating. This portion of the study requires one to think critically and to make conscious, deliberate decisions. Ironically, some choices that may harm the *validity* of the study may in fact increase its *reliability*, and vice versa, so sometimes "give-and-take" decisions must be made. The choices researchers make will establish their competence and originality as researchers, as well as determining the strength of the study. This part of the process should not be viewed as being "black or white" or "right or wrong"; the choices are simply value decisions that must be made by the researcher. The more knowledge a person has about the potential threats, the better prepared they are to make the best decisions for a particular study.

VALIDITY AND RELIABILITY

The opening paragraphs to this chapter use the words *validity* and *reliability* in ways that may appear confusing. This possible confusion is caused by semantic ambiguity (i.e., the uncertainty of words' meanings). Like other research terminology, the words *validity* and *reliability* have very specific and unique meanings when applied to research methods.

Validity: The ability to accurately measure what one is intending to measure.

Validity, as applied to research methods, is "the best available approximation to the truth," according to Cook and Campbell (1979, p. 37). The key word is *approximation*, since actual truth is often elusive. What the researcher may consider "true," "accurate," or "right" today may be proven false tomorrow when there are better measuring instruments or analytical techniques. For example, scientists once thought it was "true" that removing blood, called *bloodletting*, was the best way to cure many illnesses. Later medical breakthroughs, based on scientific studies, found this practice to be ineffective and actually harmful. This compilation of knowledge over time is what has caused researchers to realize that "truth" can be relative, and that accurate studies focus more on verifying that the concept under consideration cannot be proven "false" (Popper, 1959).

Operationalization: The process of taking abstract concepts and converting them into measurable variables.

The easiest way to conceptualize validity is to continually ask the question, Is the researcher really measuring what he or she *thinks* is being measured? *Accuracy* is a good way to think of research validity. Semantics play a key role when trying to determine, for example, whether a researcher is actually measuring "frustration" when they think they are measuring "anger." This is related to the principle of **operationalization**, which is how one precisely defines the variable(s) being measured. For example, how would a competent researcher measure the construct "love"? Hatfield, Bensman, and Rapson (2012) writing on the "history of social scientists' attempts to measure passionate love," state that in the 1940s social scientists began to create tools designed to measure this emotion. Since that time numerous constructs have been created, but there still exist no one definite measure. The authors also show how scholars' conceptualization of love has changed over the years, which demonstrates how social, cultural, political, and temporal factors influence the ideology of "love." By reviewing this article, students can see a listing of 33 different measures (scales) of love. Importantly, students can also see how such constructs are gauged for a scale's reliability and validity information. In other words, how well does the scale actually measure love? To be discussed later, for example, is a statistical procedure called Cronbach's alpha which can help assess a scale's accuracy.

Source: takasuu

While the aforementioned research primarily focuses on a form of romantic love, there are in fact many different types of love, and of course with each type there are many possible ways to measure love as well as many different hypotheses that could be developed around the notion that love (or the lack of it) influences behavior in some way. One could hypothesize that a juvenile who is loved less (by parents, by family, by teachers, by significant others, by self, etc.) is more likely to engage in violent crime than are those youths whose experiences with love are positive. But in order to test such a hypothesis, the first thing a researcher must do is to determine exactly what he or she means by *love*, and the researcher needs to measure it exactly as intended. First, the researcher must define what *type* of love is being examined. There are many types of love (e.g., love for pets, family, snowboarding, pizza, country). Each of these types of love is quite different from romantic love, although romantic love is perhaps the most commonly used meaning of the word in American culture, and probably the one the reader conceptualized when the term was initially introduced. After considering how variables are constructed they must then be operationalized in a way that measures exactly what the researcher intends (validity). Considering the preceding example, it could be hypothesized that a teen that feels loved by their parent could be one predictor or independent variable explaining a reduced probability of violent crime. A teen that loves and respects himself or herself could also be an independent variable that might influence a propensity for violent crime. Alternatively, a teen who is in a romantic relationship, and thus feels romantic love, may also influence the rate of violent crime. Yet, a teen that loves excitement, or an adrenalin rush, might also participate in higher rates of violent crime in the quest for excitement. Each of these forms of "love" must be measured separately and uniquely to have a valid study regarding the relationship between the construct of love and violent crime. The word *love* is subjective and means different things to different people, so even something as simple as this construct must be carefully evaluated.

When defining variables, it is important to keep in mind the imprecise and ever-changing nature of language, particularly the English language. The vast majority of classical literature has been translated from Greek or Latin texts. Unfortunately, by the time these texts are published in English, they have lost much of their original meaning and subtlety. For purposes of this illustration, consider four separate and distinct Greek words (*agape*: sacrificial, altruistic regard; *eros*: erotic, sensual longing; *philia*: the feeling of brotherly friendship or loyalty; and *storge*: natural affection for family), all of which are often translated into one ambiguous English word, *love*. The imprecise nature of language is but one example of the difficulty in assessing the validity of variables, which are discussed later.

Suppose, though, that romantic love is specifically the variable of interest and is the topic of the researcher's study. How can romantic love be accurately measured? A person may sense or just "know" he or she is in love, but a researcher examining romantic love must be able to *operationalize*, or measure, the concept of romantic love. This is a much harder task than merely feeling "love." Some possible measures of romantic love might include (1) the amount and quality of time spent with the person; (2) the percentage of money spent on the person; (3) the importance of the love recipient (is the person on speed dial?); (4) the priority given to the subject (which person is texted the most?); (5) the extent, frequency, and degree of physical intimacy; (6) the amount of time spent thinking about the other person; and (7) the degree of "sacrifice" that one would make for the other. Can a researcher distinguish between true love and infatuation in a research study? Are the variables different? Most would argue that they are.

Taken *individually*, the seven items of love just presented may not be a valid measure of the existence or degree of romantic love. For example, a person may spend considerable time with an employer, but not even like that person. One may have several work-related numbers on speed dial or may text a coworker often (but not *love* the coworker). A single measure may not provide a true measure; however, if the researcher accumulates all the preceding measures and combines them in what is called a scale, index, or **composite measure**, then a more valid, and perhaps reliable, measure of "romantic love" might be created. Hopefully, it is becoming clear that many analytical and critical thinking skills are necessary in order to construct valid and reliable studies. Now, consider the equally important concept of reliability.

Composite measure: A collection of questions to better measure a research concept (commonly called a scale).

Reliability: The ability to consistently reproduce the same results under similar research conditions; the repeatability of findings and measures, or measurement consistency.

Reliability can be thought of as the "consistency" or "repeatability" of a measuring instrument or study. In other words, researchers want to make sure that the survey instrument is capable of producing the same (and hopefully correct) responses with repeated applications to different study respondents or to the same respondents over time. Singleton, Straits, Straits, and McAllister (1988) add to this definition that reliability is "concerned with questions of stability and consistency. Is the operational definition measuring 'something' consistently and dependably, whatever the 'something' may be? Do repeated applications of the operational definition under similar circumstances yield consistent results?" (p. 111). Or, put more simply, reliability is when a measurement technique (such as a questionnaire) gives the same consistent results on repeated applications. If the questions are worded correctly (valid and reliable) on a survey instrument, the respondent should give the same response today as next week. In other words, reliability gives precision or *confidence* in consistency of results. If a cell phone works only part of the time, it is *not* reliable. If the brakes on a motorcycle only work occasionally, the vehicle is not very reliable and should *not* be used.

In quantitative research especially, researchers need to be able to trust that the techniques and research instruments used (such as surveys) are in fact reliable and valid.

The index or scale discussed earlier as a way to measure romantic love, can be statistically examined to measure the degree of reliability it possesses. For future reference, an actual statistical procedure for measuring scale reliability is **Cronbach's alpha,** which produces a numerical value (e.g., .89 would be excellent, whereas .3 would be a low reliability coefficient) indicating how well, or reliably, the scale is actually measuring what it intends to measure. Cronbach's work (1951) can be reviewed for the mechanics on how to statistically assess scales; ultimately, however, he reminds us that even those researchers who are more focused on ensuring validity should not avoid considering the reliability of their measures. Both must be considered for quality research studies.

Cronbach's alpha: A statistical procedure to measure the strength of a particular scale or index (e.g., how good is the measure?).

The researcher can improve, or hurt, the reliability of a scale by adding or removing items on the scale. In the hypothetical scale created earlier, suppose an eighth item is included, such as "(8) number of hours spent watching television together." If this question is a good indicator of romantic love, then the Cronbach's alpha value for the scale would increase (because the higher the number, the better the measure). If it is a poor measure, the value would decrease, and the researcher would know to avoid including "watching television" in the romantic love scale. There are other ways to measure the accuracy of the items in a scale designed to assess a concept, but Cronbach's alpha is the most common and is the one generally taught.

Many researchers have made a useful analogy to help understand validity (accuracy) and reliability (repeatability) when developing a scale by comparing them to a target and marksmanship (Figure 4.1). The analogy to target practice is insightful. The tightness of the bullet holes (the pattern) reflects precision, consistency, or "reliability"; "validity" is reflected by how close the center of the pattern is to the actual bull's-eye (Streiner & Norman, 2006, p. 327). If a person is sighting in a rifle and the shots group very tightly together every time, then both the rifle and the shooter are reliable. If the bullets scatter about on the target, then reliability is lacking. Alternatively, if the shots cluster *on the center* of the target, validity exists. Visualize the "bull's-eye" as representing the concept (romantic love) the researcher is attempting to measure. Each dot, or "shot," represents a measure of the concept. The closer one comes to the center of the target, with all bullets grouped tightly together, the better the measurement (strong reliability and validity). Figure 4.1 shows the possible outcomes. In the first target, the measure (shots) is reliable but not valid, since the shots are tightly grouped but do not hit the desired bull's-eye (measure the correct construct). The middle target reflects some validity, but it is hard to say how much, since it lacks reliability. The third target is both reliable and valid.

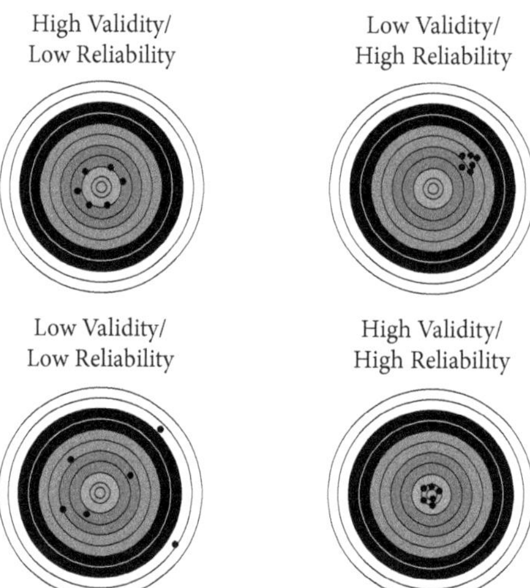

Figure 4.1
Validity and Reliability

Retrieved on May 31, 2010, from: http://ccnmtl.columbia.edu/projects/qmss/measurement/validity_and_reliability.html

In other words, to be valid, a measure must be reliable, since if shots were scattered all over, the validity could not be determined. There can be reliability without validity, as the tight groupings away from the center in the first target indicate. Researchers could get the same results on a testing instrument (survey questions) today as next week, but those questions may not be accurately measuring what was intended (reliability, but not validity). The goal is to achieve both.

Test-retest reliability: When two separate researchers generate the same outcome of the same measure—or the same measure produces the same results with multiple testing (e.g., testing instrument).

Intraobserver reliability: When two separate researchers at different times observe the same results or behavior.

Test-retest reliability occurs when two identical measures are taken on two separate occasions and the results are the same, or when two separate researchers administer a test and obtain the same results. If a student takes a research methods exam and then takes the same exam three weeks later and receives approximately the same score, then the exam is assumed to be reliable. Of course, during the interim period the research subject cannot have done anything to influence the score—such as studying, reading methods texts, or attending lectures. If more than one observer, or a team of qualitative researchers, are making observations (instead of using a questionnaire or exam), and the same result is achieved from each, this phenomenon is called **intraobserver reliability.** As mentioned earlier, Punch (1986) goes so far as to call the qualitative researcher an "instrument." Intraobserver reliability, then, provides an indication of the stability of responses from the same research subjects when they are collected at different points in time. The greater the variation (or the differences between responses), the lower the reliability. In statistical analysis, the technique to measure this, or provide a numerical value, is called a *correlation coefficient*.

The second common way to determine reliability is to take multiple items, or questions, to measure the factor of interest. This is called a measure of internal consistency, or **interitem reliability** (see Bachman & Schutt, 2011). Returning to the earlier example, recall how "romantic love" was measured. Each of the seven indices or measures of romantic love should be highly correlated with one another; simple statistical procedures taught in statistics classes (and in the data analysis chapter in this text) expand on these techniques designed to demonstrate the actual degree to which the measures are correlated with one another. These variables should be correlated, but not too closely or they may in fact just be measuring the same construct.

Interitem reliability: The process of measuring concepts or items in multiple ways to help ensure reliability of the measure.

Alternate-forms reliability is measured when researcher subjects are given slightly different questions, or measures, of the same concept. The differences can be as minor as simply reversing the order of questions or answers. If the instrument is reliable, then the results will be the same regardless of question or answer order. These are good to include in questionnaires to assess the reliability of the measurement instrument.

Alternate-forms reliability: The process of creating variation in the way a concept or item is measured in order to assess the consistency of the measure.

Intercoder reliability is a problem when two researchers interview the same subject but get different results or responses. It is also when researchers interpret a single subject's behavior differently. Intercoder reliability issues also can occur in the data entry phase when results are entered inaccurately. This reliability threat can occur in qualitative as well as quantitative studies. More specifically, in quantitative data, intercoder reliability can occur when multiple raters (coders or data entry personnel) are used to assign a code (numerical data) to findings, causing inconsistencies and inaccuracies. In qualitative data, for example, it is a similar problem when interviewing five different witnesses at a crime scene and five different interpretations of the event occur (people's attention to details and observation can vary), or when multiple researchers observe behavior (research) but qualify the data differently. Typically this can be prevented with proper training and by utilizing research assistants who are motivated and conscientious. Even in the example of the crime witnesses, one can be trained to pay more attention to details. That is why it is important, if a researcher relies on research assistants, to take the time to train and reinforce the importance of reducing reliability issues. Do not assume that everyone will be as attentive as others. Taking steps to reduce the potential threats early in the research development stage will prevent problems with reliability of the study later.

Intercoder reliability: A research threat when inconsistencies exist in the data collection stage or the data entry stage; for example, two interviewers may interview the same research subject yet have different findings.

TYPES OF VALIDITY

Donald Campbell and Julian Stanley (1963), along with Thomas Cook and Donald Campbell (1979), are best known for their description and explanation of the varied types of validity, including both threats and potential solutions. The first means of differentiating between types of validity is by "internal" and "external" validity.

Internal validity: Addresses whether two variables are in fact related. If they are related, then when one variable changes (increases or decreases), so does the other.

According to Cook and Campbell, **internal validity** deals with the need to determine if "a relationship between two variables is causal that the absence of a relationship implies the absence of cause" (1979, p. 37). In others words, each of the variables (independent and dependent) must covary or move together; this means that as one variable "moves," so does the other. The direction of the movement or change does not matter so long as one (the independent variable, or X) influences the other (the dependent variable, or Y). For example, the more a student studies (X), the better grades he or she will receive (Y). Since more of X causes an increase in Y, it is called a positive (+) relationship. If the opposite occurs, an inverse or negative (–) relationship exists. For example, the more a student studies (X), the less time he or she will spend sleeping (Y). As one rises the other falls; this is an example of variables covarying in an inverse relationship. It shows how factors can help aid in understand phenomena or behavior.

Exogenous variables: Those factors external to the study that influence the relationship between the variables being examined.

Statistical conclusion validity: The attempt to statistically account for all the variables that could be influencing the variable of interest (dependent variable).

The problem is that other, unknown variables may also influence the dependent (Y) variable. These other, often unknown, variables are called **exogenous variables** (Z). If there is more than one exogenous variable, and there usually is, then a subscript number (1) is often used to designate which variable it identifies. The problem these other variables create for the study is termed **statistical conclusion validity.** For example, what else might influence a student who is making better grades? Obviously, the amount of time spent studying is one of many possible variables. Other variables that could influence grades are how individuals study (Z_1), what they study (Z_2), the attitude they have toward school (Z_3), the quality of the instructor's lecture (Z_4), and even intelligence levels (Z_5). It could even by analyzed that if a student is in a romantic relationship (Z_6), grades may change in one direction or the other. A well-designed research study will account for, or control, the influence of these other variables, but they may not all be known (what if the respondent had a copy of the test and the researcher did not know it?). This is a good example of an unknown exogenous variable. Another way to think of internal validity is as anything that jeopardizes the researcher's confidence in knowing that it was *only* the treatment (stimulus) that produced the change in the dependent variable (Kraska & Neuman, 2011, p. 164).

External validity: The ability of a specific study outcome to be generalizable to a larger population or setting.

External validity is concerned with how well the study findings are "generalizable" to other people, places, and times. For example, if a researcher determines that students at XYZ University, during fall semester 2018, are more likely to cheat in online classes than in traditional lecture classes, that does not mean that students at ABC University are also more likely to cheat in online classes. It does not even mean that students at XYZ University are more prone to cheating in online classes during the summer of 2019. However, the better job a researcher does of selecting a "representative" sample, the fewer problems with external validity he or she will have; this is discussed in greater detail in chapter 8 on sampling strategies. For now, remember that both internal and external validity face different threats and require different solutions.

Specific Validity Threats

Cook and Campbell (1979) described 13 different threats to internal validity. While each threat is genuine, only the more common ones relevant for social science research are presented here; these threats are also not presented in any order of importance. Some solutions to the most common threats are provided; however, each study will require different solutions depending on the nature of the study and the topic of the research. The relative importance of each threat will vary depending on the topic of the study, the sample, how the topic was selected, and many other variables, some of which, like the weather, are completely out of the control of the researcher; but others are in potential control and must be considered and addressed.

History is the first threat to validity presented by Cook and Campbell. **History** is anything that happens during the course of a study (between the pretest and posttest) that may affect the outcome or study results. Singleton et al. (1988) note that history affecting a study can be something major, such as an assassination of a public figure or terror attack, to something very minor, such as a hostile remark made by a subject or researcher. If a researcher was conducting a longitudinal study of poverty or crime in New Orleans and Hurricane Katrina destroyed the economy and much of the city during the study, what effect would that have on the outcome of the study? Clearly, the economy was devastated, and crime rose significantly after the hurricane, so much so that crime was not even reported to the Federal Bureau of Investigations (FBI)'s Uniform Crime Reports (UCR) for that period. Carefully read the following insert by Wendy Hicks and try to identify other threats to research.

History: In a research study it is when external events that occur may influence the study findings.

INSERT 4.1

History and Other Threats to Research: The Stage Is Set

Wendy L. Hicks, PhD
University of Loyola
New Orleans, Louisiana

As a researcher or project team embarks on any specific study, individual focus soon becomes narrowed, as the demands of the project become all encompassing. However, it is the savvy

continued

Insert 4.1 *continued*

researcher, that extravagant individual with a penchant for observation for whom research is far more than mere recorded observations in a notebook, who is able to maintain a broad stance, focusing acute awareness on the external world beyond the confines of the laboratory or university, keenly on the alert for signs of any possible threats to the validity or reliability of their precious research.

There are a myriad of potential threats to a research project. However, it is often the items and events least expected by a researcher that prove the most damaging to the outcomes of any specific project. It can seem a daunting task trying to predict and identify threats to reliability and validity in a research project. All too often it can seem as though the elements of chaos theory have conspired in an attempt to derail a valued research endeavor. After all, one must not forget the basic tenets of chaos: if a butterfly flaps its wings in Beijing the subsequent hurricane season in Havana is extraordinarily extreme.

In order for a researcher to mature and hone his or her craft to a fine precision, it is necessary to embark on a study of just one such threat to valid and reliable research: history. The effects of historical events are all too often easily overlooked as potential threats to experimental reliability and validity. One might be forced to question how the emergence of a historical event can give rise to any threats to research validity or reliability. Or, in this example, how could an overly active Gulf of Mexico hurricane season possibly affect scholarly research on a worldwide scale? We will briefly discuss here the hurricane ferocity and the subsequent widespread effects on scholarly research on a global scale. First the stage must be set.

Hurricane Katrina

When Hurricane Katrina roared ashore on August 29, 2005, few could foresee the ultimate destruction that would be wrought by storm's end. While Katrina isn't the most powerful storm to ever strike the Gulf Coast, its effects continue to be felt over a much more extensive area than even Hurricane Camille in 1969 (National Weather Service, 2005). Damage extended into western Louisiana, eastward into Florida, and farther northward than Interstate Highway 10. Entire sections of St. Bernard Parish are no longer habitable, and the small towns of Waveland, Long Beach, and Bay St. Louis, Mississippi, are little more than memories of times past. Apart from damage to smaller cities and towns along the Louisiana and Mississippi Gulf Coast were the extensive flooding and damage to the cities of New Orleans, Metairie, and Kenner. The world watched as levees designed to protect the metropolis of New Orleans were breached and most of the city plunged into darkness as power and water systems failed.

Most residents of the city of New Orleans will readily state that the media was primarily responsible for the sensational stories of murders, rapes, and pillaging perpetrated by and against the evacuees sheltered inside the Superdome. To date there has been little direct evidence of any such behavior occurring inside the Superdome during the onslaught of the hurricane. While the response to the aftermath of the storm was admittedly less than desirable, one important fact remains: the effects of Hurricane Katrina displayed before all a surprising look into the underbelly of America's welfare state. As the authorities pointed fingers and tried to decide upon a proper course of action, looting and lawlessness were unleashed on the devastated city. Police officials were without proper equipment, communication was nonexistent, and there existed no discernible plan for the evacuation of stranded residents, deployment of rescue forces, or distribution of much needed food, water, and supplies.

For the uninitiated to get an adequate appreciation for the extent and severity of the problems facing the entire Gulf Coast, perhaps some background information on the characteristics of Hurricane Katrina are in order. Putting the severity of the storm into a scientific context provides a better description of the storm's rampage through the states of Louisiana, Mississippi, and Alabama.

The most powerful hurricane to hit the Gulf Coast to date was Hurricane Camille. Camille roared ashore on August 17, 1969, as a full Category 5 storm with sustained winds of 190 mph. Hurricane Camille had the lowest pressure ever recorded in the Gulf of Mexico at 909 mb (National Weather Service, 2005).

Hurricane Katrina roared ashore as a strong Category 3 storm near Waveland, Mississippi, on August 29, 2005 (National Weather Service, 2005). The third lowest pressure ever recorded in the Gulf of Mexico was documented during Katrina at 920 mb. At landfall the NASA Michoud facility recorded a pressure of 949.88 mb, while the University of South Alabama at Pascagoula documented a pressure of 976 mb (Knabb, Rhome, & Brown, 2005). Hurricane Katrina had 2-minute sustained winds of 126.5 mph (107 kt) recorded at the NASA Michoud facility. The wind gauge at the Eastern New Orleans Air Products Facility recorded sustained winds of 119.6 mph (104 kt) before finally failing, and winds at Long Beach, Mississippi, were recorded at 121.9 mph (106 kt). New Orleans's Algiers area experienced 12.49 inches of rainfall by day's end on August 31, 2005 (Knabb, Rhome, & Brown, 2005).

While wind damage was certainly to blame for some of the severe storm damage, the storm surge was an additional problem encountered by residents along the storm's path. Hancock County, Mississippi, experienced a storm surge of 22 feet, resulting in the near-total destruction of Waveland and Bay St. Louis. The Biloxi River was recorded at a level of 26 feet near the I-10 bay bridge, and Pascagoula, Mississippi, recorded a storm front of 16.1 feet. Lake Pontchartrain experienced a midlake storm surge of 6.8 feet, with Lake Maurepas recording a surge of 3.08 feet before the gauge finally failed (National Oceanic Atmospheric Administration, 2005). Finally, the small town of Grand Isle recorded a 12-foot storm surge (National Weather Service, 2005).

continued

Insert 4.1 *continued*

While Hurricane Katrina is astonishing on a scientific level, the resulting property losses and damage are equally astounding. Communities up to 76 miles east of the center of Hurricane Katrina experienced severe damage resulting from high winds and flooding (National Weather Service, 2005). According to the National Weather Service, "Almost total destruction was observed along the immediate coast in Hancock and Harrison [counties] with storm surge damage extending North along bays and bayous to Interstate Highway 10" (2006, p. 1). High storm surge was observed over a much more extensive area than even seen in Hurricane Camille. Insured property losses in the State of Louisiana totaled $22.6 billion, with the State of Mississippi experiencing an additional $9.8 billion in damages (National Weather Service, 2006). By October 30, 2005, there were a total of 1,053 deaths in Louisiana and 228 in Mississippi (National Weather Service, 2005).

Academia's Response to Katrina

As I sat in the Internet café in Krakow, Poland, that fateful evening of August 29, 2005, I couldn't help but question my colleague as he sat back in his chair, mouth agape, stating quietly but emphatically, "The levee broke." That was it. The levee broke. The city of New Orleans was under 20 feet of seawater. We sat in silence as the seconds ticked by on the nearby wall-mounted clock. Finally, without uttering a word, we both got up and headed back to our respective hotels, unsure of how to proceed with our scheduled conference presentation the following morning.

As CNN, Fox, BBC, and even the Chinese News Service broadcast news of the unfolding disaster, my party of four university professors from New Orleans was quickly besieged with questions, comments, and critiques on a vast array of social issues. Racism, cultural isolation, crime, law enforcement, weather patterns, and military intervention were among the inquiries we all tried to field as we made our way across the tree-lined avenues of Jagiellonian University. Finally, we sat in our research panel trying in vain to explain the culture of New Orleans, the nuances of southern law enforcement, race relations, geographic isolation, and the very real dangers local wildlife presented to survivors and rescuers in the disaster.

Later, as I sat in the Air France aircraft along with several hundred Swiss and French Red Cross workers and military officials, slowly trying to make my way to the home of my parents in Illinois, I couldn't help but notice the throng of academics crammed in with the contingency of relief workers and military police officers. It seemed as though my home of New Orleans had suddenly become a hotbed of research, a Petri dish, if you will, of sodden infrastructure, flooded streets, and exhausted survivors.

The Aftermath

I was finally able to get back to my university in October, five weeks after the hurricane made landfall. As I sat in my office, I began to notice that my previous research projects that had been placed aside as I was forced to contend with issues pertaining to locating groceries, clean water, and gasoline were no longer quite as important as I had once considered them.

Researchers from a vast array of American universities descended on the New Orleans area as they tried to provide explanations for the events that transpired in the Superdome as thousands of people fleeing their homes were forced to contend with a lack of food, water, and plumbing facilities. Others tried to shed light on the detrimental effects of geographic isolation that has been problematic for the metropolitan area since the colonial era. Still more tried in vain to explain the phenomenon of looting and violence that swept the city and continued to be problematic months after the storm.

I couldn't help but notice that almost none of the research to be published after the hurricane was work emanating from local scholars, but rather studies conducted by foreign or domestic academics that had often never visited the city prior to the ravages of the storm. As a researcher I was forced to question the results of most of these studies, as I was quite certain the investigators had little intimate knowledge of the city, its history, or its dynamic cultural roots.

In one fateful afternoon, research agendas across the globe had switched from efforts to explain gender roles in crime, societal nuances of consumerism, or personality factors in choice of fashion attire to more immediate interests pertaining to brutality in law enforcement, disaster relief, race relations, social isolationism, disaster recovery, FEMA preparedness, and an additional array of interesting, thought-provoking matters pertaining to the many issues and problems facing the Gulf Coast communities, especially the urban areas surrounding New Orleans.

In addition, the general public seemed to switch gears nearly instantaneously from identifying economic woes or international relations as the most pressing issues of the day to topics more in line with what they were witnessing on their televised news stations and reading in the newspapers of their respective regions. Now surveys proctored to elicit information and opinions pertaining to social and political phenomena were skewed as Katrina-related issues dominated the public psyche. In one fell swoop research on many timely societal topics became biased, with results facing numerous threats to both reliability and validity all due in no small part to one factor: history.

Research, much like technology or the fashion world, is very much driven by the latest trend. There is a certain style encountered when conducting research or trying to obtain funding. It is often the latest couture that is able to secure funding and ultimately publication. Attendance at scholarly conferences necessitates an interesting agenda for a researcher, as audiences tend to

continued

Insert 4.1 *continued*

gravitate to those studies addressing sensational and timely topics. It was the events occurring during and after Hurricane Katrina that caught the scholarly world's attention for several years after the storm. The latest trend in research was aimed at disasters, recovery, law enforcement, violence, and other mitigating factors that are often key ingredients in any catastrophic event. One only had to peruse the table of contents of any magazine or academic journal, and entries offering critiques, assessments, and essays on the effects of Hurricane Katrina abounded.

In the aftermath of the storm and the many publications arising from the storm-ravaged front lines, there are many lessons to be learned. It is first and foremost important to note that research does, most definitely, contain a fashion-forward front. Those researchers able to glom onto the latest trend in their discipline are generally the ones who are most successful at obtaining goodly amounts of funding and prime publication opportunities. Additionally, it is important for a researcher to be able to generate new ideas or new perspectives on the current trendy topic. Only through creativity will a scholar truly be successful in following research fashions or trends. Audiences and colleagues are often unenthusiastic to hear repeated catch phrases and worn-out hypotheses. It is the new and tantalizing take on the latest phenomenon that attracts interest. It is the savvy scholar that attends to nightly news reports and pop culture trends and undercurrents, as these can often be the springboards for interesting, thought-provoking research projects. Also essential to a successful research project is an investigator capable of full consideration of the effects of history on the reliability and validity of the study. One fateful event can change public opinion, perception, and academic perspective.

References

Knabb, R. D., Rhome, J. R., & Brown, D. P. (2005). *Tropical cyclones report Hurricane Katrina 23–30 August 2005*. Atlanta, GA: National Oceanic Atmospheric Administration, National Hurricane Center.

National Weather Service. (2005). *Tropical cyclone report*. Atlanta, GA: National Oceanic Atmospheric Administration. http://www.nws.noaa.gov

National Weather Service. (2006). *Tropical cyclone report*. Atlanta, GA: National Oceanic Atmospheric Administration. http://www.nws.noaa.gov

Natural disaster or climate change is but one example of history threatening internal validity. History can be any event such as war, political upheaval, terrorism, death of a public figure, or any other number of extraneous variables beyond the control of the researcher. A doctoral candidate in the 1990s was studying police-community relations in Michigan when the Rodney King police beating occurred in Los Angeles. Due to the widespread media coverage and repeated airing of the actual videotape, police all over the country suffered decreased community support, especially among economically challenged minority communities. Clearly, a televised police beating or shooting would impact any study on police-community relations. The same was true in 2015–2017 with the media coverage of use of force by police, and the resultant civil protest. Certainly, people paying attention to the media and news events (also the source of the news [liberal or conservative news] itself must now be considered) are likely to have a different impression of the police than those who are not, so these events would need to be considered, and controlled for, on any study regarding public perception of law enforcement. A serious researcher would critically question media accounts and look to empirical data to measure police use of force.

What can be done to mitigate the effect of history influencing a study? Honestly, not much. This is probably the most difficult threat to internal validity to resolve. Often the researcher must simply acknowledge its existence and try to measure the impact. It is always important to acknowledge any potential problem, and being honest and transparent is the best strategy. A good conclusion to any research study, honestly and openly, addresses any potential problems to the study. Never leave it to someone else to identify the potential weakness of a study. The researcher should be the first to identify the potential threats and problems associated with the study. There are no perfect studies and good researchers first do everything possible to eliminate problems, but second make sure that they identify for readers what potential problems may still exist with the study. This is also important to allow future studies to improve upon the initial study.

The second threat to internal validity is maturation. **Maturation** is any change in the respondent due to maturity, socialization, age, or education. This includes "any psychological or physical changes taking place within subjects that occur with the passing of time regardless of the experimental manipulation" (Singleton et al., 1988, p. 202). Kraska and Neuman (2011) interject that a respondent's *emotional makeup* may also influence a study's outcome, and emotions can change over time. Again, imagine how one's perception of police may change if it is one of their own family members that they believe was unfairly beaten or killed by police. Or imagine how an officer's opinion of their job and the people they serve might be influenced if he or she is being unjustly accused of police brutality when in fact it was a justified use of force.

Maturation: The changes to a respondent (e.g., age, maturity) during the course of a study that can influence the findings.

The National Center for Community Policing in the 1990's received a grant to study community policing in Michigan. At the start of the study, 10,000 Vietnamese refugees were settled in Lansing and Grand Rapids (great expense and trouble were taken to print questionnaires in Vietnamese). Most of the refugees spoke little

English, and many feared the police during the pretest study period. A year later, when the follow-up posttest was conducted, many of the "Viet Americans" were socialized to American ways and feared the police much less. The study results indicated a clear and statistically significant improvement in community and police relations. Was this improvement solely due to community policing, or did maturation (changes in the subjects themselves) play a role? In summary, maturation may be due to "respondents growing older, wiser, stronger, more experienced" (Cook & Campbell, 1979, p. 52). Fortunately, a solution to this threat, and most other threats, to internal validity exists. When the researcher can randomly divide subjects into a treatment (X) and a control or comparison group, the two groups should be equivalent, and then each would experience the same environmental and maturation stimuli. The sole difference should then be the treatment or applied stimulus, and the difference between the two groups can be assessed. Thus, randomization of samples is the solution to many internal validity threats (this is covered in greater detail in chapter eight on sampling).

Testing effect: Typically occurs in pretesting and posttesting studies when the familiarity of the test instrument influences the outcome of the posttest.

The third threat cited by Cook and Campbell is a **testing effect**, which may occur when respondents become so familiar with the survey instrument that their answers are influenced, as in the example of someone who knew what questions were going to be asked. The testing effect happens because of the pretest itself. More often than not, people "will score better and give more socially desirable or psychologically healthier responses the second time a test . . . is administered to them" (Singleton et al., 1988, p. 203). For example, if respondents were given the same exam or questionnaire once a week for 10 weeks, they may infer, over time, which are the desired responses and adjust their answers accordingly as opposed to giving an honest and sincere response.

Would applicants interviewing for a job with a law enforcement agency willingly admit on a questionnaire to having low self-control and a violent temper and to being aggressive? Not if they want the job! According to Singleton et al.:

> On some measures such as an intelligence test, the tasks simply become easier after practice. Attitude scales on the other hand, may alert subjects to the purpose of the scale, causing them to give socially desirable responses or perhaps to reexamine their own attitudes.
>
> *(1988, p. 203)*

One solution to this problem of testing effect is carefully crafting questions in different ways and using different versions of questions on repeated applications. Mixing the offering, design, and wording can reduce potential issues. Asking scenario questions might access self-control more accurately than just asking someone if they have it or not. The researcher may also find he or she gets a more reliable and honest response, which serves as a better measure.

The process of ascertaining validity and reliability is a research skill necessary in all disciplines, not only in criminology or criminal justice. Psychologists are especially adept at addressing this problem, and they have made many methodological contributions in a field of study called *psychometrics*. For example, a psychological test often administered in career or relationship counseling is the Myers-Briggs Type Indicator (MBTI). This test is designed to measure personality types in a manner that prohibits self-deception by asking the question in a variety of ways for the purpose of making the reason for the question imperceptible to the subject.

> Approximately two dozen recent published studies . . . examined reliability and validity of the Myers-Briggs Type Indicator (MBTI) in clinical, counseling, and research settings. Several assessments of split-half and test-retest reliability of the . . . inventory have yielded generally satisfactory correlations for all four scales. A larger number of studies of construct validity of the MBTI have yielded support for research hypotheses in situations ranging from correlations of the MBTI with a personality inventory, to couples' problems in a counseling setting, to line judgments in groups, and others.
>
> *(Kovar, Ott, & Fisher, 2003, p. 2)*

The next threat to internal validity is **instrumentation**, which is a problem when a change, or alteration, in the measuring instrument is made between the applications. If a pretest is given and the researcher subsequently discovers additional questions or a better way to measure a topic of interest (and so alters the posttest instrument to include these improved measures), then he or she has created a problem with instrumentation. The pretest and posttest should not be altered. The two should not be different, as discussed in the first few paragraphs of this chapter.

Instrumentation: A threat to the quality of a study when changes are made to the testing instrument (e.g., between the pretest and posttest).

The threat of instrumentation might be illustrated by the use of the Gallup Poll to compare the popularity of former Democratic President John Kennedy with Republican President Donald Trump. The questions asked by the Gallup Poll in 2018 about President Trump are quite different from the questions asked in 1964 about President Kennedy. Not only have the questions changed, but so has the terminology used. It is therefore hard to compare these two presidents' relative popularity. A Gallup Poll addressing popularity or acceptance of decisions made by President Donald Trump is likely to be very different and thus cannot be reliability compared to polls about earlier presidents. The solution to this internal validity problem is relatively simple: do not change the survey instrument between the pretest and posttest! If a comparison is desired, this may be easier said than done, however, because of what was discussed earlier about how language and words change over time. Sometimes alterations have to occur. Simply do a Google search of new terms or evaluate the changes made to dictionaries over time to appreciate that terminology changes. Trying to avoid slang words can be important to consider for several reasons, but especially in terms of instrument reliability.

In some cases, the *measuring instrument* might be an actual person instead of a questionnaire (as mentioned earlier when discussing qualitative research). For example, perhaps a researcher is hired to observe police recruits enrolled in a semester-long police academy. The instrument (observer) may become more skilled at "observing" and recording over the course of the training program; alternatively; he or she may become bored and less observant over time. These changes in skill or motivation in the instrument (observer) create a unique instrumentation problem called *intraobserver reliability* (this was mentioned earlier, as was intercoder reliability).

Statistical regression: When statistical outliers move closer to the average response; also known as regression to the mean.

The next threat to validity deals with statistics. This threat is called **statistical regression,** or *regression to the mean.* It occurs when outliers (extremes of the sample) move (regress) closer to the mean, or average, on subsequent testing. Consider, for example, intelligence. The average intelligence quotient (IQ) is 100; people typically vary slightly above and below the mean. In a sample, the average of everyone's IQ can be recorded (or plotted), and should be arranged in what is called a **bell-shaped curve** (Figure 4.2).

Bell-shaped curve: A normal distribution of data.

Outlier(s): The extreme scores that influence a normal distribution of data (e.g., bell-shaped curve).

Outlier(s) are those people with a very low (under 55) or a very high (over 145) intelligence quotient (IQ) (Chapter 9 provides more discussion on outliers). If an IQ test is really reliable and valid, then the IQ score of people taking the test should remain relatively constant. Not all measures are reliable and valid, however; furthermore, people change and mature over time. Even changing the testing conditions can alter responses. When respondents become more familiar and comfortable

Figure 4.2
Bell Curves

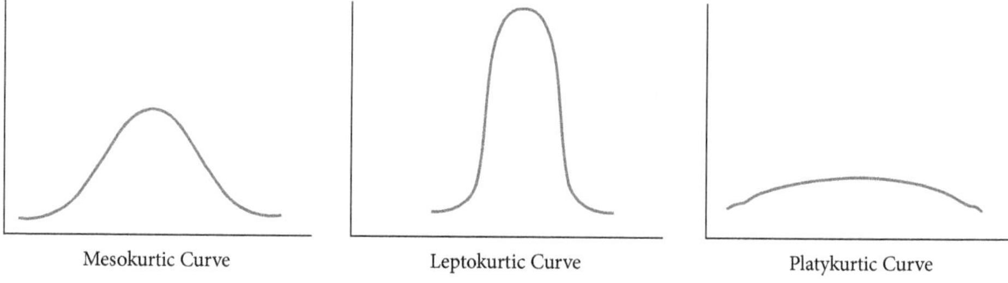

with the testing environment, scores can increase and therefore move closer to the average score.

Consider the scores of students on their first research methods exam. There may have been students who scored extremely high, say a 107, or very low, perhaps a 7 (yes these are actual scores) on the first research methods exam. Assume the class average was 78. On the second exam, the student who made the 7 probably dropped the class, but if not, what do you think they made? According to regression to the mean, the student would make closer to the class average of 78, perhaps a 55. What about the student who made a 107? This student also "regressed," or moved closer to the average, perhaps scoring a 99. These two extreme scores regressed, or moved closer to the overall average.

So, statistical regression or regression to the mean is nothing more complicated than when extreme high and low scores move to closer to the mean (or average) on subsequent testing.

INSERT 4.2

Regression to the Mean and Owning Some Chumps

William R. Smith, PhD
North Carolina State University
Raleigh, NC

Let's say that you've hired a coach to help you improve your Slayer game in Halo 3. I've heard of stranger things. Let's say this coach looks like Mr. Miyagi (from *The Karate Kid* films) but he curses WAY more. He uses a variety of training and motivational techniques, ranging from grenade throwing drills to trigger finger sprints, doing everything he can to drive you toward perfection. You notice, though, that he eventually stops praising you whenever you rank at the top of a match. He did at first, but now when you earn more than your usual number of kills your coach stands stoically by, straight faced and not giving you a single word of praise for those outstanding rounds.

Eventually, you ask him why he never praises you when you do a really good job. "Because," he says, "I've noticed that praise doesn't work. Every time I praised you for a really good round, your next round is always mediocre. And what's more, when I yell at you for playing poorly, next round you always do better. Praising not only doesn't make you better, it makes you worse." You pause for a second, then cry, "You're not my real dad!" and run out of the room, bawling like a child. Yes, you do. That emotional outburst aside, though, is your coach's logic sound, given that you DO in fact perform worse every time he praises you for doing well and perform better whenever he rebukes you for doing poorly? Praise makes you do worse and berating makes you better, right? Nope. Your performance following stellar rounds of Halo or Starcraft II or any other game involving skill can be best explained not by the effects of praise or punishment, but by something called "regression to the mean."

continued

Insert 4.2 *continued*

Let's assume that if we looked at your performance over a bunch of matches and plotted them out with ending scores along the *X*-axis and how often you end a match with that particular score on the *Y*-axis. They'd probably form something close to a normal, bell-shaped distribution. If we were to pick any single match at random, it's more likely that your performance would be about in the middle somewhere—somewhere near the "mean," which is basically another word for "average." In this example, that's 10 frags. It's rare that you're at the very top (17 frags) or bottom (3 frags). In fact, if your performance follows a normal distribution [like the one in Figure 4.2], then the following will be true:

- 68% of your matches will end with scores between 8 and 12
- 95% will be between 6 and 14
- Only 0.6% will be under 4 or over 16

And even if your distribution is a little skewed because you do well more often than you do poorly, the numbers won't change much until things get REALLY skewed. At which point no amount of coaching is going to change your game in either direction.

This is the reason that you seem to do worse after good matches and better after bad ones. The particularly good or bad matches are rare, and because they're rare it's improbable that you'd have two in a row no matter what your coach does. So don't get discouraged when you can't consistently come out on top multiple times in a row in any game of skill. You may be able to move your distribution up the right-hand side of the scale and/or squish it together so that there's less variation, but you're always going to regress to the mean somewhat because every round can't be your best (or worst) round. Now go give your dad a hug.

http://www.psychologyofgames.com/2010/03/30/regression-to-the-mean-and-owning-some-chumps/ (retrieved November 26, 2012)

1. Actually, in statistical parlance "average" is a vague term, but most normal people use it in the same sense that statisticians use the word "mean." So let's not make a big deal about it, okay?
2. For the advanced students in the audience, these numbers refer to one, two, and three standard deviations above/below the mean.

The phenomenon of regression to the mean occurs outside the classroom as well. Consider this true story illustrating regression to the mean. Years ago a woman took the LSAT, the exam required for admission to law school. The woman did extremely well, scoring in the top two percentile of everyone who took the exam that year. This was an outstanding score that would have gained her admission to any law school. For some unknown reason, she decided to retake the exam. Perhaps she wanted to prove that she really was that smart, wanted to see if she could improve upon her score, or had some other personal or hidden reason.

Her boyfriend, a professor who taught statistics, was shocked that she would even consider retaking the exam and argued strongly against the idea (perhaps providing further motivation for her to retake it). In addition to his concern for her future, the boyfriend understood about regression to the mean and advised that in this case, it was not a risk worth taking. His efforts at persuasion were to no avail, and the woman retook the LSAT. It is not hard to guess what happened. She never went to law school. When the lower test score was taken into consideration, her average score no longer guaranteed her admission. And, no, they are no longer dating.

What is the remedy to this problem of statistical regression? The most obvious solution is relatively simple; the researcher may merely remove the top and bottom 5% from the study (the outliers). For example, he or she may only examine or analyze the middle 90% and eliminate the top 5% and lowest 5% of study respondents. This removal of outliers eliminates the problems of high and low scores impacting the mean, or average. Think about taking the average age of a freshman college class, for example. Typically, the student's age would be 18 or 19; however, what if a 65-year-old female was also enrolled in the class? If her age were included, it would pull the class average age much higher than what is the true representation of the class. It is important to analyze the data for outliers and consider their effects and evaluate how they should be addressed; as will be covered more thoroughly in statistics courses, some statisticians suggest substituting the *mean value* (attribute average) for the value of the outlier rather than *eliminating* the outlier. Sometimes outliers can be eliminated from the study, but sometimes this is not the best option. Fortunately, outliers can be addressed in a variety of ways.

A criminal justice researcher was once conducting a study of incarcerated adolescents' knowledge of, attitudes toward, and behavior related to HIV/AIDS. Due to the nature of the study, one question asked the number of sexual partners of each juvenile. Assume for purposes of this illustration that the overall average was eight, but a small group of juveniles had been intimate with a much greater number of sexual partners. Unfortunately, closer examination showed that this latter group of juveniles had been professional sex workers (often unwillingly and against their will). These extremely sexually active teens would greatly inflate the overall average number of sex partners for *everyone* in the study if they were included. The obvious solution would be to simply remove those in the extremes. Is this a good solution? Not in this case, because it is the very sexually active respondents who are most likely to come into contact with, contract, and spread HIV. Because the study was about HIV, these were probably the most important people to include in the study, and taking them out would be counterproductive and foolish, even if it did solve the problem of statistical regression. Further, removing them would be a methodological as well as moral mistake. The solution used to overcome or address this type of dilemma differentiates poor or mediocre researchers from good researchers. The choice to eliminate respondents from the sample must be *critically* evaluated. Each study will be different, and researchers must separately ascertain what the best course of action is for each particular study.

Selection bias: Occurs in the sampling process when selection to a research group or assignment to research groups, experimental or control, is poorly done and compatibility is lacking.

The next threat to internal validity is **selection bias,** which occurs when unequal groups are chosen for comparison. The research subjects in the experimental group (the group receiving the intervention, test, stimulus, or independent variable [X]) should be as similar as possible to the subjects in the control group (the comparison group, which does not get the experimental treatment). As stated earlier, the best way to achieve this is through the use of randomization, which is described later in the chapter on sampling. Quasi-experimental designs, which by definition lack randomization, are especially susceptible to the threat of selection bias. R. A. Berk finds that "whenever one has a nonrandom sample, the potential for sample selection bias exists. . . . The difficulty is that one risks confounding the substantive phenomenon of interest with the selection process" (1983, p. 391). Berk provides another insightful illustration of the threat of selection bias:

> The impact of a mother's level of education on a child's college grade point average may be confounded with its impact on the child's likelihood of getting into college. The impact of a husband's income on the amount of leisure time a couple shares may be confounded with its impact on the likelihood that the couple will be married at all. The impact of seniority on output per hour may be confounded with its impact on the likelihood of being employed. Finally, the impact of a respondent's race on any of these phenomena may be confounded with its impact on the likelihood of responding to a questionnaire.
>
> *(1983, pp. 391–392)*

Mortality is another threat to the internal validity of a study. Again, it is important to keep in mind technical definitions when terms are applied to specific scientific endeavors such as research methods. Mortality, by general definition, relates to proportion of deaths to population; in research methods, there are other technical or esoteric meanings of the word.

Experimental Mortality in research occurs when research subjects drop out, or are otherwise lost from the study, before its conclusion. Sadly, when conducting long-term AIDS research, some subjects may actually succumb to the disease. Another AIDS-related example of mortality occurred during the corrections demonstration project called Linking Inmates Needing Care (LINC). This was a five-year study that followed subjects after release from prison and jail to determine if the HIV-positive inmates continued to take HIV medication following their release (Braithwaite & Arriola, 2005).

Experimental Mortality: A research threat when original participants in a study drop out, die, or are otherwise missing from the research before the study is complete.

Assume that the LINC investigators wanted to follow 5,000 inmates for five years. Think about how many would drop out or be lost due to name change, being re-arrested, diminishing desire to participate upon release from jail, homelessness, and many other factors. How could the LINC researchers make sure that they had 5,000 inmates to track over the course of the study?

The solution is relatively simple. If the researchers desire to finish with 5,000 research subjects, they should begin the study with as many as 10,000 subjects. This solution, called *oversampling*, is a commonly used technique. The problem, of course, is that researchers can never be certain how many respondents will be lost due to mortality. Barring economic concerns, it is better to have an overabundance of subjects than an inadequate number of study participants in order to compensate for potential mortality threats.

Consider a study on inmates in rehabilitation programs while incarcerated. Inmates are released early, transferred to different prisons often, receive disciplinary sanctions or solitary confinement, or may simply decide to stop participating in programs. Those participants that the researcher started the study with may not reflect the same number for the duration of the study. This can be problematic and must be addressed. At a minimal, the researcher must explain this loss of participants as a weakness of that study, and they should address how exactly the loss of these participants could influence the overall findings of the research.

How about a study on the homeless? A researcher in a large city may access homeless shelters to gather voluntary and willing participants in order to track life style, health care, emotional and mental assessments, past life experiences, relationships, job progress, and the like. Often this population is not easily tractable as they are often very transient. In addition, homeless shelters, by practice, do not release names and information about their clients. If one research participant moved from one shelter to another, or decided to live in a vacated premise, wooded area, abandoned structure, or even under a bridge, they may likely be lost from inclusion in the study. If those who drop out of the study are somehow different from the subjects who remain for the duration of the study, this presents a unique problem for the researcher to address. If some of the study dropouts can be located and measured, then the researcher can statistically compare their demographics and characteristics with those of the subjects who remained in the study. If the researcher is lucky, few differences will be found; if there are significant differences, then the ethical researcher must report and attempt to explain how the dropouts differ from those who completed the study, and infer implications of how it affected the research outcome. In the example provided previously, those who drop out of homeless shelters and decide to live under a bridge on their own without any public assistance may be uniquely different from those homeless who are securely located in one single shelter trying to secure reliable employment. It could be hypothesized that these individuals are more likely to be suffering from drug, alcohol, mental, emotional, or health problems. Others may be homeless for strictly financial, or hardship, reasons. Sounds like an interesting research study, does it not? These are things that an astute, analytical, and well-trained researcher will try to anticipate and address.

Diffusion of treatment: Can occur if a respondent learns too much information about the study or experiment and it influences his or her response to the study.

Diffusion of treatment is basically when too much information is revealed about the research, and in this case specifically about the treatment being introduced. If the effect of the treatment is the focus of the study, and the control and experimental groups know about the testing of the "treatment," the quality of the study could be affected. This can occur if researchers reveal too much detail about the study or if subjects in the control and experimental groups converse with one another and learn about the treatment themselves. The problem arises when the control group learns from, mimics, or incorporates knowledge or behavior, impacting and contaminating the study outcome. The simple solution is to keep the two groups separate; however, this is often very difficult to accomplish. For example, in prison and jail research, subjects and control subjects often interact and communicate in a variety of ways. Even though they may be instructed to not discuss details of the research study with one another, human nature may dictate otherwise. That communication can jeopardize the study.

Compensatory rivalry: When control group participants learn of potential benefits of the experimental group's "treatment" or stimuli and then alter their own behavior based on that information; they may "compensate" and perform in an atypical manner.

Closely related to the diffusion of treatment problem is the impact of compensatory rivalry on behavior. **Compensatory rivalry** occurs when subjects in the control or comparison group learn of special treatment or consideration given to the experimental group and consequently alter their behavior. In a study of inmates taking medication for HIV/AIDS, other HIV-positive inmates may alter their behavior in an effort to also receive the medication. Particularly in studies directly impacting the health (or even life) of the participants, it is crucial to be aware of the threat of compensatory rivalry.

Alternatively, take for example a study on teacher instruction and students' reading success. One group (Group A) of teachers is given extra compensation for every child that learns to read above grade level while in that particular class. In fact, Group A teachers are paid an additional bonus for *every* grade level improvement that is achieved by *every* child. The other group of teachers in the study receives no compensation for reading improvement by their students. The design of the study is to compare control groups with experimental groups to see if providing bonuses to teachers increases the rate of reading success for the students. Imagine what might occur should Group A share with Group B that they are receiving extra compensation when group B is not. Could this even create a "backlash" effect in Group B in regards to morale and teaching motivation? Could it, in fact, be possible for Group B's reading scores for their students to be lower than they would have been normally once the teachers learned of this inequity? Alternatively, it might actually *motivate* Group B to get their students to perform better. Many things have to be considered in good research studies.

Finally, there is the problem of experimenter expectancy, which could be considered a threat to internal or external validity. In **experimenter expectancy** the researcher (perhaps subconsciously and unintentionally) makes the subjects aware of the hypothesis, or expected outcome, thereby influencing the subjects' behavior. For example, the directions and information given to the respondent might provide so many details of the study that is obvious what the researcher expects, influencing the results that a respondent provides. Another form of experimenter expectancy is the **halo effect,** which occurs when the researcher subconsciously evaluates his or her subjects. For example, in a study of drug resistance techniques for incarcerated juveniles, the criminal justice researchers expected the juveniles in the experimental group (with whom the researchers had frequent contact) to perform better than the control group (located 250 miles away and with whom the researchers never had any contact). Ultimately, the data showed no difference between the two groups despite the researchers' "halo effect" expectations; it is important to remember, however, that halo effects *may* inadvertently influence decisions that researchers make, so good researchers guard against personal bias influencing a study.

Experimenter expectancy: A threat to research when the researcher makes too much information known to the respondents about the study that can bias or influence the participants' behavior or opinions.

Halo effect: A threat when a researcher's judgment, opinions, or personal bias about research subjects or the topic influences the outcome of the study.

These are some of the more commonly encountered threats to validity. Be aware, though, that others exist, and also remember that it is not uncommon for researchers to use different terminology to represent such threats. Once the basic concepts are learned, it is relatively easy to follow variation in terms. Note that not every researcher breaks these threats into *internal or external* threats, and that such dichotomous categorization need not be the focus. While it is a way to help process information, what is most important is to be aware of the different factors that weaken validity and reliability, take them into account, and address all that are possible.

Confounding interactions: When more than one threat to validity interacts with another threat (both occur at the same time); it is not uncommon to have two or more threats in a study.

Be cognizant of the fact that quite often there will be **confounding interactions** (Singleton et al., 1988). In other words, more than one threat to validity may be occurring simultaneously. To make matters worse, *fixing* one threat may actually increase another. It is important, and typically the best approach, to be aware of the threats and make the best decisions that are the least harmful to the study.

Take, for example, a study where a researcher encounters problems with both "experimental mortality" and "regression to the mean." The researcher may decide to resolve the problem of statistical regression by eliminating the high 5% and low 5% scores; however, this solution removed 10% of the study participants, thereby exacerbating the mortality problem (too many respondents are omitted).

More About External Validity

To review, recall that external validity "has to do with generalizing to particular individuals' settings and times, as well as generalizing across types of persons, settings and times" (Cook & Campbell, 1979, p. 71). A problem with external validity means the researcher cannot generalize findings beyond the group originally studied. For some studies, a goal of research is to be able to make inferences about the total population (generalize to the larger population). Problems with internal validity affect the ability to generalize (external validity). For example, take the problem of respondents knowing they are being studied. Would this potential "contamination" influence the ability of the research to make inferences to larger populations?

Reactivity: When respondents change their behavior because they know they are being studied.

Hawthorne effect: A label given when respondents know they are being studied and somehow alter their normal or typical behavior or opinion.

Reactivity occurs when subjects are aware that they are participants in a study and thus alter their behavior. The best-known study demonstrating reactivity (where subjects altered their behavior because they knew they were being studied) was conducted in Hawthorne, Illinois, and resulted in a new research term, **Hawthorne effect.** An academic search of this study reveals many interesting details, but to summarize briefly, in the 1920s and 1930s, Elton Mayo was a researcher who manipulated the work environment in the Hawthorne, Illinois, Westinghouse electric plant. The goal of the study was to determine what ecological manipulations would increase workers' productivity. But no matter what Mayo did to alter the subjects' work environment, productivity increased! He explained the occurrence of this phenomenon by the influence that the subject's knowledge they were being studied had on their performance. The concept and study became so influential that, over time, whenever research subjects alter their behavior because they know they are being studied, it is called the *Hawthorne effect*, after the Westinghouse plant location.

Another form of reactivity is the **placebo effect** (Beecher, 1955). A placebo is a "neutral" substance or stimulus given to the control group instead of the experimental substance or stimulus. In medical research, Beecher's placebo effect has been generally accepted as a scientific fact for decades. Why is it that some people who receive a placebo, or sugar pill, instead of the real experimental drug, will actually improve or be healed? Although no one knows why, it is perhaps due to their body reacting to their mind's expectation of being healed (aka the placebo effect). This supposition is an interesting research study in itself.

Placebo effect: When a respondent is given a "make-believe" treatment or stimulus and believes the effects are real.

It should be noted in keeping with the critical aspect of this text, however, that the validity of the placebo effect has been disputed. In a persuasive article, Kienle and Kiene note:

> Recently Beecher's article was reanalyzed with surprising results: In contrast to his claim, no evidence was found of any placebo effect in any of the studies cited by him. There were many other factors that could account for the reported improvements in patients in these trials, but most likely there was no placebo effect whatsoever. False impressions of placebo effects can be produced in various ways. Spontaneous improvement, fluctuation of symptoms, regression to the mean, additional treatment, conditional switching of placebo treatment, scaling bias, irrelevant response variables, answers of politeness, experimental subordination, conditioned answers, neurotic or psychotic misjudgment, psychosomatic phenomena, misquotation, etc.
>
> *(1997, p. 1311)*

Kienle and Kiene further contended that the placebo issue causes weak methodological thinking and that Beecher's misinterpretation should be a learning event in understanding the "interpretation of current placebo literature." Setting aside this dispute for now, the placebo effect is when the subject's belief in the effectiveness of the placebo may alter his or her behavior, opinion, and even health. In order for a treatment or experimental drug to be considered effective, more people in the treatment group (who get the real treatment) must improve or be healed than in the control group (who receive the placebo). Even the researcher may influence the findings, and so a **double-blind experiment** may be conducted where even the researcher does not know which group receives the placebo and which group receives the real treatment. This eliminates several potential problems.

Double-blind experiment: Excludes the participants and the researcher from knowing which groups of respondents belong to the control and which belong to the experimental group; this reduces many threats.

There is also the issue of "population validity." Just because a group in one study responds to stimuli or treatment, this does not mean that other groups will respond the same way. Consider a custodial technique (a method of controlling inmates) used in one prison. While it might work at one location with a certain type of inmate, one cannot assume that the same technique would be effective at every prison or with every inmate. Assuming so is a serious threat to external validity, and in order to control for this potential weakness, multiple sites should be studied and subjects should be selected by random selection. It is also important to replicate the study using different subjects and geographic locations and compare the results to see if they are similar.

Additional Types of Validity

Criterion validity: Utilizes a well-established measure (criterion) to compare to an alternative measure, which together can provide more predictability.

While there are also other forms of validity, the most commonly referenced are criterion validity, construct validity, and content validity. **Criterion validity** is also called *predictive validity*, since it deals with the ability of an instrument to *predict* some future occurrence. For example, the Graduate Record Examination (GRE) is argued by some to predict students' potential for success in graduate school. Likewise, the Law School Admission Test (LSAT) is used to predict which law school applicants will do well in their future legal studies, and the Scholastic Aptitude Test (SAT) and the American College Testing (ACT) exams are used to predict high school students' success in college. Past grades could also be used to predict someone's chances of getting into secondary and graduate schools, and they can be used to predict someone's future grades. Previous grades and standardized testing are criteria (independent variables) that are often used in admission decisions. When such measures are logically related, this refers to construct validity.

Construct validity: Determines if the instrument measures the intended concept accurately.

Construct validity determines if the measures used are actually measuring the concept under examination. For example, hair color is not logically related to athletic ability, but body type might be. Thus, body type might provide construct validity as a predictor of athletic success. The National Football League (NFL) "combine" tests college players on a number of athletic activities that presumably help predict success as a professional player. Measurements of the time needed to run 40 yards and the number of times 225 pounds can be benched pressed are used to compare athletes and assess overall athletic ability. Describing the texture of one's hair or one's eye color is not a likely predictor of future athletic success.

Consider also the conditions that might help prevent teens whose parents are in prison from becoming criminals themselves. Measuring the quality of food served where the parents are incarcerated will not likely predict the child's delinquent or criminal behavior; however, measuring the relationship with the parents, the child's social support system, and the child's experience at school might. Social support and school experience are logically related. Construct validity basically deals with being focused on how variables are measured and logically related to each other. It can be difficult to distinguish between criterion validity and construct validity. For both of these forms of validity, the scores on one variable should be related to the scores on the other if they both intend to inform some outcome. For example, for a person to be accepted to law school, grades and scores on the LSAT should be similar and in the higher percentiles.

Finally, **content validity** addresses the *range* of related measures. At the NFL combine, measures of strength, speed, and agility (assessments) are combined to determine a player's potential. The combination of *all* these measures enhances the content validity of the NFL's assessment at the combine.

Content validity: Deals with how well the measure covers the breadth of the concept.

Exams for college and graduate school admission contain content validity, since they cover a range of topics in one assessment, from math to English to writing ability. Another form of content validity can be seen in the review process itself. Graduate school committees evaluate more than just GRE scores in order to determine who is selected for master's degree opportunities. Committees will evaluate the applicant's grades, extracurricular activities, volunteer work, presentations, publications, and letters of recommendation. Typically, these measures are related and indicative of motivated students. So it is the "breadth" of the related measures that helps give content validity.

OTHER RESEARCH THREATS

There are a few additional concerns of which the competent researcher must be aware. Cook and Campbell note, "The definitional operationalism of logical positivists has supported the uncritical reification of measures and has encouraged research practitioners to overlook the measures' inevitable shortcomings and the consequences of these shortcomings" (1979, p. 93). For example, consider the scales created to measure romantic love earlier in this chapter. Does that measure *really* measure romantic love? It probably does not. It merely provides a proxy, or alternative, measure. Importantly, quality researchers recognize the limitations of their constructs (measures) and overall studies. Again, honesty, transparency, and critical thinking skills are imperative!

Reify: To treat something abstract as if it were concrete, or to treat something as being real when it is in fact not real.

To **reify** something means to treat something that is not real as if it were real. For example, a common measure of police performance is the number of arrests that an officer makes. But does this really measure who is the better-performing officer? What about the officer who has reduced the crime in his or her patrol area to virtually zero and so makes very few arrests? Hasn't that officer done a better job of policing? Likewise, many law enforcement agencies like to report their "average response time" as if this were indicative of good policing. Because most victims wait an average of 20 minutes before even calling the police, does a 2-minute faster response time really matter? Consider students accepting as fact that "Rate My Professor" is giving an accurate analysis of quality instruction and passion for student success. A high rating might just reflect a professor who is considered "easy." This is yet another reminder to be critical consumers of knowledge.

Ex post facto hypothesizing: Creating hypotheses to predict relationships after they have already been observed or measured.

Finally, there is **ex post facto hypothesizing,** which is creating hypotheses concerning the relationship between variables after the quantitative data is already collected and analyzed. This is generally considered unethical with quantitative research (see chapter 3). However, with qualitative research there is a form of ex post facto hypothesizing that is acceptable and even necessary. Adam Lankford (2013) studies the motivations behind suicide terrorists and mass murders. Since, by definition, his research subjects have expired, no strategy exists except for trying to "ex post," or retroactively, recreate the events and psychological profiles that motivated these mass murderers (his research subjects). The importance and uniqueness of this research demands ex post facto hypothesizing, and he has successfully created these type profiles.

Chapter 5 explores sampling strategies for both quantitative and qualitative studies, and chapter 6 addresses how the various research designs minimize the detrimental effects of reliability and validity threats. So many different forms of validity and reliability are covered in this chapter that it might be a bit overwhelming to distinguish the difference. For now, at least memorize what is meant by *validity* (are researchers really measuring what is intended?) and *reliability* (would the same results occur over time?). Both validity and reliability are very important to achieve in a well-designed research study. Likewise, critical thinking skills will only enhance one's ability to conduct good research. Continually think about all the things that *could* go wrong, could *weaken* the quality of the study, and use some of the techniques discussed in this chapter to defuse potential problems. The great thing about science is that, over time, new information and new techniques will emerge to help advance research studies. Perhaps *you* will be the very one to determine what they are!

KEY TERMS

Alternate-forms reliability
Bell-shaped curve
Compensatory rivalry
Composite measure
Confounding interactions
Construct validity
Content validity
Criterion validity
Cronbach's alpha
Diffusion of treatment
Double-blind experiment
Ex post facto hypothesizing
Exogenous variables
Experimental Mortality
Experimenter expectancy

External validity
Halo effect
Hawthorne effect
History
Instrumentation
Intercoder reliability
Interitem reliability
Internal validity
Intraobserver reliability
Maturation
Operationalization
Outlier(s)
Placebo effect
Reactivity
Reify
Reliability
Selection bias
Statistical conclusion validity
Statistical regression
Testing effect
Test-retest reliability
Threats
Validity

CRITICAL THINKING EXERCISES

1. Why is it important to evaluate and address "outliers"? How might one recognize and address the issue with outliers?
2. Explain, in your own words, what reliability and validity mean. Can you think of an analogy to help you describe and remember these two concepts?
3. What does Cronbach's alpha tell us? Why is it a useful statistic? How does it work?
4. If a researcher provides the respondent with too many details of the study, what problems can this present? What is this threat called? How might it be addressed?
5. There could be an association between amount of time studying and the grade received on a test. The independent variable (study behavior) influences the dependent variable (test score). It is specifically hypothesized that as time spent studying increases, so will the test grade; however, other variables besides study time may influence the dependent variable. These are referred to as *exogenous* variables (such as a student having a copy of the test). Describe an expected association between two *other* variables. Then, consider at least four exogenous variables that could actually be influencing the dependent variable. For example, consider two variables that you think might influence one another. Specifically decide which you think might be influencing the other. Now critically consider what other variables might actually be involved.
6. Provide an example of how fixing one threat can make another one worse. How does a researcher determine which threat to fix?

CHAPTER 5

Qualitative Research Strategies

CHAPTER OBJECTIVES

After reading this chapter students should:

- Be able to describe the philosophical basis for qualitative research.
- Discuss the historical foundations of qualitative research.
- Understand what "field research" is and how it is conducted.
- Articulate the benefits and risks of ethnography.
- Have a better understanding of the factors influencing qualitative data collection.
- Know the drawbacks to qualitative research.
- Understand the different types of qualitative research.
- Be aware of unique challenges qualitative research presents for Institutional Review Boards (IRBs).

In the previous chapter on validity and reliability (threats to research), it should have been clear that, in general, qualitative research has greater *validity* while quantitative research is more *reliable*, although each is just a matter of degree. The overall strength of a study, particularly with regard to validly and reliability, is to a large extent determined by how well the researcher conceptualizes and "sets up" the study before beginning the data collection process. No matter how well it is initially organized, once the investigation is under way, flexibility is a defining characteristic of a successful qualitative study—although flexibility is difficult for some Institutional Review Boards (IRBs) to approve. This chapter provides a historical and philosophical basis, and then outlines and describes some of the more common *qualitative* data collection strategies.

There is no "one" qualitative method. Tewksbury notes the following:

> The data that [are] used in qualitative research come from a range of collection methods. These include interviews with individuals, observations of people, places and actions/interactions, immersion in settings so as to understand the what, how, when and where of social structure and action/interaction, the analysis of media (written, spoken, drawn, etc.) content and guided conversations with groups of individuals (focus groups).
>
> *(2010, p. 43)*

Social science researchers have utilized all of these strategies, and more.

Given the importance of the initial construction of the study, good researchers must understand the research design process. The rest of this chapter presents the basic strategies commonly employed by qualitative researchers. The strategies enumerated here are not exhaustive. One of the primary factors influencing the choice of research strategy is the research topic itself. Ideally, the topic will be the first consideration when selecting a research strategy. Subsequently, other factors such as time, research opportunity (access and location), finances, and training are also important; sometimes even politics influence choices about research designs.

HISTORICAL SYNOPSIS OF QUALITATIVE RESEARCH

Qualitative research has a long history and predates positivism, which is the underlying basis for quantitative research. In fact, some types of qualitative research such as oral history (a means of transmitting knowledge from generation to generation, often as stories, legends, or fables) are among the oldest known mechanisms for conveying knowledge. In any qualitative study, the purpose is to ultimately be able to provide an *in-depth* and *complete* understanding of the subject. Max Weber (1864–1920), one of the founders of sociology, used the term ***verstehen***, a German word that loosely translates to "interpretive understanding" or "deep understanding," to help explain qualitative research. To Weber, *verstehen* was important as a means of differentiating the qualitative methods often used in the social sciences from the quantitative methods traditionally employed in the natural, or hard, sciences. Weber also argued that while quantitative methodologies might be able to describe phenomena, quantitative methods often fail to provide *deep* meaning to socially constructed, contextualized behavior. This tension between the two methods and natural/social science persists even today.

Verstehen: German term meaning a deeper understanding of the social world.

Tewksbury described qualitative researchers as seeking "to provide a fully rounded empathetic understanding of issues, concepts, processes and experiences" (2010, p. 51). The more fully one can participate in the subject being examined, the better understanding (or *verstehen*) one has of the event, situation, or subject. For example, a researcher may hold focus group discussions, conduct interviews, and participate in police "ride-alongs" to better understand the sensation of being arrested; however, nothing will really convey the experience like actually being arrested! One could share details of this experience and provide understanding to others.

Geertz (1973) borrowed the term *thick description* from British anthropologist Ryle (1971) to define this type of intellectual effort (as cited in Mark & Eisgruber, 1988). Geertz believes the political culture needs to be taken into account in order to truly understand human behavior. In order to interpret behavior, one must take into consideration not only the *action* but also the *motivations* or contributing factors causing the behavior (e.g., physical, social, psychological, and other influences).

As discussed in chapter 3, it is important to remember two things regarding researcher participation in qualitative studies, according to Punch: (1) the impact upon a study when "the investigator engages in a close relationship during a considerable period of time with those he or she observes" and (2) that "the researcher is his own research instrument" (1986, p. 12). With qualitative research, since this *deep* understanding and thick description are the primary objectives, it is important to be mindful of the biasing effects that can occur when one is "too close" or has too much of an influence on the study. For example, with qualitative research the mere presence of the researcher may have an impact on the study, since the researcher is typically involved in the processes of observing behavior and collecting data. As pointed out in the earlier chapter, if researcher characteristics are suspected of having a mitigating or aggravating effect on responses or respondents' behavior, they must be explicitly acknowledged in the resulting report or research article. Because often there are more personal relationships (typically more personal contact occurs between the researcher and the subject in qualitative research), it is especially important that a researcher maintain his or her role as *researcher.* A researcher can inadvertently influence the outcome of the study by having preconceived notions about the direction of the data, or by providing too much information regarding the study to the respondents. Even small gestures (such as note taking, raised eyebrows, etc.) or comments by the researcher can change the opinion or behavior of research subjects. Researchers' errors in note taking can influence the reported outcome of the study, as well (some steps to note taking are covered later in this chapter in the section on research tools). For example, field observations (data) should be recorded exactly as they occur in the natural environment—and not as the researcher thinks they should, or wants them to occur. A quality researcher is skilled at note taking and considers *accuracy* to be imperative. These are just a few problems that can occur with qualitative research. It is worth repeating that qualitative researchers need to guard against any biasing effect that they may have on the study and to always remember their role as *researchers*. While some may question whether biasing effects can be removed completely from research, and some even argue whether it is really that important anyway, in the end, studies are much more likely to be "trusted" as actually contributing to science when the researcher has taken precautions to eliminate biasing effects.

Qualitative research as applied to the social sciences (in particular sociology, social work, political science, anthropology, criminal justice, and criminology) has a much more recent history than do quantitative methods. Members of the Department of Sociology and Anthropology at the University of Chicago from the 1930s to the 1950s deserve the most credit for making qualitative research relevant, popular, and useful (Bachman & Schutt, 2011). These founding pioneers, including (but not limited to) Robert Park, Clifford Shaw, Henry McKay, Ernest Burgess, W. I. Thomas, Florian Znaniecki, Frederic Thrasher, Howard Becker, and Erving Goffman, were often social reformers, newspaper writers, and social workers—and most obviously scholars—who conveyed their history and experiences into social scientific research primarily through qualitative methods. Never before or since has there been such a critical mass of like-minded social science researchers located in one department. The School of Criminology at Berkeley in the late 1960s had an equally strong contingent, but it was in the area of critical criminological theory (Lanier & Henry, 2010). The contemporary practice is for academic departments to employ faculty with *variations* in research approaches, rather than have strictly one approach represented.

For better or worse, it has been the practice of academic departments for the last 30 or so years to employ faculty with diverse skill sets. In other words, contemporary departments are much more likely to have a combination of quantitative, qualitative, critical, liberal, and conservative researchers. While this brings balance to the department and contributes to mixed methods research, it may spark intense debate among these scholars (affording a rich opportunity for new ideas and progress), and it does create an environment less conducive to producing extensive, comprehensive, in-depth studies in a single field, or subset of a field, as occurred at the Chicago school and at Berkeley.

Fortunately, the Chicago school researchers were able to demonstrate the value of qualitative research methods, which remain widely accepted today, even if not as commonly applied. Consider that

> the numerous advantages of qualitative methods provide a depth of understanding of crime, criminals and justice system operations and processing that far exceeds that offered by detached, statistical analyses. Because of the differences in the data, how data is collected and analyzed, and what the data and analyses are able to tell us about our subjects of study, the knowledge gained through qualitative investigations is more informative, richer and offers enhanced understandings compared to that which can be obtained via quantitative research.
>
> *(Tewksbury, 2010, p. 38)*

It is apparent from Tewksbury's statement that there is an ongoing spirited debate between proponents of qualitative methods and those who favor quantitative methods. For an alternative view, see Worrall's thought-provoking article (2000, pp. 353–360), where Worrall provides his arguments in support of quantitative over qualitative research in the field of criminal justice. The debate will likely continue, but more recently we have been seeing a merging of the two approaches in a single study.

REQUISITE QUALITATIVE RESEARCH TOOLS

One paramount requirement for *all* types of research is an intense curiosity. The actual process of conducting qualitative research involves skills most people already possess. Becoming a competent qualitative researcher often only requires honing these skills and learning systematic means of recording, storing, and codifying the collected data. The most difficult part of qualitative research is *interpretation*; the actual process of making "sense" of the data and developing or using theory to explain the themes, patterns, or findings the study generated—again, another reason that critical thinking skills are so important. Ultimately, making use of good communication skills and paying attention to detail are hallmarks of a good qualitative researcher.

Bachman and Schutt begin their description of qualitative research by noting that

> some of our greatest insights into social processes can result from what appear to be very ordinary activities: observing, participating, listening and talking. . . . Qualitative researchers must keenly observe respondents, sensitively plan their participation, systematically take notes, and strategically question respondents. They must also prepare to spend more time and invest more of their whole selves than often occurs with experiments or surveys.
>
> *(2011, p. 253)*

FIELD RESEARCH

The strategies for collecting data in a purely qualitative study are often termed **field research.** Initially and historically, most qualitative research took place among remote tribal villages, primarily by anthropologists. With time and more qualitatively trained researchers the "field" grew to include deviant subcultures (street corner societies, jazz [concert] halls, motorcycle clubs, etc.). These often involved recreational pursuits. The more recent practice has expanded the field to include common workplace locales like offices, factories, and police departments. Today, the social world provides a plethora of qualitative research possibilities. All this real-world data collection takes place in the natural working or living habitat of the research subjects, termed the *field.* A variety of techniques and strategies have been used to capture this type of field analysis. Technology has, not surprisingly, altered those strategies and tools.

Field research/ fieldwork: Observing behavior in its natural environment through direct personal observation by the researcher.

The first cultural anthropologists who immersed themselves in foreign cultures relied on pen and paper for documentation. It was not unusual for qualitative researchers "in the field" to amass thousands of pages of hand-scribbled notes. The task was to review that mass of files, make sense of it, and develop a reasonable explanation (theory) for the behaviors they observed. With the advent of computers and handheld data collection devices, the task is made easier, but the overriding objectives remain the same: to record the data as they occur in the natural setting. *Note taking* is a somewhat generic term, based on historical precedent that encompasses how data are recorded in the field. Traditionally, pad and pencil were used to jot down observations, reflections, and bits of information, while on scene or in the field. Immediately upon returning to the office, dorm room, or hotel (so that memory was still fresh), the researcher would take the scribbling and convert it into longer, more detailed narratives. Later these long narratives would be reviewed in an effort to identify themes and patterns and to develop theory or explanations to interpret the data. Note-taking practices have evolved over time with technology, as has data management.

The concept of good data managment continues to evolve, but what will remain at the core is an attention to detail and a dedication to organization. Huberman and Miles define as data management as, ". . . .the operations needed for a systematic, coherent process of data collection, storage and retrieval" (1994, p. 428). Data management is perhaps the area most subject to error, in part due to the large amount of information collected, and potential errors on the part of those observing and entering data. Data collection is a process where "raw experience is converted into words, typically compiled into extended text" (Huberman & Miles, 1994, p. 430).

These *words* can be created from observation, interviews, or even documents. In the "old days," field notes were scribbled onto note cards, and other paper-and-pencil devices were used, as noted earlier. Today it is much more common for researchers to rely on iPads, portable computers, video and tape recorders, and even cell phones. Regardless of the devices used, the end result is thousands of pieces of data or words that the researcher must condense in order to make sense of them.

Data reduction is when the data are reduced to manageable bits and pieces that the researcher can use to create a conceptual framework. This sorting of the data is more easily accomplished if the researcher uses the five storage and retrieval functions first suggested by H. G. Levine in 1985. These are, according to Huberman and Miles (1994, p. 430), *formatting* (how materials are laid out, physically embodied, and structured into types of files); *cross-referral* (linkage across different files); *indexing* (defining codes, organizing them into a structure; and pairing codes with specific parts of a database); *abstracting* (summaries of larger materials, such as documents or extended field notes); and *pagination* (numbers and letters locating specific material in field notes).

One of the defining characteristics of qualitative research is that it takes place outside of a laboratory setting—typically in the natural environment. In other words, it is conducted in the "field." Peter Manning defined **fieldwork** as "systematic gathering of data on specific aspects of social life by means other than social surveys, demographic techniques, and experimentation that includes an ongoing relationship with those studied" (1987, p. 9). It could be inferred, then, that qualitative methods are everything that quantitative methods are not.

The collection of qualitative data is by necessity different from quantitative data collection, which often occurs in a predetermined series of steps in a linear pattern. Qualitative research is nonlinear and, if performed properly, relies on an interactive model. Huberman and Miles (1994) suggest the components of this model are data collection, data reduction (see earlier mention), data display, and conclusions (both making and verifying the conclusions). Unlike in quantitative research, data reduction, display, and conclusions all influence one another and so often change, as shown in Figure 5.1.

Manning added to his previous description of fieldwork by elaborating that

> fieldwork does not give way easily to lists, steps, or stages in spite of what many textbooks suggest. Lists assume that one thing leads to another, that the first precedes the second, that the stages of the investigation are mutually exclusive and that the progress from "top" to "bottom" is linear and cumulative.
>
> *(1987)*

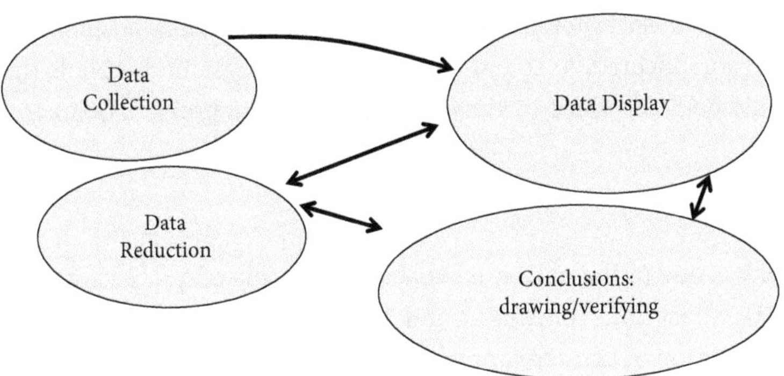

Figure 5.1
Components of Data Analysis Interactive Model

Adapted from Huberman and Miles (1994), p. 429

In essence, flexibility is key! Qualitative fieldwork is not concerned with amassing high volumes of research subjects as in quantitative research, but instead with obtaining in-depth, quality research from the subjects being studied.

OTHER TYPES OF QUALITATIVE RESEARCH

The nomenclature or naming protocol used in some of the primary qualitative research designs accurately describes the process. Consider the meaning of the terms *performance ethnography, public ethnography, participatory action research, focus group interviews, historiography, oral traditions, content analysis,* and *case studies.* The terminology itself conveys the strategy. Other terms may require explanation, since the research design title, or type, may not clearly express what the research strategy actually entails, usually because of the terms' scarcity of use in the common language or their cryptic meaning. For example, *standpoint epistemology, dramaturgy, narrative authority, semiotics,* and *grounded theory* are not necessarily self-explanatory and so they require elaboration.

Someone once noted, "There are as many different qualitative designs as there are qualitative researchers." While this is an exaggeration, it does make the point that each qualitative study is unique, will have a different focus, and should not follow any particular pattern. As the study progresses, findings evolve, and so strategies will also need to evolve. Data collection strategies may be altered as the data and findings dictate. This is one reason there are so many identified research designs. Researchers have attempted to articulate and label the processes as they have emerged over time, thus the terminology.

While there are many types of qualitative research designs, the major, or more commonly employed, strategies are considered in this section. They are presented in no particular order, so it should not be assumed that the first is most important or the last the most complicated. As stated several times throughout this book, the research design should be determined by the particular research problem being examined.

Ethnography

Ethnography: Research whereby the data collector immerses himself or herself in the study.

Ethnography is one of the oldest, most accepted forms of qualitative research. It is also one of the most time-consuming and difficult. It is also not without controversy. The basic definition of **ethnography** shows that "the practice places researchers in the midst of whatever it is they study" (Berg, 2004, p. 148). Ethnography was originally developed by cultural anthropologists as the best means to examine foreign cultures (Lanier, Henry, & Anastasai, 2015). The motion picture *Avatar* is a popular example of ethnography. The researchers' goal was to immerse themselves in the culture so as to learn more explicitly.

The purpose of any ethnographic strategy is to examine the phenomenon from the perspective of the study participants. The researcher may engage in the behavior studied to varying degrees. He or she may simply observe (nonparticipant observation) or may actively participate in the activities of the research subjects (participant observation). Think of a continuum from *pure researcher* to *pure participant*. A *pure researcher* would not participate in any way with the events or people being studied. By contrast, a *pure participant* would engage in every facet of the topic under study, completely being engaged in the focus of interest in order to gain

Source: Courtesy Everett Collection

the deepest understanding. Another term for this type of participation is *immersion*. According to Tewksbury, "Immersion in a setting, for purposes of gaining an understanding of how that setting operates, is the data collection method that drives the production of ethnography" (2010, p. 45). The more deeply a researcher can "immerse" himself or herself, the better, resulting in a more complete understanding of the subject.

Immersion takes time and unique, specific skills. Once the researcher has become imbedded, or immersed, in the study group, observations can be made, and data recorded, coded, and analyzed. For example, wartime correspondents who are "embedded" with combat units in a war zone are actually conducting ethnographic studies of troops in action. Research conducted in an active war zone would be utilizing what Miller and Tewksbury (2000) refer to as "extreme methods." **Extreme methods** are "dangerous approaches" and, as Miller and Tewksbury's title *Extreme Methods: Innovative Approaches to Social Science Research* indicates, "innovative approaches" to conducting research. The difficult part is "making sense" of these shared experiences and observations, or developing explanatory theory. Think of a researcher who "runs" with a violent gang in order to have a better understanding of gang behavior, or a researcher who is incarcerated to learn about prisonization.

Extreme methods: Creative, but often risky, data collection processes.

There are cautionary issues with these types of studies. As mentioned in earlier chapters, IRB processes are now often designed in ways that make it difficult to get approval for participant observation research. In addition, because groups typically have to be informed they are being studied, this could influence their behavior. Also, an ethnographic researcher needs to overcome much personal background, tradition, beliefs, and other forms of bias before being able to explain the behavior from the perspective of the group studied. Kraska and Neuman explain:

> Ethnography assumes that people make inferences—that is, go beyond what is explicitly seen or said to what is meant or implied. People display their culture (what people think, ponder or believe) through actions, language, or rituals. These do not give meaning; rather meaning is inferred, or someone figures out something. Moving what is heard or *observed* to what is *meant* is at the center of ethnography. (2011, p. 220, emphasis added)

A simple example helps illustrate this. In Orlando, Florida, the firefighters at Station X "require" every new rookie assigned to their firehouse to receive a tattoo from a specific tattoo artist ("Miss Heidi"). It is a "forced" rite of passage, and the rookie has no choice but to comply or face hazing and retaliatory consequences. Mere *observation* of this practice, which suggests forced compliance with what may be deemed a deeply personal, perhaps painful, and for the most part permanent decision, may disconcert or even severely disturb someone analyzing the behavior (aka the "researcher"). The researcher's personal, cultural, or religious beliefs about the tattoo ritual might conflict with, or support, the observations made regarding this conduct. Basically, one researcher may think this required hazing is totally acceptable, while another researcher may be appalled that a professional organization would engage in such behavior. If the researcher has strong personal opinions—one way or the other—the research findings and evaluations could be biased. These personal beliefs must be minimized in order to conduct good qualitative analysis. Even if a researcher becomes a participant observer, maintaining a neutral perspective helps reduce biased work. It is important for researchers to keep themselves "in check."

As Berg (2004) notes, the good researcher will alert the audience to the preexisting biases of which the researcher is aware that might influence the outcome of the study. For the firefighters, the *meaning* of the practice and ritual, which began as a tribute after the 9/11 terrorist attacks, is to develop a sense of camaraderie. This takes on a deep, "thick" meaning once the culture of firefighters is better understood. For someone who has worked as a firefighter, the ritual makes perfect sense; others, however, cannot comprehend this practice at all, considering it "barbaric," "unethical," and perhaps even "criminal."

The first sentence of David Fetterman's book describing ethnography reads, "Ethnography is the art and science of describing a group or culture" (1989, p. 11). This observation is accurate. Ethnography and other social science research methodologies are part "art" and part "science." The art aspect reflects the unique perspective, skills, and abilities of individual researchers. These skills can be cultivated and expanded, but they are difficult to teach. The science is more easily taught, as this and many other books and lectures affirm. There are other factors to consider as well.

Like all research strategies, ethnomethodology has some limitations. Getting arrested is one way to conduct research on police arrest practices, bail procedures, or inmate socialization; however, it is not a good idea. There are other limitations to ethnography as well. A researcher's age, gender, race, personality characteristics, and ethnicity can also dictate what can, and cannot, be effectively or safely studied. A middle-aged, undersized female could not, and should not, do a participant observation ethnographic study of a National Football League (NFL) training camp due to the risk of serious injury (of course, a younger, less vulnerable female athlete might attempt to do so). Likewise, men will never know by participant observation what it is really like to give birth to a baby. How, then, does a researcher excluded by factors such as age, gender, race, or personal characteristics study these apparently restricted topics?

One solution is to hire, recruit, or utilize research helpers, or "confederates," who can participate in these activities and report on the experience. **Confederates,** who are part of the group being studied, often provide a richer understanding of what is observed (explaining gang initiation, or the physical demands of NFL training camp, for example). Confederates may also facilitate entry to the study site or subjects. This type of confederate, called a **gatekeeper,** often introduces the researcher to the study population and vouches for the researcher's good intent. Consider how some researchers gain access to deviant subcultures, for example.

Confederates: Members of the research group who provide even richer insight into the topic of study and often assist with aspects of the study.

Gatekeeper: A member of the research group who enables the researcher's access to the group of interest.

A less rigorous form of ethnography relies on secondhand information when the researcher cannot fully participate. Embedded wartime news correspondents rarely kill someone and are therefore unable to fully comprehend the psychological effect of taking a human life. John Paul Vann was a participant in the Vietnam War and was the subject of an excellent book by Neal Sheehan, *A Bright Shining Lie*, which provides rich detail of the practice and "thick description" of the feelings associated with jungle combat. Sheehan was not a trained ethnographer, nor was he the actual participant, but he contributed to knowledge from secondhand information.

According to one review of Sheehan's book:

> This passionate, epic account of the Vietnam War centers on Lt. Col. John Paul Vann, whose story illuminates America's failures and disillusionment in Southeast Asia. Vann was a field adviser to the army when American involvement was just beginning. He quickly became appalled at the corruption of the South Vietnamese regime, their incompetence in fighting the Communists, and their brutal alienation of their own people. Finding his superiors too blinded by political lies to understand that the war was being thrown away, he secretly briefed reporters on what was really happening. One of those reporters was Neil Sheehan. This definitive expose on why America lost the war won the Pulitzer Prize for nonfiction in 1989.
>
> *(http://www.amazon.com/Bright-Shining-Lie-America-Vietnam/dp/0679724141 [accessed May 27, 2010])*

Despite this shining review of a shining lie, the actual author never participated in the tale being told. It was through the lives of others that the researcher was able to describe the experience.

Other examples are easily made. Several former students, and perhaps even those currently reading this chapter, have participated in Basic Law Enforcement Training (BLET). Many other former students are now mothers and may recall the childbirth delivery experience; yet, these "participant observers," unless educated in research methodology, lack the experience and training required to accurately

Source: Everett Historical

narrate, document, or report their experiences while exposing typologies or themes. Therefore, the relationship between the participant and researcher is an important one to science. The qualitative researcher is the vehicle by which knowledge can be gained by the lived experience of others.

The skills a trained ethnographer can provide are essential. Obviously, while the experience of the firsthand BLET trainee or birthing mother is richer, their lack of training in conducting research typically prohibits a useful study. The well-trained ethnographer, on the other hand, while possessing the skills necessary to conduct a useful study, must rely on secondhand data that are not as accurate, or as valid, as actual participation—but are, nevertheless, a close second.

Regardless of whether the data are personally collected or confederates are utilized, the process is very time-consuming. Time, however, is an essential feature of good qualitative research. The more time spent in the "field" (research setting), the more opportunities for observing the phenomenon will present themselves. Thus, the length of time expended for qualitative data collection is often equated to the strength and validity of a study. What if the researcher does have an extended period of time available to devote to the study, but the research subjects are available only for short periods of time (e.g., people arrested for driving under the influence [DUI] are rarely held in jails longer than 24 hours)? How can the researcher use qualitative measures to study the experiences of subjects such as these who are available for a limited amount of time? One solution is focus group interviewing.

Focus Group Interviewing

According to Berg, **focus group interviews** are an "interview style designed for small groups" (2004, p. 123). They can be guided or unguided discussions that revolve around the research topic. If the focus group is led or guided, the person who leads the discussion is called a **moderator.** The primary task facing the moderator is to solicit, or "draw out," information from the participants (Berg, 2004), as opposed to letting the respondents simply dictate the content. The moderator must take care not to influence or bias the subjects in any way, however. For example, the moderator can never convey moral or ethical feelings about the topic. Doing so could bias and jeopardize the results. As mentioned earlier, maintaining neutrality can be very difficult when addressing topics on which the moderator holds strong personal convictions. Imagine holding a focus group with a child sex molester. Although it may be extremely difficult or uncomfortable, as a good moderator one must work hard to mask any negative personal opinions. The goal as a research moderator is not to alter or change behavior or responses, but to better understand the existing behavior, feelings, or motivations.

Focus group interviews: Interviews with small groups in order to explore in greater detail issues or questions raised in the study.

Moderator: A person who leads discussion, often in focus groups.

There are several benefits to employing focus groups. The first benefit to this research strategy is that it is highly flexible and can be used in conjunction with other research strategies, such as participant observation. As is the case with the Orlando Fire Department, if a researcher has immersed himself or herself in participant observation about the socialization of a rookie fireman, focus groups could also be used to explore a deeper analysis of being tattooed as part of the indoctrination into the "brotherhood." According to Berg, focus groups allow "researchers to access substantive content of verbally expressed views, opinions, experiences, and attitudes" (2004, p. 126). They are a relatively quick means of collecting valuable data and are particularly useful for examining *transient* populations, which are those subjects that can "come and go" quickly (like the DUI subjects in jail). Due to the relatively short period of time necessary to conduct a focus group study, it is much cheaper than other prolonged types of qualitative data collection strategies. Lichtenstein further argues:

> Qualitative research has advantages over more traditional modes of data collection in several important respects: it presents the subjects' views and behaviors in a narrative format and in culturally sensitive modalities, and identifies the context of issues in a way that may be opaque in quantitative studies.
>
> *(2000, p. 116)*

Lichtenstein used focus groups to interview 51 HIV-positive and 84 HIV-negative men and women in rural Alabama, most of whom were either incarcerated or in treatment centers. Twenty-three correctional staff and other treatment providers then supplemented the initial information gained from these subjects. Lichtenstein decided that these additional 23 key informants needed to be studied in order to "gain insight into the nature of HIV infection in the local area from a broader (structural) perspective than could be elicited from the focus groups or individual interviews" (2000, p. 113). The combination of data received from the HIV study participants and from those "serving" the population provided a deeper analysis of treatment center or incarcerated HIV populations.

While the benefits of utilizing focus groups as a research strategy for collecting data are great, it is important to remember, and guard against, the shortcomings of this approach. As mentioned previously, the potential exists for the researcher or moderator to contaminate (harmfully influence) the research by interjecting views and opinions. Many of us have a natural tendency to do so; the competent researcher must work hard to avoid this. Second, meeting in a focus group, or even a series of focus groups, simply does not allow the same type of in-depth understanding that a longer qualitative strategy would permit. Thus, it does not provide "rich observational data" (Berg, 2004, p. 126). Because focus group meetings are briefer, it is imperative that the time be used as wisely as possible. For example, it might be valuable to utilize a *guided interview question* format if information on a specific topic is needed, as opposed to completely *open-ended, free-flowing format.* Question design is a crucial part of any study, whether qualitative or quantitative. Sometimes, "role playing," as can be seen in the following insert, can aid a researcher in being prepared for guided interviews.

INSERT 5.1
Interviewing "Role Play"

Doreen Morici
Western Carolina University
Cullowhee, North Carolina

A goal in conducting interviews (personal or telephone) is to *guide* respondents, but prevent *leading* them in any way. In order to do this, it is important to be prepared for what on types of comments (by the respondent) may trigger inappropriate responses from the researcher. Also, in qualitative research, where more open-ended questions are typically used, it can be challenging to keep a respondent "on track." Role-playing can help prepare a researcher for these types of problems.

Also, in interviews and telephone survey research, people may be a little less likely to be completely honest. It could have something to do with an unconscious fear of being "judged." Therefore, researchers should avoid personal "interjections" when conducting research. This helps ensure more accurate data are collected, and also helps minimize potential bias that may be caused because of the researcher's *presence* in the interview (in person or on the phone).

In order to practice role-play, select a partner, and one assumes the role of researcher and the other assumes the role of respondent. A team can switch roles, allowing both participants to practice conducting interviews.

1. Interviewer (researcher), please introduce yourself and let the respondent know that you appreciate their time. For example, please say:

Interviewer:

"My name is [*your name*], and I will be recording your responses. I know you are very busy, so thank you in advance for taking the time to complete this interview. It should take approximately [10] minutes." Note: be honest about approximately how long the interview should take.

The respondent may say something like, "You're welcome" and be ready to begin. However, he or she may say something like, "Well, I know you don't want to do this any more than I do" or "I bet you hate having to conduct interviews," or may ask you a question like "Are you a criminal justice major?" or "Do you like being a student at your university?" They may even ask the goal of the research.

Consider all the possible comments the respondent may make and how to respond appropriately. Remember, the key is to keep the respondent "on track" and not say anything that may put him or her in a biased frame of mind. For example, you would not respond by saying, "Being a student here sucks because there is nothing to do and the professors make us do bull crap."

You are not asked to lie, but you are expected to *divert* attention back to the interview/questionnaire. Keep in mind that the respondent is probably just being polite and not expecting an editorial anyway. You could simply say, "There are positive and negative things about being a student; it is pretty cool that I actually get experience in conducting research. Would you like to begin now?" *Your* response is all about balance; don't be too short (rude), but you want to avoid editorials (potential bias).

Practice how you would address the following comments from the respondent:

"Your voice sounds really good on the phone. I bet you are cute."

"I went to your university. I had Professor X. Boy I hated them. Do you like them?"

"What is this survey going to be used for, anyway?"

"How do you know my responses are going to be kept confidential?"

"I don't think questionnaires are very reliable, do you?"

In other words, a good researcher/interviewer will be prepared for potential questions and know in advance the best way to deal with them.

continued

Insert 5.1 *continued*

Another potential "trap" is to avoid comments related to specific questions. What if the respondent says, "Boy that is a stupid question"? Or asks your opinion on a question? Or gives a response that seems like he or she is just joking or not taking the interview seriously?

Here are some tips to remember:

- Avoid interjecting your *opinion* at any point. If it is done for one, it would have to be done for every single interview, and it has the potential of biasing the respondent anyway. Just avoid the temptation. Practice the interview several times before actually "going live."
- Practice will also improve your communication skills.
- Try to be friendly in your greeting, yet not *too* friendly. Avoid laughing, and remember that in this situation, you are the professional!
- Have a professional tone, not too "stiff" and not too casual—practice finding a "happy medium."
- It may be challenging to keep a "talker" on track, and it may be challenging to avoid your own personal interjections. Be ready by practicing how you would deal with potential comments.
- Be aware of "overempathizing," and avoid editorial comments. If the respondent says, "We don't even have any place to put dead bodies in our county," don't say, "You got to be kidding." Avoid editorial comments! It is harder than you think.
- Above all else, avoid biasing the respondent. Don't agree that the question is stupid or unclear, for example.
- If you are asking questions that have a specific scale as the response categories (e.g., typically closed-ended questions), such as very satisfied, somewhat satisfied, somewhat dissatisfied, and very dissatisfied, and the respondent says "somewhat" (does not want you to read all the responses because he or she is getting impatient), help the respondent to the applicable category. Ask, "Would you say somewhat *satisfied* or somewhat *dissatisfied*?" Avoid seeming angry or impatient in your own response. Your patience can help "pull" the respondent back "on track."
- Keep in mind that each question should be read exactly as it appears to each respondent.
- Avoid talking too fast. It may be natural to want to complete an interview quickly, but the "pace" should be appropriate (not too fast and not too slow). Remember that most respondents appreciate having an opportunity to have someone pay attention to their needs and opinions—so avoid the rush.

- If the respondent seems frustrated and wants to comment more than what is provided, make it clear that at the end of the interview you will write the comments down *exactly* as he or she states them, and you will make sure the principal investigators receive them.
- Most important, whether in the field taking notes or conducting an interview with subjects, record the data as they actually occur or are stated by the respondent. The data collection stage is no time to try to make sense of the data (interpretation); simply record the data exactly as they occur. Interpretation of qualitative research will come later.

Historiography and Oral Traditions

Recall the well-known statement "Those who refuse to learn from history are destined to repeat it." Although this quote, with some variations, has been attributed to a variety of philosophers, including the great statesman Edmund Burke, founding father Thomas Jefferson, and philosopher George Santayana, the statement also applies appropriately to research methods. This important "pearl of wisdom," even though it is in print and is now available online, is an example of an *oral tradition*. The philosopher spoke the words to pass along an insightful sentiment. The quote was conveyed verbally over many years until it has become a part of the national consciousness. Centuries later, we continue to be reminded of the value of learning from history, although there is much variation in the degree to which history is utilized to inform current understandings and decisions.

History has a valuable place in research methods, though many texts commonly omit it from serious consideration. Consider that oral traditions predate *scientific* research methods by thousands of years. Indeed, in some cultures that lacked the ability or tools to create written documents, **oral histories** were the primary means of conveying information, mores (long-established customs), norms, traditions, and laws. In fact, before laws were codified (written down), oral histories were the only means of passing them from one generation to the next. Native Americans are an example of a culture with a rich oral history. Much can be learned from this method of inquiry, but it has been underutilized in criminal justice research.

Oral histories: Precede other forms of recorded history, using information passed verbally from one generation to the next.

Historical research is simply "a process that examines events or combinations of events in order to uncover accounts of what happened in the past" (Berg, 2004, p. 234). The disadvantage can be that it is difficult to assess the authenticity or accuracy of historical evidence. Who writes and records the history can be unknown, as well as written only from the perspective of the person codifying the account.

Historical research: Attempts to contribute to science by understanding the past.

Generally, most written, official, or government "history" is written by the people in power, which consequently means it may omit the vantage point of the oppressed, defeated, or marginalized in society.

An often-repeated axiom is "History is written by the winners" (Orwell, 1944) or "If all records told the same tale—then the lie is passed into history and becomes truth." "Who controls the past," ran the Party slogan, "controls the future: who controls the present controls the past" (Orwell, 1944). The concept contained in these quotes from George Orwell is conveyed by many similar statements such as, "History is the polemics of the victor" (Buckley, cited in Loewen, 1995); "Of course history will be kind to me, for I intend to write it" (Winston Churchill, http://tvtropes.org/pmwiki/pmwiki.php/Main/WrittenByTheWinners [accessed June 7, 2010]); "'I have done that,' says my memory. 'I cannot have done that,' says my pride, and remains adamant. In the end, memory yields" (Nietzsche, 2009); "The history of a nation is, unfortunately, too easily written as the history of its dominant class" (Nkrumah, 1964); and, finally, "History is a set of lies agreed upon" (Napoleon Bonaparte, c. 1814). All these quotes about history reflect that power has influence on what is documented, and what is presented as history is limited by the memory of persons providing the perspective. It is through careful linguistic analyses that period-specific differentials are revealed. In other words, there are research benefits associated with conducting historiographies in and of themselves, but also in investigating account variations and why they occur.

Had Nazi Germany won World War II, Adolf Hitler would have been portrayed much differently. Many are not aware that the American government also practiced eugenics (forced sterilization) and other atrocities, albeit on a smaller scale, as Nazi Germany did. Americans know well the human desecration in Germany, but much less is known about violations committed by the United States and its allies. Samuel noted, "It is remarkable how much history has been written from the vantage point of those who have had the charge of running—or attempting to run—other people's lives, and how little from the real life experience of the people themselves" (Samuel, 1975, p. xii, cited in Berg, 2004, p. 244). It is only of late that we are learning more about American eugenics victims from their own perspectives; recently they have even testified before Congress. Oral traditions are the vehicle providing voice and illumination from the perspective of the average person, and are therefore important to exemplify and represent a broader representation of reality.

An example of historical analysis in criminal justice research is Dobash, Dobash, and Gutteridge's book *The Imprisonment of Women* (1986) on the treatment of female inmates. The authors state, "Our historical analysis is meant to serve two main purposes: to present evidence where little or none has been widely available before, and to provide a background for understanding the development of the imprisonment of women today." Part of their rationale for using a historical analysis was that "researchers usually fail to explore the relationship between historical patterns and contemporary forms of imprisonment" (1986, p. 11). Their work merges practices of the past to the present. So the combination of history and oral traditions is an appropriate qualitative approach to science.

One excellent repository of historical documents related to crime and justice is the Folger Institute in Washington, D.C., which freely provides archives to social science researchers; for example, it offers a manuscript containing all the old English common laws (see http://shakespeare.folger.edu/cgi-bin/Pwebrecon.cgi?BBID=170243). Another example, written before England had an actual police force, was created when citizens depended on proclamations made "by the king" (or queen) that were enforced by the constables and petty constables (http://shakespeare.folger.edu/cgi-bin/Pwebrecon.cgi?BBID=16422). Other informative historical documentation available at the Folger Institute concerns the debate about *who* should have the authority to decide laws, the church or the secular court (http://shakespeare.folger.edu/cgi-bin/Pwebrecon.cgi?BBID=160619). This debate was a contributing factor in Henry VIII's break with Rome. Reviewing the documents provides fascinating insight into a huge data set on crime and justice that has been preserved for hundreds of years, and that typifies historical research. Evaluating and analyzing such documents can be referred to as **content analysis.**

Content analysis: Examines existing books, letters, websites, documents, and other sources of data (e.g., graffiti) in order to identify commonalities or themes.

Content Analysis

Content analysis is a common and popular form of qualitative research. Unlike most data collection strategies, some researchers who rely on content analysis conduct data collection, entry, and analysis all in one process; other researchers have three, or more, distinct methodological steps. With either approach, the ultimate goal is to identify common patterns or themes within the data. The range of materials that can be analyzed is very broad. The materials archived at the Folger Institute are excellent examples, but the possibilities are vast. Consider themes that can be identified in news reports, video games, television programs, or music genres. Do themes in country music differ from themes in rap or heavy metal? Recently, the words to rap music have been analyzed from a research perspective (Ballard & Coates, 1995; Fried, 1996). There are distinct differences in music genres that can be revealed by a simple content analysis.

The more traditional areas of content analysis have included books, government documents, both private and public letters, and memos. A criminal justice example is provided by Baro and Eigenberg (1993), who conducted a content analysis of criminal justice and criminology textbooks, demonstrating how they graphically depict women. Sloan, Smykla, and Rush (2004) conducted a content analysis of case files from a family court in Jefferson County, Alabama. These secondary qualitative data were then compared with another data set from a random sample of juveniles who had completed a substance abuse program. The combination of data sets provides a more rich analysis.

Tewksbury provides a detailed explication:

> Content analysis is the examination of some form of media or communications for purposes of identifying how such messages reflect construct and are a part of culture. Scholars who engage in content analysis take as their data a collection of similar types of media (magazine articles, television sitcoms, suicide notes, criminal confessions, etc.) and work within a structured, systematic process to identify patterns and trends in what is included, what meanings are being communicated, the type of vocabulary/images used to convey particular types of messages or how various types of messages are contextualized within their particular form of media.
>
> *(2010, p. 48)*

In the next insert, Christine Ivie describes the content analysis she conducted for her doctoral dissertation study on human trafficking.

INSERT 5.2

Reimagining and Remapping the Gendered Geography of Human Trafficking: Surveying Documentary and Fictional Films

Christine Ivie, MS
Doctoral Candidate
Indiana University
Bloomington, Indiana

A student of criminal justice may question the merits of studying cinema in understanding crime and law. Such skepticism is warranted, given the deeply entrenched positivistic history of criminal justice scholarship, one in which measurement and prediction of crime, often ascertained through experimentation, are mainstays. However, as attested to by our government's demonstrated difficulties in quantifying and, concomitantly, combating human trafficking, certain crime problems require thinking outside of the positivist box. Despite federal and state human trafficking legislation authorizing extensive allocation of law enforcement and social service provisions, the 50,000 victims estimated by the State Department as being annually trafficked within U.S. borders have yet to be documented in official counts. This disjuncture between the perceived and the actual has not gone undetected or undiscussed. In his scathing 2007 article on federal (mis)handling of trafficking in persons, *Washington Post* columnist Jerry Markon indicted Congress for peppering the nation with nearly four dozen task forces, funded in excess of $150 million, to fight a largely unfounded domestic war on human trafficking. Markon assails the State Department's calculation of trafficking victims as hyperbolic, given that (at the time of his article) a mere 1,362 victims had been identified and a scant 148 federal cases filed since congressional passage of the seminal anti-human trafficking legislation, the Victims of Trafficking and Violence Protection Act of 2000.

The Victims of Trafficking and Violence Protection Act has been reauthorized three times. The Trafficking Victims Protection Reauthorization Act (TVPA) of 2005 mandates biennial reporting by state and local authorities to Congress on all reported incidents of suspected human trafficking. The Department of Justice provided the first synthesis of these data in January 2009. Of the 1,229 incidents reported, law enforcement verified only 112 as instances of human trafficking. These confirmed incidents involved 216 arrests, 328 victims, 140 prosecutions, and 61 convictions. Per Markon, the story told by these numbers, or lack thereof, is one of governmental largesse and inefficiency, another installment in an extensive history of state ineptitude or what Schram and Neisser (1997) deem the "meta story" of the "incompetent, but glorious state." Despite his overt doubting of governmental integrity in managing this matter, he appears to place tremendous stock in the official numbers imparted in this report. Perhaps such figures should be more critically assessed. To be deserving of deference, these tallies of human trafficking victims, arrests, prosecutions, and convictions require nuanced elucidation as to how cases come to be counted, or not. Statistics, descriptive and otherwise, should not be exempted from narrative analysis. As Schram and Neisser (1997) caution, "research results," while facially more valid than mere "rumor," involve their own degree of storytelling.

In my dissertation work, I propose that limited clarity, comprehensiveness, and consensus in the "imagining" of human trafficking victims by lawmakers and law enforcers conceivably impede suppression of what the State Department regards as "modern day slavery." Through analysis of cultural artifacts, these being congressional testimony and films, I employ British criminologist Alison Young's (1996) usage of the term *imagining* augmenting, and possibly overwriting, codified constructions of human trafficking victimization. Much scholarship elucidates how definitional deficiencies in antitrafficking legislation preclude detection of victims and prosecution of offenders. These deficits include both ambiguity and rigidity suffusing the legal

continued

Insert 5.2 *continued*

constructs of trafficking in persons, with the issue of ambiguity casting the greater pall on successful reduction of this societal malady. Attesting to the indistinctness of human trafficking legislation is invocation of the terms *force*, *fraud*, and *coercion*, one of which must be convincingly demonstrated to distinguish a trafficking victim from an offender (e.g., prostitute, illegal immigrant). While the parameters of these concepts are skeletally sketched within the policies, law enforcement exercises considerable discretion in the interpretation and application of these nebulous legal terms, which oftentimes do not seamlessly affix to the panoply of human trafficking possibilities. Stringency of such laws manifests in insistence that victim assistance hinge on the designation of "severe trafficking" status and on cooperation with authorities, neither of these terms being immune to subjective application. In sum, the legal frameworks accorded law enforcement by legislators leave much to be imagined in visualizing who is to be declared a human trafficking victim.

Before piecing together the puzzle of who potentially constitutes such victims, these pieces must first be gathered and organized. From what sources are these pieces culled, and what alternative sites could and should be consulted in reimagining trafficking victims? Copious congressional testimony over the last decade presumably informed existing legislation governing designation and classification of those trafficked. For this reason, I explore testimonial texts as one means of mapping out the existing and disjointed geography of trafficking in persons into and within the United States. However, as referenced in critiques of pertinent domestic policies, the picture of human trafficking victims may be obscured by either the opacity or the inflexibility inhering in these laws. Utilizing the emergent interdisciplinary field of law and film, I move beyond legal constructions, drawing also from the interpretations of artists and activists, to develop a more holistic mosaic of the human trafficking victim. But what insight into human trafficking victimization can be gleaned from analyzing movies on the topic? Film, not unlike testimony, constitutes a body of cultural documents that can either reflect or mediate societal conditions, including various inequities (Reinharz, 1992). More cogently, these cultural artifacts can shape, not merely signify, social norms. As with law, film makes meaning through "storytelling, performance and ritualistic patterning envisioning and constructing human subjects and social groups, individuals and worlds" (Kamir, 2005, p. 257).

Law professor Jessica Silbey has written extensively on the relevance of film to the understanding of law. She dichotomizes the study of film and law as taking one of two trajectories: "law-in-film" or "film-as-law" (Silbey, 2009), the latter of these being the approach I adopt in my own work. While "law-as-film" analysis involves critiquing cinematic representations of law and legal processes, "film-as-law" assumes that a law constitutes a legal culture external to the film. Scholarship on "film-as-law" assesses how movies propagate particular worldviews, advancing beliefs that certain people and/or practices are desirable, objectionable, and so forth. Further, this means of studying law and film examines how audiences are actively engaged to relate to proposed viewpoints.

Following the "film-as-law" tradition, my dissertation research employs feminist multitext analysis of 10 movies chronicling the subject of human trafficking. This methodological approach can be distinguished from its more easily recognizable cousin, content analysis, given its focus on discerning evidence, within and/or between texts, emblematic of structural inequalities historically challenged by and through feminism: classism, patriarchy, racism, xenophobia, and so on. Though an array of injustices pervades the problem of trafficking in persons, I am particularly interested in the decidedly gendered tone of human trafficking discourse. Assessment of the extent to which these movies reify and/or challenge gender, and other types of, discrimination ascends as central to my analysis. In selecting films to analyze, I defer to the recommendations made by Amanda Kloer, an abolitionist who trains civil attorneys representing human trafficking victims. On the Change.org website, Kloer identifies these 10 films, an amalgam of documentaries and fictional movies, as potent in fostering awareness of trafficking in persons. Of note, international sexual trafficking, especially of children, features prominently in Kloer's selections and in human trafficking discourse, despite labor trafficking materializing as the more capacious problem globally. Also of interest is that Kloer's cinematic selections characterize human trafficking as primarily involving persons from outside of the United States. How does the viewer of these movies come to conceive the problem of human trafficking? Kloer recommends these films to educate the public and those in the legal system working to eradicate trafficking in persons. What quality of education do these cinematic representations of human trafficking provide? This and other epistemological queries are explored in my dissertation.

References

Kamir, O. (2005). Why "law-and-film" and what does it actually mean? A perspective. *Continuum: Journal of Media & Cultural Studies, 19*(2), 255–278.

Markon, J. (2007, September 23). Human trafficking evokes outrage, little evidence: U.S. estimates thousands of victims, but efforts to find them fall short. *Washington Post*, p. A01.

Reinharz, S. (1992). *Feminist methods in social research.* New York, NY: Oxford University Press.

Schram, S., & Neisser, P. (Eds.). (1997). *Tales of the state: Narrative in contemporary U.S. politics and public policy.* New York, NY: Rowman and Littlefield.

Silbey, J. (2009). The politics of law and film study: An introduction to the symposium on legal outsiders in American film. *Suffolk University Law Review, 42*(4), 755–768.

Young, A. (1996). *Imagining crime.* Thousand Oaks, CA: Sage.

Content analysis has traditionally been included as a version or type of qualitative study; however, the recent trend of this methodology is to incorporate very elegant and often sophisticated statistical analyses. Further technological changes have allowed greater sampling with larger groups (remember that smaller sample size has typically been a characteristic of qualitative research). The larger sample size affords even stronger statistical strategies to be used. Due to these changes, there are very real reasons to include content analysis as a quantitative research strategy. Data collected from increasingly prevalent (and invasive) cameras at traffic intersections are an example. Lange, Johnson, and Voas (2005) did a large-scale (n = 4,656) analysis of the photographs of drivers passing through toll plazas on the New Jersey Turnpike. The demographics of people receiving tickets issued by the New Jersey State Police on the same part of the turnpike were then compared to examine racial profiling. Little about this very well designed study could be categorized as qualitative, and so it is indicative of how analytical strategies and technology have increasingly blurred the distinction between quantitative and qualitative designs. One might also make the argument that their research exemplifies a mixed methods study.

Finally, some innovative qualitative researchers are utilizing the internet in novel ways to conduct qualitative research. Holt, for example, finds:

> As the Internet and computer-mediated communications (CMCs), such as email and instant messaging, are rapidly adopted by all manner of criminals and deviants, it is critical that qualitative criminologists recognize how this data may be examined in order to understand social phenomena.
>
> *(2010, p. 466)*

Presumably, content analysis would be the apparent methodology of choice. The online data sources identified by Holt include forums, bulletin boards, news groups, email and instant messaging (IM), websites, blogs, and online text, all of which qualitative researchers can easily access.

Standpoint epistemology: Learning about the perspective of another from the unique experience of the actual person(s) being studied; "walk a mile in my shoes."

Standpoint Epistemology

Another type of qualitative study is **standpoint epistemology,** which is essentially a qualitative research method in which only the research subject, himself or herself, can understand and explain the topic under study. It is from the subject's own "standpoint" or position that insightful analysis is revealed.

Standpoint epistemology is founded on the premise that no one, other than the actual research subject, can actually fully comprehend or understand the *lived* experiences of the individual. The old expression "You can't understand me unless you have walked a mile in my shoes" provides a good colloquial description of standpoint epistemology. Recall from chapter 1, epistemology examines the question of how we know what we know (Flavin, 2001), or, as Harding states, epistemology is "theories of what knowledge is, what makes it possible, and how to get it" (1991, p. 308). Standpoint epistemology can be understood as valuing the perspective of the subject because a deeper knowledge can be gleaned from those who have lived the experience themselves. This form of insight is especially useful for understanding groups that have been or are suppressed in society.

Standpoint epistemology was developed, and has most often been used, by feminist theorists, or researchers who examine the unique experiences of women from a critical viewpoint (Lanier & Henry 2010, p. 347). Any subgroup, subculture, minority, or other distinct group could rely on the concept, however. Standpoint epistemology claims that

> the construction of knowledge requires many voices; especially those that have been marginalized by racism, sexism or class privilege. No one standpoint is given greater honor over others; together they give a rough understanding of the many ways to grasp the incredible complexity and ever-changing patterns of social life. Standpoint epistemology reveals a neglected or forgotten point of view, it empowers those excluded.
>
> *(Young 1995, p. 730)*

Flavin adds, "Standpoint feminists try to construct knowledge from the perspectives of the persons being studied on the grounds that the perspective of the oppressed or marginalized tends to be less distorted" (2001, p. 274).

Quite often the theories that underlie social science research are complementary and rely on empirical analysis for validation; however, standpoint epistemologists do not accept standard social science methodologies, since these strategies treat people (research subjects) as "objects" (Denzin & Lincoln, 1994, p. 101). Objectification devalues the feelings, thoughts, joys, sorrows, and physical, financial, and emotional realities of an individual's experience; who better to describe these events than the actual person living it?

There is, however, no one specific research strategy employed by standpoint epistemologists to garner this insight. Case studies, participant observation, interviews, and content analysis often are used. Lanier and Henry note that relative to standpoint epistemology, "this attention to a diversity of experiences, multiple knowledges, and the social construction of difference has led some to the view that a new nonexclusionary paradigm is necessary. One such approach is postmodernism" (2010, p. 345). Opponents of this strategy (notably positivists) hold that epistemology has an inherent definition that cannot be modified by the word *standpoint*. Should standpoint epistemology simply be labeled "viewpoint," "perspective," or "paradigm"? Or, as sci-fi writer Philip K. Dick (1978) stated, "The basic tool for the manipulation of reality is the manipulation of words. If you can control the meaning of words, you can control the people who must use the words" (see later section on semiotics for more on this). One of the more common complaints against standpoint epistemology is that there is no way to remove bias. This is not meant to discourage the use of standpoint epistemology as a research strategy, but simply to present the essential critical perspective or point of view. As always, application of critical thinking is imperative when making decisions about research strategies.

Dramaturgy

Dramaturgy: A research methodology in which the researcher scripts, or plays a role, based on the subjects' reactions and the research setting.

Dramaturgy is a research strategy that derives from a theoretical perspective called *symbolic interactionism* (common theory of understanding human interaction in sociology). It is basically a theatrical metaphor to help understand why and how people (and organizations) behave the way they do. The dramaturgical argument is that human actions are often dependent upon who is watching and the time and place of the behavior. Basically, behavior fluctuates based on many factors but primarily upon how the "actor" wants to be portrayed by the "audience." Important to this concept is the idea of "self" and "other," meaning that how one presents oneself to another person is based on symbolic interaction by which culture, norms, mores, and expectations influence human action directly. Thinking of the world as the stage and each of us as actors/performers helps describe this qualitative approach to research. Researchers (and others) may script a role based on the audience or subjects with whom they interact. This is done in part to gain access so that a deeper, richer story can be told.

Arguably, a researcher examining a deviant biker subculture would be privy to a deeper analysis if he or she fit the role. For example, it would be beneficial if the researcher knows a good deal about motorcycles, especially those typically ridden by outlaw clubs, and has disdain for those bikes not ridden by the deviant group. A male researcher may be afforded more access (and research success) than a female, since many accounts of the negative experiences of female bikers exist; a specific presentation in appearance could gain trust by which the member of the group feels more connected to the researcher. Typically, in this situation, having tattoos, leathers, or headgear provides a stronger identity, or connection, to the group and affirmation of belonging. Ultimately, this "presentation of self" is intended to gain credibility among the "other." If it is successful, much insight can be achieved by using the strategy of dramaturgy.

Hunter S. Thompson (1966) conducted this type of study on the outlaw motorcycle club the Hells Angels. Though not formally trained in either ethnography or dramaturgy, Thompson nonetheless relied on the strategies and techniques associated with this mode of study Thompson prefaced his observations of the Hells Angels in often less than flattering terms (which resulted in his being severely beaten by members of the gang). Obviously, the research strategy of putting oneself in a dangerous environment to present "self" to "other" in order to gain a deeper understanding can have serious ramifications (and can now be difficult to have approved by IRB committees).

Thompson was criticized by some, and applauded by others, for engaging in a style of reporting he dubbed "gonzo journalism," in which reporters involve themselves in the action to such a degree that they become central figures of the stories. Despite the criticism, Thompson's observations provide a rich and complete (deep) understanding of the Hells Angels Motorcycle Club. Thompson also wrote *Fear and Loathing in Las Vegas* (1996), which contains a character named Dr. Gonzo. Although *Fear and Loathing* is considered a prime example of gonzo journalism (and in fact is the source of that term, which later acquired negative connotations), Thompson regarded it as a failed experiment (1996, p. 210).

When researchers present themselves in a way that connects with those who are the focus of the study, based on symbolic interactionism, the subjects are less likely to change their usual behavior. Had the outlaw motorcycle club been researched by someone not having the relatable characteristics, the members' (the actors') behavior may have changed to fit better with the culture, mores, and expectation of the "other" (the audience). Imagine the most conservative, law-abiding, strict-looking female teacher as the researcher of the outlaw gang as opposed to Dr. Gonzo, who fit the script. Could the behavior of the gang change because its members were trying to project a certain image to this conservative-looking female researcher?

Semiotics

One of the oldest and most widely utilized qualitative research methods is the field of study called **semiotics,** which is fundamentally the interpretation of signs or linguistic analysis (study of words). Manning defines semiotics as

Semiotics: The study of signs and symbols (including words and language) as forms of communicative behavior.

> an approach to the analysis of social life that assumes that language is a model for other systems of signs and that seeks to identify the rules or principles that guide *signification* (the process by which objects in the world communicate meaning).
>
> *(1987, p. 9)*

This study of the contextual nature of words can be used to explain the example of rap music analysis mentioned earlier. The study of semiotics is also useful for understanding how professional organizations and groups use language to create divisions. For example, researchers speak a certain language in a certain context. Even common words take on a different meaning for someone who is trained and educated as a researcher. Consider, for example, the term *operationalization*. The layperson would likely not understand this term or would use it in a different context with a different meaning than a researcher would. Lawyers and those in the medical field also have semiotics that can intentionally or unintentionally exclude others from full comprehension. Try reading a medical journal or legal brief. Critical semiotics is used to critique how people in power use words and phrases as a means of subjugation or control. This is essentially all that is meant by the term *critical semiotics*. The theoretical underpinning of semiotics is symbolic interactionism, which is the same as mentioned in the discussion of dramaturgy. It is one way of making sense of how and why people interact with one another the way they do. To be a good qualitative researcher, an understanding of these forms of symbolic interaction is important. It can aid in the *interpretation* of the data, and being prepared for typical human reactions to researchers can allow a good game plan or strategy (research design and ways to deal with potential problems) to be in place.

Grounded Theory

Grounded theory is best understood as a method for theory development that is created ("grounded") as the data are both collected and analyzed. Grounded theory was first coined and presented in 1967 in the seminal text by Barney Glaser and Anselm L. Strauss. Grounded theory, while primarily used by qualitative researchers, could also be used in quantitative studies. The basic principle is simply that the theory is "grounded," or based, on the data as they are collected. In other words, instead of generating hypotheses and then collecting data to test them (the positivistic scientific method), the data themselves generate the theory—the opposite of the traditional research process. Recall that theory consists of "plausible relationships proposed among concepts and sets of concepts" (Strauss & Corbin, 1994, p. 278).

Grounded theory has several defining characteristics. First, it is conceptually dense or has many conceptual relationships (many of which may change). Second, grounded theory researchers examine and seek "patterns of action and interactions between and among various types of social units (i.e., actors)" (Strauss & Corbin, 1994, p. 278). They are consequently not so focused on individuals or specific events, but rather on discovering process. By process, they do not mean stages or steps but, rather, "reciprocal changes in patterns of action/interaction and in relationships with changes of conditions either internal or external to the process itself" (p. 278). Because grounded theory is based on the data, the data analyses are thus crucial to theory development. With grounded theory it is an ongoing and constantly evolving theory development process suggested by what the data show. Finally, grounded theory is very "fluid," since it emphasizes temporality and processes.

All interpretations are temporally restricted. First, theory is temporally limited in two respects. It is provisional; because theory is not static it should always be changed, elaborated on, and even negated. Second, theories are restricted by time and place. Different eras and different societies may lead to the creation of different theoretical development with everything else being equal.

In summary, grounded theory is more method than theory. It was considered a hallmark event when first introduced in 1967. For the reasons cited earlier, grounded theory is inherently an inductive approach to research. Grounded theory is less concerned with detailed descriptions and is focused instead on generalized explanations. Some have criticized the method for this, and others applaud it for this very reason. Another potential problem for some is the lack of codified, uniformly applied rules, steps, or procedures for data collection and theory development. Despite these concerns, grounded theory has enjoyed support among many qualitative researchers.

Triangulation

Triangulation is not a research method or study design, but it is a research *strategy*. **Triangulation** is including two or more research strategies in one study. These combinations may be all quantitative, all qualitative, or a combination of the two approaches. Typically, however, at least one qualitative component is included (hence the inclusion in this chapter, plus, the sooner the concept is introduced, the more useful it may be). For example, consider a study of hate crime, "Goode and Ben-Yehuda's (1999) indicators of a moral panic by triangulating sample data, official statistics, and editorial/opinion polls" (as cited in Colomb & Damphousse, 2004, p. 147). Each data source can be used individually; however, the combination can assist in verification of facts and accuracy of findings.

Triangulation: Using multiple research methodologies in one study.

Another common application of triangulation is using two or more data sources, often derived from different methodologies, to examine one topic. Hickman, Piquero, and Garner (2008) used computer-assisted jail interviews coupled with the National Crime Victimization Survey (NCVS) to better understand police use of force. The data gathered were used in combination to provide a more accurate understanding of the issue.

FACTORS INFLUENCING THE QUALITATIVE DATA COLLECTION PROCESS

Regardless of the research design employed, with a qualitative study, there are important factors the researcher must be aware of during data compilation. Maurice Punch (1986) outlined eight specific factors that will influence the value of the qualitative data collection process. The astute researcher will try to account for the effects of each. Many of these are also equally applicable to the quantitative strategies outlined in the subsequent chapter. All these are factors to be evaluated, and in some cases guarded against, by the researcher.

The first mitigating factor is the personality of the researcher. According to Punch, this is important because the researcher's personality influences "the selection of topics, intellectual approach, and ability in the field" (1986, p. 22). In other words, greater clarification as to why and how qualitative researchers select their research topic and location is needed. It is valuable to share what factors contribute to the topic selection. Punch, for example, argues that geographic proximity (location) is often a significant factor for why a topic is actually selected (e.g., a study on topless adult entertainment being chosen because the establishments are in close proximity to the researcher), and yet rarely is this type information presented in the research description. Since qualitative work is about a deep examination, revealing the *reasons* a topic is chosen can also provide value. Thus, having transparency in factors that contribute to topic choice and direction of research in qualitative research is beneficial.

Punch also notes that whether it is acknowledged or not, the nature and reputation of the research institution and of the researcher himself or herself are also likely to play a role in the direction of the research. The academic reputation of the affiliated research institution and the reputation of the researcher may garner additional liberties and have increased opportunities for conducting research, for example. To illustrate, it is likely, due to the high esteem of the agency, that the Centers for Disease Control and Prevention (CDC) would have considerable creditability for conducting HIV/AIDS research.

Conversely, during the Vietnam War era, the "radical" criminology researchers at Berkeley, while they may have been correct in their analysis, probably would not have been successful in presenting to the Defense Department a qualitative study regarding the effects of political conflicts or the necessity (or lack thereof) of military engagement. Since many of the qualitatively trained research faculty were very vocal in their *opposition* to the Vietnam conflict, their objective credibility with both state and federal government was at issue; therefore, they were not a likely choice to receive government funding or support for their research. Ultimately, student activism and the radical nature of the faculty directly led to the demise of the School of Criminology at the University of California, Berkeley, in 1976. While this example digresses a bit, it is a good illustration of some "real-world" effects, often unintended, of research. The example also lends itself to qualitative research possibilities.

While the faculty at Berkeley were practicing "praxis" (social change through human action) and leading by example, many of them paid a heavy price, losing hard-earned tenure positions at a major American university and demonstrating that research does have consequences. This is a fascinating story in itself. One perspective of the history, nature, and reasons for Berkeley's School of Criminology termination is told in the *Social Justice Journal* (1976). The editors state the following:

> The struggle to retain the School of Criminology was militant and spirited. Thousands of students participated in demonstrations and there was a broad base of community support for the progressive activities within the School. But the tendency of the movement to "bow to spontaneity" in the absence of a stable left organization capable of uniting various struggles seriously undermined the possibility of victory. Consequently, the movement to save the School of Criminology was no match for the administration's repressive, hegemonic, and tactical superiority.
>
> *(p. 1)*

Basically, because of the activism of the researchers and their vocal stance against the Vietnam War, the political consequences were large. Jobs were lost, and the whole department was eliminated (despite student support).

To relate this example to qualitative research, consider the things that could be investigated and studied. Consider how this example influenced future protocol. Consider whether the (relatively) recent collaboration between Berkeley (in departments outside of criminology) and the various governmental agencies is indicative of a shift in the political climate, changes within the university (policy, faculty attitudes and actions, alumni input, control and decisions of governing boards etc.), the board composition and objectives of funding sources reevaluation of goals by the government, the particular party holding government offices at given time, political influence, freedom of speech issues, dynamics of activism, or any number of other factors that could be studied directly. The possible options to study are vast regarding this single event. It should be obvious that many factors (such as political and economic) must be taken into consideration in conducting a qualitative study. A deep analysis is necessary in order to "pull back the layers of meaning" and gain a better understanding of the many embedded factors that influence outcomes. This is what qualitative analysis is all about. Some researchers and institutions will be afforded more opportunities than others, but possibilities do exist for all. While the methods of research may be somewhat restricted by economics and politics, even in the single example provided here one can see how the options for study are endless. Logically, right or wrong, politics play a part and are another reason that critical thinking skills are important.

The third mitigating factor impacting a qualitative study is the allocation of resources and access to (research) opportunities. Punch offers this explanation for why some projects are supported while others are not:

> The intellectual development of the discipline, academic imperialism, the institutional division of labor, the selection and availability of specific supervisors, backstage bargaining, pre-contract lobbying, departmental distribution of perks (research assistance, travel money, typing support) and patronage can all play a role.
>
> *(1986, pp. 22–23)*

The process of peer review evaluation was established, in part, to alleviate some of the problems with funding being allocated to unethical, or simply less competent, researchers. As mentioned in chapter 2, peer review is a process to help promote quality research. For example, in this book we have encouraged the use of peer-reviewed journals for literature reviews because, at least, the work is reviewed by "experts" and improvements are required before the work is accepted for publication. The peer review process also exists to aid in deciding which research projects get funded:

> Peer review has its well-discussed flaws and problems, but to date no better system has been devised to ensure quality. The argument for peer review is not that it is perfect, but is the best system we have yet to devise. It can, perhaps, be compared with Winston Churchill's opinion of democracy: "No one pretends that democracy is perfect or all-wise. Indeed, it has been said that democracy is the worst form of Government except all those others that have been tried from time to time.
>
> *(Fraser, 2007, p. 2)*

The process of funding can be frustrating and political, and no perfect system for determining who and what get financial support exists. Many times, however, qualitative studies are negatively impacted more than quantitative studies by these decisions (Cheek, 2008).

It is not unusual for a qualitative researcher to feel slighted when grant money is distributed, whether the reason for being overlooked, underfunded, or denied research funding is academic imperialism, backstage bargaining, precontract lobbying, politics, or another reason. For instance, Cheek argued, "It is still true that most funding is attracted to research projects using traditional (quantitative) scientific methods. This means that it is relatively harder to obtain funding for qualitative research" (2008, p. 71). While we have indicated several times in this book that the "purpose" of one's study should dictate which methodology is employed (qualitative, quantitative, or mixed), it is nevertheless a reality that political and economic factors weigh heavily on decisions, especially when funding is an issue; hopefully, however, one's purpose is not simply to secure grant money. In a perfect world, the research topic itself dictates the decisions made.

The fourth factor is that of how the "status" of the researcher impacts the field setting. For instance, a hired researcher with a large staff and much equipment will bias, or contaminate, a research setting more than what Punch terms a "lone wolf" researcher who travels light, blends in, and leaves a small "footprint." By "status" Punch seems to mean "presence." In order to reduce biasing influences, the field setting needs to remain as "pure" as possible, so it is important for the observer (researcher) to minimize his or her presence and other factors that could contaminate the research results.

Fifth is the influence of being part of, or the leader of, a research team. Punch believes most academic researchers are not trained to be, nor do they have the inclination to be, good team managers. When researchers do not work alone, it is imperative that they manage their team members effectively. As mentioned earlier, large teams of researchers pose their own sets of problems. We mentioned contamination issues, but any number of factors such as "workloads, ownership of data, rights of publication, and career and status issues are all affected by the constraints of team research" (Punch, 1986, p. 23), and even things such as a failed personal relationship between team members can have detrimental effects on the success of a research project. Managing people and research projects can be challenging, and most academic researchers do not have the leadership training or experience that would equip them to handle these stressors. A good qualitative researcher will be cognitive of these factors, deal effectively with issues, and often make personal sacrifices and compromises to be an effective manager and team leader.

The sixth factor cited by Punch is the "personality, appearance and luck" of the researcher (p. 24). This factor really deals with the personal characteristics of the researcher and makes the point that even gender and appearance will hinder some research projects while facilitating others (this point is also made elsewhere in this chapter). The "luck" factor suggests that the observant, astute scholar will recognize and seize research opportunities as they present themselves. Some researchers are just luckier than others, but an old quote exemplifies it best: "Luck is when preparation meets opportunity." A trained researcher will be observant of details and be prepared and ready to seize research opportunities as they afford themselves. It is really about paying attention to one's social world and making use of personal characteristics to enhance research opportunities.

Seventh is the fact that a good research team can disintegrate, collapse, or otherwise cease to be functional after the research products appear in print (presumably in peer-reviewed journals). Quite often the research subjects, fellow researchers, sponsoring agency, and university may take offense at the way they are presented in the published work (Punch, 1986, p. 24). This factor is related to the eighth and final one.

Eighth, fieldwork generates "social and moral obligations," which is a twofold problem: "On one hand there is the nature of the researcher's personal relationship with people he encounters in the field. On the other hand, there are moral and ethical aspects related to the purpose and conduct of research" (Punch, 1986, p. 25). In other words, how much can the researcher engage, participate in, and observe deviant or illegal activity while maintaining research ethics integrity and complying with IRB requirements? This has been a focal issue throughout this text. Difficult decisions have to be made.

Each of these eight factors, ethical considerations (presented in chapter 3), and threats to validity and reliability (presented in chapter 4) may influence research; the direct influence will vary based on the specific study, however. Regardless of the topic or strategy employed, an appropriate method to minimize negative influences is to pay attention to details and remain flexible, especially in qualitative work. Sometimes modifications to research projects are necessary throughout the research project itself, which is why some researchers promote *fluid* research processes.

Consider an example of an easy qualitative study that requires modification. Suppose a student researcher is using participant observation to study how other students in a typical class respond to lectures. Do they rely on a laptop to take notes? Do they handwrite notes? Do they just listen? Do they use a tape recorder? Do they just sleep? Do the students in the back of the room take as many notes as the ones up front? Do some ask questions to clarify lecture points? Do others frown on students asking questions to clarify notes? As the students' behavior is closely observed, the researcher may find that some are actually *not* taking notes at all, but are checking Facebook or Myspace, surfing the internet, or texting. Now, the astute and flexible researcher will make this observation, change the research methodology, and interview the classmates (research subjects), using focus groups, to best determine why they are not taking notes. These *direct personal* interviews may reveal that because lecture notes are available online, students attend the class only to get "attendance credit" or do not want to risk missing material *not* provided in the online lecture notes.

In other words, the student researcher noted common themes or occurrences, explored them, and then attempted to develop a theoretical explanation by continuing to "dig deeper" into the analysis. Basically, the researcher attempted to make sense of the data and had to adopt a flexible approach in order to fully investigate the issue. This theory development of attempting to *explain* the observed behavior is the hallmark of a good *qualitative* investigator. Had the researcher failed to conduct focus group interviews, the outcome of the study would be much different, and an important reason for some students' behavior (lectures were available online) would have been misrepresented.

SUMMARY

A lot of information has been presented in this chapter, and when possible it has been presented in a manner true to *qualitative* research: quoting the "voice" of others rather than paraphrasing -allowing the ability to keep exact the words of the original authors. Those skilled in the refencing style of the American Psychological Assoication (APA) might note this variation as APA recommends to paraphrase when referencing others, unless the true meaning would be forfeited by doing so. Paraphrasing is the typical approach in research papers in the social sciences.

Hopefully it is becoming clearer, as this text is read, that there are some unique differences between qualitative and quantitative approaches in research methods. It should be clear that qualitative analysis is about providing a *rich* understanding that deeply reflects the opinions and experiences of others.

Recapping some of those differences are in the way data is colleted, for example. Qualitative research is not about providing closed-ended questions on surveys given out to large numbers of respondents.The researchers are more concerned with capturing the experience through the lived experience of those being studied, and not in survey research analyzed by statistical procedures.

Typically, when exploring social issues qualitatively, this means that smaller samples and more time-consuming studies are conducted. Despite the long history of qualitative inquiry (and the quality of the work), the number of recent research publications utilizing quantitative methods greatly exceeds those relying on qualitative strategies. Most estimates agree that 85% of all peer-reviewed publications are based on quantitative methods (Tewksbury, DeMichele, & Miller, 2005). The next chapter explains *those* research strategies; and as presented in this text- the goal of combining qualitative and quantitative methods (mixed methods); will be discussed further. There are political, economic, and social trends that influence the application of research designs. Understanding all approaches makes for a better-prepared researcher.

KEY TERMS

Confederates	Field research/fieldwork	Oral histories
Content analysis	Focus group interviews	Semiotics
Dramaturgy	Gatekeeper	Standpoint epistemology
Ethnography	Historical research	Triangulation
Extreme methods	Moderator	*Verstehen*

CRITICAL THINKING EXERCISES

1. Describe at least three characteristics of qualitative studies.
2. Identify and describe at least three different types of qualitative research designs.
3. How have Weber, Geertz, and Tewksbury contributed to the understanding of qualitative research?
4. Why was the University of Chicago significant to qualitative research?
5. With qualitative research methods in mind, design a study to best investigate college social life. What factors should be considered to ensure the highest quality?
6. Compare and contrast quantitative methods with qualitative methods.
7. How does the philosophical basis for qualitative research differ from that for quantitative research?
8. Why is there sometime tension between natural and social sciences? Quantitative and qualitative researchers?

CHAPTER 6

Research Designs and Survey Research

CHAPTER OBJECTIVES

After reading this chapter students should:

- Continue to learn the differences between qualitative and quantitative research, and how combining research designs can at times produce more robust studies.
- Understand how validity and reliability connect to research designs.
- Conceptualize what "coding" refers to and why it is an important factor in data analysis.
- Comprehend the process of operationalization of variables.
- Be able to identify experimental and quasi (pre-) experimental research designs.
- Describe the differences between experimental and quasi-experimental designs.
- Articulate why experimental designs are sometimes preferred over the alternative methods.
- Identify and draw the corresponding diagrams of quantitative research designs and understand what the symbols represent.
- List and describe the pros and cons of different data sets used for secondary data analysis.
- Identify the advantages and disadvantages of longitudinal designs.
- Recognize and understand scenario methodology.
- Identify and measure exogenous variables.
- Be able to describe why randomization is important to research.

- Be able to create valid and reliable survey instruments.
- Appreciate why survey research is such a popular method of collecting data in many fields of study in the social sciences.

The first thing a student of research methods should comprehend is that there are many ways to address research questions and to contribute to the scientific field. There are many types of research designs and more and more these methods are being combined in attempts to develop a more robust study (mixed methods). In the first section of this chapter, the more common *quantitative* research strategies are presented, but attention is given to how alternatively qualitative approaches can be used to address research questions. In the second section, survey research is discussed in detail (typically quantitatively based), but survey research is also common in qualitative research, which is often facilitated through personal interviews with respondents rather than large-scale closed-ended questions that are typical of quantitatively designed instruments.

As mentioned throughout this book, when selecting a methodology (research design), the overriding consideration is that the research *topic/question* should always dictate which quantitative, qualitative, or mixed methods research strategy is most appropriate. Other factors, such as time constraints, training, publication goals, and economic realities, also influence which research design is selected.

The research designs presented in the first section of this chapter outline the primary means of capturing quantitative data, that is, data based on numerical representation. In the social sciences many concepts can be measured, and analyzed, statistically using quantitative methods. A person's attitude on the death penalty, a political evaluation of tax reform, the effectiveness of an offender rehabilitation program, the perceptions of preparedness of first responders to respond to natural disaster and terrorist attack, the development of anti-government regimes, the nutrition quality of the inhabitants of third-world countries, the social effects of nuclear weapons threats, the voting behavior of people aggregated by age, race ethnicity, and geographic location, and factors that influence a teen's probability of having unprotected sex, binge drinking, and drug use are all examples of research topics that can be quantitatively assessed. Without question these same topics can be analyzed through qualitative techniques as well. As mentioned many times in this book, the research topic and goals of the research project should dictate the research design. Being trained in both can facilitate those choices. With either approach, solid techniques of inquiry are key.

An intellectual exercise is to start questioning everything and begin to contemplate how the answers to those inquires can best be assessed. The point should also be becoming clear that there are several ways to design research studies, whether it be qualitatively, quantitatively, or by combining both approaches into mixed methods. With any study, a focus on details is important. Breaking the whole into its parts helps one begin to think about how the concepts should be understood and measured. One of the challenges in conducting research is taking abstract thoughts or concepts and putting them in ways that can be effectively measured. These are known as research "variables," and figuring out how to operationalize them (put them into measurable terms) is very important, especially in quantitative research designs, because validity and reliability of the research depends on how well these variables are conceptualized and measured (aka operationalized).

Before a specific discussion begins on the process of operationalization of variables and on coding of variables, it is a worthy effort to show how one can approach a research topic from either a quantitative or qualitative approach (or both). Recall that some qualitative methodologies include fieldwork, ethnography, unstructured interviews, life histories, textual analysis, discourse analysis, critical histography, participant observation, and so forth (Auerbach & Silverstein, 2003). If one were to simplify a variety of qualitative techniques into a brief definition, qualitative research is best understood as analyzing phenomenon, interpreting text, and evaluating open-ended interviews and behaviors in order to reveal consistent patterns designed to more fully describe the focus of study.

Auerbach and Silverstein (2003) summize that quantitative research leads to "hypothesis-testing" research as opposed to the "hypothesis-generating" research captured in qualitative work. They use their "Haitian Fathers Study" to highlight the difference. Their initial interest in the study of fathers occurred in an "ah ha" moment recognizing that traditional theories of child development had neglected the role of the father. Original research suggested the role of the mother as being most important in a child's life, and the role of the father was simply in an adjunct role to the maternal parent. Not only did Auerbach and Silverstein decide to study fathers, but they wanted to do so from the perspectives of ethnicity, sexual orientation, and cultural variations. One of their main research goals was to study fatherhood from a multicultural diversity perspective. In order to accomplish intended goals they found the typical quantitative research approaches limiting. Recall the focus of quantitative research as:

> Hypothesis testing research investigates a phenomenon in terms of relationships between independent and dependent variables, both of which are measurable

> numerically. This relationship is called a hypothesis. The aim of the research is to statistically test whether the hypothesized relationship between the variables exists by more than just chance.
>
> *(Auerbach & Silverstein, 2003 p. 5)*

A quantitative research design might approach a study on fatherhood by defining some measure of fatherhood (e.g., operationalizing the dependent variable: the dependent variable is that which the researcher is trying to explain). The researcher might design questions on a survey instrument to assess the commitment to the father's children (different measures could be combined to assess time commitment, emotional commitment, financial commitment, and so forth). Questions would typically be designed as closed-ended questions and ask the respondent to rank or score his levels of commitment with provided attributes (answers) from which to choose. Then, the researcher would need to create measures of independent variables that he or she hypothesizes to have influence on the dependent variable of "fatherhood." For example, the researcher may "predict" that the relationship the respondent had with his own father might be important to try to assess as having influence on how the respondent approaches fatherhood. He or she would need to operationalize this construct, perhaps through questions that assess the presence of the father in the respondent's own life as he was growing up as a child. The researcher would then make educated guesses (develop hypotheses) about the relationship between the dependent and independent variables, knowing that it is possible to statistically measure how a series of independent variables could explain the variance in how one approaches fatherhood. Something like this: It is hypothesized that the father's emotional commitment with his children is influenced by how much time his own father spent with him when he was a child. Statistical procedures would determine if true correlations exist between the variables.

Auerbach and Silverstein conceptualized they were somewhat limited in such approaches if they were trying to gain a better understanding of multicultural differences in fatherhood. They admittedly did not know enough about cultural variation in parenting to establish meaningful quantitative hypotheses, stating, for example:

> A middle class white male might be able to make enough money at one job to support his family and have flexibility for free time spent with his children. Alternatively, a lower working class Latino immigrant father may have to work two full-time jobs, or work out of his own country to provide the financial support to provide extra tutoring lessons in order to increase his child's success academically, or provide

> for his children financially. Thus "affection" for the child might cause the Latino father to spend less time with his children rather than more!
>
> *(2003, p. 6).*

The construct of "good" fatherhood is complex, subjective, and a multifaceted variable. This led the researchers to conduct *hypothesis-generating* research using Grounded Theory, rather than *hypothesis-testing* quantitative research. The first step is listening to what respondents say in an unstructured interview and then coding themes in the qualitative analysis process. Grounded Theory uses the research participant as a source to gather knowledge first; it involves questioning rather than measuring and then generating hypotheses using theoretical coding (identifying themes present in the research findings). With technologies such as NVIVO, which is a qualitative data analysis program, the importance of coding proves central to qualitative research methodology. It is a misconception that modern qualitative researchers do not analyze data; they just go about it differently (see chapter 10).

This fatherhood study is a great example of utilizing strengths from both qualitative and quantitative methods to provide a richer research design. Since chapter 10 focuses on qualitative data analysis in greater detail, the focus for now will be on the sometimes challenging task of operationalizing abstract concepts for statistical analysis.

OPERATIONALIZATION AND CODING

In the physical sciences, research concepts are typically "concrete" (objective) and lend themselves easily to statistical analysis. Take, for example, determining the point of boiling liquid: the degree of heat can be *measured* directly. Or take, for example, a gene mutation that can serve as a marker to predict certain types of cancer. Typically few question the ability to statistically observe (quantify) concepts in the physical sciences because they appear to be more objective and measurable. In the social sciences, concepts are typically more abstract (subjective), and some people have reservations about the ability to *accurately* measure more abstract variables, such as love or fatherhood.

While it can be a tedious task that demands intellectual attention, operationalizing social concepts can be done in a way that allows quantitative and qualitative assessment. Importantly, researchers have to make sure that what they think they are measuring is actually what is being measured (validity), and that those measures would lend themselves to consistent responses when retested (reliability). Equally important is that one must "code" those concepts (variables) in a way that transposes words into numbers that can be statistically analyzed. A researcher may want to compare how much education males and females in a state prison obtained the year before they were incarcerated. Gender is not a number, so how can it be captured in a quantitative study? As discussed earlier, it can be done very easily. The researcher simply has to develop a measure (question) assessing "gender" and then convert the answers (attributes) into a number. For example, a question could ask respondents to self-assign their gender; the responses can later be converted to 1s and 2s. In the coding process, the researcher would merely assign the number 1 to all who identified themselves as females and the number 2 to all identifying as males (or vice versa). The biological "attributes" for gender are male and female, and because of coding, the variable can now be *quantified*. A biological determination of gender might look at chromosomes to determine sex. A social determination (socially constructed) or self-determination is more complex. Decisions must be made to address transgender by allowing an additional category (3) or by simply allowing the respondent to select the gender (male, 2 or female, 1) to which they currently identify. Some researchers classify this variable as "sex" and some as "gender." Some see it as a biological phenomenon and some as more socially constructed. Both are different than "gender roles," however. Construction of variables are intellectual decisions. How to operationalize variables must be made well in advance of administering the survey, and in the setting of a political and cultural climates. The context of the research study itself can often help make such decisions

The variable (question) assessing education level can also be converted numerically. A researcher could ask about number of years of school completed and have the response options represent the *actual* number of years (recall that this was discussed in chapter 2 as interval-level data). More typically, however, the researcher may provide categories for the respondents representing *levels* of education, such as "some high school," "high school GED," "high school graduate," "some technical college," "technical college degree," "some four-year college," "four-year degree," and so forth. These measures are ordinal level because one can be ranked higher than the other, but the exact distance between them is unknown. At the coding stage, these categories would be represented by a numerical value such as some high school = 1, high school GED = 2, high school graduate = 3, some technical college = 4, technical college degree = 5, some four-year college = 6, four-year degree graduate = 7, and so on. It is helpful if the variable attributes and the represented numeric move in a logical sequence. In the example just provided, the numbers increase in an ascending sequence, as do the education categories. Doing this makes the data analysis process easier. This is a little key about direction of coding that makes analyzing the data easier in bivariate and multivariate statistical analysis. It is easier if both move in the same direction, typically. This process of coding in quantitative research designs takes places at the data entry phase of the study and will generally involve some type of data analysis software. Of course, operationalization of variables comes prior to the coding process, and in chapter 9, the process of coding variables is explained further; for now, more discussion is provided regarding the process of *operationalizing* variables because this can be one of the most important tasks, and often the most difficult for students of research methods to grasp, so further discussion is warranted.

Prior to designing a quality study, good researchers will focus on exactly *what* they are studying and how best to measure (**operationalize**) the concepts involved. The concept of "love" is a construct that most people presume to know and understand. For a researcher, the challenge is to actually *measure* this concept. Recall this topic from an earlier example in chapter 4: How would a scholar measure love? First, the *type* of love must be established. The love a person feels for his or her favorite college course, music artist, or vehicle is qualitatively different from the love someone may feel for a "significant other." If the researcher is interested in romantic love, the variables (questions) measuring it will need to be designed accordingly. For the sake of simplicity, focus on the concept of love for a significant other (romantic love). One could hypothesize, for example, that as romantic love for another increases, a released inmate will be less likely to return to prison if the inmate returns to that loved one upon release, and assuming of course that the significant other does not engage in illegal behavior.

Operationalize: The process of converting abstract concepts into measurable variables.

Alternatively, assume that a sociologist wants to study infidelity among married couples; infidelity can be measured as having sexual relationships outside of the marriage—with or without the spouse's knowledge. What independent variables predict infidelity, and how would a researcher measure them? Perhaps the couple does not conceptualize intimate relationships with others as "infidelity" at all. Are there cultural, ethnic, age, or gender differences that need to be considered in developing the most robust research design? What variables need to be considered, and how will they be operationalized? Does the researcher need to conduct Grounded Theory before the study begins so he or she can have a better concept regarding intimate relationships? One logical hypothesis might be that the greater the love between the married couple, the less likely it is that infidelity will occur. Alternatively, some may view allowing open marriages is a real sign of love. Measuring "love" and measuring "infidelity" are more complex that the novice researcher might think. It is also worth mentioning that one construct of love is not likely enough to truly measure "love." Great care needs to be given to these types of details long before an actual research study begins.

COMPOSITE MEASURES

A common research strategy to assist with the operationalization process is to list various indicators of the construct. This was mentioned in chapter 4 regarding the construct of love. If the researcher combines all of the items that indicate love, he or she creates what is known as a *scale* or a *composite measure* of "love." After the data are collected, the researcher can conduct a statistical analysis (e.g., Cronbach's alpha) that determines how strong, or reliable, the "love" scale actually is. Invalid items would be identified and removed from the scale. With a social construct like love, it is often better to avoid trying to measure the concept with a single indicator. A composite scale is a better measurement option. Fortunately, there are statistical procedures available to assess the accuracy of the scales. It is worth noting that when creating questions that assess a construct which will be used later to create a composite measure, it is helpful that all attributes are created on the same scale. For example, if one were to try to measure "love" it is helpful if all of the questions have the same attributes for the respondent to choose from, for example, "How often a day do you think about kissing your partner," "How many times a day do you tell your partner that you love them," "How many times a day do you text or call your partner to tell them something kind," and so forth. If all answers are on a scale of 0 to 100+ then the questions can just be computed to reflect an "intimacy" scale. Alternatively, and perhaps more simply, the researcher could have the attributes set up on a Likert scale: "unsure," "never," "seldom," "often," and "very often." These too can be created into a composite scale. The more the person self-selects "very often" instead of "never" on the questions regarding their "intimacy" with their partner, the higher the respondent would be rated on the intimacy scale. It is hoped that the astute reader is questioning this logic, however! Perhaps a person can have a high level of intimacy with his or her partner and never text them, never tell them they love them, and never think about kissing them while at work? What about a person who works at a job that leaves little room for "day dreaming," texting, talking, and so forth. What if they do not have a phone? Is it possible that some cultures, some strata, do not use phones the way the typical American college student does? One could still have intimacy with their partner, right? The measures discussed earlier might fail to measure intimacy. The first task of a good researcher is to consider all factors such as this, and then figure the best methods to address issues in the research construction and design.

CHOOSING A RESEARCH DESIGN

After crucial decisions are made, like what are the main research questions to be addressed in the study, are locating and evaluating what academic research already exists on the topic (or vice versa). It is also important to anticipate things that can influence the quality of the study, such as those discussed earlier regarding operationalization of variables. While no research study is perfect, taking the time to eliminate as many shortcomings as possible is important. One way to do that is by understanding the different types of research designs. Some types are more robust than others, and while each method has strengths in some areas it has weakness in others. Understanding the pros and cons of each approach is an important first step in making quality decisions. There are also other decisions that influence choice of design such as time, money, politics, ethics, access, research skill, and so forth. While one's job is to be a neutral researcher and let the data "speak for itself," one would be remiss not to mention that decisions do come into play other than picking the very best research design, a true unfortunate fact.

Chapter 10 addresses analysis in qualitative research, while this chapter focuses primarily on quantitative approaches to designing research. The first requirement is to determine if the study should be "experimental," "quasi-experimental," or what is often called "pre-experimental." As discussed in this book, the decision could also be made to combine qualitative and quantitative designs to promote a mixed methods approach to research.

Typically, most people conceptualize an experiment as research designed to discover something, which involves *controlled* testing to examine a hypothesis. Both experimental and pre-experimental designs can be important and effective research strategies. The primary, but not the sole, distinction is based on how the sample is selected; sample selection is discussed in detail in chapter 8, but before one makes a decision on the sample selection best suited to address the research question, an overview of the different types of research designs is warranted.

In an **experimental design** the research participants are *randomly* selected (this term has a very specific meaning relative to research), whereas **quasi-experimental designs** use other means of selecting study subjects. It is not unusual for researchers to rely on a nonexperimental (or quasi-experimental) study due to factors beyond their control. For example, Sloan, Smykla, and Rush were forced to abandon randomization. As they report, "Because the presiding judge requested an ex post evaluation and was not swayed with offers of an experimental design involving random assignment, it was not possible to use a true experimental design involving random assignment" (2004, pp. 104–105). In this illustration, Sloan et al. wanted to use an experimental design recognizing that more definitive conclusions could have been made; however, extenuating circumstances (the judge's decision) made this research strategy impossible.

Experimental studies are typically considered better, or "stronger," than quasi-experimental studies for a number of reasons. As just mentioned, samples with everyone having an equal chance of being selected (randomization) are typically valued over other sample selection techniques. The use of randomization in an experimental design helps eliminate many of the common threats to validity. Also, more advanced and predictive statistical techniques can be used with experimental

Experimental design: A research design that assesses the relationship between dependent and independent variables by utilizing a statistical comparison between groups, with one receiving the "experimental intervention" and one not. For true experimental research, the subjects are randomly assigned to these two groups and then compared.

Quasi-experimental design: A research design with the ability to compare a group that receives the treatment (experiment) with one that does not (control); however, there is no random selection to group membership. Often called pre-experimental.

studies, while quasi-experimental studies must use more basic analytical strategies. The other, related, major distinction is the use (or absence) of a comparison group. Being able to compare a randomly selected group that receives the "stimulus," "experimental variable," or "program" with a randomly selected group that does not receive it does have its benefits. In addition, the difference lies in the ability (or not) to make **generalization** to the larger population of study. Typically, research findings that try to suggest the outcome is representative of everyone in the study population would have to have higher statistical criteria such as everyone having equal chance to be in the sample through the use of random selection. This cannot be accomplished with some types of research designs.

Generalization: Making inferences about a larger group from a smaller studied group.

Independent variable (IV): What is thought to cause change in an outcome variable. IVs are hypothesized to influence the dependent variable (DV); as the IV increases or decreases, so does the DV.

Dependent variable (DV): The variable that the researcher is trying to explain in a research project and is thought to be caused by independent variables.

Pretest: Measures the dependent variable *before* the experimental treatment is administered.

EXPERIMENTAL RESEARCH

According to Kraska and Neuman (2011), an experiment will have seven main parts; however, there are variations of these seven depending on the design selected. Before the specific designs are examined, the components and the symbols used to designate them need to be defined.

The first part of an experiment is the treatment, the independent variable, or the part of the experiment that is manipulated in order to evaluate its effect. The **independent variable** (X) is the experimental stimulus; in other words, it is the cause, intervention, treatment, or "thing" hypothesized to change the outcome. The dependent variable (Y) is what the researcher is trying to explain (outcome), and the independent variable is what is expected to explain it. For example, if a researcher is trying to understand recidivism (dependent variable) of drug offenders, the independent variable (X) is what is expected to help "predict" who is likely to return to prison (recidivate). For example, it may be hypothesized that an individual participating in a drug treatment program while incarcerated will be less likely to return to prison after release.

The dependent variable is designated with a "Y." It is called the **dependent variable** because it "depends" on the independent variable(s). It is also sometimes called the effect, outcome, or result variable. The best way to measure the effect of the independent variable on the dependent variable is by taking two measures, one before the treatment and one after the treatment (X), or by comparing an experimental group with a control group. For example, one group of drug offenders receives drug therapy, and one does not; then their recidivism rates are compared to assess the effectiveness of drug therapy on recidivism of incarcerated drug offenders.

The third part of the research project is a **pretest**, which measures the dependent variable before the treatment is administered or before application of the independent variable. After the treatment, or after the group is exposed to the independent variable, a posttest is taken. The **posttest** (part four of an experiment) is therefore a measurement of the dependent variable *after* the treatment.

Posttest: Measures the dependent variable *after* the experimental treatment. The pretest and posttest are identical assessments, with one being given before the "intervention" and one given after.

Some simple research designs use only one group of research subjects; however, this is usually a less effective approach. A much stronger design is when the researcher can compare two groups of research subjects. The researcher measures the effect of the stimulus (X) by giving it to one group but not the other. The group receiving the intervention (X) is the **experimental group.** This group represents the fifth part of a basic research design.

Experimental group: The group that receives the "intervention" in a research analysis.

The control group is the sixth vital part to an experiment. A second group of study participants who are not exposed to the independent variable (or "stimulus") are considered the **control group;** in order to know if the intervention or stimulus is effective, the researcher needs to have such a comparison group. Members of the control group should be as similar to the experimental group as possible; the more similar they are, the more comparable they are, and the stronger the study is. For example, subjects in each group should be the same gender, age, race or ethnicity, and so on. Depending on the topic of the study, other variables might need to be similar between the control and experimental group, such as arrest record, years employed, or drug history. In the case mentioned earlier, for example, it would be important for both groups of drug offenders, once released from prison, to have similar support systems, living conditions, and exposure to drug use temptations. If the two groups have many differences (e.g., one group returns to a high-crime neighborhood, and the other does not), then those differences may account for the study results—not the independent variable (X) examined in the study. The best way to make sure that the two groups are equal or compatible is by using the sampling process called **randomization.**

Control group: The comparison group in an experimental study that does not receive the "intervention."

Randomization: Means that every participant has an equal chance of being selected for study (for assignment to control or experimental groups). It is a criterion of a true experimental design. There are various specified steps that must be followed to attain true randomization.

The previous chapter presented the idea of exogenous variables. The **exogenous variables** (there are often more than one) are any another factors or variables that may influence the outcome of a study and are usually designated with a "Z." Each additional exogenous variable will have a subscript numeral (Z_1, Z_2, Z_3, etc.), which designates which variable it represents. Likewise, in the case of observations (O), the subscript indicates the time the data were collected. For example, O_1 would designate the pretest or initial survey, while O_7 would represent the seventh observation.

Here is an example of an exogenous variable: hospitalization or terminal illness. In the example mentioned previously regarding fatherhood, a researcher asks how much time the father spends in leisure activities with his child in the past year, expecting this to be a measure of love or dedication to the child. There could be another variable that explains why the father is not spending time with his child which has nothing to do with love or dedication to fatherhood. If the father has a medical condition that incapacitates him, of course his leisure activity would be limited.

Exogenous variables: Those variables that influence the dependent variable.

Hypothesis: An informed, educated statement about the relationship between variables.

Experiments tests a hypothesis or, in many cases, multiple hypotheses. Recall that a **hypothesis** is an educated prediction (guess) about the relationship between two or more variables, and what effect the independent variable may have on the dependent variable. The hypotheses should be based on prior research findings shown in the literature review. The insert by Christiaan Bezuidenhout describes how hypotheses are created.

INSERT 6.1

Formulating Hypotheses

Christiaan Bezuidenhout, PhD
Department of Social Work and Criminology
University of Pretoria
Pretoria, South Africa

A hypothesis can be defined as a tentative generalization of which the validity has not been proven. For example, to study the influence of social class on the committing of property crimes, the hypothesis that the affluent class will commit significantly less property crime than the disadvantaged class could be formulated. The difference between a hypothesis and a statement is that the person making a statement knows that it is either true or false. In the case of a hypothesis, the person suspects that his or her prediction will be correct. Whether or not economic class is related to the committing of property crime is unknown, and therefore the prediction that a relationship exists is a hypothesis and not a statement. As soon as information becomes available that proves that the prediction is correct (e.g., that economic class is related to the committing of property crime), the hypothesis becomes a statement, which is accepted as a fact. Many facts of which the validity was proven by empirical verification were originally stated in terms of hypotheses.

Hypotheses can be formulated on almost any subject. Although many inexperienced researchers believe that hypotheses only have meaning if they are supported, this assumption is incorrect. Whether or not a hypothesis is supported by the research findings, the finding is of scientific importance. Should the researcher know the validity of a hypothesis when it is formulated, the hypothesis makes no contribution toward gaining new knowledge.

Therefore, the scientific value of the research could be questioned—why research what is already known?

Types of Hypotheses

The primary hypothesis used in research in the social sciences is the research or scientific hypothesis. Before the research hypothesis can be tested, it has to be reformulated as a statistical hypothesis because the research hypothesis merely postulates that a tentative relationship exists between two or more variables. This means that the statistical hypothesis makes a statement about the numerical value(s) of the parameter(s) of one or more populations. With regard to the statistical hypothesis, a distinction can be made between the null hypothesis (H_o) and the alternative hypothesis (H_1). The null hypothesis means that no differences will occur between that which is compared. The alternative hypothesis, on the other hand, predicts that significant differences will occur. In the case of the alternative hypothesis, a distinction can also be made between a hypothesis that predicts direction and one that does not predict direction. Should a hypothesis, for example, be formulated that the crime patterns of men and women differ significantly, direction is not predicted, because the nature of the difference is not indicated. If this hypothesis is, however, changed to read that men commit significantly more crimes than do women, direction is predicted.

Note that the statistical hypothesis only shows whether or not statistically significant differences occur. In order to interpret the finding of the statistical hypothesis, the researcher has to revert to the research (scientific) hypothesis.

Functions of Hypotheses

The primary functions of hypotheses are to

- test theories
- supply guidelines (with regard to the theories) that can be used to explain a certain phenomenon
- describe social phenomena.

Hypotheses also have certain secondary functions. Results obtained by testing hypotheses could, for example, contribute toward the formulation of social policy; changes or improvement in prison systems; the introduction of new methods of education; and the submission of proposals to the government, which provide solutions for various social problems. Testing hypotheses may in some instances lead to change in certain general assumptions regarding human behavior, or it may, to a greater or lesser degree, influence the way in which individuals are oriented toward their environment.

continued

Insert 6.1 *continued*

Advantages of Hypotheses for the Study

- Hypotheses give direction to research; they limit or demarcate the field of study by formulating particular hypotheses, which serve as a systematic basis for the selection of information.
- Hypotheses sharpen the researcher's perception and help him or her to focus on facts relevant to the study.
- Hypotheses enable the researcher to see a relationship between phenomena that may otherwise appear to be unrelated. Life is so complex and the phenomena involved in it so numerous that it is not always possible to see such relationships. They become easier to see, however, when a hypothesis sharpens the researcher's ability to observe.

Suggestions for the Formulation of Suitable Hypotheses

First, to be able to formulate a hypothesis, the researcher needs extensive background knowledge of the subject (in this case criminology), as well as related subjects such as psychology and sociology. As a result of his or her background knowledge, the researcher becomes aware of limitations within his or her own field of study. The broad knowledge and extensive literature review on the intended topic to be researched also allow the researcher to formulate good hypotheses and even subhypotheses about the phenomenon. This knowledge also allows the researcher to write a rationale for why he or she is predicting the outcome of the hypothesis. This means the researcher can predict direction in the hypothesis based on related research. Once this has been done, the researcher can test the hypothesis by means of a questionnaire. The questionnaire will be analyzed, and the hypothesis will be tested by means of inferential statistical formulas. Only after the hypothesis has been supported can H_1 be accepted. Remember that an opposite finding is also possible which does not support your hypothesis. In this case, no direction is supported, and the researcher needs to accept H_0. This is also important because your finding is not in line with related research and with your prediction. The researcher now needs to be creative to find a rationale for this unexpected finding. It is necessary to ask, "Why did I get an opposite finding?"

Second, the cultural background in which a science is developed and the cultural background of the researcher give rise to issues that can be studied and from which hypotheses can be formulated. In this case, the researcher from a dominant culture can have the idea that his or her culture is superior to the minority culture that is researched. It is thus important that individuals who want to undertake scientific research should be able to distance themselves from their own cultural views and norms to ensure objectivity and a critical approach to the subject.

Third, researchers should learn to distinguish between the unique and the ordinary. The uncommon draws more attention than everyday occurrences, and therefore it is understandable that researchers will be inclined to focus their research on the unusual. For example, if a newspaper headline reads, "Grandmother of 76 Years Robs a Bank at Gunpoint," your attention is already on this unusual feat. Researchers should avoid this human tendency to focus on the extraordinary, bizarre, unusual, or macabre phenomenon and be wary not to ignore everyday issues that occur regularly and are actually threats to society. Usually issues that occur regularly (e.g., snatching of children at shopping malls) need to be investigated as a priority. The snatching of children at shopping malls may in fact require research, as the solution to many human trafficking problems may depend on knowing more about this social problem. Care should be taken not to explore what seems on the surface to be the answer to certain issues. Researchers need to be wary of underlying factors that are not so obvious, because the causes of many phenomena are hidden.

Fourth, researchers should continuously search for relationships between phenomena that occur together or consecutively.

Finally, one of the most important requirements to formulate a satisfactory hypothesis is intensive brain work. If the observed facts cannot be processed and interpreted with creativity and intelligence, the statistical analysis of data has little value.

Characteristics of a Good Hypothesis

1. A hypothesis should not contain any value judgments.
2. A hypothesis should be in agreement with observed facts. In other words, it should not clash with known facts. For example, if the researcher formulates a hypothesis that "females commit significantly more rapes than males," the hypothesis will immediately be frowned upon by other scientists. A researcher could, however, present known facts in a new light and, in doing so, make a valuable contribution. When a researcher formulates a hypothesis that is in opposition to generally accepted universal laws, the rationale for it must be extremely good. In this case, the researcher can hypothesize that females are getting more involved in spousal abuse as the abuser compared with the pre-1970s generation. The rationale for the researchers' thinking is the fact that middle-class females rapidly started entering the economic sector by 1970. Before the 1970s, it was a societal norm that the male was the breadwinner of the family and the head of the home. As they entered the economic sector, women started earning equivalent salaries to men and were also given positions in the managerial corps. These developments contributed to a change in lifestyle and the acquisition of more luxury goods, and both husband and wife starting to grapple with the prescribed norms of the role of the breadwinner and the head of the house. This role confusion and power struggle can indirectly contribute to family discord and probably spousal abuse. A female can feel that she is working just

continued

Insert 6.1 *continued*

as hard as her partner and that she also deserves respect. In addition, her "power" at work can be transferred to the family situation, which can cause frustration and abuse. In this context, the researcher could find that the female abuses her partner psychologically or even physically. Nevertheless, proper research is necessary to test this hypothesis.

3. A good hypothesis should be short, concise and stated in simple terms. The concepts used in a hypothesis must be clear and easy to understand. It is therefore essential that the phrasing and formulation of a hypothesis should not be ambiguous (e.g., "variable A [poverty] has a significant impact on variable B [property crime]"). The correct way to formulate this hypothesis is: "The level of poverty of an individual has a significant influence on his or her motivation to commit property crime." The not so correct way to formulate this hypothesis is: "Poor people steal more than rich people."
4. Available research procedures should be kept in mind when formulating a hypothesis. In some instances, a hypothesis may lead to the development of new techniques of testing it. The researcher should at all times be aware of his or her limitations.
5. The hypothesis should contribute toward theory (e.g., criminological theory) in that it tests, extends, or refutes existing theory. This means that, to a certain extent, a relationship should exist between the hypothesis and existing theory or theories. The researcher can test whether Travis Hirschi's social bond theory is valid, for example. This can be done by testing hypotheses about the attachment, commitment, involvement, and beliefs of juvenile offenders against those of their significant others, the school, and other primary role players.

Testing Hypotheses

The testing of a hypothesis means that it has to be subjected to some form of empirical evaluation. By using empirical evaluation, it is determined whether or not the hypothesis can be supported. A hypothesis has to fulfill the following two criteria to be tested:

First, the researcher must be sure that an actual situation exists in which the hypothesis can be tested. If the researcher, for example, formulated a hypothesis on the corruptive behavior of prison wardens, it should be possible for him or her to visit a number of prisons where the behavior of wardens can be observed. The identification of an appropriate environment or situation for testing is a difficult task because permission must be obtained from the organizations where the research will be conducted, and the proposed respondents must agree to cooperate (e.g., sign a letter of consent). If a researcher wishes to test a hypothesis on the behavior of arrested juvenile delinquents, he or she may find that it is extremely difficult to convince the juveniles to participate in the research. Even if they agree to participate (e.g., sign a letter of consent), further permission must be obtained from their parents (e.g., a parent or guardian should sign a letter of consent because the juvenile is still underage), the court, and the police. These specific requirements refer to the phase in which the researcher needs to gain access to information that will enable him or her to test the hypotheses that were formulated.

The researcher should also make sure that his or her hypotheses are testable. This means that the researcher has to limit the research to phenomena or events that can be observed on a sensory level. In other words, it must be possible to test the variables referred to in the hypotheses. If it is impossible to apply some form of measurement to the variables, the hypotheses are not testable. A researcher who, for example, hypothesizes that evil powers cause juvenile delinquency will not be able to test the hypothesis by means of conventional scientific methods. Although empirical methods exist with which the researcher could determine the extent to which juvenile delinquents are involved in supernatural practices, it is impossible to determine to what extent evil forces have an impact on their behavior.

EXPERIMENTAL, QUASI-EXPERIMENTAL, AND PRE-EXPERIMENTAL DESIGNS

As mentioned previously, the key distinction between types of research design is whether the studies are "experimental" or "quasi-experimental," and typically the primary distinction that determines this is how the samples are selected. The use of randomization is how research subjects are selected to be in either the experimental group or the control group and is what characterizes experimental designs. Experimental designs are considered stronger, or "better," but pre-experimental studies are more common, since they are quicker and less expensive to conduct.

Pre-experimental Designs

Sometimes there are reasons that prevent a researcher from conducting a true experimental design; say, for example, a researcher wants to introduce stimuli to the experimental group and deny stimuli to the control group to study the influence of the independent variable (stimuli). It is not likely that the study would be approved by IRB, nor would it be ethical to conduct anyway, if that study involved testing the effects of parents dying in a child's early life and assessing its effect on delinquency. The researcher questions if juveniles who lose loving parents would influence the dependent variable of criminal behavior and is a reasonable hypothesis; however, the researcher could not carry out this research study by using a true experimental design. The researcher might instead assess related questions on a survey instrument and analyze the beta coefficients of particular variables (such as loss of parents) on the variance in criminality.

Perhaps a professor wants to evaluate whether exam reviews are really valuable for students. To test this hypothesis, he or she may want to divide students into two separate groups to measure the effect of a review. Many students think that a review prior to each exam improves their exam score. The instructor may not be so sure and so conducts a simple study. Because students are already in one class, and due to ethical concerns, randomization might not be an option. For example, it would be potentially unfair to exclude some of the students from a class review if they wanted to attend it (the control group). This research topic, whether or not to use an exam review before a test, is worth examining, but can professors test this hypothesis? If the seven factors described earlier for experimental design are not available to the researcher, he or she may decide to use what are commonly referred to as *pre-experimental designs.*

One-shot case study: When one group is studied at one point in time after the "intervention" has been given.

One-Shot Case Study. A **one-shot case study** is a very common research design despite having several validity threats. Under this design, a treatment (X) is given to a group of research subjects, and the group is observed, measured, or otherwise tested to see what effect the treatment has, as shown in Table 6.1.

$$X \quad O_1$$

TABLE 6.1 *One Shot Case Study*

In the preceding example, the professor could offer an *optional* review session and compare the test grades for the students who participated in the review against those who did not participate, to determine any differences. Importantly, however, there are other unknown factors (exogenous variables) that could actually lead to the differences between the scores, but that are not measured in this particular research design. For example, the hardworking, dedicated students are more likely to participate in a *voluntary* scholastic event. Would they be more likely to score better anyway? Are there differences between those students who would voluntarily participate and those students who would not voluntarily partake in extra study time that could account for test score variations? With such studies, it is hard to control for all influencing factors. Clearly, this is a weaker design, but it is often used and can have some benefits. If positive effects of the review were apparent in the test scores, the professor could instruct the students that showing up and participating in a review is a logically good decision. The professor may motivate some students by demonstrating the difference between the scores of those students who utilized an exam review versus those who did not; scientifically, however, the instructor is very limited in the ability to *prove* the effectiveness of the review.

To further clarify the one-shot case study design, consider if the researcher takes a group of subjects and shows them a video on animal rights or veganism, and then gives the research subjects a questionnaire to see what the students think about these topics. This would allow for a quick, cheap, and easy study where some information could be gathered, but an obvious problem in assessing the influence of the video is that the researcher has no idea what the subjects' opinions on veganism or animal rights were *before* seeing the video. There is no baseline measure. This example demonstrates that the one-shot case study will often face threats due to mortality, maturation, and history (Singleton et al., 1988). As mentioned previously, such studies can be interesting and beneficial, but they typically are limited in the conclusions that can be made.

Table 6.2 shows one solution to the problem of not having baseline data in the one-shot case study. This improved design is called the *one-group pretest/posttest design*. The researcher gives a pretest, then introduces the stimulus, gives a posttest, and compares the two measures. In the earlier example, a pretest could have been given to the research subjects prior to showing the video (X). This pretest measure, questionnaire, interview, or other form of measurement gives a good idea of what subjects knew, thought, or believed prior to seeing the video. After the students watch the intervention (video), the posttest measure provides an indication of change due to the intervention, in this example, the video. This is a stronger design than the one-shot case study, but it still presents some problems.

$$O_1 \quad X \quad O_2$$

TABLE 6.2 *One-Group Pretest/Posttest Design*

One threat to the validity of this design is experimental mortality, since some subjects may "drop out" between the pretest and posttest. With the one-group pretest/posttest design, the threat to mortality or the impact of dropouts can be mitigated, controlled, or accounted for by paying attention to the mortality threat and not allowing those who drop out to be analyzed. Only the data from those participants who received both the pretest and posttest should be evaluated in regard to the effects of the stimulus or independent variable. Also, because pretests were collected from the participants before they dropped out, the data on that assessment can be compared to determine if those who did not participate in the posttest differed initially and significantly from those who received the second intervention (Singleton et al., 1988, 207). Like the one-shot case study, this design also might have threats due to maturation and history. In fact, the more time between the pretest and the posttest, the more likely, and the more significant, these problems might be. For example, if a substantial amount of time elapsed between the two assessments, other influences could not likely be controlled. Perhaps another video, news article, discussion, or television show on animal rights or veganism was observed between the pretest and posttest. The influence of the posttest would be tainted if this were the case.

Other threats to internal validity may also exist, such as testing, instrumentation, and statistical regression (Singleton et al., 1988). One problem is that the pretest may have influenced or biased the respondents. For example, simply asking a series of questions before the video is shown could influence how the participants respond on the posttest. The obvious solution to this threat to validity is to remove, or eliminate, the pretest. If the researcher elects to do this, the design is called a *static group comparison*.

Static group comparison: When two groups are studied at one point in time; one receives the "intervention," and the other does not. The differences between the groups are then analyzed.

Static Group Comparison. The **static group comparison** is an "improvement over the One-Shot Case Study in that it provides a set of data with which to compare the treatment scores," according to Singleton et al. (1988, p. 207). Basically, the participants are divided into two groups. One group is exposed to the stimulus and their results are evaluated and compared with those of the control group that did not receive, in this example, the intervention. Then, the effects of the posttest can be compared to help determine its influence. Note that the posttest could also be a treatment, stimulus, or other independent variable. In the static group comparison (Table 6.3), each group is measured just one time, making this a quick, easy, and inexpensive study to conduct.

X	O_1
	O_1

TABLE 6.3 *Static Group Comparison*

An additional benefit to this design is that, since there is no pretest, validity threats due to testing and statistical regression (scores moving closer to the mean) are eliminated. Instrumentation should not be a problem either, since with only one application there is no opportunity to alter the data collection instrument (see chapter 4). There are, however, other threats that must be acknowledged; for instance, experimental mortality cannot be accounted for because there was no pretest. In other words, since there are no pretest data, it is impossible to compare the subjects who drop out between the intervention and measurement. Maturation may also be a factor if the two groups are changing (maturing) in different ways or at different rates. The most serious threat, however, is selection bias. If randomization is lacking, it is difficult to have equal, or comparable, study groups. Because these studies do not ensure that each participant has an equal chance to be selected for the group receiving the stimulus, it is difficult to control for all influencing variables. Alternatively, using the experimental designs presented next can eliminate most of these threats.

Experimental Designs

Classic Experimental Design. If a study includes all seven components, as mentioned previously, then it would be considered a **classic experimental design** (Table 6.4). This simple example should illustrate how a basic experiment works. Recall the research methods instructor mentioned earlier who questioned the value of giving a review before each exam. The instructor can easily "test" the effectiveness of the review by doing a simple experiment. The first step would be to randomly (R) divide one large group of students into two separate groups. Next, he or she would give each group of students a comprehensive exam on the first day of class (the pretest). One group of students, the experimental group, would be given a review (the independent variable) before each subsequent exam during the rest of the semester. The second group of students would not receive a review and would therefore be considered the control group. A simple comparison of the exam scores (the dependent variable) should suggest the value of the test review. These exam scores would be the Y, or result, of the review given by the instructor. The overall class averages at the end of the semester and the score on the final comprehensive exam (identical to the one given on day one) would serve as two dependent variables, each showing the value of giving a test review. Obviously, the lectures would have to be identical for each group, and all external variables (the exogenous variables) controlled, such as the influence of one class receiving a guest lecture and not the other, canceled classes, individual attention from the professor outside of class, and so on. Basically, the two groups need to receive an identical experience except for the review sessions. For example, the classes should ideally meet at the same time of day, since students may not perform as well in early mornings (Z_1). The classes should also meet in the same room, since the physical environment (scenery Z_2, room color Z_3, temperature Z_4, type of furniture Z_5) might also influence learning. The astute researcher would to try to identify and measure the effect of these other factors that might influence the grades. This hypothetical instructor/researcher would also try to anticipate any other confounding or exogenous variables.

Classic experimental design: Is designed with random assignment of two groups, with measures taken to ensure that the experimental and control groups are similar. The experimental group receives the intervention (DV), and each group gets a pretest and posttest.

R	O_1	X	O_2
R	O_1		O_2

TABLE 6.4 *Classic Experimental Design*

The ethical researcher would also consider whether it is unethical to withhold a desirable treatment (the exam review) from a control group, since doing so might adversely affect their grade. One ethical solution could be to adjust all the grades for the control group by the amount of improvement shown in the experimental group—if there was any. In other words, if a review resulted in the class average being 8 points higher for the experimental (review) group, then students in the other group (control) might have 8 points added to their final grade. The curve eliminates unfairness to the control group. This of course assumes that the hypothesis (that a review improves performance) is supported. Alternatively, what if the exam review was found to lower the class average? Would the control group also have their grades lowered by the same amount?

This design might have potential threats due to compensatory rivalry and testing effects. A good researcher will identify these threats in advance and try to either eliminate them or reduce the impact they may have. The design itself eliminates many internal validity threats, and at least for those that do exist, it is not a factor in one group and not the other because the mere act of randomization of the respondents addresses that potential problem. According to Singleton et al.:

> Consider history first, any event in the general environment that produces a difference between the pretest and posttest in the experimental group would produce about the same difference in the control group. Similarly, changes due to maturation, testing, or instrumentation would be felt equally in both groups. . . . Random selection also eliminates the factors of selection and regression.
>
> *(1988, p. 209)*

Clearly, this design is much stronger than the designs covered previously; however, as stressed elsewhere in this book, perfect studies are rare. Even with this design, the pretest can pose some potential problems. It may bias or influence research subjects. It may also alert them to the purpose or intent of the study, which can also cause them to alter their responses or behavior. The astute researcher considers all factors that might influence results.

Two-Group Posttest-Only Design. In the classic experimental design described earlier, suppose that the researcher/instructor was concerned that giving each group of students the comprehensive final exam as a pretest might create a problem (threat) with testing bias or even with cheating by some students. Simply removing the pretest could control this validity threat. In other words, leave the classic experimental design the same, but do not give either group the pretest (final comprehensive exam at the first day of class), thereby creating a **two-group posttest-only design** (Table 6.5). Note that the two groups are still randomly (R) divided.

Two-group posttest-only design: An experimental design, but with no pretest given, only the posttest; respondents are randomly assigned to groups.

R	X	O_1
R		O_1

TABLE 6.5 *Two-Group Posttest Design*

This design is very similar to the static group comparison except that randomization is used to create the two groups. This important randomization step eliminates many threats to validity. This design has other benefits as well. First, it is easier and therefore cheaper to conduct than a classic experiment design. It also takes care of the potential interaction between the pretest and the experimental manipulation (Singleton et al. 1988, p. 210). The next design eliminates all the threats to validity and therefore is considered the strongest of all experimental research strategies.

Solomon Four-Group Design. The **Solomon four-group design** (Table 6.6) eliminates virtually all threats to validity. Basically, this design is merely a combination of the classic experimental design (see Table 6.4) with the two-group posttest design (see Table 6.5). It allows the researcher to measure for the effect (threat) or impact that the pretest may have had on the respondents. The test bias is thus eliminated, or can be accounted for and measured, when the researcher compares the group receiving the pretest with those not receiving a pretest.

Solomon four-group design: Is when the study is designed with two experimental and two control groups, and one group of two receives the pretest and the others do not. Subjects are randomly assigned to the groups, making the study a strong experimental design.

R	O_1	X	O_2
R	O_1		O_2
R		X	O_1
R		X	O_1

TABLE 6.6 *Solomon Four-Group Design*

Despite the strength of the Solomon four-group design, it does have two major flaws. First, it is very complicated to conduct in a "real-world" setting such as prison, jail, hospital, drug rehabilitation facility, or school system. For that reason it is not used often. Several threats to validity, such as compensatory rivalry, diffusion of treatment, and the Hawthorne effect, may also create problems. Second, the Solomon four-group design only collects data at two points in time. A person who is trying to lose or gain weight will probably weigh himself or herself more than just twice. A person who invests in the stock market will probably check the performance of the stock on more than just two occasions. So, in order to measure trends over time, a researcher must rely on another type of research design, called a time series or longitudinal analysis.

Time series designs: Research studies conducted over an extended period of time.

Time Series Designs. Research designs that take place and collect data over an extended period are called interrupted time series or longitudinal studies (Table 6.7). This type of study can be experimental as the project has two groups (experimental and control) that are randomly selected or divided. If two study groups are used but they are not randomly divided, the same design is considered quasi-experimental.

$$O_1 \quad O_2 \quad O_3 \quad X \quad O_4 \quad O_5 \quad O_6$$

TABLE 6.7 *Simple Interrupted Time Series Design*

With this design a researcher can study one group of people over time to see what effect the independent variable or treatment (X) has. While Table 6.7 shows that six measurements are taken at different times, the actual number might be much greater. Often the longer the time frame used to measure the impact of an intervention, the stronger the study is (see the study by Braga, Pierce, McDevitt, Bond, & Cronin, 2008, described later). Perhaps the most comprehensive contemporary example of a longitudinal study is provided by Petras, Nieuwbeerta, and Piquero, who examined study participants over a long period of time. They described the study as follows:

> Using data from the Criminal Career and Life Course Study—including information on criminal convictions across 60 years of almost 5,000 persons convicted in the Netherlands—and applying a two-part growth model that explicitly distinguishes between participation and frequency, the study . . . assessed the participation-frequency debate.
>
> *(2010, p. 607)*

The biggest drawback to this design is that there is no comparison group, so adding a second group results in a simple interrupted time series with nonequivalent comparison group (Table 6.8).

$$\begin{array}{ccccccc} O_1 & O_2 & O_3 & X & O_4 & O_5 & O_6 \\ O_1 & O_2 & O_3 & & O_4 & O_5 & O_6 \end{array}$$

TABLE 6.8 *Simple Interrupted Time Series with Nonequivalent Comparison Group*

Braga et al. (2008) were interested in examining the effects of a program designed to reduce the criminal use of firearms. The stimulus, or independent variable, they wanted to examine was called "pulling levers." They examined gun violence in Lowell, Massachusetts, from 1996 to 2005 by comparing their time series data to other similar cities. They used a nonrandomized quasi-experimental design comparing trends in youth homicide in Lowell to trends of gun violence in other Massachusetts cities. The intervention measured was a "pulling levers strategy," which they describe as follows:

> In its simplest form, the approach consists of selecting a particular crime problem, such as youth homicide; convening an interagency working group of law-enforcement practitioners; conducting research to identify key offenders, groups, and behavior patterns; framing a response to offenders and groups of offenders that uses a varied menu of sanctions ("pulling levers") to stop them from continuing their violent behavior; focusing social services and community resources on targeted offenders and groups to match law-enforcement prevention efforts; and directly and repeatedly communicating with offenders to make them understand why they are receiving this special attention.
>
> *(Braga et al., 2008, p. 134)*

Theirs is a well-designed and well-implemented one-group time series study in criminal justice, even though the authors admit they did not follow the preferable randomized controlled experimental approach. Two features made the study strong: (1) the length of time the subjects were examined, and (2) the comparison with other cities not receiving the intervention (pulling levers). The problem with the simple interrupted time series with nonequivalent group comparison (see Table 6.8) is that the researcher (e.g., Braga et al.) cannot be sure that the two groups (the experimental and control groups) are in fact similar to one another.

The solution to having nonequivalent groups for comparison is actually quite simple: the researcher would merely take one large group, then randomly (R) divide it into two equal groups; one would get the treatment (X) and the other would not, thus serving as the control group (Table 6.9). Because the two groups are randomly divided, this type of longitudinal design could be considered experimental. Note that the sole difference is that the two groups are divided randomly (R).

$$RO_1 \quad O_2 \quad O_3 \quad X \quad O_4 \quad O_5 \quad O_6$$
$$RO_1 \quad O_2 \quad O_3 \quad \quad O_4 \quad O_5 \quad O_6$$

TABLE 6.9 *Simple Interrupted Time Series with Equivalent Comparison Group*

Factorial Designs. Remember also that the classic experimental design that was laid out by the researcher/instructor recognized several other variables that may have an effect on test grades besides the review sessions. For example, early morning classes (Z_1), the students' IQs (Z_2), room color (Z_3), temperature (Z_4), and even type of furniture (Z_5) might impact exam scores. Rather than considering these exogenous variables, the researcher may instead consider them additional independent variables that might influence the dependent variable which in this case is grades. The sum total of all the variables' effects would be greater than just the variable of exam review, each having its own beta coefficient that shows the magnitude of influence on the dependent variable. For example, one classroom may be a portable trailer and so might be hot, uncomfortable, and painted a dull gray (which has been shown to inhibit learning), while the other classroom, perhaps in a new air-conditioned building, would have a much better physical environment, which might enhance learning. Which classroom characteristics would be hypothesized to produce better performance? A combination of factors considered collectively can better predict the dependent variable. The Solomon four-group design can be considered a type of **factorial design** if the effects of all these other variables are accounted for, or "factored in."

Factorial designs: Designed to assess more than one treatment or different levels of the same treatment in a single study.

OTHER RESEARCH STRATEGIES

In addition to the pre-experimental, experimental, and time series designs just discussed, there are other very commonly employed strategies, or research designs, for examining numerical data. Secondary data analysis is one of the most prevalent, while "scenario research" is gaining in popularity with some researchers. These forms of data collection can also be used in qualitative studies. Also very common in both qualitative and quantitative data is survey research. The last section of this chapter is dedicated to survey research, since it is one of the most popular methods used in the social sciences, but first a more detailed discussion on secondary analysis is warranted.

Secondary Data Analysis

The reanalysis of data that were collected by someone else has a long history and is still very commonly employed in research. Utilizing existing data, as opposed to collecting original data, is referred to as **secondary data analysis.** The data may be used to examine the original research question for which it was collected, or it can be used to examine, or test, different research hypotheses and questions. Large-scale data sets are collected for the purpose of being broad based and available to researchers to examine a large number of variables and varied research topics. Sociologists have long taken advantage of large-scale survey secondary data

Secondary data analysis: The use of data that have been previously collected, often for another purpose.

analysis to examine macrolevel phenomena. For example, Joanne Kaufman (2005) utilized the Add Health database from the University of North Carolina (Udry, 1998) to measure the effects of race and ethnicity on violence in personal relationships. Secondary data analysis is also popular in criminal justice research. Thomas Stucky (2005), for instance, used census data collected by the U.S. Department of Commerce to examine 1,083 cities to gauge how the form, or type, of local government (e.g., mayor-council, city council), percentage of minority members in the population, and crime rates affected the number of police employees per 1,000 residents (police strength). The International Search and Rescue Incident Data set (ISRID) is currently one of few data sets that those interested in search probability theory for locating missing persons can use to analyze probability statistics (Koester, 2008).

Data sets are available in almost any scientific field, especially in the social sciences. For example, data are already available specifically designed to examine crime and justice topics, political voting patterns, family structure issues, effectiveness of rehabilitation programs, and government funded projects—and the list goes on. The use of existing, often government data sets, is a very common practice among social science researchers. Traci Schlesinger, while a doctoral candidate at Princeton University, used the data collected by the Bureau of Justice Statistics (BJS). This data set is called the "State Court Processing Statistics, 1990–2006: Felony Defendants in Large Urban Counties" (2004). The data provided in this government source were then further categorized and reanalyzed by Schlesinger (2005) to measure the impact of racial and ethnic effects on criminal court processing. The Schlesinger study is discussed again in chapter 9 on statistics.

Perhaps the most commonly used secondary data set for those researchers interested in crime are the Uniform Crime Reports (UCR) compiled by the Federal Bureau of Investigation (FBI). These data have been collected since 1930 and for a long time were the sole source of crime data, albeit perplexed with methodological weakness especially in its early days of inception. These types of data provide several benefits for researchers overall, however. First, trends can be documented over a long period of time. Second, since some of these sources of data are "official" government-funded and -collected data, they are widely available for researchers to use. It is important for researchers to recognize, and evaluate, the weakness with any data set. It is a fallacy to assume that any data is free of methodological flaw (yes, even those collected by governments!). Virtually every textbook on crime, criminal justice, criminology, sociology, political science, social work, psychology, and so forth laments such problems; in fact, some argue that Uniform Crime Report (UCR) data are so inaccurate they should not be used as an indicator of criminal behavior (Loftin & McDowall, 2010, p. 527). Loftin and McDowall summarize the primary criticisms:

1. The procedures and definitions of crime are not consistent across agencies.
2. Many crimes are not included because citizens do not report them to the police, and the likelihood of citizen reporting varies in systematic ways. The crimes that are unreported are not accounted for.
3. The police are selective in reporting crime, and this filtering process is biased (not constant across social groups or areas).
4. Some agencies do not report, or they report incompletely, and missing data are poorly documented.
5. The major data collections do not provide information on the characteristics of offenders (such as age, race, and gender), and these must be inferred from arrest data.
6. The UCR is not a statistical program in the usual sense of the term. Rather, it is a "house organ" of the police (Lejins, 1966, p. 1016) and reflects the organizational interests of agencies that may use the data to further those interests.

Nevertheless, despite these well-documented problems, UCR data are still widely used, in part because not much better exists—especially for documenting crime trends *over time*.

The revised National Incident Based Reporting System (NIBRS) attempts to address many of the obvious problems with the UCR. NIBRS contributes more information than UCR data do, and provides data on specific incidents rather than just aggregate data. Another improvement over the UCR is that the raw data, rather than just being compiled into summaries, are provided to researchers. This has allowed new research opportunities for those interested in studying public issues related to crime.

Self-Report Data. Another valuable type of secondary data available to researchers is self-report data. This methodology entails asking people to self-report their involvement in particular activities. Researchers can learn about criminal and/or delinquent behavior, victimization, exercise habits, eating behaviors, stress management techniques, relationships, mental health, cultural variation, personality characteristics, habits and hobbies, drug use, physical health, vacation practices, religious practices— the options are endless! This offers many advantages over large data sets like the UCR. For one thing, much greater detail is provided in self-report data, as opposed to knowing only about things that are publically documented like crime or participation in government-funded programs. One historical reason for the development of self-report data actually emerged because the relationships between the victim and the offender were unknown in the standard Uniform Crime Reports. With the development of self-report data, much was learned by being able to ask individuals about their relationship to the perpetrator of the crime. Krohn, Thornberry, Gibson, and Baldwin (2010) argue that the development of self-report data is probably the biggest methodological advancement that has occurred this century. It allows the potential for a more realistic "picture" of reality by allowing a deeper analysis of personal perspective. This applies to any subject area, because asking the person to tell about their own perspective, their own experience, might well give a deeper understanding than counting occurrences in a pre-existing government or academic institution collected data set. Combining data sets might result in an even more robust research design, and researchers are beginning to employ this practice more often.

Another large improvement in data has been the ability to study behavior, and social phenomenon overtime. While most self-report data is collected at one point in time, called the cross-sectional study, a major improvement has been in studying the same group of people over an extended period. The National Youth Survey (NYS) provides a nationally representative group of subjects, who were surveyed initially during their teen years and analyzed until their thirties. Another popular data set is the National Longitudinal Survey of Youth (NLSY). These types of studies are called *longitudinal panel designs* because they study subjects *over time*. The NLSY, for example, includes data on the *children* of the original subjects, making it a multi-generational set of data comprised of numerous research categories of interest and thousands of variables. These two data sets are especially popular with researchers in the social sciences.

Because many topics in fields like crime, social work, sociology, political science, psychology, history, emergency and disaster management, and so forth may generate interest in material that might seem sensitive, politically fueled, private, or otherwise difficult to assess or obtain, another research option is to utilize something known in research methods as scenario methodology.

Scenario Methodology

Conducting crime and deviance research is often difficult due to the nature of the topics examined. A researcher could be interested in how people might react to a person being victimized, but very few researchers would be presented with an opportunity to collect data on this specific type of event. A researcher interested in how people respond to a tragic event, natural disaster, or terrorist attack may find it difficult to study those events in progress as they occur in time. For this reason, a research strategy that asks a large number of people to anticipate their reactions to certain events or situations is a reasonable, though imperfect, substitute for actual observation or participation. This is not a new strategy, as it has been employed in many disciplines, including business, psychology, sociology, legal studies, and criminology for a while (Piquero, Exum, & Simpson, 2005), but its popularity seems to be growing. Scenario methodology is usually carried out by research subjects being given questionnaires or forms to complete that reflect how they *anticipate* they would respond to specific scenarios that are presented. Piquero et al. (2005) provide an example of scenario research by giving respondents hypothetical situations using scenarios, or vignettes, and once these are read, asking the respondents to reflect and report on how they would respond in the given situation. Here is an example of one of their scenarios:

> Lee, a manager at Steelcorp, considers whether to order an employee to meet with competitors to discuss product pricing for the next year. Lee thinks that the law governing this act is unreasonably applied to companies like Steelcorp. Steelcorp is a diversified company, currently experiencing growing sales and revenues in an industry that is losing ground to foreign competitors. If successful, the act may result in a positive impression of Lee by top management. Lee also believes the act will greatly increase firm revenues. The firm had mandatory ethics training, and an employee was severely reprimanded after being discovered by the firm engaging in a similar act. Lee decides to order an employee to meet with competitors to discuss product pricing for the next year.
>
> *(Piquero et al., 2005, p. 279)*

After scenarios are provided to respondents, the researchers gather descriptions of all the vignette dimensions, variables, and responses; data are then coded, entered, and analyzed.

Obviously, there are some disadvantages to scenario research, such as potential bias from respondents who simply provide the "socially desirable response" instead of an actual honest response. By wanting to impress, gain the approval of, or perhaps even anger others, the subject may respond in an artificial way; this is called "experimenter expectancy." Also, research respondents and people in general cannot always anticipate how they might react in any given situation. Soldiers do not go into combat with the intent of running away, having an emotional breakdown, shooting the innocent, or giving up—yet some do. Police do not intend to go into undercover work only to "join the criminal side," yet it happens. Doctors to not intend to become desensitized to the medical woes of their patients, yet some do. Bystanders probably would not report that they would walk away or fail assist a victim in distress, but it is a reality. While someone may think they know how they would respond, in truth their actions may be much different. These weaknesses in this type of data collection must be considered, accounted for, and addressed in the best way possible. While asking respondents questions and expecting honest answers has some weakness, it is nevertheless a common methodology. Some research even supports that most people are typically honest on surveys, especially if the respondent's identity is protected. There are steps that can be taken like building in reliability questions that can help gauge honesty and making sure the respondent knows their responses are anonymous.

SURVEY RESEARCH

Throughout this chapter, research designs have been discussed. This chapter elaborates on the specific measurement devices that can be used for gathering the data. Survey research is perhaps the most common form of data collection strategy, and because survey research can utilize questionnaires or interviews, it can be categorized as both quantitative and qualitative research in its approach.

The purpose of survey research can be descriptive, explanatory, or exploratory, as discussed in chapter 1. **Survey research** is merely a broad, inclusive term, but it usually signifies that the researcher utilizes either questionnaires or personal interviews to gather data. Again, *typically*, questionnaires are considered quantitative data, while interviews are typically categorized as a qualitative methodology. Whichever format the researcher selects, the data collection instrument should be designed so that the validity and reliability can be determined. In other words, the instrument needs to actually measure what is intended and should be designed in such a way that the same responses would be given if the measurement instrument were repeated. The way in which the questions are worded is extremely important.

Survey research: A method of collecting data, typically through personal interviews or questionnaires.

Recall from earlier chapters, and the first few paragraphs of this chapter, that the results of a questionnaire have to be "coded" and entered into statistical analysis software for quantitatively designed studies. This is where the responses to the questions are transposed into numbers so that statistical analysis can be conducted. Quite often qualitative interview data are also "coded" so that they can be entered into a computer and analyzed using statistical techniques, as well. It should be interjected here, however, that many qualitative scholars oppose this process on philosophical grounds; others embrace it. As a general notion, survey research is regarded as quantitative, as the primary goal is to mathematically analyze the data and report on statistically supported relationships between the variables. Analyzing qualitative survey data is typically carried out by noting themes or patterns in the sample response. As mentioned earlier, responses from open-ended surveys or personal interviews can inform hypothesis development (hypothesis generating) for researchers.

Questionnaires

Questionnaire: A form of obtaining information (data) by providing a series of questions given to respondents with pen and paper, online, in person, or over the telephone.

Questionnaires are used often in the social sciences. Most college students are familiar with questionnaires because they are often targeted as survey respondents for researchers. A **questionnaire,** which is an option of gathering data, has many benefits and so is used more often than personal, in-depth interviews. The primary benefit is that a large amount of information can be collected quickly and with little expense. Personal interviews can take a large quantity of time. A further benefit is that respondents can remain anonymous, leading to a greater probability they will be honest with their responses.

There are also several methods of administering a questionnaire which may enhance the probability of participation (response rates). Questionnaires may be conducted over the telephone, mailed to respondents, delivered in person, or facilitated online. For example, surveys can be provided through a website such as "Survey Monkey," "Qualtrics," or "Ultimate Survey" that is specifically designed to distribute surveys through internet links. Other websites such as Facebook can even be used to dispense questionnaires, albeit with some methodological concerns such as selection bias, of course. In some situations, the questions can be read over the phone to a respondent and answers recorded accordingly, or they can simply be sent through the mail. Surveys can be given in prisons, jails, courts, hospitals, churches, recreation centers, public health facilities, libraries, classroom, or work settings and even handed out in any public place.

The method and targeted audience depends on whether or not the researcher wants the results to be *representative* of the total population. As mentioned earlier, for the results to be generalizable to the total population, the respondents need to be randomly selected; everyone needs an equal chance of selection for participation. In some research, generalizability is not the objective, and respondents are *chosen* specifically. Perhaps the goal is to study a specific program or agency, such as evaluating the opinion and practices of participants in public assistance programs. With either approach, however, an important goal of survey research is to have an acceptable *response rate*. A sufficient number of respondents need to participate, and certainly, the information gathered needs to accurately reflect reality. Achieving these objectives requires proper training, preparation, and knowledge on the part of the researcher.

Despite the common usage and many benefits of survey research, there are disadvantages to using this form of data collection. As mentioned earlier, perhaps the biggest obstacle is obtaining a sufficient response rate. Many potential research subjects simply do not want to take the time to complete a questionnaire. Sometimes, additional time and money have to be allocated to sending *reminders* to respondents to help bolster participation. In some instances, various types of incentives may prove useful. For example, respondents may be given a small token, food voucher, or even cash in exchange for their time. As discussed in the ethics chapter, this practice is not, in itself, unethical as long as the incentive is not coercive and IRB protocol is followed. The bottom line is that a study is jeopardized if response rates are low, so care and resources are necessary allocations to enhance participation.

Language barriers and limited reading ability are also potential problems in survey research. The subject must be able to understand the questions. During grant-awarded research, the National Center for Community Policing once had to print 10,000 questionnaires in Vietnamese due to an influx of refugees in two of their study areas (Grand Rapids and East Lansing, Michigan). Not everyone reads English or is on the same reading level, so reading comprehension must also be considered. For example, many youths who are incarcerated read at a lower reading level than similar-aged youths (Briggs, 2008). Therefore, the sample (respondents) should be considered when drafting the wording of the survey instrument (questionnaire) itself. If the survey is targeted toward career professionals or college students, higher level language could be considered; if the audience is the general public or correctional populations, the words utilized typically should be at a sixth-grade reading level. Regardless of the audience, subjective language should be avoided; respondents interpreting words differently needs to be avoided. Language barriers, reading comprehension levels, and the way questions are worded should all be considered.

One word may have several meanings; therefore, the questions need to be constructed so that the subjects in the sample interpret the researcher's intended meaning of the word. If, for example, a group of surfers are asked what a "barrel" means to them, they would likely indicate the inside "tube" part of a wave—a highly desirable place for a surfer to find oneself. Another person may interpret it to mean trouble or difficulty, as in "I'm in a barrel," a less-than-desirable place to be. A football player may "barrel" someone over, while a rodeo participant may race "barrels."

An avid hunter or shooter may conceptualize a barrel as a part of a gun, as in "they look down the barrel of their gun." One could even make the "stretch" that the term to a researcher could trigger them to think about questionnaire development as in "a double-barreled question," which means that the question is asking two questions at once (which should be avoided). The key is to think through the fact that words can be interpreted differently based on the "audience"; however, when the survey instrument is created, the researcher may not "catch" this potential problem. That is one reason it is always a good idea to *pretest* the survey instrument on a group of people who are similar or identical to the study respondents. The feedback from the pretest can assist in identifying issues such as the construction of questions and the terminology used; a researcher may not notice potential problems without the use of pretesting. It is worth the time to do so, rather than to find out that the question can not be used later or that data results are based on poorly constructed questions.

Types of Survey Questions and Some Associated Problems

There are two primary types of questions in survey research: "open-ended" and "closed-ended" (basically multiple choices). As mentioned earlier, closed-ended questions are more common in quantitative research, and open-ended questions are more common in qualitative work. An example of an open-ended question would be, "Why did you take research methods?" This type of question allows the respondent to answer in his or her own words, therefore, allowing a much broader range of answers or responses. This allows the researcher to examine in-depth what each subject really thinks. Perhaps respondents will provide answers that the researcher never even thought about. **Open-ended questions** are often known as "free response" questions, since they allow respondents to answer in whatever way they want. Open-ended questions can provide a wealth of information to researchers and may even produce unexpected patterns and ideas (Singleton et al., 1988). Open-ended questions are, however, more difficult and time-consuming to analyze than closed questions and typically involve analyzing all subjects' responses for patterns and similarities. Difficulties also arise if respondents write illegibly or give answers that are ambiguous. Some respondents are also more reluctant to answer open-ended questions due to the greater amount of work and self-exposure entailed. For that reason, some researchers believe that open-ended questions should be used sparingly in questionnaires.

Open-ended questions: Survey questions that do not provide predetermined options but that prompt respondents to answer the questions as they wish.

Another issue to consider with an open-ended format is that the amount of information collected can be overwhelming. What if a researcher asks in a general population survey what people think about President Trump; the responses would likely be across the board. Suppose a researcher is concerned about explaining criminal behavior, and so provides an open-ended questionnaire to 150 inmates, asking, "Why did you engage in criminal behavior?" What if the researcher received 150 different responses? This would be a mass of "raw" data to process, which could also be very confusing. The researcher may decide to look for themes and identify the most common reasons given, perhaps the top five explanations. This process is called *parsimony*. **Parsimony** (as related to this topic) is when multiple explanations for understanding a construct or question are provided, and the researcher must select the few that have the most empirical support. Let's say a researcher asks a class of 50 students why they took a research methods class. While many different responses could be given, a review of the data could be simplified into the most common, most logical responses. For example, while 50 different responses could be given, many students would probably answer that they took research methods because it is a required course. Others may have taken it because of the professor's reputation, or it may have simply fit the student's schedule, and some may have enrolled by mistake or just followed the advice of friends. From the responses, the answers having the most rational and empirical support would be the ones the researcher utilizes to inform the question. This process of parsimony helps manage and make sense of the data; it is a way to scale back to the simplest forms. It is common in qualitative research.

Parsimony: Reducing many possible explanations to the one, or fewest, which make the most sense and have the most empirical support.

Alternative, **closed-ended questions** provide a listing of possible response options. This is what students have experience with when they take multiple-choice exams that provide a, b, c, and d or true/false options. Likert options are typical in closed-ended question formats, for example. **Likert scales** allow respondents to select a response that reflects their opinion or attitude. These responses typically run from "strongly agree" to "agree" to "disagree" and "strongly disagree," for example.

Closed-ended questions: Survey questions that provide the answer options for a respondent to select.

This closed-ended format solves the dilemma of having too many varied responses, as mentioned earlier, but it introduces another potential problem of *limiting* results. What if the answer the respondent would prefer to give is not listed as an option? One of the complaints about closed-ended format is that it forces respondents "into boxes." Some even argue that if sufficient options are not provided, it "sways" the outcome by limiting it to only what the researcher provides. One way to address this is to make sure to offer a fairly *exhaustive* listing and to provide an option for the respondent to select "other" or "N/A" (not applicable). There may even be times when the option of "other" allows for the respondent to write in the desired response. This does cause some "coding" issues, but these can be easily managed and the "other" option reduces the problem of forcing respondents into limited options.

Likert scale: A type of closed-ended answer format where the responses are "rankable," such as "strongly agree," "agree," "unsure," "disagree," and "strongly disagree."

Fowler (1995) outlines the strategies for improving survey measures, which include being mindful of offering "mutually exclusive" and "exhaustive" categories. Here's an easy example. If a researcher wants to know a respondent's religious background, he or she may ask, "What is your religious affiliation? (A) Baptist, (B) Catholic, (C) Jewish, or (D) Protestant." The most obvious problem is that not all religions are listed. If someone practices no religion, Wicca, or atheism, for example, what category should be selected? One solution is for the researcher to list more religions (there are obviously many more than four religious groups) and to include an option for the respondent who does not practice any religion at all. An **exhaustive** question has all possible answers provided for the respondent. It often requires a bit of homework for the researcher but reduces potential problems. Another solution is having the final attribute option of "other" to allow the respondent to "fill in the blank" and provide a response that was not offered as a category.

Exhaustive: Means every possible answer or response is provided for selection by the respondent.

Consider what else is wrong with the question: "What is your religious affiliation? A. Baptist, B. Catholic, C. Jewish, or D. Protestant." If a person is a Baptist or Protestant, the answer is obvious. Someone who worships as a "Baptist" can also be considered a "Protestant." Since either could be correct, the options are not *mutually exclusive.* One of the options should be omitted from the possible answers. **Mutually exclusive** means there can be only one correct answer, and it does not overlap with another.

Mutually exclusive: Answer options provided that do not overlap with one another; in other words, there is only one correct response.

A researcher should be especially careful when the answer options involve numeric ranges. Consider the example asking how much sleep, on average, a respondent receives each night: A. 0–2 hours, B. 2–4 hours, C. 4–6 hours, D. 6–8 hours, E. 8–10 hours, F. 10 hours or more. Notice how these options are *not* mutually exclusive; for example, a person who sleeps 2 hours could select category A or B, a person who sleeps four hours could select B or C, and so on.

Another common problem is called a **double-barreled question,** as mentioned before, which is simply asking two questions at once. If a researcher asks, "What is your religion, and how often do you go to church?" the problem is that two inquiries are asked at the same time. It also erroneously assumes that one question infers the other, which may not even be true. A person can have a religion but not go to church, or go to church but not have a religion. Here is another example: "Do you drink or smoke?" A person may drink, but not smoke. Another respondent may smoke, but not drink. Yet another research subject may smoke, but only when drinking! Double-barreled questions should always be avoided. The solution is simply to ask two separate questions. Ask only one question at a time.

Double-barreled questions: Questions that inadvertently ask two questions in one.

In addition, while most typically infer that the question is referring to drinking alcohol and smoking tobacco, the vagueness of the question leaves room for individual interpretation. Could it also mean drinking coffee and smoking marijuana? Vagueness and subjectiveness should be avoided. This question is also vague in that it lacks qualifying the behavior to a time frame (a day, a week, a month, etc.). Questions should be worded to assess exactly what is intended. If the researcher is interested in alcohol and tobacco use, he or she should first ask how often the respondent drinks alcoholic beverages in a given week. Then, ask how often the respondent smokes tobacco (and select the intended time frame, for example, in a given week). If the researcher wants to include the act of dipping or chewing tobacco, it would be necessary to assess that question as well. Remember, there may be respondents who do not do either, so they would need an option to indicate that or else the survey needs to provide skip patterns if subsequent questions are based on the assumption that the respondent does partake in the activity when in fact they may not.

Contingency questions and **skip patterns** direct the respondent to skip certain questions or items, which are used on a questionnaire if some of the questions do not apply to all respondents. In the earlier case, a person who does not drink alcohol could be directed to skip the related questions. Similarly, if a person does not identify with a religion they would skip questions asking about affiliations with specific denominations. Here is another example of a contingency question: "Have you ever been the victim of a robbery? If so, proceed to the next question; if not, skip to question number X." The next questions might ask about the respondent's experience as a victim, which would not apply to those respondents who had never been a victim of robbery. Respondents can get frustrated if they are asked to respond to questions that do not apply to them and dismiss themselves from participation, so be mindful of this.

Contingency questions: Questions that should be answered only by those meeting or fulfilling a particular condition or requirement.

Skip patterns: Involve allowing (and directing) respondents to skip a question, or series of questions, if the questions are not applicable to them.

Respondents may not be able to agree or disagree with overly complex questions. For example, problems could arise if a questionnaire were to ask respondents whether they agreed or disagreed with the following statement: "Legislators should legalize and regulate marijuana and use the revenue to fund government health care." Respondents may agree with marijuana legalization but be against government health care and thus cannot agree *or* disagree with the statement. This question is thus too complex, which might jeopardize reliability. It also combines two questions in one (double barreled).

Questions should also avoid **biased terminology.** These are expressions that could automatically trigger the respondent to think either negatively or positively. For example, "income tax increase" and "assistance to the poor" are more neutral terms than "tax hike" and "food stamps." If the question asks whether the respondent agrees with the state's recent tax hike, the word *hike* infers unfairness, which could influence the respondent's opinion. Ethical researchers must be careful that the questionnaire does not influence respondents so that they answer a certain way. The choice of wording is very important. It needs to be phrased in a neutral manner (regardless of the researcher's own opinion).

Biased terminology: Words that can influence the research subject in a particular direction.

Related to biased terminology is what can be referred to as *emotion* words (also referred to as **value-laden terminology**). Emotion words should be avoided. An example would be adding a descriptor before a noun such as asking a question about drug use and putting the word *dangerous* next to the identified drug. "Do you use dangerous cocaine?" is an example. Emotion words and value-laden words can "lead" the respondent into a particular response. They infer "judgment," which can influence the outcome of the study.

Value-laden terminology: Words that convey a personal opinion on the part of the researcher, which may sway the respondent's answers.

The same is true for **slang terminology.** While there are some audiences for which exceptions may be made, typically the formal word needs to be used and not its slang form or nickname. Slang is used much more than people realize. It has almost become habitual, so researchers need to be careful to avoid using it. For example, if the researcher is interested in marijuana use, he or she needs to use that word and not *blunt*, *dope*, *pot*, *weed*, or *Mary Jane*. If a researcher is interested in offender correctional alternatives, use the words *incarcerated*, *served time in a correctional facility*, or *placed in jail* instead of *thrown in the slammer*, *sent to the big house*, and so forth. Certainly, if the formal word is unfamiliar, exceptions may need to be made (this often depends on the audience). As a general rule, however, slang should be avoided.

Slang terminology: An alternative, informal word that is substituted for the literal, formal term.

The order of questions in a questionnaire is essential in reducing bias. For example, a set of questions about the quality of education in the United States followed immediately by a question asking respondents to identify what they think is the most critical issue in America today could result in a biased response (they would likely say "education" because they were *led* that way). Although the effect of some questions on subsequent responses cannot be eliminated, careful questionnaire construction can minimize this effect.

Question order can also be used to help maximize questionnaire response rates. As a rule, the most interesting questions should be placed first in a questionnaire. This ordering captures the respondents' attention and makes them more likely to finish the questionnaire. Initial questions should not be threatening to avoid offending the respondent, and questions regarding demographic information (race/ethnicity, income, gender) should be placed at the end of the questionnaire. Placing such questions at the beginning will make the questionnaire seem dull and will not motivate the respondent to complete it. While there are exceptions to the placement of demographic questions, typically it is a good practice to avoid starting a survey with these traditional identifiers. The ordering of the questions is important for response rates, and question wording is important for reliability of results.

As mentioned earlier, advanced terminology that might be unfamiliar to the respondent should be circumvented or at least defined (as long as defining a word does not influence the respondent). For example, instead of using the word *circumvented*, we could have used *avoided*. Most readers of this text probably know what *circumvent* means, but everyone likely knows what *avoid* means. It is safer when there is a possibility that a word could be unknown, subjective, or misunderstood to replace it. If it cannot be substituted, then it may be necessary to define the word for the respondent. Here is another example. What if a researcher wants to assess how many respondents are ambidextrous? Rather than assuming everyone knows the term, a brief definition could be provided or the question could be phrased without the use of the word (e.g., a person who can effectively use their right hand or left hand). Providing this definition does not *lead* the respondent and reduces the problem of misunderstanding; however, sometimes providing a definition could *bias* the respondent, so be careful. If it is necessary to provide a definition, do so in a neutral and factual manner. If a researcher provides the definition for *pedophile* as a "scumbag that sexually victimizes children," the question or study may be jeopardized by use of the word *scumbag*. It could bias the respondent and does not represent neutrality, which is paramount in science.

Invalid conclusions can also occur if a respondent has read the question too quickly and fails to grasp the true meaning of the sentence. Survey developers should evaluate whether a particular question is at risk for this. Consider a question asking whether a respondent agrees with the following statement: "Teachers shouldn't make political statements to their students." A respondent who fails to read the word *not* might answer differently than one who had noticed the word. Avoiding conjunctions can help, and sometimes italics might help the respondent focus (e.g., teachers should *not* make political statements to their students). This practice can be tricky depending on how attention is drawn to a word; it could do more harm than good because it might actually bias the respondent. Carefully think through the decision.

Important decisions have to be made at *every* stage of a research project; it is hoped that the point has been made that a survey instrument should not just be "thrown together." Great care and diligence need to be given to its development. Many of the things that a person is interested in researching have likely been studied before; it is worth the time to see if there is a preexisting questionnaire on the chosen topic. Luckily, this is not considered "cheating" or "plagiarism." Quite the contrary, there are actually some very strong and valid reasons for identifying preexisting questionnaires.

One benefit to using a preexisting questionnaire is that, if it was done correctly, the instrument has already had content validity assessed—in other words, it measures what is it supposed to measure and asks the "right" questions. The researcher who first developed the questionnaire may also have run statistical tests to measure the instrument's reliability. Published articles will typically report this.

Another benefit to using a preexisting questionnaire is that comparisons are possible. One researcher can compare the results of his or her study with any other study that used the same instrument. As mentioned in other chapters, *research* often involves evaluating prior studies to validate or refute their conclusions. If the same survey instrument is used, such comparisons are possible. As is true in every case, just "give credit where credit is due."

Longitudinal comparisons allow a researcher to measure changes over time. For example, if juveniles are given a questionnaire asking about their knowledge of HIV/AIDS, and then 10 years later the same survey is given again, their knowledge can be compared over time. Did their opinion or knowledge change as they aged? Another type of research comparison might be by location, such as comparing juveniles in Alabama (a low-risk area for HIV infection) with juveniles in San Francisco (a high-risk area for HIV infection).

There are many advantages to reviewing existing questionnaires, but do not assume that just because they exist, they are of high quality. Many times they can be used as a starting point but need improvement. If a preexisting questionnaire is not available or cannot be located, researchers will need to create an original survey instrument; if all guidelines are followed to ensure validity and reliability, then theirs may be used for others to follow.

Note that a student should check with the research methods professor as he or she might want the student to go through the intellectual exercise of actually creating survey questions.

Survey research is a common, effective way to gather data. As discussed, there are several methods of deploying questionnaires. Both questionnaires and interviews come with responsibility. As discussed in chapter 3 on ethics, when interviewing abused subjects, crime victims, mental health or physical health patients, children, etc. it is vital to maintain respect and to observe ethical considerations. This requires researchers to "walk a fine line." Although ethics are paramount and sensitivity to respondents' feelings is important, at the same time questions must be specific. For instance,

> Questions should be designed to avoid use of vague or ambiguous terms such as abuse, rape, and violence, and instead, directly ask respondents about whether or not they have experienced certain specific acts, such as being hit, slapped, or forced to have sex against their will.
>
> *(Ellsberg & Heise, 2002, p. 1601)*

Clearly, researchers must practice empathy along with sound science. Gathering data through interviews may require a heightened sensitivity due to the nature of the more personal connection. While the topic of interviews could be appropriately included in this chapter on research designs, the detailed discussion will be delayed until chapter 7 on mixed methods. Personal interviews are common in qualitative designs but are now being combined with other quantitative data techniques, which results in this third category of research designs, which is commonly referred to as *mixed methods*. Because the mixed method approach is the newest and most controversial, a separate chapter is devoted to the topic.

SUMMARY

This chapter has presented several types of research designs and data collection devices, and covered common problems with survey instruments. It should be evident that some methods and tools are preferable to others in regard to "scientific" quality. While each offers its own level of contributions to knowledge, choosing designs that eliminate potential threats allows conclusions to be made with a higher level of confidence.

There is a lot of material covered in this chapter, which reflects the fact that there are many choices available to researchers, and each decision comes with its own techniques and best practices. Ultimately, it is the research problem that should determine the research design, survey instrument, and analysis. However, as discussed throughout the book, many decisions affect the approach that is chosen. As is discussed in the next chapter, increasingly, researchers are using a combination of approaches in one study (mixed methods). In such designs, the best aspects of qualitative work are combined with the best aspects of quantitative research.

KEY TERMS

Biased terminology
Classic experimental design
Closed-ended questions
Contingency questions
Control group
Dependent variable (DV)
Double-barreled questions
Exhaustive
Exogenous variables
Experimental design
Experimental group
Factorial designs
Generalization
Hypothesis
Independent variable (IV)
Likert scale
Mutually exclusive
One-shot case study
Open-ended questions
Operationalize
Parsimony
Posttest
Pretest
Quasi-experimental design
Questionnaire
Randomization
Secondary data analysis
Skip patterns
Slang terminology
Solomon four-group design
Static group comparison
Survey research
Time series designs
Two-group posttest-only design
Value-laden terminology

CRITICAL THINKING EXERCISES

1. Identify each research design presented in this chapter, draw the corresponding diagram, and describe in detail what the symbols represent. Make sure each specific design is fully described.
2. What are the differences between experimental and quasi-experimental design?
3. Identify why some researchers prefer experimental designs over quasi-experimental ones.
4. List and describe the pros and cons to three different data sets that researchers utilize for secondary data analysis.
5. What are the advantages and disadvantages to using scenario methodology?
6. What is longitudinal analysis, and what are the associated research benefits of it?
7. Is the one-shot case study pre-experimental or experimental? Why?
8. Identify the strengths and weaknesses of survey research.
9. What is the difference between open-ended and closed-ended questions? What are the benefits associated with each approach? What are the weaknesses?
10. In questionnaire construction, describe the problems associated with using the following: biased language, emotion words, value-laden terminology, words with multiple meaning, and slang wording.
11. Describe why it is important to pretest a survey instrument before implementing it.
12. List the principles to follow when creating questions for survey instruments. At a minimum, five "rules" should be discussed.
13. For the following variables, create a way to *measure* them (survey question) using first an open-ended approach, and then using a closed-ended approach. Be sure to apply the "rules" discussed in this chapter, such as avoiding subjective language, double-barreled questions, biased terminology, and so on. The concepts to measure are alcohol use and crime victimization. Now, evaluate whether the questions developed meet the guidelines of survey research. It may be necessary to create more than just one question.
14. What is the difference between "hypothesis-testing" research and "hypothesis-generating" research? Discuss and provide an example of each, that was not an example provided in the chapter.

CHAPTER 7

Mixed Methods

CHAPTER OBJECTIVES

After reading this chapter students should:

- Be able to compare and contrast differences between qualitative and quantitative approaches to research, and describe why division occurs between some "camps."
- Articulate what mixed methods are, as well as the potential benefits and potential problems associated with them.
- Identify research topics that are less, and better, suited to mixed methods.
- Understand the need for fluid research and the problems created by fluid research.
- Show how reliance on only one data source is often unreliable.
- Demonstrate how politics, ethics and the media might affect research.

A deliberate attempt has been made to present the various approaches to research and to avoid favoring either quantitative or qualitative methods so that students can make informed decisions after being exposed to the benefits and shortcomings of both approaches. As mentioned earlier, the typical practice is for one methodology to be chosen, often at the cost of losing any beneficial qualities of the other. Understanding both quantitative and qualitative research strategies may lead to asking why each type of research cannot be employed in a single study. For example, wouldn't relying on firsthand experience coupled with a large-scale survey of respondents provide the most definitive answer to many research questions? Doesn't even a cursory understanding of research methods suggest this combined approach? Also, when considering the various threats to validity and reliability, would some be reduced, or eliminated, if varied methods were used in one study? All these questions would seem to suggest an affirmation. A combined qualitative and quantitative study should be preferable; however, if it was such a good idea to combine multiple methods in one study, why hasn't it become the preferred research strategy for all, or at least, most researchers? The reality is the vast majority of published research relies on one method or the other, and not a combination.

There are other constraining factors, such as the hallmark of good research being the ability to adapt to changing social or experimental conditions; yet a rigid research design, which is required by IRBs and many researchers, does not permit the flexibility to take advantage of changes or new opportunities. An example of this occurred during a simple descriptive study of juveniles' attitudes and knowledge about HIV/AIDS. The state correctional system, presumably in an effort to increase the juveniles' knowledge base, quickly implemented an AIDS education course at the start of the study. Luckily, only a third of the students completed the five-day course, a third completed three days' worth of AIDS education, and a third received no AIDS education. The researcher then altered the existing descriptive research design to measure the *impact* of AIDS education and ended up with a much better study than originally intended (Lanier & McCarthy, 1989). This fluid approach allowed the study to continue and actually resulted in much better research. However the IRB requirements in 1989 were much less precise than today, which might have hindered the fluid research strategy employed.

This chapter outlines some of the reasons fluid mixed methods *should* be the preferred research strategy for some studies; keeping with the necessary critical approach of this book, though, it also examines why mixed methods and fluid designs are not more commonly used.

In general, **qualitative research** involves data collection that focuses on an *in-depth personal experience* or understanding and affords more flexibility than methods for collecting quantitative data. Furthermore, the validity is often high with a qualitative study, since the researcher has a deeper understanding of the topic being examined. Alternatively, because that deeper understanding is gained from considerable time spent in one (or at best a few) research locations; the reliability will often be lower than with a quantitative study. Alternatively, a **quantitative research** study relies on the numerical data collected and so provides *a numerical or statistical analysis* of the research topic. This method allows a large number to be studied in a short amount of time. For example, a quantitative focused study might survey 500 health and human services departments to learn about gender differences among staff at various levels. A qualitative approach may take place in only one city or county, but over a two-year period. The same topic can be studied by two distinct approaches;

Qualitative research: A method of research designed to gather data of the lived experience of the research subject; primarily achieved through an *in-depth personal experience* or understanding of social issues.

Quantitative research: A method of research focused on statistical procedures to assist in making sense of the numerical data collected; provides *a numerical or statistical analysis* of social issues.

the type of data collected naturally varies. Alternatively, an approach for combining the two methodologies, qualitative and quantitative, into one study, is termed **mixed methods research.** As will be shown, this strategy often provides "the best of both worlds," despite some pragmatic and philosophical challenges. Before too much detail is provided on combining approaches, we present a brief review of the primary difference between qualitative and quantitative research.

Mixed methods research: Combines qualitative and quantitative research techniques into one study or a series of studies.

Chapter 5 focused on qualitative research designs and Chapter 6 on quantitative methods. To help consolidate the basic premises, consider Table 7.1:

As shown in Table 7.1, quantitative and qualitative research can be distinguished by several key factors. Quantitative research tends to be more objective, whereas qualitative research tends to be more subjective. Objective research tends to be more factual and not influenced by personal feelings or opinions. This type of research tends to rely on closed-ended questions, where there are a limited number of responses to choose from (most commonly used in survey research or secondary data). A limited number of fixed responses create impartial interpretation by the researcher. This is valuable since subjective research is more likely (than quantitative) to be influenced by the personal opinions and experiences of the researcher. Qualitative research is more dependent upon researcher interpretation and requires more investigation when classifying responses. Researchers hope to immerse themselves in the subject matter and develop sensitizing concepts that enhance their understanding and explanation of reality. Qualitative research is demonstrated in field studies, interviews, and participant observation studies. These

TABLE 7.1 *Quantitative and Qualitative Comparison*

	Quantatative	Qualitative
Definition:	Amount of something	Nature of things
Orientation:	Objective	Subjective
Focus:	Deductive	Inductive
Type:	Applied	Pure
Time:	Quicker	Longer
Theory:	Positivism	Post Modernism, Symbolic Interaction
Methods:	Questionnaires, Secondary data,	Ethnography, Observation, Interview
Popularity:	Dominant	Waning

types of research involve the researcher experiencing a group's way of life from the group's perspective.

Quantitative research is deductive, often starting with abstract concepts or a theoretical proposition, that outlines the logical connection among concepts, then evaluates the concepts against concrete evidence (Neuman, 2011). This type of research moves from ideas, theory, or a mental state to observable empirical evidence. By contrast, qualitative research uses inductive direction, beginning with observing the empirical world then reflecting on what is taking place and thinking in more abstract ways (Neuman, 2011). Qualitative research thus moves from concrete empirical evidence and works toward more abstract concepts and theory development.

Quantitative research is most often applied research. Applied research is practical research concerned with solving immediate policy problems (Hagan, 2014). On the other hand, qualitative research uses pure, or basic, research and is concerned with the acquisition of new knowledge.

Quantitative research encompasses positivism, which developed from the natural science approach that favors studying outcomes that can be measured, or objectified, empirically. Qualitative research uses mechanisms such as symbolic interaction, suggesting that people transmit and receive symbolic communication when they socially interact (Neuman, 2011). People create perceptions of each other and social settings, then largely act on their perceptions. This suggests that how people think about themselves and others is based on their interactions (Neuman, 2011). This shows a stark contrast between the methodologies, however the disparities can be addressed and used to strengthen a study.

Interview: Interaction between researcher and subject in order to elicit information. Often occurs face-to-face but can be by Skype, videoconference, phone call, or other methods. It is a method of gathering data that is typically more common in qualitative research, which allows the researcher and respondent to come together in a conversational setting.

The primary difference between the two methods is that quantitative studies are typically larger in scale and involve research designs that afford the ability to analyze the data collected with statistical procedures. With qualitative research studies, the samples are typically smaller, they involve more time commitment with the study participants, and there is less (or even no) motivation to use mathematical formulas to analyze the data. While this description is an extreme simplification, hopefully it triggers an image of the two, often opposing, positions taken by researchers who prefer one method to the other.

Consider, however, the use of questionnaires and interviews to demonstrate how qualitative and quantitative methods may be combined into a single mixed methods research approach. Recall that in quantitative designs, typically a questionnaire is created that is targeted at larger samples with closed-ended questions, written in a way that tries to produce maximum reliability (refer to chapter 4 for review); qualitative research would more likely *not* be as restrained to closed-ended responses and might often be conducted in an *interview* setting between the researcher and respondent, increasing validity.

Essentially, an **interview** is a conversation between the research participant(s) and a researcher for the sake of conveying and receiving knowledge. An interview is very similar to a questionnaire, with many of the same threats, rules, and procedures. There are several types of interviews, and the most common method of differentiating between them is based on the level of formality and structure: formal, semiformal, or informal, as well as structured, semistructured, or unstructured—the terms used to describe interviews are essentially interchangeable.

Formal or structured interview: A type of interview that is preplanned, with questions that are structured in advance, and does not allow deviation from set scripts. The exact same questions, in the same order, are asked of all respondents.

A formal interview is possible when the researcher has a considerable knowledge base of the topic prior to conducting the study. **Formal interviews** are structured and ask all respondents the same questions in the same order, with no variation. When Arriola et al. (2002) examined AIDS issues among inmates; they were funded (in part) by the Centers for Disease Control and Prevention (CDC), which brought together health researchers, correctional staff, and criminologists. Drawing from the diverse and comprehensive knowledge base, this interdisciplinary team preassessed what information they wanted to gain and created a formal interview prior to questioning a single inmate. The resultant instrument was basically a questionnaire that could be read aloud to facilitate inmates who could not read well. This methodology allows multiple research sites to use the same instrument. A preconstructed, structured interview does have limitations, primarily that it is restrictive. Researchers should not deviate from the instrument and should not ask for additional content. It is not designed to probe for further information or clarification. If these tools are needed, a less formal interview is preferable.

Semiformal or semistructured interview: Affords some flexibility to explore issues that develop; allows more open, flowing communication but still relies on preconceived questions and areas to explore.

A **semiformal** or **semistructured interview** is often chosen when the researcher has some knowledge of the topic (at least enough to prepare questions in advance) but wants to allow flexibility to probe for clarification on responses and diverge from the preset questions. In other words, questions and categories of questions are developed in advance, but latitude is afforded to expand and seek detailed responses; some variation in the format of the interview is common, accepted, and even expected.

Unstructured or informal interview: An interview that is more free-flowing and not constrained by preconceived questions; often used with exploratory research.

The **unstructured** or **informal interview** is most likely to be used when the researcher knows little or nothing about the research subject yet wants to explore it. With this format, considerable freedom exists to discover topics the respondent is willing to share. It allows for probing, and it allows for the *respondent* to dictate the direction of the dialogue. Researchers explore and examine topics as the respondent introduces them. For example, once when a researcher was interviewing a convicted, notorious "vampire killer" (on something unrelated), the topic of "feeding circles" was brought up by the research subject; the researcher was then able to inquire about what a feeding circle was, and what benefit was gained by participants in feeding circles (Lanier & Henry, 2010). An unstructured interview is thus basically an open-ended format whereby the researcher will follow up with more detailed questioning after initial responses are given, if needed.

After an interview is conducted, the data are typically "coded" and analyzed in some way. What happens after the interview is often determined by the goals of the research, but some form of processing the data will need to occur after the data have been gathered. This provides opportunities to demonstrate qualitative, quantitative, or mixed approaches to research.

Some qualitative researchers choose *not* to *quantify* their interview data and instead rely on the traditional analytical strategy of noting, developing, and describing commonalities or "themes" identified in the data. This is the traditional qualitative analytical strategy and provides numerous advantages. The primary benefit is that researchers develop a deep understanding of, and appreciation for, the data. This depth of knowledge conveys itself in richer, more explanatory descriptions of the research, respondents, and study.

For example, Strydom and Kivedo (2009) presented a combined research approach. In a study of the psychosocial needs of children whose parents are incarcerated, Strydom and Kivedo note that their study can primarily be considered qualitative, although the *measuring instrument* used would be considered quantitative. Psychological researchers are best known for creating scales and inventories that can be used to differentiate "normal" people from the "abnormal." For instance, depressive states of mind can only be identified if there are *baseline* measures of what non-depressed people "look like." Such *scales* are typically considered quantitative in nature when measured against each other; by *observing* children and *interacting* with them, a more complete understanding is gained than would be possible just through reliance on a scale. This part of the study is considered more qualitative research. Later in this chapter, much more attention is given to examples of mixed methods, as well as identifying some of the positive and negative issues surrounding the use of mixed methods.

A theme that is hopefully becoming apparent is that a triad exists in survey research. The three components to this triad are as follows: (1) typically, preconstructed questionnaires with response options provided are characteristic of quantitative research methods. This makes the data easier to code and enter into statistical software packages. (2) Interviews, structured or unstructured, are more commonly associated with qualitative designs. Typically, researchers critically examine the data for themes and patterns and seek data results that will exemplify the "lived" experience of the respondent. (3) Increasingly, qualitative researchers are employing coding techniques and statistical analysis software, making their work more quantitative in nature, and quantitative researchers are employing techniques to capture a richer experience from the research subjects. This combination of what were once two distinct approaches results in what is commonly described as *mixed methods*. Equally important to mixed methods is the idea that research can be modified at various stages, or is fluid.

The insert by Eugene Paoline and William Terrill provides an excellent illustration of the need for a flexible and fluid research strategy, supporting the mixed methods rationale. Mixed methods are, however, not without controversy, as will be discussed after the methods are explained.

INSERT 7.1

A Practical Lesson from the Assessing Police Use of Force Policies and Outcomes Project

Eugene A. Paoline III, PhD and
University of Central Florida
Orlando, Florida
and
William Terrill, PhD
Michigan State University
Lansing, Michigan

Before undertaking a research project, you need to have a plan of action. Much like a blueprint for building a house, this happens before you set foot on site. While this blueprint serves as a course of action, at times you find that things can change once you are in the field. In the end, we often realize that the research process is about compromise. In our example, we highlight a lesson from a project designed to explore the impact of different use of force policies on a variety of police outcomes. As part of a two-stage research strategy, we realized that our "planned" approach for our second phase needed to be altered from the initial research proposal, based on evidence that was presented to us during phase one. What follows is a summary of how this played out.

The Research Plan

Our original research proposal was designed to accomplish two goals: (1) determine the various types of nondeadly force policies being used by police agencies throughout the country

continued

Insert 7.1 *continued*

(particularly those employing a force continuum approach),[1] and (2) determine if certain types of policies offer more beneficial outcomes to police practitioners (e.g., less force and fewer complaints, injuries, and lawsuits, as well as improved officer attitudes regarding policy utility). To accomplish the first goal, we planned to administer an agency mail survey to police agencies across the United States using a disproportionate stratified random sample based on department size and type. The results from this survey would then allow us to identify and more closely study eight police departments, which would differ in terms of their use of force policy *design* (e.g., linear, matrix/box, wheel/circular) and the *placement of tactics* within the policy (i.e., when various force options could be used).

Selection of the eight agencies would be broken down into four clusters of two agencies. Cluster one would consist of two agencies that employ a linear design but that differ in terms of tactical placement (e.g., one agency that permits the use of a Taser on passively resisting suspects, and one agency that permits the use of a Taser only on aggressively resisting suspects); cluster two would contain two agencies employing a matrix/box continuum design, but differ in terms of tactical placement; and the third cluster would contain two agencies employing a circular/wheel continuum design, but differ in terms of tactical placement. The fourth and final cluster was to contain two agencies not employing a continuum design, but it relied solely on individual policies concerning varying forceful tactics (e.g., empty hand strike, takedown maneuver, chemical spray, baton, Taser).

The Empirical Reality

After distributing the national mail survey to 1,083 police agencies, 662 were returned. We immediately noticed that the practical reality of the use of force policies in operation was vastly different than what we hypothesized and proposed as part of the original research design. That is, more than 80% of the responding agencies noted that they used a force continuum approach within their policy, with 77.4% explaining that they utilized a linear design. Moreover, of the 80% that were using a force continuum, only 10.1% were matrix/box designs and 9.3% circular/wheel designs. Of the roughly 19% of agencies reporting that they did not use any type of force continuum (our fourth category besides linear, matrix/box, and circular/wheel), they either did not require officers to systematically document use of force incidents with a report (our main data source), or they were very small in size, which would have hindered comparisons to the other agencies. Based on these empirical results, we decided to revisit our plan in the second phase of the project with respect to selecting equally proportionate use of force policy designs.

The Revised Plan

Our revised plan still included eight agencies for in-depth study, but we oversampled departments that used a linear design to more adequately reflect use of force policies nationally, rather than imposing our own artificial standard. To mirror the percentage of policy types noted in the mail survey results, we chose six agencies using a linear design, one using a matrix/box design, and one using a circular/wheel design. In the end, we also chose to concentrate more on the variation in the tactical placement of force options over the design type. The primary lesson that can be learned from this experience is that researchers need to go into a project with a well-thought-out plan of action. At the same time, this plan should not be too rigid, in the event that important changes need to be made that would ultimately work to produce a better overall research product. In our case, the proposed plan was more symmetrical and tidy, but it would not have resulted in an accurate portrayal of the majority of use of force policy designs that were being implemented by American police departments.

Note

1. A force continuum is a policy tool that attempts to ordinally link varying types of force tactics with varying types of subject resistance in terms of severity.

Paoline and Terrill have reputations for being methodological purists and adherents to social science's version of positivism. Their recognition that "things change" and their willingness to adapt to, and take advantage of, departmental realties (fluidity) led to a much stronger study than originally envisioned. As discussed in the chapter on ethics, how does this work with the rigidly defined criterion demanded by IRBs?

As mentioned, many researchers limit themselves to one type of research design (either qualitative or quantitative); reasons for this have already been mentioned. Brent and Kraska (2010) argue, however, that this polarization is unnecessary, and that a mixed methods approach can be desirable:

> Crime and criminal justice studies have embedded under this surface, then, with what Roth (1987) refers to as methodological exclusivism: an ideological orientation that presumes a single paradigm for generating credible and legitimate scholarship. These conditions have consequently meant the construction of rigid methodological boundaries that maintain the opposition between qualitative and

> quantitative paradigms. Instead of utilizing a multi-faceted approach to conducting research, these boundaries eschew any methodological tools that fall beyond their territory. This traditional perspective of "quants versus quals" is, as Kraska and Neuman argue, both greatly "unnecessary and inhibiting. . . .
>
> *(pp. 412–413)*

This methodological exclusionism is prevalent and entrenched, yet it is easily exposed as limiting to an overall quest for knowledge. There is a long historical precedent based on "epistemological, philosophical, and methodological grounds" (Popper, 1972, cited in Brent & Kraska, 2010, p. 415). Fortunately, there is a resolution.

While Brent and Kraska (2010), along with Creswell (1994, 2003), Nastasi and Hitchcock, (2016), Curry and Nunez-Smith (2015), and Plano Clark (2010), have been the most prominent recent proponents of mixed methods research, the use of mixed research methods dates back to at least 1959 (Campbell & Fiske, 1959). Various terms have been used to describe the approach, and occasionally researchers use combined research methods, but do not provide a specific term for the practice.

Creswell and Plano Clark define mixed methods research as

> a research design with philosophical assumptions as well as methods of inquiry. As a methodology, it involves philosophical assumptions that guide the direction of the collection and analysis of data and the mixture of qualitative and quantitative approaches in many phases in the research process. As a method it focuses on collecting, analyzing, and mixing both qualitative and quantitative data in a single study or series of studies.
>
> *(2007, p. 5)*

In short, a combined research approach includes the use of both qualitative and quantitative designs and methods in a single project to gather data or information. Curry and Nunez-Smith (2015, p. 4) accept the definition provided by Johnson, Onwuegbuzie, and Turner: "Mixed methods is the type of research in which a researcher or team of researchers combines elements of qualitative and quantitative research approaches (e.g., use of quantitative and qualitative viewpoints, data collection, analysis, inference techniques) for the broad purposes of depth of understanding and corroboration" (2007). Often this results in a stronger study. Kraska and Neuman add, "Valuing diversity can be seen as a form of triangulation, in which crime and justice phenomenon [*sic*] can be studied and viewed from different angles, allowing for a more holistic and rigorous answer" (2011, p. 269). These scholars predict that the utility of mixed methods is so great that it is destined to become the third major type of study (quantitative and qualitative being the first two types).

One major strength of this research practice is that many of the concerns related to the individual methods are overcome when each method is used in the same study; in fact, "mixing quantitative and qualitative methods draws on the strengths of each while minimizing their weaknesses" (Kraska & Neuman, 2011, p. 271). Some specific strengths are highlighted by Brent and Kraska: "Qualitative information such as words, pictures, and narratives can add meaning and depth to quantitative data [while] quantitative data have the ability of enhancing clarity and precision to collected words, pictures, and narratives" (2010, p. 419). At this point, it would be helpful to review Table 1.1 in Chapter 1 prior to studying mixed methods further.

Another benefit to mixed methods research is that the findings from one part of the study may guide or channel the rest of the study. Kraska and Cubellis (1997, pp. 607–629) provided an excellent illustration of this in their study of the increasing prevalence and role of police SWAT teams. They noted the following:

1. "The ethnography was invaluable for developing a knowledge survey instrument, based on insider information, ensuring a high response rate and the ability to document a host of important trends that only an insider would have known about."
2. "The survey data were invaluable for establishing hard data about the growth and normalization of SWAT teams in the United States."
3. "The follow-up interviews provided context and qualitative depth to some of the more surprising findings and controversial quantitative findings."

The relevance of this finding is contrasted by the growing law enforcement trend for the past quarter-century or so toward the use of community policing (CP) or problem-oriented policing (POP). It would logically seem that the parallel growth of SWAT teams would be antithetical to this trend:

> At first glance one might assume that a trend toward militarization must be in opposition to the community policing "revolution." In the real world of policing however, some police officers are interpreting the reformers' call to adopt a proactive stance . . . as requiring a more aggressive, indeed militaristic approach.
>
> *(Kraska & Cubellis, 1997, p. 624)*

Only the interviews and qualitative aspects of this mixed methods study allowed this revelation. The creators and early advocates of community policing would be shocked and dismayed to learn of this development (Trojanowicz & Bucqueroux, 1990). Theirs is an excellent example of the use not just of mixed methods but also of theory in practice and some of the unintended consequences of a policy, such as community policing.

Source: bibiphoto

There are major considerations that must be addressed in any mixed methods study. The first is a "timing effect," in other words, should the methods be used concurrently or sequentially? Next, a decision must be made to use one data set more than the other—will the study be primarily quantitative or qualitative? This has been termed a *weighing decision*, but it really focuses on which method receives more emphasis. Finally, exactly how will the two methods be combined?

Three means of conducing mixed methods studies are commonly employed. The first strategy is to use the qualitative data to explain the quantitative findings. The converse technique is to utilize quantitative data to show that the qualitative findings are not an isolated phenomenon. Finally, some mixed methods researchers use each method equally and in conjunction with one another.

The researcher must also consider whether the study should be mixed methods at the "design" level, when the study is first set up, or at the "data" level, where two separate studies (one qualitative and the other quantitative) might be combined in one. The stronger design would be the strategy in which the original study employed each method and accounted for the other. Under this model, measures would be congruent and presumably measure the same construct. Some examples might help clarify this.

ILLUSTRATIONS OF MIXED METHODS

As a hypothetical example of using mixed research methods using a real-world tragedy, say that a researcher decides to examine the Pulse Night Club shooting that occurred on Orange Avenue in Orlando, Florida, on June 12, 2016. The number of victims (quantitative) of the shooting, 49 killed and 53 wounded, is not difficult to determine because police and medical reports are available to provide the necessary information. The nature (qualitative) of the act, which includes the motivation for the mass shooting, cannot necessarily be determined from the official records, nor can the motivations of the criminal, much less the feelings of the crime victims, survivors, and family members, be ascertained from official reports, as first shown by Steve Berman (2016). Traditionally the mass media could be used to check government abuses, excesses, and crimes (e.g., Watergate). However, a recent trend is that much of the media has become a tool for the government to relay a particular message—which may or may not be true. Consider these words by Berman:

> "The false narrative emerging from the media seeks to make a few points, all of which are red herrings and straw men designed to take attention from the truth.
>
> - The shooter, Omar Mateen, was homophobic because he hated gays.
> - Mateen was unstable because he was mean and beat his wife
> - Mateen had too much unfettered access to guns
> - Mateen was not religiously motivated"
>
> *(Berman, 2016).*

As thinking mixed methods scholars, and as citizens of any country besieged by terrorism, it might be both prudent and methodically correct to follow Berman's admonishment that we either accept the media version or we critically make our own conclusion based on known facts. In the Pulse shooting, these "facts" were:

> Mateen had a clean record, worked as a security guard, kept himself in excellent physical condition, and trained for his jihad. This was not a crime of opportunity, or of passion. It was a planned operation. The "mentally ill" narrative offers no hard evidence at this point. He bought weapons because, despite the FBI having investigated him, nothing of concern was noted that would prevent him from doing so. This is a failure of the intelligence and law enforcement system, not our Second Amendment rights. . . . The simplest explanation is that Mateen was a radicalized Muslim, who moved easily with other radicalized Muslims, some of whom are probably living their lives in Orlando. Only now would the FBI be interviewing those people and find connections. The press is weaving a false narrative to fashion a complex explanation for a simple problem. . . . Political correctness, the inability of our president to accept the problem because of his beliefs about Islam being a religion of peace, and impossible restrictions placed on federal, state and local law enforcement have made this crime possible. http://www.foxnews.com/opinion/2016/06/13/orlando-mainstream-media-serves-up-false-narrative-about-terror-attack.html

According to one source, The terrorist killer, Omar Mateen, was yelling "Allah Akbar" during his rampage and professed allegiance to a fringe Radical Islamic group. However, presumably for political reasons, the Federal authorities tried to portray it as an isolated homophobic act against gays and lesbians. This false narrative was quickly dispelled when eyewitness accounts (including definitive cell phone recordings and Mateen's own statement) clearly showed an attack by a supporter of Radical Islam.

The more appropriate way to find out about the nature of the attack and the response to it (consider the first responders on the scene) would be to interview a number of people directly involved. By using both methods (official government records coupled with interviews of victims and the offender) in one study, a much deeper and more valuable understanding of unprovoked mass shootings is possible. The political aspects of the attack and misrepresentation of the event by the media would make reliance on official government records a weak research strategy. Can the media and government narratives be considered reliable sources for mixed methods researchers?

The more recent Las Vegas attack further strains the government's creditability (and the media have not critically investigated this shooting, either). This highlights the need for independent objective social science researchers to operate autonomously. It also underscores our belief in critical scholarship. While this research example is hypothetical, but based on an actual event, many real mixed methods studies do exist (generally, see Creswell & Plano Clark, 2007, and *Journal of Mixed Methods Research* in particular) that draw from multiple data sources.

Consider one example of a strong mixed methods research strategy from Communication Studies in Insert 7.2. The primary methodology employed was Social Network Analysis (SNA). Can this mixed methods strategy be also applied to the Pulse shooting? Could Pulse result in copycat attacks to unprotected soft targets?

Source: John Panella

INSERT 7.2

Werther Effect in School Shooter Events? Examining Potential Copycat Behavior.

D.R. Hughes, MS
D.J. Griffin, PhD
University of Alabama
Tuscaloosa, AL

M.J. Egnoto, PhD
Walter Reed Army Institute of Research
Washington DC

Abstract

If it bleeds, it leads—this is an unfortunate but real mentality in the industry of news media. Reporting practices have led to what is perceived as sensationalism of negative events. The Werther effect establishes the connection between publicized suicide events and a spike in incidents of suicide that follow (see Kim et al., 2013). Given the established behavior of the Werther effect, investigations should seek to understand what impact, if any, media publicizing has on copycat behavior of other life-ending incidents. Recently, active shooter events have become heavily publicized in the media. This begets a logical question: Are there copycat active shooters that seem to be motivated by media? This study served to explore the possible presence of copycat phenomena of contemporary active shooters through media sensationalism. Through the analysis of shooters' written manifestos available through public record we examined references made within their writings to previous active shooters. This relational data was input into social network analysis software (i.e., UCINET) to construct a network visualization. Google Trend analytics were also used to explore whether media portrayals might be driving interest in past active shooters—especially Columbine and Virginia Tech (VT). Findings support the notion of an *idolization effect* in the context of active shooters with the focus being on the large shootings of the past. The need for journalist ethics in active shooting contexts is discussed.

RQ1: Is there a copycat effect occurring between school shooters?

RQ2: Do journalistic or media practices potentially influence the perpetration of active shooter incidents?

Social Network Analysis

Social network analysis (SNA) is a method to establish and understand relations between individuals (or nodes) in a network of some type. Applications of SNA are almost limitless. Application in the communication discipline has been to examine bibliometric (citation) behaviors of authors in a networks; the hiring behavior of departments in the discipline have also

continued

Insert 7.2 *continued*

been examined (e.g., see Barnett, Danowski, Feeley, & Stalker, 2010). In applied mathematics, researchers are generally interested in how some item (e.g., information) might flow through some type of network, such as a banking database. Here we rely on SNA to see how interest of other shooters might reveal the focus on previous acts through the shooters' manifestos.

Overall, SNA is a robust tool for identifying associations between cases within a dataset to identify different patterns and structures in information. SNA is ideal for identifying key players in a variety of different types of social networks (Borgatti, 2006), making its application to understanding the potential for copycat active shooters an excellent choice. Unlike other tools that may only identify if some relation exists between media and copycat active shooters, SNA provides a tool that shows which actors have the most troubling media portrayals, giving a more targeted tool for creating best practices in preventing any Werther-like effects.

Centrality is a core concept in the use of SNA and it is easily understood. Centrality is best explained as how a node, or actor, is in the *thick of things*. That is, an individual in a network is central if they are connected to more others in the network, or if they can act as a gatekeeper for the flow of the network, or if they are connected to others who are also themselves highly connected. Examples are plentiful for illustrations about centrality and a great deal is published about SNA and centrality; readers interested in an in-depth discussion of these matters should visit other volumes (e.g., Wasserman & Faust, 1994). For our purposes we were interested in which shooters were referenced by the most other shooters—that is, who were the central shooters known and studied by others. For this reason we rely on degree centrality—which is simply a count of the number of ties an individual (node) has in a network.

Method

To answer the research questions posed, the first author analyzed manifestos and other written material by school shooters available publically. Specifically, the website shoolshooters.info (Langman, 2015) was a useful resource as it complied a great deal of information about school shootings in one location. The website contains information about past school shootings that are categorized by shooter. A list of shooters from the site was compiled into a spreadsheet and the shooters' names were then placed into a data matrix. This matrix contained the names of the shooters in the columns and all the same names were input across the row headings; this created a matrix that allowed any two shooters to be related in a cell in the matrix (referred to as a co-occurrence matrix). To examine the research questions the authors decided that it was theoretically meaningful to incorporate ten years of documentation about school shootings. That is, the earliest shooter in the matrix enacted his crime in 2005 and the most recent was of February 2015.

For each of the shooters researched documentation from the site schoolshooters.info was reviewed for any mention of another violent offender. The references of violent offender included: school shooters, mass murderers, terrorists, and serial killers. The inclusion of these allow for the relational map to reflect the interest and focus of the school shooter being studied. For example, many of the shooters referenced Adolf Hitler. Other mentions such as locations (high school, college), weapons (gun type, ammunition, or purchase location), music (genre and artist preference), clothing (brand, style, or purchase location), or date of planned attack were excluded (not used to document a relation) to prevent coincidental or unintentional references from being collected. If the writings of the shooter contained mention of another violent offender, a placeholder was used in the relational matrix to indicate the reference made to that past shooter. After reviewing available documentation for the time period selected for study the completed relational matrix was processed using UCINET social network analysis software (Borgatti, 2002). To explore the first research question the tool was used to conduct centrality scores and to construct a network visualization of the studied shooters. A line showing centrality was added to the visualization to help make reference for viewing the most central persons on the map; this highlights the most frequently referenced offenders. The relational matrix was also used to mathematically calculate quantitative centrality scores for each of the shooters. Specifically, we relied on degree centrality; this centrality is a count of the raw number of connections a node has within the network. Degree centrality allowed us to explore who were the most referenced school shooters within the network.

To explore the second research question, the events linked to the two shooting events with the highest centrality scores were analyzed using Google Trends. In this analysis, postings from news and media sites referencing Columbine and or Virginia Tech (VT) were visualized such that an occurrence of searches for these terms were shown in correlation to media stories about school shootings (that also referenced the two shooting events). Moreover, Google Trends allows users to see how web searches of terms varies across time—and in this case how these trends pattern themselves around media stories.

Results

RQ1: Is there a copycat effect occurring between school shooters?

In answering our first research question, we created a ranking of the most shooters based on centrality scores output by UCINET. In addition, a visualization of the shooter network was created with the software and can be seen in Figure 1. The centrality rankings and network visualization were used to examine if a Werther type effect might be occurring in the context of school shootings. The four most central nodes in the network were the two Columbine shooters (Eric Harris and Dylan Klebold), the VT shooter (Seung-Hui Cho), and Adolf Hitler. These four killers out-ranked all of the other criminals and were the centermost nodes. From these findings and from viewing the visualization it can be seen that a copycat effect that resembles the nature of a recent shooting influencing a shooter to enact their crime is likely not the nature of what is occurring amongst school shooters. Instead, it seems that these shooters put much thought and planning into their crimes—as seen by their references to the bigger crimes in the historical lens

continued

Insert 7.2 *continued*

of these types of killings. The majority of shooters within the network did not make reference of shootings occurring closer to the commission of their own crimes. Instead, they tended to cite Columbine and VT (two most central nodes) in their writings.

To further illustrate the point that most shooters were citing Columbine and VT we removed these nodes from the network using a function in UCINET that allows for the removal of any selected nodes from the network. This resulted in a complete collapse of the relational network wherein the shooters became sparsely connected and many small cliques formed in the network—central shooters are the core or backbone of the shooter network based on their references to one another in their legacy tokens.

It does appear that an *idolization phenomenon* is occurring amongst school shooters. That is, shooters are not enacting their crimes because of a previous/recent school shooter, but instead they are enacting copycat behaviors that are motivated by the *best* or *biggest* shooters from the past. Shooters planning their attacks seem to want to be similar to the well-known shootings such as Columbine or VT. Also of note is that the shooters write about Adolf Hitler and because of this he was also highly central in the network. We believe that school shooters may be experiencing the need to overcome a perceived injustice or settle a need for a perceived reparation towards others who they believe have wronged them—much like Hitler is known for doing in his speeches and writing (e.g., his book *Mein Kampf*).

RQ2: Do journalistic or media practices potentially influence the perpetration of active shooter incidents?

Our second research question focused on media and portrayals of shooters—whether this might be adding to the incidence of new shootings. The findings align closely with what we found about a potential idolization effect; that the media also continues to idolize the *big* active shooters in history. The results from the Google Trends revealed that mention of Columbine and VT are republished when similar shooting events occur, further perpetuating the legacy of past-idolized shooters. To continue to mention these events likely influences new Internet searches—shown in the spikes in the data trends. These responses to media (re)portrayals might instigate new shootings and continue their focus on the more well-known shootings—which likely ends up in their written manifestos.

Discussion

In asking if there is a copycat effect occurring with school shooters, there were many factors to consider. After running the network analysis and accessing the network centrality scores it is shown that there is likely not a Werther type effect or traditional copycat effect occurring with school shooters. Instead, our findings of the network analysis from shooter manifestos

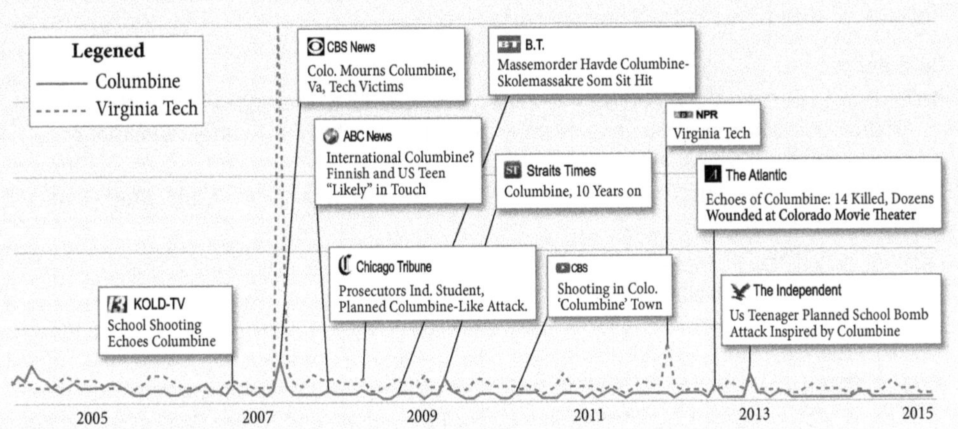

Figure 7.1 Quantatative and Qualatative Comparison

(referencing previous shooters) revealed that shooters were more concerned and focused (in their writings) with the well-known shooters and killers. By relying on the visualization and centrality rankings, we conclude that there is an *idolization phenomenon* occurring in our data. While this may be seen as a type of copycat behavior, it is unlike what is found with traditional Werther effects influenced by media (e.g., in the context of suicides). Coleman (2004) previously discussed this type of idolization effect amongst school shooters and stated that the fame given to school shooters is a social problem. This idolization effect is likely being driven by the fame from coverage provided by the media. Evidence for this is shown in the network map (Figure 7.1).

To answer our second research question we used Google Trends analytics to explore potential correlations in Internet searches surrounding media coverage of active shooting events. What we found aligns with our findings taken from the network visualization. For each event that spiked on the graph (searches of Columbine or VT) there was a recent school shooting that had occurred. At these times there were media reports that made mention or a direct comparison to a larger or more prominent shooting event, further giving fame to the big perpetuators of *classic* active shooting events. In reviewing the network visualization, it becomes clear that every shooter studied made mention of the Columbine school shooters in their written materials analyzed. Together, this relational data with the Google Trends analytics suggests that the media attention contribute to the notoriety of the Columbine attackers by creating an idolization effect. Holding that this is accurate, it is important that ethical journalistic practices be developed to aid in minimalizing the coverage of active shooter events at their occurrence, aftermaths, and into the future. There is a clear need for the development of ethical journalistic practices surrounding the media's coverage of active shooting events.

continued

Insert 7.2 *continued*

References

Barnett, G. A., Danowski, J. A., Feeley, T. H., & Stalker, J. (2010). Measuring quality in communication doctoral education using network analysis of faculty hiring patterns. *Journal of Communication, 60*, 388–411.

Borgatti, S. P. (2006). Identifying sets of key players in a social network. *Computer Mathematics Organization Theory, 12*, 21–34.

Coleman, L. (2004). *The copycat effect: How the media and popular culture trigger the mayhem in tomorrow's headlines.* New York: Simon and Schuster.

Kim, J. H., et al. (2013). The Werther effect of two celebrity suicides: An entertainer and a politician. *PLOS One, 8.*

Pirkis, J., Blood, R. W., Beautrais, A., Burgess, P., & Skehan, J. (2006). Media guidelines on the reporting of suicide. *Crisis: The Journal of Crisis Intervention and Suicide Prevention, 27*, 82.

Wasserman, S., & Galaskiewicz, J. (Eds.). (1994). *Advances in social network analysis: Research in the social and behavioral sciences* (Vol. 171). Chicago: Sage Publications.

This blending of strategies has been done successfully with many social science topics, as shown in both inserts. Mixed methods are applicable to any type of research (see chapter 1). To highlight the usefulness of mixed methods, we present an illustration for its use in program evaluation. The increasing popularity (in part due to economic pressures facing government at all levels) of program evaluation and some unique realities are reasons we use it for illustrative purposes; however, the lessons are applicable to all forms of mixed methods research. Program evaluations are important in criminal justice, when funds are limited, when political parties may disagree on resource allocation, and when decisions need to be made regarding the effectiveness (or lack thereof) of programs or policies. Mixed methods approaches can serve both the research and policy agendas.

MIXED METHODS FOR PROGRAM EVALUATION

By its very nature, program evaluation is inherently political. In fact, some argue that political aspects are the single most defining feature of program evaluation (Patton, 1987, cited in Greene, 1994). Greene (1987) argued, correctly, that politics and science are intertwined in all evaluation research, since

> social programs are manifest responses to priority individual and community needs and are themselves "the creatures of political decisions. They [are] proposed, defined, debated, enacted, and funded through political processes, and in implementation they remain subject to [political] pressures—both

> supportive and hostile" (Weiss, 1987, p. 47). So program evaluation is integrally intertwined with political decision making about societal priorities, resource allocation, and power.
>
> (p. 531)

So, by accepting the reality of the *politics* of program evaluation, how can researchers best maintain an *objective, neutral* position?

This is where mixed methods are beneficial. First, qualitative researchers explicitly acknowledge their biases up front (as do many quantitative researchers). In a mixed methods study, biases for or against methods are mitigated, since *multiple* methods are employed and the study does not rely solely on one approach. Second, both validity and reliability are enhanced by reliance on mixed methods (see chapter 4). Finally, nonscientific communities (such as media, politicians, and average individuals) can better understand illustrative case examples, quotes, and narratives from the qualitative aspects of the study. Economists and government "bean counters," alternatively, will appreciate the rigorous quantitative aspects and statistical analyses. The approach of offering a deep qualitative analysis of the true "experience" combined with the benefits of evaluating program outcomes statistically provides richer conclusions to be drawn and has the potential to allow more individuals to better evaluate the merits of the program.

Another excellent example of how criminal justice researchers describe their research problem and present the rationale for a mixed methods study is provided by Brezina, Tekin, and Topalli (2009). The following is the abstract that preceded their research article:

> Several researchers point to the anticipation of early death, or a sense of "futurelessness," as a contributing factor to youth crime. It is argued that young people who perceive a high probability of early death may have little reason to delay gratification for the promise of future benefits, as the future itself is discounted. Consequently, these young people tend to pursue high-risk behaviors associated with immediate rewards, which include crime and violence. Although existing studies lend support to these arguments and show a statistical relationship between anticipated early death and youth crime, this support remains tentative. Moreover, several questions remain regarding the interpretation of this relationship; the meanings that offenders attach to the prospect of early death; and the cognitive processes that link anticipated early death to youth crime. In this article, we address the limitations of previous studies using a Multimethods approach, which involves the analyses of national survey data and in-depth interviews with active street offenders.
>
> (p. 1091)

Is it possible that the Aurora, Colorado, shooter was motivated by what Brezina, Tekin, and Topalli found in their study? Could "futurelessness" have motivated the recently failed doctoral student? Many are curious why and how this college student could kill innocent people, and many will theorize to relevant causes. Hopefully, the importance of knowing how to conduct research methods is becoming clearer as answers are sought for aberrant, seemingly inexplicable behavior.

Recall that a theme in this book is that all research problems and studies should be guided by prior research and theorizing. It is one important reason for conducting the literature review. Mixed methods research requires this same basic step. Aside from a comprehensive literature review, what else is required for a mixed methods study?

STEPS TO MIXED METHODS RESEARCH

Mixed methods research is more complex, more difficult, yet ultimately more rewarding than monomethod research. Because of its very nature, expertise and procedures from both qualitative and quantitative paradigms must be utilized, doubling the work—or so it would seem. In reality, it does not require double the work, but we argue that researchers and funding agencies receive double the benefit! These are the steps to follow to conduct a scientifically valid, ethical, and useful mixed methods study. They are neither drastically different from nor more demanding than those employed in a monomethod study.

First, the researcher must become conversant with the research topic. All the scientific and even some popular culture literature (written and online) must be assessed. This will be used to help compile the literature review, identify topics to examine, and suggest the best data-collecting strategy.

Second, a research team must be compiled. It is rare to find one individual who is "expert" at all aspects of both quantitative and qualitative research (though some may exist). Even if one is an expert in each field, more "bodies" divide the labor, broaden the lenses, and strengthen the study. A team is also useful for performing mundane tasks, such as the responsibility of double data entry to be divided among researchers. We advocate research teams having different fields and areas of expertise. Having a quantitatively trained psychologist work with an anthropologist trained in ethnography is better than having two criminologists with identical skill sets. For example, one of the authors of this text just completed an international study on human trafficking in which a medical sociologist, lawyer, criminologist, and social worker all participated. All had varying skill sets, knew different theories, and had very different ideas about the problems (and solutions) related to human trafficking.

Once the literature is surveyed and the research team created, a research design or study strategy must be laid out. The most rigorous, tightly defined study design is preferable, yet always be aware that later changes will occur; thus, fluidity is important. Decide if it is best to use existing survey instruments or to create new ones, or use a combination. Existing questionnaires and interviews have the benefit of prior statistical validation. They also allow longitudinal comparisons and comparison with earlier studies in different locations. However, a new instrument may be needed if none of the existing ones measure the variables being examined. If participant observation is one method employed, this must be explained and justified. For example, how many hours will be spent in the research setting? Will the researcher make his or her presence known? Next, a sampling strategy or identification of the population to study must be made. The next step is to acquire support letters (e.g., get a letter from the county sheriff stating he or she will allow department staff to participate in the study).

Next seek IRB approval. A tightly designed study will also gain IRB approval more easily. Our recent experience has been that the IRB process is the most lengthy and difficult step of the entire research process (others have echoed this observation). It is even harder for a mixed methods study that uses qualitative components. The study design should include specific measures, types of instruments, sampling strategies, ethical protection of subjects, and anticipated analytical strategies.

Finally, the data collection can begin. This is the real core of the study. Once data are collected, they must be cleaned, analyzed, and interpreted, just as with any other study. The difference is, of course, that data will be of multiple types. By mixing the data, the researcher gets more accurate results. Creswell and Plano Clark argue that

> there are three ways in which mixing occurs: merging or converging the two datasets by actually bringing them together, connecting the two datasets by having one build on the other, or embedding one dataset within the other so that one type of data provides a supportive role for the other dataset.
>
> *(2007, p. 7)*

During analysis, hopefully one type of finding can be used to explain the other. For example, Moncrief (2012) found that African American correctional officers respected the job more, but inmates less, than did a comparable sample of Caucasian officers. Focus groups and interviews revealed the reason for this counterintuitive and wholly unanticipated finding.

This step-by-step guide to mixed methods research is obviously very much abbreviated. Creswell and Plano Clark (2007) devoted an entire textbook to describing the steps used in mixed methods research. The basic steps outlined here are similar to those for any other study. The differences are subtle, yet important. These minor differences are what lead to criticism of mixed methods, as shown next.

CRITICAL SUMMARY OF THE MIXED METHODS APPROACH

There are some problems with mixed methods research. Most of these criticisms focus not on the method itself, but on the researcher's skill, training, philosophy, and aptitude. However, there are arguments that, because of the nature of a quantitative method versus a qualitative method, the two are incompatible. Be aware that many researchers do not accept that the two methods can be combined:

> Both sets of purists [qualitative and quantitative] view their paradigms as the ideal for research, and, implicitly if not explicitly, they advocate the incompatibility thesis (Howe, 1988), which posits that qualitative and quantitative research paradigms, including their associated methods, cannot and should not be mixed.
>
> *(Johnson & Onwuegbuzie, 2004, p. 14)*

Methodological "purists" simply do not see a combination, or merging, of methods as being possible. For instance, some qualitative researchers adamantly reject the precepts of positivists, which form the foundations of all quantitative research. Brent and Kraska summarized this argument: "Proponents of this thesis often point to the contrasting notions of reality, truth, and good evidence that formulate each paradigm's methodological toolbox that renders them contradictory" (2010, p. 416).

A related problem is that many researchers are not equally and sufficiently trained in both quantitative and qualitative research skills. This often occurs because many research texts, courses, and even academic programs favor one method over the other. A course taught by a pure quantitative researcher is not likely to promote the merit of (or even teach) qualitative skills, and vice versa. A pure qualitative researcher will not likely endorse quantitative approaches either. Not only are the skill sets required diverse, but also sometimes they are even contradictory, as the earlier quotation suggests. Many adhere to the logic that in order to effectively implement one method, the other method must be abandoned because the principles are diametrically opposed.

By contrast, mixed methods advocates do not promote one method (quantitative or qualitative) over the other. Rather, they highlight the strengths of each:

> The ultimate goal of examining the mixed methods approach is to change the status quo. In our view this movement is essential for redirecting our field's pedagogical compass toward inclusion and compatibility. Debating quantitative versus qualitative ultimately implies that one is superior while the other is misguided. A more conducive avenue would be to examine differences for purpose of comparison and to illuminate their compatible and mutually reinforcing qualities. This approach harbors better potential to legitimize and clarify both valued traditions.
> *(Brent & Kraska, 2010, p. 427)*

Mixed methods, in summary, utilize the strengths of each method, allowing the weakness of each to be counteracted. If creativity is not stifled, perhaps new approaches will continue to evolve and create new ways to address social issues and contribute to science. The use of mixed methods is in fact growing, and scholars have even devoted a journal—the *Journal of Mixed Methods Research*—to exploring best strategies and highlighting the best mixed methods research.

SUMMARY

This chapter provides an explanation for the rapidly evolving and increasing use of mixed methods research. This research strategy offers many of the benefits of both quantitative and qualitative studies. It also reduces many of the threats to validity and reliability; however, some researchers object to it on philosophical grounds, and others lack adequate training in both methods. As always, it should be the research question that ultimately dictates the methodology selected. If mixed methods are chosen, then a single researcher needs to be cross-trained, or better yet, interdisciplinary research teams, with multiple researchers, should be employed.

KEY TERMS

Formal or structured interview
Interview
Mixed methods research
Qualitative research
Quantitative research
Semiformal or semistructured interview
Unstructured or informal interview

CRITICAL THINKING EXERCISES

1. Write one paragraph describing what qualitative research means, another paragraph describing a quantitative approach, and then another describing what mixed methods are.
2. Why would some researchers be opposed to combining qualitative and quantitative research into one study?
3. Why would some researchers be in support of the mixed methods approach?
4. Are there some research projects and situations that would not be suited for mixed methods? Provide an example.
5. What does fluid research mean, and what are the positive and negative aspects associated with it?
6. Create a research question and design that might employ a combined approach of qualitative and quantitative research in the same study.
7. How can you reconcile the need for fluid research with the rigorous, nonflexible strategies required by IRBs?
8. Why is evaluation research a good venue for using mixed methods?
9. Can the government and media be used as reliable data sources?

CHAPTER 8

Sampling Strategies

CHAPTER OBJECTIVES

After reading this chapter students should:

- Be able to identify the benefits of selecting a sample of the population as opposed to studying the entire population.
- Be able to distinguish the difference between probability and nonprobability sampling.
- Be able to specify what it means to *generalize* to the population.
- Be able to appreciate that perfect probability samples are probably nonexistent.
- State the techniques necessary to draw a probability sample.
- Judge if samples are representative.
- Identify the different types of probability sampling.
- Identify the different types of nonprobability sampling.
- Know the strengths and weaknesses of various sampling strategies.

Sabrina Newsome (1993) was preparing to write her master's thesis at Michigan State University on the goth subculture. She was particularly interested in the dark or supposedly satanic aspect to this youth subculture. She was competent with statistical analyses, writing, assessment, and reviewing prior literature. No data set existed for her to analyze, however, and there were presumably few goth devotees in the towns of East Lansing and Lansing, Michigan. How could she collect her data? This chapter explains how she did it. The key is the identification of respondents.

The prior chapters have often made reference to *respondents or participants*, whether in qualitative or quantitative designs, as those subjects who participate in research studies. This chapter examines how they are selected or chosen. The methods for selecting participants are important for a variety of reasons, but they often center on the ability to make generalizations to the larger population (or not) and determine what statistical procedures can be applied. Typically, sampling strategies are discussed in conjunction with quantitative studies; however, many of the techniques presented are equally useful for qualitative research. Because the type of sample selected is contingent upon the research design and, more important, the research *question*, the various designs have been covered first in this book prior to a discussion on sampling.

Sampling is the term that refers to "who or what and what method" is chosen as the focus of the study. Sampling often occurs via one of two ways: (1) by trying to be "mathematical" in the way the sample is chosen so that advanced statistics can be utilized and inferences can be made to larger populations, or (2) by being less focused on representation of larger populations (and widespread generalizations of findings) but more committed to studying targeted or selected groups. Each method has strengths and weaknesses.

Sampling: A strategy or set of strategies that permit the researcher to select a portion of the total population to be studied, as opposed to studying the entire group.

Sampling is the means by which a researcher chooses a subgroup of the overall study population to examine. There are many obvious benefits to studying a sample as opposed to studying the entire population. The most frequent reasons for using a sample are economy of time and resources, and ability to utilize specific statistical procedures. It is much easier and less expensive to interview a portion of the group instead of the entire group. If a scientifically valid sample is selected, following standardized and tested procedures, then the researcher can be confident that the sample is probably representative of the study population. In other words, if properly selected, a sample can be generalized to the total population, and there is no need to have to study every person in that specific population of interest. This means, however, that a probability sample must be conducted, which is discussed in more detail later in the chapter.

In probability sampling, an objective is to select a sample from the population that is as similar as possible to that overall group. The characteristics of the total population and the sample need to match in terms of age, gender, socioeconomic status, race/ethnicity, and so forth. These are often referred to as *demographics*. Sometimes the sample will need to be compatible in areas in addition to standard demographics, such as when a researcher wants to study female legislatures with more than 20 years of experience. In this case, 20 years of elected political experience, in addition to gender, would serve as the defining variables of interest. Rather than including *every* female elected official in the nation with more than 20 years of experience in the study, a *representative* sample could be drawn. Note that in this, however, it is likely that oversampling will have to occur, as there are not a lot of females with over 20 years of elected political experience.

The astute reader will note that the word *probably* appeared within the description of the characteristics of a sample. This is because rarely is a selected sample perfectly reflective of, or exactly like, the larger population. There normally are differences between the sample selected and the study population; these differences are called **sampling error.** All samples will contain some error. All the strategies presented here are designed to mitigate or minimize the inherent inaccuracy of sampling. In general, the better the sampling strategy selected by the researcher, the less sampling error there will be. Circumstances, resources, time, or other "real-world" events often influence what sampling strategy the researcher utilizes, however. Sometimes researchers *purposively* target specific populations and worry less about the sample being able to generalize to the total population (and more about being sure to focus on the intended group). For example, a researcher may have access to a specific group of "at-risk teens involved with goth subculture" and gather data specific to those teens' personal experience. The researcher does not intend to infer that the data represent *all* at-risk teens; the study findings are only specific to the people selected for study.

Sampling error: Occurs when the chosen sample does not exactly represent the total population. It is the amount of difference between the sample selected and the actual population.

Researchers must be careful in the sample selection process, especially when making references to larger populations. It is important that a study is reflective of the actual unit of analysis. For example, if the sample is drawn at the individual level, references and conclusions are limited to that level of analysis. To do otherwise would result in what is known as an **ecological fallacy.** If, for example, a researcher is interested in voting patterns across countries and uses data from individuals at XYZ University, it would be erroneous to infer that the data set at the individual level informs knowledge about geographic variations in voting practices.

Ecological fallacy: Making a judgment or assertion about an individual (specific person) based on group data or group-level characteristics (e.g., all professors must be smart).

Secondary data analysis is a common approach to securing data. Some researchers may purposively target existing *data sets* or existing programs because they have characteristics deemed important by the researchers. ISRID (International Search and Rescue Incident Data) is a large set of data collected to assist with search probability theory and missing-persons searches. Several subcategories of missing persons exist in the data set so probability theory can be understood based on certain characteristics, such as hunters, hikers, berry pickers, despondent, elderly, child, teen, those with disability, and so forth. The data set already exists, so there is no data collection needed on the part of the researcher that wishes to utilize the existing data. The researcher will simply access the data that fulfills his or her specific research interest.

Another example is the Child and Young Adult Supplement of the National Longitudinal Study of Youth (NLSY79) that was used by Carter Hay and Walter

Forrest because "the study was designed to oversample Blacks, Hispanics, and economically disadvantaged non-Hispanic whites, who were expected to be at greater risk for experiencing problems in the transition from adolescence to adulthood" (2008, p. 1048). Because having minority group status means that their numbers are smaller, resulting in not having an equal chance of being selected for inclusion in a study (via random selection), then *oversampling* is needed to ensure representation. This was also referenced in the earlier example of studying females with over 20 years of legislative experience. Because of the minority status of this population, oversampling of elected officials in the United States will likely have to occur until a satisfactory quota of the sample "females with over 20 years of experience" is collected.

The list from which characteristics of the larger population are denoted is called the *sampling frame*. Commonly, the sample is selected based on variables that exist in the population (which the sampling frame will reveal). For example, one may wish to study college seniors who live off campus. The registrar would have a *list* of active students who could be categorized according to class rank, and the office of student housing should be able to identify residency. Noting the characteristics of interest and selecting samples from the larger population based on these identifiers (housing and class standing) is what is referred to as the sampling. The sampling frame would be the entire student population. A researcher may wish to study emergency management directors in the United States; a list of all those persons who hold that status would need to be gathered first if the researcher wants the findings to be able to generalize back to the entire population of American Emergency Managers. If a sample of those emergency managers is drawn everyone must have equal chance of being selected for the study. If a study wants to focus on just emergency managers in urban areas, or in the south, or in rural areas, or in small-populated jurisdictions, then the sampling frame would be further refined. Plan early in the research process about decisions to be able generalize back to the entire population of study. Recognize that the sample selection will determine what can be inferred about the research findings and what statistical procedures can be utilized later.

Nonprobability sampling: Does not involve processes of random selection when selecting the sample; often used in qualitative studies, or when a random sample is not possible or desired.

In summary, a variety of sampling strategies can be used to help accomplish the goals of the researcher. First, the researcher needs to determine whether the sample will be a **probability sample** or a **nonprobability sample** (discussed next). In probability sampling, the research draws samples with some degree of mathematical certainty of representativeness; in nonprobability sampling, mathematical certainty is not the main objective.

PROBABILITY OR NONPROBABILITY SAMPLES?

The choice of whether the sample is a probability or nonprobability sample will have considerable impact on every stage of the research. As mentioned, if a nonprobability sampling strategy is selected, the results are not "likely" generalizable to the larger population. Furthermore, only the more basic descriptive statistics can be used in the analytical phase of the research. The word *likely* is used because there are some techniques that can be employed with a nonprobability sample that allow *some* level of representation to the larger population; these methods are discussed later.

The selection of a **probability sampling** strategy helps the researcher be able to make inferences to the larger population, as well as to use the more powerful, or robust, inferential statistics (this difference is explained in the next chapter). For this reason, probability sampling is generally preferred for quantitative research, though a qualitative researcher can also use these strategies. A qualitative researcher may be more likely to rely on nonprobability samples, since typically inferential statistics are not the primary analytical strategy anyway, and since the topics studied and subjects often do not lend themselves to pure randomization in the sample selection process. Sometimes, researchers will also employ nonprobability sampling, especially when they have been charged to evaluate a specific program or agency or when a complete listing of the total population is not available (but it is more often used in studies of things like prostitution, where no "list" exists at all). As mentioned several times, the subject matter under consideration, the research topic, and the goals of the research project should dictate which sampling strategy is the most appropriate. It is important to realize, however, that often extraneous factors will influence the sampling decision including, perhaps, access, training, time, resources, and even politics.

Probability sampling: Utilizes random selection of the population to help ensure equal chance of representation in the sample.

Here is a way to conceptualize the difference between probability and nonprobability sampling. If a researcher wants to study a *specific* population, perhaps one that is *convenient*, a nonprobability sample may be drawn. With nonprobability sampling there is less concern over representation or generalizability and more focus on simply studying a *targeted* group. While there are some techniques that can be used to enhance the representativeness of nonprobability samples, the primary design is specific to one population, such as a researcher being asked to evaluate job satisfaction at a specific location or to evaluate a specific social service program at a specific city. Very often programs or agency evaluations are based on nonprobability sampling. Examples of this type of research design include purposive sample, quota sample, snowball sample, and convenience sample.

If one wants to be able to make inferences to the larger population from which the sample is drawn, all respondents need to have an *equal* chance of selection and be representative of the entire study population. In other words, the sample participants have to be chosen by random selection and be reflective of the *overall target* group. If a researcher wants to have a study representing study habits of all college students in the United States, he or she could not just study students at one university. A sample of students from every university would need to be used. Of course the sampling frame could be reduced to be reflective of certain-size universities, or certain geographic locations such as midsize regional public universities in the south. The methods of probability sampling and examples of research designs include simple random sample, stratified random sample, cluster sampling (area probability sampling), and systematic sampling, which can be probability or nonprobability in design. Let us first elaborate on probability sampling.

Probability Sampling Strategies

Randomization: A process to allow "participants" equal chance of representation from the total population to be included in the sample; the sampling process has very specific requirements.

The defining feature of a probability sample is the use of randomization. In this context, **randomization** means that each and every element (person, artifact, document, case, record, etc.) in the population has an *equal* and fair chance of being selected for inclusion in the sample. For the random sample to be scientifically valid, it can only be chosen through the process of randomization. It should be restated that while great attempts and mathematical procedures may be utilized, errors can always occur, and *unrepresentative* samples can result even in probability sampling. This is what *sampling error* means, but true randomization helps reduce sampling error. Four steps are required to select a random sample.

Steps to Randomization. Most researchers rely on computer software to generate a random sample selection. If the population to be studied is large, such as every person in the United States, then a computer program is the only feasible means of selecting a random sample. (For smaller populations, like the project students may be conducting in a research methods course, other options are available for selecting participants.) It is important to note, however, that some purists (traditionalists) argue that the computer is designed on a binary system, and so true randomization does not really occur in any computer-generated random sample. While there are some merits to this argument, it is doubtful that the slight error that such software might introduce would have more than a negligible impact. Even with the slight chance of introducing error via the computer-generated random samples, this method is better than the alternative methods and is best for very large samples.

All methods are limited to the "master list," which, if it is not a complete listing of the total survey population, will affect sampling errors. The four steps are relatively simple, but each must be undertaken to select a representative sample.

The first step is that every element in the population has to be assigned a number. For instance, if the research methods class comprised the study population and there are 123 students in the course, then the researcher would assign each student a number from 1 to 123. Often in government agencies, employees will already have numbers assigned to them. For example, fire fighters have badge numbers. The researcher can use sometimes these numbers, but usually it is better to assign numbers. The possibility has to be eliminated that the way numbers are assigned does not favor or exclude the possibility of random selection, so it is best to simply assign numbers and then use a random start, and pattern, for the selection of the sample.

After each member of the population is assigned a number, the researcher will utilize a **table of random numbers.** The researcher arbitrarily selects (e.g., by throwing a dart, or closing their eyes and pointing to a spot on the table) a starting point. It is important that this point be arbitrarily chosen in case a later study uses the same population. If the starting point were the same in the subsequent study, then the resulting sample, or group chosen to study, would be identical to the first sample selected. Today, computer programs are designed to generate simple random samples. The researcher would just have to have a master list to input into the program.

Table of random numbers: A table or chart used to select random samples. Today online random number generators are available to promote randomization in the selection process.

If the researcher does not use a computer-generated random sample, and chooses to select the sample manually, the third step will be to select numbers from the chart in a systematic way, either horizontal or vertical. A member of the study population whose number is selected becomes part of the sample. This process will continue until a predetermined number of participants, or a percentage of the total population, is selected. If the class numbered 123 people and the researcher wanted a sample of 20%, then 25 students would be chosen. If the researcher suspects the study may have a validity threat due to mortality (respondents' dropout), then he or she might oversample, or increase the size of the initial study sample, to compensate for respondents who do not remain in the study (e.g., "lost," unaccounted for, refused to participate, or deceased). It is important to acknowledge here that sample size can be key in what statistics can be generated, so this is also an important consideration. This is an area where qualitative and quantitative studies can vary greatly. A qualitative study may have few elements in the sample (smaller sample size), whereas quantitative studies typically have larger sample sizes. While there is no set number in regard to the number of participants or elements in a quantitative study, it i important to remember that the effect of sample size on statistics is an important consideration.

Fortunately, technology has greatly simplified the random selection of samples. For example, to randomly select 100 cases, a researcher can use a random number generator. Because the numbers are presented at random, the researcher will simply move down or across the list. Table 8.1 is generated from http://stattrek.com/Tables/Random.aspx, which is one of the better websites devoted to creating tables of random numbers for various purposes.

Again, the use of a simple random sample is dependent on having a valid list of the entire population. Everyone, or every item, depending on the study, must be represented on this list. Sometimes more than one list may be required. Shaun Gabbidon was interested in knowing how American criminal justice and criminology department heads and chairpersons viewed their jobs. To comprehensively cover each group, "the author randomly selected 145 universities from the 1999–2000 Academy of Criminal Justice Sciences (ACJS) membership directory and the 2001 American Society of Criminology (ASC) annual meeting directory" (Gabbidon, 2005, p. 7). By utilizing the membership rolls of the two largest American criminal justice and criminology organizations, he was able to draw a random sample from the most accurate sampling frame available for all department heads of criminal justice/criminology programs. Had Gabbidon used only one list, he would have had incomplete information about the total sample. Even with this approach, we can see how there is always a

TABLE 8.1 *100 Random Numbers**

67505	60028	82459	15166	43601	84854	61096	79254	24779
14762	71373	74982	37597	76309	86731	02349	82054	42938
60287	61355	58151	67764	12366	25443	39329	97672	22643
21170	52146	59219	64559	48537	96603	25848	11557	80986
46142	50674	90195	45074	53878	80581	73914	40801	66696
15571	15830	68168	84595	08757	62828	00617	60691	07026
41465	91263	41870	63491	51742	86990	54687	98481	67100
87799	99144	91667	14098	46806	75241	89936	92735	10894
56419	46401	03012	06621	69236	81390	18371	33988	13694
74577	65368	66437	63232	72845	44006	57082	70968	02753
54283	52810	83786	64300	69641	53619	01685	57487	16639
12625								

* This table of 100 random numbers was produced according to the following specifications: Numbers were randomly selected from within the range of 0 to 99999. Duplicate numbers were allowed.

possibility of sampling error because there may be department heads in the criminal justice field that were not currently on *either* list and therefore did not have an equal chance to participate in the study. Being on the membership roster is dependent upon paying annual membership dues. Those chairs who are not paying yearly dues for either professional organization may be more likely to be unhappy or dissatisfied chairs, so omission of this group could result in sampling bias. We must acknowledge such shortcomings and proceed with the best method possible, which in this case was the combined list from the ASC and ACJS. Researchers are responsible for describing any potential weaknesses in their study, and the possibility of sampling error is a good example. Imagine that a researcher is trying to make generalizations about people involved in human trafficking. Since it is unknown who is involved in the act of using humans as a commodity (such as in farm, factory, household, or sex capacities) then a large percentage of error could exist. This is because the researcher might try to form conclusions from their data that suggest the findings are reflective of the total population of people who traffic in humans. There is no list of these people. Consequently, a simple random sample is not likely the sampling technique of choice in this situation. It is important for researchers to choose the best research design and sampling technique, to be honest about strengths and weaknesses in the study, and to use sound sampling techniques. Presented next are some of the more common sampling strategies, and the benefits and weaknesses of using each.

Simple random sample is a sample from the population in which every member in the total population has an equal chance of being selected for participation. A simple random sample is the first type of probability sample and is a basic, first component of each of the more complicated, subsequent random probability samples. The simple random sample, with everyone in the research population having equal chance of selection, is a good sampling strategy and meets all the necessary requirements to be considered a true probability sample. It is important to remember however, that for everyone to have an equal chance of being randomly selected for the sample, those persons, units, or things must be known to the researcher. If political scientists wanted to gather data on the sleep patterns, stress levels, education levels, religious affiliations, and so forth of every gubernatorial candidate in the United States in the last 20 years, that list could be compiled (unlike knowing every criminal involved in human trafficking). The two main conditions of this Simple Random Sample are to have a master list of the population of study and for everyone in that population to have an equal chance to be a participant in the sample. Random selection must occur, and there are various methods can be employed to help accomplish it.

Simple random sample: The most basic probability sample; ensures that everyone in the study population has an equal chance of selection.

A real-world example highlights problems with representative samples and sampling error. If sociological research was being conducted the day after a major disaster such as Hurricane Katrina, and the focus was on including everyone whose person or property was affected by the storm, researchers would not likely have access to all victims. Some had likely perished, relocated to safer areas, or were otherwise missing. If the researcher interviewed only those victims who were present in the center of New Orleans one day after the disaster, there could be a lot of selection bias. In this case, a sociologist would note that stratification issues are prevalent and should consider that the upper class is more likely to have left after initial warnings of pending disaster. Because of some residents having higher status in the strata, they were more likely to have had the capital (social, political, cultural, and economic) to secure alternative accommodations and means of revenue, and made decisions to leave the area altogether. For those who had poor access to communication, finances, education, and even transportation, they are more likely to be the residents who did not leave the area prior to the storm. Therefore, drawing a sample of those present initially after the disaster would not result in a probability sample with everyone in the population having equal chance to be randomly selected for the study. The study would not be generalizable to the entire population of victims of Hurricane Katrina and would have a high level of selection bias and sampling error. Even if the research secured a master list of all homeowners and renters in the affected area, and conducted the study once those individuals were able to be "tracked down," some level of sampling error would exist, as homeless victims would not likely have been on an official listing of homeowners/renters—yet they were also victims of the disaster. Obtaining this list of property owners/renters would be a better method than what was described earlier, if the researcher wanted to *attempt* to have a probability sample. Yet there are still weaknesses with the study that the researcher should address and report in his or her findings. Once the master list of residents was obtained and all homeowners/renters identified, the process of random selection of participants would need to begin.

Using a table of random numbers is one method to assist in this type of sampling design. Another increasingly used variation of the simple random sample is a procedure called ***random digit dialing.***

Random digit dialing: A process of selecting participants for telephone surveys by generating the numbers at random. Computers can be used to do this.

Organizations and researchers who conduct telephone surveys use random digit dialing. The researcher will select numbers within a phone prefix area, and a computer will randomly select numbers to be dialed in order to choose respondents to be surveyed. With random digit dialing, even unlisted numbers are included in the sample, so it is a preferred method over using a master list such as a phone book. Again, however, it is not a *perfect* method because the strategy cannot include people who lack a telephone (which causes sampling error). It also has other potential problems, such as cases being eliminated because of answering machines, busy signals, disconnected numbers, business and fax lines, and of course nonanswered calls (Mears, Hay, Gertz, & Mancini, 2007, p. 235). In this time of unlisted cell phone data, and now that this is many people's primary means of communication, this also sets up issues to resolve. Of course, the astute reader should also question if random digit dialing would be an appropriate process of selecting a sample from the Katrina example described earlier. Of course it would not—as cell phone towers and phone lines were down for an extended period of time, and it is likely that some areas secured service well before others (and yes, probably based on stratification and political factors) which would continue to influence sampling bias and error.

Software and technology are making telephone- and computer-accessed surveys easier and more accurate. Mears et al. note in their study, "Interviewing was conducted using the Ci3 Sawtooth computer-assisted telephone interviewing (CATI) software . . . to insure accuracy in recording data collected" (2007, p. 235). As technology continues to increase, so will the options for generating research.

Stratified Random Sample. Despite the value of a simple random sample, it is not the best approach for all research projects. Say, for example, a researcher wants to follow the logic of William Sheldon about variations in body types and hypothesizes that body type is correlated to criminal behavior (albeit not much support exists for such logic). Nevertheless, the researcher suspects that adult males under 5 feet 2 inches are more likely to be involved in crimes involving fraud. If randomly surveying the population, how would the researcher be sure that all heights would be represented in the sample, especially the shorter males? Oversampling would need to occur. The males would need to be divided by height categories, and sufficient numbers from each category would need to be randomly selected. Here is another example. If a researcher desires to compare student grade point averages based on the students' year in college (freshmen, sophomore, junior, or senior), the simple random sample *might* provide a balanced and equal number of students in the respective categories, but it is doubtful it would happen just by chance. To ensure that adequate numbers of students are represented in each category of interest, the method of choice is **stratified random sampling.** If the researcher hypothesizes that "year in college" has an impact on grades, the independent variable (X) is assumed to influence the dependent variable (Y): grades. To measure this presumed effect, grades for freshmen, sophomores, juniors, and seniors would need to be compared. A sufficient sample would have to be available in every category.

Stratified random sampling: Divides the population into specific strata or group characteristics and then draws a random sample from each category.

Thinking more about this study at the university level, four lists (or strata) of students would need to be compiled. One list includes names of all the freshmen, the second list represents all the sophomores, and so forth. Next, a simple random sample is taken from each individual list; each person in each stratum (or group) has an equal chance of being selected for participation in the study. Because the four groups are now randomly divided, a representative sample can be selected from each category. This ensures that there are as many freshmen in the sample as there are seniors; any other type of sampling technique would not likely ensure this.

Lange, Johnson, and Voas (2005) were interested in studying whether New Jersey state police used racial profiling to issue tickets. They conducted an informative and creative study by comparing the photographs taken at toll plazas with the citation data from the New Jersey police. According to Lange et al.:

> The data-collection structure first was stratified as a function of weekend versus weekday under the assumption that the demographics of drivers might differ according to day of week. Second, stratification occurred according to the geographic section of the turnpike. . . . Random selection of the exits with levels of stratification was accomplished through a random number generator in the SPSS package.
> *(2005, pp. 198–199)*

The researchers realized there may be some differences that needed to be taken into consideration and categories that needed to be represented through stratification. Therefore, they chose a stratified random sampling approach.

In the insert, Amber Perenzin describes another stratified random sample strategy. Her study examines the dissimilarities between institutional review boards (IRBs) among American universities.

INSERT 8.1
How Institutional Review Board (IRB) Standards Vary between Types of Universities

Amber Perenzin, MS
University of Central Florida
Orlando, Florida

Partially as a result of unethical biomedical studies, government regulations now control any federally funded research conducted in the United States involving human subjects, including research in the social sciences. Most universities and colleges have adopted the federal standards for conducting research and have modified them to fit their needs. A stratified random sample of 10% of the universities in the United States (N = 4,392) was used to examine how institutional review boards (IRBs) vary in terms of policy and structure (Perenzin, 2010). This essay describes how schools were stratified, the rationale, and the criteria.

Contemporary social science research has evolved over the years to ensure optimal protection of human subjects in research. The horrific biomedical experiments conducted on concentration camp internees during the Nazi regime highlighted the need for research oversight. Gruesome experiments were practiced by Nazi doctors, who forced prisoners to endure excruciating pain and caused irreversible psychological and physical damage (Oakes, 2002; Parvizi, Tarity, Conner, & Smith, 2007; Jacques & Wright, 2010). In the Tuskegee syphilis study in the United States, 399 African Americans who had been diagnosed with a curable disease were unknowingly denied treatment and suffered with syphilis for almost 40 years (McClure, Delorio, Schmidt, Chiodo, & Gorman, 2007). In light of these and other unethical experiments, the need for federal guidelines for biomedical research studies was certainly understandable (White, 2007). Strict standards for medical research protect human subjects from unethical studies to help assure that participants are not harmed in any way. It is the responsibility of an IRB to enforce the standards for conducting research and to provide oversight. Although these regulations were created for use with biomedical research, they have been increasingly applied to research in the social sciences as well, with mixed reviews.

Some problems are related to uniformity of standards. For example, although the need for informed consent is consistent across all IRBs, there are a number of ways in which IRBs vary. The procedures for evaluating research proposals are not standardized and can vary between institutions. Some institutions allow a researcher to have an IRB member critique a research proposal prior to the full board meeting. In some cases, a subcommittee will review the proposal, and then provide recommendations for the study. Some IRBs provide written critiques of research proposals, while others provide verbal critiques (Jones, White, Pool, & Dougherty, 1996; Parvizi et al., 2007). The number of proposals a committee reviews every year also varies. While some schools may review just a handful of studies over a given time, another school may review hundreds of research proposals in that same period.

The purpose of this study was to determine how IRBs vary between types of universities. I hypothesize that Ivy League schools will have higher ethical standards than tier 4 or unranked schools to protect their hefty endowments from litigation by research participants. Because larger universities are able to produce a larger quantity of research, it is postulated that larger universities will have more strict IRB standards, also to prevent their researchers from litigation. It would also be logical to predict that research-based universities will take IRB approval

continued

Insert 8.1 *continued*

more seriously and will have more regulations on human subject research. Data are collected on school location, type (public or private), and rank to determine if there are any relationships between IRB standards. Religious schools and schools identified as being research-intensive institutions will also be used to compare with the other categories. The specific criterion for sampling is described next.

Stratified random sample was used for this study to obtain a representative sample of all universities according to size, location, type (public or private), and rank. A sample of religious schools and research schools—identified by the Carnegie Foundation for the Advancement of Teaching—were also collected. The Carnegie Classifications and school rankings in *U.S. News & World Report* were used to identify the population of schools targeted for this study—the population consists of all four-year universities. The Carnegie Classification has been published six times since 1970 and "has been used in the study of higher education, both as a way to represent and control for institutional differences, and also in the design of research studies to ensure adequate representation of sampled institutions" (Carnegie Foundation for the Advancement of Teaching, 2005). *U.S. News & World Report* has been in existence since 1948 and has been ranking American colleges and universities annually since 1983 (http://www.usnews.com/usnews/usinfo/history.htm [accessed July 27, 2010]). These sources were chosen because they are reputable and reliable sources of data on colleges in the United States.

Random sampling was used to ensure that an unbiased sample was collected. Each university in the sampling frame was assigned a number using Microsoft Excel 2007. Using a table of random numbers, a portion of each sampling frame was selected for inclusion in the study. Systematic sampling was not used to select the universities because, in many cases, the lists of schools were arranged in alphabetical order. Although using systematic sampling would have been more convenient, it was determined that this method would create a biased sample (Maxfield & Babbie, 2008).

Stratified sampling was used to ensure a representative sample was obtained and to decrease the probable sampling error (Maxfield & Babbie, 2008). Schools were stratified by size, location, and rank. A sample was taken from each subgroup within these categories. In regard to location, the stratified sample ensured that universities from each section of the country were included in the sample. The use of stratified sampling was particularly important with the development of the sample of schools by rank. Because there are only eight Ivy League schools, there was only a 0.002% chance that an Ivy League school would have been randomly selected had a purely random sampling strategy been used. By stratifying the school rank, such as Ivy League, top ranked, unranked, and so on, a more representative sample was developed, allowing for the comparison of Ivy League schools to unranked schools.

Size

The sample pertaining to school size was created from the data in the Carnegie Classifications on size and residential character (Carnegie Foundation for the Advancement of Teaching, 2005). Only four-year institutions were included in this study. To eliminate the variable of residential character, the Carnegie Classifications were grouped strictly according to size. Schools identified as "Very small four-year, primarily non-residential" were grouped with "Very small four year, primarily residential" to create the size category of "Very Small," since they both represent enrollment of fewer than 1,000 students. Similarly, small nonresidential, residential, and highly residential schools were grouped into one category representing schools with enrollment between 1,000 and 2,999 students. The same was done for medium and large schools. These institutions were broken down into four categories, including Very Small (fewer than 1,000 students enrolled) (N = 432); Small (1,000–2,999 students) (N = 647); Medium (3,000–9,999 students) (N = 447); and Large (enrollment greater than 10,000 students) (N = 246). Ten percent of schools from each category were randomly selected to be included in the sample.

Location

The 2005 Carnegie Classifications were used to create the sample of schools by location. The country was divided into eight regions, which were labeled the Far West (AK, CA, HI, NV, OR, WA) (N = 598); the Rocky Mountains (CO, ID, MT, UT, WY) (N = 149); the Southwest (AZ, NM, OK, TX) (N = 378), the Southeast (AL, AR, FL, GA, KY, LA, MS, NC, SC, TN, VA, WV) (N = 1,059); the Plains (IA, KS, MN, MO, NE, ND, SD) (N = 443); the Great Lakes (IL, IN, MI, OH, WI) (N = 649); the Mid East (DE, DC, MD, NJ, NY, PA) (N = 726); and New England (CT, ME, MA, NH, RI, VT) (N = 268). Ten percent of the schools were randomly selected from each of the eight regions.

Type (Public/Private)

The Carnegie Classifications also divided schools into two types; private (N = 2,654) and public (N = 1,737). The private sample included schools categorized as private nonprofit and private for-profit. A random sample consisting of 10% of the schools from each of these categories was collected from the 2005 Carnegie data.

Rank

Lists of schools by rank were taken from the *U.S. News & World Report* National Universities Ranking from 2010. Rank was determined by using 15 indicators that assess the quality of academics offered at the university. Each indicator produced a score. The sum of the scores from

continued

Insert 8.1 *continued*

each indicator determined the rank of the school. This list enabled us to compile a list of Top Ranked, Tier 3, Tier 4, and unranked schools (http://colleges.usnews.rankingsandreviews.com/best-colleges/national-universities-rankings/ [accessed February 24, 2010]). Ten percent of the schools in each category were selected to be included in the study. The sample of Ivy League schools was compiled by randomly selecting 10% of the eight Ivy League schools listed on the Ivy League Universities website (http://www.go4ivy.com/ivy.asp [accessed February 24, 2010]).

Other Classifications

Religious schools (N = 314) and research schools (N = 199) will be compared with other types of schools in this study. Religious schools were taken from the "theological seminaries, Bible colleges, and other faith-related institutions" sample in the Carnegie Classifications. The Carnegie Classification system classifies schools as having "very high research activity" and "high research activity." These two groups were combined to get the research school sample. A 10% sample was taken from each of these categories as well.

Instrument

A 25-question instrument was developed to determine the level of thoroughness of each IRB. Standards listed in the Belmont Report, a document consisting of federal guidelines and ethical principles that all researchers are mandated to follow, were used to develop this measure. The measure was pretested with IRB procedures of two schools (Marymount University and Northeastern University). Additionally, content validity of the instrument was assessed by having an established researcher review the instrument questions. Additional questions were included in the instrument as a result of this pretest (NCPHSBBR, 1979; Regina, 2010; Robbers, 2010). In addition to demographic information, the instrument gathers information about each university's IRB standards. The questions address training requirements for IRB members, requirements for informed consent, vulnerable populations, and requirements for confidentiality. Procedures for reviewing student research are also a part of the instrument, along with questions pertaining to the use of on-site monitoring to ensure research procedures and processes are being followed properly.

References

Carnegie Foundation for the Advancement of Teaching. (2005). The Carnegie Classification of Institutions of Higher Education. http://classifications.carnegiefoundation.org/ (accessed March 15, 2010).

Jacques, S., & Wright, R. (2010). Right or wrong? Toward a theory of IRBs' (dis)approval of research. *Journal of Criminal Justice Education, 21*(1), 42–59.

Jones, J. S., White, L. J., Pool, L. C., & Dougherty, J. M. (1996). Structure and practice of institutional review boards in the United States. *Academic Emergency Medicine, 3*(8), 804–809.

Maxfield, M. G., & Babbie, E. (2008). *Research methods for criminal justice and criminology.* Belmont, CA: Thompson Wadsworth.

McClure, K. B., Delorio, N. M., Schmidt, T. A., Chiodo, G., & Gorman, P. (2007). A qualitative study of institutional review board members' experience reviewing research proposals using emergency exception from informed consent. *Journal of Medical Ethics, 33*, 289–293.

National Commission for the Protection of Human Subjects of Biomedical and Behavioral Research (NCPHSBBR). 1979. *The Belmont Report: Ethical principles and guidelines for the protection of human subjects of research.* Washington, DC: U.S. Government Printing Office.

Oakes, J. M. (2002). Risks and wrongs in social science research: An evaluator's guide to the IRB. *Evaluation Review, 26*(5), 443–479.

Parvizi, J., Tarity, D. T., Conner, K., & Smith, J. B. (2007). Institutional review board approval: Why it matters. *Journal of Bone and Joint Surgery, 26*, 418–426.

Perenzin, A. (2010, October). *Institutional review boards: Structural variations.* Paper presented at the annual meeting of the Southern Criminal Justice Association, Clearwater, Florida.

Regina, N. C. (2010). Policies and procedures for human research protections. Northeastern University research website. http://www.northeastern.edu/research/research_integrity/human_subjects/

Robbers, M. (2010). Institutional review board. Marymount University IRB website. http://marymount.edu/discover/irb/

White, R. F. (2007). Institutional review board mission creep: The common rule, social science and the nanny state. *Independent Review, 11*(4), 547–564.

Another probability sampling strategy that is especially good for large samples is the *cluster sample*. A cluster sample is useful for large populations located in a large geographic area, such as the citizens of a particular state. While cluster sampling is less common in criminology and criminal justice, it is very common when studying voting behavior or in research projects that involve comparing neighborhoods or zip code zones. Researchers from virtually every academic discipline can benefit from cluster sampling. A cluster is "a naturally occurring, mixed aggregate of elements of the population, with each element appearing in one and only one cluster" (Bachman & Schutt, 2011, p. 125). If a researcher desires to know what residents of Colorado think about marijuana legalization, he or she may divide the state into clusters (perhaps cities), or divide cities into blocks, and then randomly select which clusters to study. Each city may be given a number; then, using a table of random numbers, cities would be selected for inclusion based on random selection. This enables large populations to be broken down into clusters so that representative samples can still be managed. Cluster sampling is also known as *area probability sampling* and typically consists of sampling *groups* rather than individual persons or items. This is useful, for example, if a researcher wants to study the resiliency of a community to "bounce back" after a natural disaster or terrorist attack; communities and/or disasters, not the individual, would be the unit of study.

Another, more useful variation of a cluster sample is the *multistage cluster sample*, in which several *stages* of the cluster strategy are used. Donna Hale (Hale & Wyland, 1993) once submitted a research grant proposal to the Department of Justice to study female police officers. Her proposal included the use of a multistage cluster sample. The plan was to first list every police department in the United States based on size. Large departments would have more than 5,000 officers, medium-size departments would have between 501 and 4,999 officers, and small departments would have fewer than 500 officers. A random sample of 10% of the departments would be selected from each category (stratum). Hale decided that 10% was better than a specified number, since there are many more small departments than large ones, and using a percentage would provide a more accurate sample and better representation of the departments. Once the three lists were selected, each department would be contacted and asked to provide a list of all its female police officers. From the provided lists, another random sample would be drawn, and this final list would comprise the actual research subjects. The cluster sampling occurs in various stages, thus the label ***multistage stratified random sample.*** Alternatively, there is also a *stratified* sample that occurs in various stages as well.

Multistage stratified random sampling: Allows categories in the stratified sample to be further subdivided to ensure equal representation of subjects who otherwise might not be selected for participation.

Multistage Stratified Random Sample. A good illustration of a multistage stratified random sample is Kaufman's (2005) study of how the race and ethnicity disparities in violence are explained by macro-level variables. To accomplish this, Kaufman first had to locate a data set that contained all the variables she needed to consider, and she had to make sure the categories of interest had enough subjects reflected in them. As mentioned earlier, sometimes this requires oversampling of a targeted group. The data set Add Health database, which was collected by Udry in 1998,

> offers several advantages, including a large sample size, oversampling for many ethnic groups (well-educated Blacks, Cubans, Puerto Ricans) and a wide variety of measures at both the individual and the community level. . . . The data were collected using a multistage, stratified, cluster survey design.
>
> *(Kaufman, 2005, p. 231)*

The most important thing about a stratified sample is that it allows for representation of a suitable number of subjects in categories that might not otherwise have an equal chance of being selected if oversampling of the group did not occur. If it is a *random* stratified sample, even though oversampling occurs, everyone within the category still has an equal chance of being selected for participation.

Systematic Sample

A systematic sample can be either a probability or a nonprobability sampling strategy. Either way, systematic samples are very popular. **Systematic sampling** is when the researcher relies on a list and chooses every *n*th person. As a reminder, *n*th represents a random number, and every time that number repeats itself, it indicates selection for participation, for example, every *fifth* number. A large, very old Gothic state prison is located in Marquette, Michigan. The city council contracted with Linda Zupan to study the economic and social impact of the prison on city residents. She utilized the Marquette telephone directory and selected every 10th person to interview (by phone). She continued to count by 10 and make selections until the sample size was satisfactory. The respondents were then telephoned and asked to answer questions regarding the impact of the local state prison on the community. If the researcher uses a random way to start the selection of subjects and adheres to the systematic process throughout, then it could be classified as a probability sample. If randomization is not guaranteed, then it is better to conceptualize it as a nonprobability sample.

Systematic sampling: A method of selecting a sample from the population by using an arbitrary starting point and then following the specific pattern until a sufficient sample is drawn. For example, every *n*th subject is selected for participation.

Nonprobability Samples

As mentioned earlier, a nonprobability sample often occurs when the researcher's goal is to study a specific sample or when a complete list of the total population is not available. Remember, a random sample cannot be successfully drawn if the entire list of the target population is not available or accessible.

Quite often social science (e.g., public health or nursing) researchers are interested in behaviors that are illegal or deviant. In these cases, the researcher will not have a list of the study population from which to randomly select participants. For example, typically no list of all the prostitutes in a given city exists. Even where prostitution is legal and prostitutes are required to register, there will be "freelance" sex workers who do not register, pay taxes, and have disease screenings. There are many reasons a prostitute may not register. Other prostitutes may do so only occasionally, and prostitutes may move in and out of the area frequently; thus, even if a list did exist, it would be a difficult population to manage. If a researcher wants to study all the various types of prostitutes, then a random sample would not be possible. There are many sex workers who are not likely to be known to the researcher, and therefore not all prostitutes will have an *equal* chance of selection. In other situations, time and resources do not permit the researcher to conduct a probability sample; therefore, he or she will most likely rely on one of the nonprobability samples, which is discussed next.

Convenience sampling: Samples that are chosen simply because subjects are accessible to the researcher. Also called an *accidental sample* because the researcher studies whoever is readily available.

Convenience Sample. The simplest (most convenient) type of a nonprobability sample is to merely study the people a researcher has access to. A **convenience sample** is a preexisting, easily accessible group. Participants are not randomly selected but are simply chosen because of availability. A researcher may go to an area where there are a significant number of people. For example, a sociologist may want to research birth control practices in Third-World countries. He or she may visit a Third-World county health clinic and try to recruit volunteers to participate in the study. The researcher may simply ask anybody who comes along what his or her method of birth control is. This is not the best method of data collection and comes with selection bias, as perhaps only certain types of people in the Third World are at health clinics, so the research has to be mindful of such weakness with the sample selection process and in the reporting of data results.

Another very common application of this type of sample is when university professors utilize the students who happen to be enrolled in their class as a study population. This type of sample is also called an *availability sample* or an *accidental sample*. Again, the participants are selected because of easy access. Despite the relative widespread use of this sampling strategy, it is clearly the weakest of all possible sampling techniques and one that many researchers try to avoid. With that said, however, depending on the research project, it may even be the *best* strategy. Michael Reisig and Christina DeJong teach in a major PhD-granting criminal justice program. One of the issues that continually arise when making graduate admissions decisions is the predictive value of the Graduate Record Exam (GRE) and the student's grade point average (GPA) to predict success in graduate programs. A great research question is whether these measures actually predict a student's ability to do well with graduate studies. Because, in this case, the study is directly relevant to criminal justice students, these students would form the best sample, not to mention the records and the students are accessible to the researchers (see Reisig & DeJong, 2005). Another good example is an undergraduate research study by Lauran Catennacci, who relied on a large group of Facebook users to provide insight into the biases created among potential jurors by the media coverage of the Casey Anthony murder case. For studies of this nature, it is reasonable to assume that a large enough sample might naturally evolve that ends up (if simply by chance) to be representative of the people who would actually be selected to serve on a jury.

The obvious problem with this, however, is that if the only participants are internet users, the data are limited to only those types of people who share their opinion publicly on the internet. Is this reflective of all people? The study population is limited to people who use computers, who visit the Facebook website, and who might have some interest in the case or in crime in general. In other words, the outcome of the data is biased toward a particular type of individual (selection bias).

This raises another important issue regarding response rates. Response rates can be understood as the number of participants who actually participated in the study as opposed to the number that is needed or desired. The ultimate goal is to have high response rates, and the type of sampling can influence the likelihood of participation. For example, a small qualitative study where the researcher *personally*, face-to-face, asks for participation may yield a higher response rate than a computer-generated telephone marketing survey. Social networking sites such as Facebook may seem like a great way to obtain high response rates (and they might be in some cases), but remember that response rates are based on percentages and are calculated based on the total number who *could* participate.

Because of *response rate* issues (the number who actually participated in the study as opposed to the number desired) and *sampling bias* (not having everyone included in the sample that "needs" to be), this type of sampling strategy might not provide extremely useful, or scientific, information. The mass media, including many internet websites, often rely on this type of sampling strategy (and, by the way, may represent it as scientific fact). Companies promoting their products might do so as well. How often do the local news media interview someone, such as a neighbor of an arrested individual, and represent that person as a credible source of information? The respondent was really selected just because he or she was available, yet the general public may accept such "samples" as reflecting real research or scientific fact.

Quota Sample. The biggest problem with a convenience sample is that the researcher must be satisfied with anyone who happens to be selected. To overcome this flaw, the researcher may select a sample that is representative of (similar to) the population being studied. Alternatively, the researcher may need to oversample until the characteristics of interest are sufficient in the sample. A **quota sample** is designed to assure that the sample is representative of the study population, at least according to the variable used to select the sample by its proportion in the population. For example, if a police department consists of 25% Hispanic officers, then the researcher will select a sample that is also 25% Hispanic. This helps maintain representativeness. One further benefit to a quota sample is that the research subjects of interest (e.g., Hispanic law enforcement officers) may be oversampled.

Quota sampling: Sampling procedures in which an effort is made to keep selecting participants until a certain quota (representation of specific characteristics) is reached.

This sampling strategy is very similar to a randomized stratified sample but is less rigorous and is not randomly selected. Quota sampling reflects its name; respondents continue to be selected until the *quota* is reached. It is likely to require oversampling, because the number of respondents will continue until enough of the desired characteristics are represented.

Due to the absence of randomization, the main flaw with a quota sample is that the researcher has no means of knowing if the sample chosen is representative on any other variables beyond the one used to select the sample. Say a student is charged with designing a research project to assess whether alcohol consumption varies by college freshman compared with college seniors. How would this student get access to these two groups? He or she could stand outside a venue on campus and question students as they enter the event. If the student is a freshman, the researcher will select that student for participation in the study, and if the student is a senior, he or she will do the same. Sophomores and juniors will not be asked to participate. The researcher will continue with the process until enough freshmen and seniors are selected—thus filling the quotas. Say, however, that the venue that the students were entering was a commercial marketing vehicle giving away free samples of tobacco. Are the students who would stand in line to receive free tobacco products representative of all freshmen and seniors? The sample may be biased, simply by where and how it is chosen. The venue where the sample is drawn needs to be critically evaluated. As always, great care has to be given to thinking through what might seem like small details.

Purposeful Sampling. A purposeful or "*purposive*" sample is often used by qualitative researchers due to some specific advantages. The researcher often knows in advance what types of characteristics or variables are needed for the study, and the sample is chosen based on those qualifications. A **purposive sample** is when the researcher has already decided the characteristics of interest for the study and intentionally seeks out those types of research subjects. Consider that many child abusers were themselves abused as children. If this were the research topic, then a researcher would seek out victims of child abuse to serve as research subjects. One obvious disadvantage to this sampling strategy is that the researcher may have no means of actually knowing who victims of child abuse are. Furthermore, even if victims could be determined, there is no means of knowing if they are representative of *all* child abuse victims—again, the reason this method is a nonprobability sample instead of a probability one.

Purposeful sample: Occurs when subjects are specifically chosen for participation.

In some other cases, it is easy to identify the sample. If a researcher is interested in job satisfaction among veteran correctional officers, the sample is more readily identified. A county department of corrections will have personnel files on all employees containing information that could be used to select a representative sample. If the researcher were interested in examining employees with more than 10 years' experience, this would be an easy sample to acquire (assuming, of course, the personnel files were available).

Alpaslan (2010) wanted to study how undergraduate students cope with a huge range of very serious social problems in South Africa. He recognized a

> dearth of information about the realities of the living conditions of . . . [u]ndergraduate students . . . their living conditions to be overcrowded, noisy, unsafe, expensive and unstable . . . furthermore they are confronted with xenophobia, crime and violence, drugs, prostitution, street children and beggars.
>
> *(p. 1)*

Because Alpaslan was very familiar with the problems and the study population, it was best to use a purposeful sample; "namely purposive sampling was used because the researcher sought participants who were information-rich because of their knowledge and ability to describe the phenomenon under study" (2010, p. 1). The purposive sample allowed the conditions of the students' experience to be collected and shared.

Qualitative researchers rely frequently on purposive samples. When describing the causal mechanisms behind drug dealing, Jacques and Wright (2008) outlined their sampling strategy indicating that "Pete" and "Christian" were recruited using a purposive sampling strategy because the two individuals were known to be involved in drug dealing. As in the South African study, the researchers' prior knowledge about the study populations and the research topic made this a good sampling tactic. Another sampling technique relies on identifying the initial respondent and then having that respondent suggest others. In the example just mentioned, *Pete and Christian* could be used to identify other drug dealers who might participate in a study. This is referred to as *snowball sampling*.

Snowball Sample. The snowball sampling strategy is robust and is very useful for many research topics. It is, in fact, the only strategy that will provide access to many subversive populations. The more secretive the group, the stronger the rationale for using a snowball sample. For that reason, it is a necessary sampling strategy. It is also easy to learn and fun. A snowball sample does, however, require strong interpersonal skills that enable the researcher to effectively convey the value, purpose, and confidentiality of the study to the participants. Strong conveyance of these will result in more willing subjects and a better-identified sample.

Snowball sample: Often occurs when the desired sample characteristics are rare or secretive (often used in deviance studies). The researcher will begin with one participant who meets the characteristics required by the study and then asks the subject to recommend more participants. The sample starts with one, and snowballs from there based on the initial subject identifying more participants.

As mentioned earlier, the **snowball sample** is when the researcher locates one or two individuals who engage in the practices that the researcher is interested in studying, or who belong to the group that the researcher wants to study. After the researcher has gained the trust and confidence of these subjects, they will introduce the researcher to other members of the group or subculture, who in turn will introduce even more subjects. Over time, the number of study participants will "snowball" and grow exponentially until a large enough sample is acquired. This is much like the way new students in a university far from their hometown will make new friends (or at least they did before the advent of online social network sites such as Facebook and Instagram!).

As described at the beginning of this chapter, Sabrina Newsome (1993) was interested in studying young people (generally of high school age) who were involved in the vampire subculture that exists on the fringes of the goth culture. If she had done any sampling strategy other than a snowball sample, she would have found few, if any, research subjects. Newsome creatively applied a snowball technique in order to study goths and adherents to the vampire subgroups. Newsome knew there was a pizza place in East Lansing, Michigan, that appealed to many young goth people. She started to frequent the location and further learned that late Friday nights were the most popular time for this particular group. Many of the staff of the establishment were also involved in the subculture and so were welcoming of the many spiked, tattooed, black-clothed (and often with a loss of financial means) youths. Most other eating establishments in the city probably would not have been as receptive. In fact, it was not unusual for the staff at this restaurant to give free food to some of the adolescents, many of whom were runaways, neglected, or simply destitute.

On Newsome's first official research session, she was very fortunate to locate a young goth girl named Kat. She bought Kat a pizza and drinks and merely talked to her for an hour or so, and during this conversation she described the purpose and objectives of her research study. During this time, Newsome was able to gain Kat's trust, gain her confidence, and become "friends." In a lucky twist of fate, or perhaps because good researchers make their own good luck, Kat was a leader of the local goth subculture. Due to the trust and friendship that developed, Kat then "vouched" for Newsome and encouraged all the other adolescents to participate in Newsome's study. Over the next few months, more than a hundred young people were identified who were involved in the goth and/or vampire practices. Researchers were even invited to a large, secret Halloween ritual practiced by the goth adherents. While some researchers may criticize the use of snowball samples, this is a clear example of how the research topic and special population dictate which sampling methods are employed. This same type of sampling may be effective for a political scientist who wants to study political activism at public engagements. Once the researcher has connected with one political activist that person may be able to introduce the researcher to others who participate in protests or other forms of political activism.

This chapter has presented the most common and useful research strategies for selecting samples. The benefits to a sample are explained and the drawbacks articulated. It should be clear that there is no single "best" sampling strategy. The researcher must choose the sampling strategy based on considerations such as the research topic, time, resources, and access to research subjects. Often the researcher must also remain flexible and willing to deviate from the sampling strategy if situational contingencies arise. Perhaps a study begins with a quota sample, but during the course of the study, group leaders are identified and used to bring other subjects into the study, becoming a snowball sampling strategy. While making such concessions is not encouraged by all researchers, or even permitted by IRB guidelines, it is congruent with the precepts of mixed methods research and the concept of research flexibility or fluidity. If the sample follows a quantitative method with a probability sample being the focus, adhering to stricter mathematical guidelines is very important.

Hopefully, a theme that has been identified in this chapter is that there are different approaches to research designs and different approaches to selecting samples, depending on the design and the researcher's goals. The field of study, criminology, criminal justice, emergency and disaster management, sociology, social work, political science, public health, nursing, interdisciplinary studies, and so forth all have initial decisions to make early in the research design process. Does the researcher want the study to be reflective of the entire population (generalizable), and does the researcher want to employ advanced statistical analysis procedures? If so, that researcher will want to adhere to guidelines that ensure that a probability sample is accomplished. If the researcher is less worried about generalizations to the larger population and/or utilizing advanced statistical procedures, then they may decide on a non-probability sample. They may focus on a sample of the population that is more specific, purposeful, and accessible to the research, especially if this were the case where a program review was at the center of the study. The fact remains that regardless of the field of study; it should be the research question that establishes the researchers' course of action, research design, and sample selection method.

KEY TERMS

Convenience sampling
Ecological fallacy
Multistage stratified random sampling
Nonprobability sampling
Probability sampling
Purposeful sample
Quota sampling
Random digit dialing
Randomization
Sampling
Sampling error
Simple random sample
Snowball sample
Stratified random sampling
Systematic sampling
Table of random numbers

CRITICAL THINKING EXERCISES

1. Identify and describe the different types of probability sampling. Be sure to include the strengths and weaknesses of each.
2. Identify and describe the different types of nonprobability sampling. Be sure to include the strengths and weaknesses of each.
3. What are the benefits of selecting a sample of the population as opposed to studying the entire population?
4. What does "representative sample" mean, and how is it accomplished?
5. Discuss why perfect probability samples are rare.
6. Consider a research project on predictors of intimate partner violence. How might samples be drawn using a probability sample and alternatively by using a nonprobability design?
7. What are the steps to selecting a random sample?
8. What is a table of random numbers? How and why would one use them in the sample selection process?
9. How do you determine which sampling strategy to use?

CHAPTER 9

Elementary and Intermediate Quantitative Data Analysis

CHAPTER OBJECTIVES

After reading this chapter students should:

- Better understand data analysis procedures for quantitative research designs.
- Appreciate the early history of statistics.
- Comprehend the levels of measurement of variables and appreciate the relevance to statistical analysis.
- Identify the basic principles of statistical procedures for univariate analysis.
- Describe and calculate the common measures of central tendency: mean, median, mode, and standard deviation.
- Have more confidence and better comprehension when reading empirical studies.
- Be able to illustrate some of the inherent problems with strict reliance on numbers, measures, and counts of statistics in general.
- Identify the logic behind bivariate and multivariate statistical analysis.
- Understand the basic principles of statistical procedures for bivariate and multivariate analysis.
- Be able to distinguish which statistical measure of association should be used with which level of data.
- Note the difference between positive and inverse statistical relationships.
- Identify the criteria required to establish causality.
- Understand the importance of significance levels and the need to reduce the likelihood of Type I and Type II errors.

- Appreciate that the ability to trust statistical analysis is dependent upon early decisions in the research design, such as how the variables are operationalized and samples selected.
- Be able to illustrate some of the inherent problems with strict reliance on numbers, measures, and counts of statistics in general.
- Have more confidence and comprehension when reading empirical studies.
- Be able to better critique the research presented by others.

This chapter presents methods of interpreting, analyzing, and presenting data for quantitative research projects. Both quantitative and qualitative research strategies require specific skills, but increasingly (primarily due to software advances) there is overlap and convergence between analytical strategies used by researchers from each domain; increasingly, a study will include both quantitative and qualitative methods (mixed methods research). Whatever analytical and statistical strategies are applied, they must be described and justified to the readers and consumers of the research. How the data are processed and presented is consequently very important.

This chapter describes some basic underlying assumptions of data analysis and presents the basic analytical strategies for quantitative studies. Full-length texts are devoted solely to just statistical analyses, and the same is true of the various qualitative analytical methods. While this chapter only "scratches the surface," it provides enough core information to foster a basic understanding about data analysis processes and should greatly enhance one's ability to comprehend and better critique the research efforts of others. The data analysis content is presented in two chapters, one for each methodology, in hopes that the material can be processed more easily. While there will naturally be some overlap between the two chapters (e.g., bivariate analysis is introduced briefly in this chapter), by dividing the discussion on data handling into two chapters, the material is less likely to be overwhelming.

This chapter presents univariate and descriptive statistics, as well as bivariate and multivariate methods of analysis. Bivariate analysis involves examining the statistical relationship between two variables, but it does not address *cause and effect.* In order to examine cause-and-effect relationships, multivariate analysis needs to be conducted. While a research methods course is not the same as a statistics course, providing a cursory introduction to data analysis can make for a better transition between the two subjects and also help in understanding empirical articles. The following chapter (10) will discuss qualitative analysis in detail.

BASIC QUANTITATIVE ANALYSIS

There is perhaps no aspect of research methods that arouses greater anxiety among many social science students than the analytical statistical strategies employed by quantitative researchers. These strategies are the statistical tools that are necessary to "make sense" of numerical data. **Statistics** are the techniques used to describe, summarize, and interpret data. If the proper learning strategy and attitude are embraced, then statistics should not be difficult to understand, and anxieties can be minimized. It can be useful to conceptualize statistics as a foreign language. People struggle when they have not had exposure to it; with practice, however, their comfort levels will increase. Once the basic language and strategies are learned, the actual statistical applications should be relatively simple. Kranzler and Moursund noted, "Learning to read statistics is somewhat analogous to learning to read music or a foreign language: impossible at first, difficult for a while, but relatively easy after some effort" (1999, p. 5).

Statistics: Methods used to examine data collected during scientific inquiry. Statistics are basically tools used to help validate research findings using math and quantitative data.

This chapter provides some tips on how to learn and use statistics. Having a core understanding of the basic definitions is important and these are presented here. We introduce the statistical procedures that are most commonly used by social scientists and criminological researchers and suggest ways to better comprehend such empirical work. Before we explore these issues, however, it is beneficial to place the practices of statistical analysis in a historical perspective.

History

The word *statistics* comes from the Latin word *statis,* which means "nation" or "state." In the original Latin, it meant a comparison of nation-states and their attributes and did not necessarily rely on numbers (Loveless, 1998, p. 3). The contemporary use of the term was by a German professor, G. Achenwald, and the first English usage appeared in a 1770 translation of a German book by W. Hooper; even then, it still referred to a study of nations (Loveless, 1998), and there was less focus on mathematical equations. Today, the word is associated with numerical representation of data and is exclusively quantitative.

The person most responsible for the use of statistics in the early nineteenth century was Adolphe Quetelet (1796–1874), who in 1819 received the first PhD in mathematics ever awarded by the University of Ghent. He became a professor and spent his career using "statistical methods to support theoretical concepts, [and] he stressed the need for interpretation, rather than simple descriptive reporting of empirical data" (Loveless, 1998, p. 8). He is well known as the person most responsible for establishing statistics as a fundamental and vital part of science.

Perhaps the first use of statistics relative to crime and the social sciences occurred in England in 1809. According to Loveless (1998), Sir Samuel Romilly was on a political quest to reduce the number of crimes punishable by death. He used numbers to support his argument, but even then, the use of statistics had its critics. Loveless notes that because statistics were used to promote particular reforms, a political divide often ensued, causing some people to despise its usage. It was during this time that the famous quote "There are lies, damned lies, and statistics" (Loveless, 1998, p. 3) emerged. The words were a protest by the prime minister of England, Benjamin Disraeli, who objected to Romilly's campaign against capital punishment.

It is not just political figures who view statistics with some apprehension. The numerical, quantitative, and mathematical properties of statistics arouse trepidation among many people, including students. Statistics, with the goal of providing a rational means of understanding the social world based on probabilities, are actually easier to understand than some other types of math. Since their humble beginnings, statistics are now vital to the operation and understanding of virtually every part of society. It is therefore important to embrace the available tools.

First Steps

Perhaps the single most important trick to learning statistics is to go slowly. Consider that a "paragraph that is full of mathematical symbols has much more information in it than an ordinary paragraph in a history book or newspaper article" (Kranzler & Moursund, 1999, p. 5). Unlike with most other academic writings, one cannot simply read a statistics book and hope to comprehend it. It demands work and patience, but once it starts to "click," it will make sense. The best way to understand statistics is to actually practice and use the strategies presented. An initial first step is to learn the symbols and then the operations used by statisticians.

In the statistical domain, *one* symbol can represent a series of mathematical and conceptual steps. If a person is attempting to learn a foreign language, then the most basic words and phrases are studied first. The elementary words have to be learned because they set the foundation for everything else. The same is true of statistics: basic symbols must be understood prior to learning the fundamental analytical strategies. After that, a basic understanding of mathematical operations is needed. For example, statistical equations must be calculated in the proper order.

Order of Operations. Parentheses are the first important symbol having a specific mathematic meaning. The rule is to calculate the mathematical operation inside of the parentheses first. For example, $3(5 - 1) = N$ would be calculated as $5 - 1 = 4$, and then 3 times $4 = 12$. So, $N = 12$. Again, note how much more efficient it is to write "$3(5 - 1) = N$" rather than a grammatical sentence that reads "five minus one multiplied by three equals what?" Note, if the numbers are manipulated or calculated in a different order, a vastly different answer or result will be given, one that is grossly misleading and wrong. Consider that the equation $3(5 - 1) = N$ could be erroneously calculated as $3 \times 5 = 15$, and then if 1 is subtracted, the result is 14 rather than the correct answer of 12. Remember, work inside the parentheses first!

Symbolic Representations. One can understand the basics of statistics when it is viewed similar to text messaging. Those who use shortcut symbols in text messaging (instead of writing the whole word) have little trouble when communicating with each other. A person who is not familiar with the texting symbols, however, will have a harder time understanding what is being said or how to respond (lmao). Individuals have to invest some time in learning the basics of the shortcut language. With practice, a person will prefer to use "texting language" rather than writing out the formal words. The same is true regarding the language of statistics; this can be referred to as *speaking statistics*. It is much more practical to use symbols than words. It is more efficient to write "3^2" than it is to write "three times three." Symbols have universal meaning and, once they are understood, greatly simplify mathematical and statistical procedures; but they can be confusing or even intimidating at first. In earlier chapters, the symbol for an independent variable (X) was presented. A second independent variable would be X_2, a third X_3, and so on. Similarly, the dependent variable is signified with the letter Y, a second dependent variable would be Y_2, a third Y_3, and so on. Someone who is not familiar with research methods might see X_3 in an equation and not know it simply means the third independent variable. Symbols are great ways to simplify, but a person who does not know what the symbols mean will be totally lost. Another example of symbol usage is in referring to a sample; a lowercase n means the number of elements in a *sample*, while an uppercase N means all the elements in a *population*. Another example would be when a letter of the Greek alphabet is used to represent a specific action. Perhaps the most common is sigma (Σ), which means to "add up" or "to sum"/"summation." When Σ occurs in a formula, it is simply letting the reader know that an action is required, namely, addition. A few other symbols are as follows: the symbol for the mean in an equation is M_x; the mean of an entire sample would be X; and the μ represents a population mean. The symbol for variance is s^2, and standard deviation is s.

Along with symbols, it is important to understand that numbers have specific characteristics; especially in the way they are measured. This is very important because it dictates what statistical formulas can be used. Variables can be collected as either discrete or continuous data. Discrete data are collected from categories and so are called categorical data. **Discrete data** has a set end point and is finite. Examples of discrete data are gender, race, and religion; these variables are simply categorical. **Continuous data,** by contrast, are not finite but can be divided and broken down into smaller values, for example, 6.2, 6.25, 6.257, and so on. Some common examples of continuous data are time and weight. For example, the weight of seized drugs can be broken down to more decimal points if a more accurate scale or measure is used. Continuous data can be "collapsed" or converted into discrete (categorical data), but discrete data cannot be turned into continuous data. For instance, the seized drugs could be classified into "less than a gram" or "more than a gram." The actual weight is converted into a category. Depending on the amount and type of drug, the various weights could be collapsed into categories such as "more than a pound" or "less than a pound," or "more than a kilo" or "less than a kilo," and so forth. We could *not* take one's gender and break it down into continuous measures, however. Gender is simply a category; people are either male or female (with the rare exception of androgynous individuals). The way variables are measured was presented earlier in this text; it is discussed again in this chapter because it dictates what can be done statistically. Let us review the different levels of measurement for variables in a data set.

Discrete data: Variables that are limited to a specific (finite) number of cases. They are expressed as whole numbers without decimal places. Number of arrests would be an example (1, 2, 3, 4).

Continuous data: Variables that can have a nonspecific (infinite) number of values, meaning the numbers can always be broken down further, for example, possible numbers indicating the weight of marijuana between 120 pounds and 121 pounds (120.1, 120.125, 120.12573, etc.).

Nominal level data: Data that are divided into mutually exclusive, and which are also exhaustive catagories; the most basic level of data collection.

Levels of Measurement. Chapter 2 introduced the different levels of measurement for variables, as well as a brief discussion on what statistics can be used for each type of variable. This explanation is worth repeating in a chapter focused on analysis because the level of measurement of variables influences not only the degree of validity, but also what statistical procedures can be used. Recall that there are four levels of measurement, each with mathematical properties. The most basic is **nominal level data.** Not a lot can be done statistically with this level of measurement, which basically allows for a simple numeric account of the attributes of a variable. In other words, a researcher can describe the frequency of the variable and provide percentages. Because of the simplistic level of mathematical analysis, some argue that the nominal level is not mathematical at all but is, rather, a qualitative level of measurement (Bachman & Schutt, 2011). In other words, nominal level measurement is more about *describing* rather than employing advanced statistical analysis. Nominal level data do not have weight or value. One cannot measure any distance or assign any value indicating that one variable attribute is quantitatively different than the other. An example would be asking whether someone's gender is male or female. Female is not considered "more than" or "less than" male; it is simply a way to describe a person (a category). One can, however, gather data on how many males are in a criminal justice class compared with how many females. Then both frequencies and percentages can be determined. Statisticians can also distinguish how many males engage in violent crime as opposed to how many females by using cross-tabulation (more on this later).

Nominal level variables are also exhaustive and mutually exclusive, meaning that the respondent "fits" or identifies with only one of the attributes of the variables, and that the attributes do not overlap in any way. This allows for some statistical comparison to be made *between* variables, such as what was just discussed (the relationship between gender and violent crime), but not much more can be done statistically. Categorical data are less robust than using variables with higher levels of measurement.

Ordinal level data are the second level of measurement and also are categorical; unlike nominal data, however, one can determine some measurement differences between the attributes of the variable. An ordinal level of measurement has the two basic mathematical properties that nominal has (exhaustive and mutually exclusive), but it is also rank ordered. In other words, it does have greater and lesser values. One example of ordinal level data is the rank of university professors. The categories are "adjunct," "instructor," "assistant professor," "associate professor," and "professor." An assistant professor is ranked higher than an instructor. This ranking, however, has no other value. For example, some associate professors, though ranked higher than an assistant professor, may earn less money. Some instructors may teach for 40 years and never rise in rank. So neither time served nor salary can be used to distinguish the *ranks* of professors. When specific values are needed to differentiate *between* ranks, a third level of measurement is needed, which is interval level data.

An **interval level measure** is exhaustive, mutually exclusive, and rank ordered and has a known, measureable, set distance between values. We could analyze the salary of university professors and be able to specifically indicate how much difference exists between the results; it is distinctly measurable. Another example of interval level data might be absolute time. Two hours are one unit more than one hour, three hours are two units more than one hour, and so on; however, there is no known, measurable start of time, or the beginning of all time. Years, months, hours, minutes, and seconds are based on a sun cycle, yet other measures of time exist. Time, at an *interval* level, is a fixed unit of measure, but it lacks a *true* zero point.

Ratio level data are considered the highest and final level of measurement and have all the properties of the first three, but also have a *true* zero as a starting point. With ratio data, all mathematical procedures can be applied. Both interval level and ratio level data are continuous, and the data are used the same way for calculations. A way to know the difference between ratio level and interval level measurement is to ask if the variable of interest has a zero point that truly means the absence of

Ordinal level data: Mutually exclusive, exhaustive data that have a rank order, but an exact measurement cannot be taken *between* the data points; the second level of data measurement.

Interval level data: Mutually exclusive, exhaustive, rank-ordered data that have a known distance between the numbers; the third level of measurement.

Ratio level data: Mutually exclusive, exhaustive, rank-ordered data with known distances between data points, but also with a *true* zero point; the fourth, or highest, level of data measurement.

anything. If it does, it is ratio; if it does not, it is interval. If a *meaningful* zero point exists in the data, then data are *ratio*. It gives a more precise count that allows the beginning point to be an absence of the property. For example, if time is considered only for a 24-hour period, then 00:00 might be a true zero point. If the time needed to run 100 meters were the unit of measure, the starting gun would designate a true zero point. In other words, when the variable has a true zero point that really means the "absence of anything," it would be considered ratio data and not interval. The meaning of the zero is really what distinguishes interval and ratio data.

Also recall the earlier discussion on "coding" variables in a sample. Data need to be numerically *coded*, making them suitable for statistical analysis. Statistical analysis software needs numerical values in order to perform statistical operations, so variable attributes are often assigned numbers. In the earlier example, we can easily compute the percentage of males and females in a class if the number 1 represents males and females are represented by the number 2. The statistician assigns the statistical software numerical codes that represent the attributes of the variables, and it is then relatively simple to generate some elementary statistics. The variables of interest in a research project collectively make up the *data set*, also a *codebook*, and statistical procedures can be conducted on entire data sets.

There are three levels of statistical analysis that can be performed: univariate, bivariate, and multivariate. Briefly, univariate statistics are descriptive, with single variables that can be described or combined to describe the makeup of the entire sample; bivariate statistics involve analyzing the relationship between two variables to determine if they are statistically associated; multivariate analysis involves determining the effect that multiple independent variables have on a dependent variable or variables. *Causality* is a greater focus in multivariate analysis. The type of analysis depends on the goal of the researcher (as well as the level of training), the level of measurement of the variables, and the research topic itself. This of course assumes that the research design has high levels of reliability and validity; the ability to have confidence in the statistical analysis of a research project depends on the quality and integrity of early decisions.

UNIVARIATE AND DESCRIPTIVE STATISTICS

While statistical procedures can be quite advanced, describing data in the simplest form is useful and is always a good starting point. Univariate analysis summarizes or describes one variable at a time and can be combined to describe group characteristics of the data set. Univariate analyses are the most commonly used (Eck &

La Vigne, 1994) and typically involve reporting measures of central tendency and variations around a mean or average. Some researchers may be interested only in the description of the data at this level, while others will conduct more advanced statistics. Either way, it is important to examine variables at the univariate level. Analyzing the variables one at a time is important for providing description of the data results and determining if the variables are normally distributed, which is important before more advanced analysis begins.

Frequency Distributions

The first step to making sense of the data is to know what the frequency distributions of the variables are. Not only can it be informative to know the raw values, but also knowing the percentage breakdown for the attributes of the variables provides a basic understanding of how the data are distributed. Frequency distributions allow the researcher to describe the data set, which is always a good launching point. For example, if the researcher were studying a group of adjudicated delinquents in a juvenile facility, it is beneficial to describe the typical characteristics of the group. Such description could sound something like this: "Of the 300 males incarcerated, 64% are 16 years of age, 82% had multiple arrests prior to the current incarceration, 68% were reared by mothers in single-parent homes, and 77% had been suspended from school at least once during high school."

Researchers can also learn a lot by analyzing one variable thoroughly. Let us say a fire department is interested in the average amount of time spent on emergency rescue calls in a month. Here are hypothetical data from 1 month.

If the time spent on each call was accurately recorded, the time, in hours spent on each call (X), might be as follows:

$$\begin{array}{c} 3 \\ 12 \\ 1 \\ 3 \\ 7 \\ 5 \\ 3 \\ \hline \Sigma X = 34 \end{array}$$

This shows that Firemedic 1 made calls on (N = 7) days, which took a total of 34 hours. Although total time is useful information, it may be incomplete. For example, if a medic spent 34 hours yet made 50 calls, then each call was handled very quickly. This might happen if a fire department changed the precinct in which the medic was assigned, or how calls were delegated. These are the kinds of things that need to be taken into consideration when analyzing data. This type of disparity presents the need for other ways to count things and is why measures of central tendency are so useful.

Measures of Central Tendency

Measures of central tendency (MOCT): A typical description of a data set, based on how the numbers compare mathematically to each other, including the mean, median, mode, and standard deviation.

Mean: Commonly known as the *average*. It is calculated by dividing the sum of the scores by the number of scores.

There are three **measures of central tendency**—the typical first description of a data set, which computes how the numbers compare mathematically to each other; these include the mean, median, mode, and standard deviation (Walker & Maddan, 2013). For example, if the local fire chief wants to know the average hours per call for the fire medic mentioned earlier, he or she can divide the total hours (34) by the number of days (7) that the officer worked. This calculation gives the mathematical average, or "mean," of time spent for each emergency call. The **mean** is the mathematical average of all the numbers in the equation. The symbol for the sample mean is M_x. This is also sometimes expressed as X when referring to the average or mean of a sample. If the average of all police arrests were calculated, this would be considered a "population mean," which is symbolized by the Greek letter μ (pronounced "mew"). If medic #1 (the research sample) spent 34 hours on 7 days, his or her average (mean) hours per day spent on calls is 4.8. The statistical formula for this sentence would be: $\Sigma X/N = M_1$ or $34/7 = 4.8$ hours per call. The rest of the time could have been spent in training, on vehicle maintenance, and on other common assignments related to fire rescue.

The "mean" or "average" is one of the three measures of central tendency. One easy way to understand the measures of central tendency is to conceptualize them as "middleness." In addition to the average, there are two other measures of central tendency, the mode and the median. Consider the grades from a research methods class. Suppose that there are 20 students in the class, and their grades on the exam are as follows:

86, 92, 92, 56, 76, 78, 45, 89, 72, 73, 74, 100, 78, 79, 67, 90, 59, 99, 98, 78

The raw frequency scores do not provide much information, except to show what the actual grades are. Some easy steps allow the numbers to make more sense and provide a better understanding of the grades on an exam. The typical first step is to arrange the numbers in rank order from low to high. Taking this step would reveal the following:

45, 56, 59, 67, 72, 72, 72, 72, 77, 78, 79, 79, 86, 89, 91, 92, 93, 99, 99, 100

When numbers are arranged in a sequence, the list is more useful. For one thing, it is easy to see the high and low scores and to identify any outliers (extreme scores). It is also easier to conduct other calculations, such as the **mode,** which is the number or category that occurs most often. Because 72 appears four times, the mode of the exam scores is 72. The final measure of central tendency is called the **median,** which is the exact middle number in a distribution. It is better to use the median when there is an even number of students in the class because there is no exact middle number. In a situation where there is no exact median (middle number), take the middle two numbers (78 and 79), add them together (78 + 79 = 157), and divide by 2(157/2 = 78.5). If there is an uneven number of cases (e.g., 21 students), there will be an exact center number or median. Just to refresh, to determine the average, as given earlier, add all the scores (1,577) and divide by the number of students (20), so 1,577 / 20 = 78.85. In this example, the median (78.5) and the mean (78.85) are virtually the same. If the data are normally distributed, then the measures of central tendency would be similar.

Mode: The number, or numbers, that occur(s) most often in a data set (and along with frequency and percentages is the only thing that can be presented for nominal level data).

Median: The midpoint in a data set. It is the value in the data set that divides the scores into two equal halves.

Deciding which measure of central tendency is most appropriate depends on what the research study is examining, and the specific variable of interest. For exam scores, the mean or average may be the best. It shows what the test average is for the whole class. For other topics, such as the average salary of all released inmates, then either the median or the mode may be a better measure of central tendency.

Variability. It is also useful to consider the range of all possible scores for a variable. Looking at the grade scores, or distribution of numbers, it shows the highest score was 100 and the lowest score was 45. If the lowest score (45) is subtracted from the highest score (100), the range or spread can be calculated: 100 – 45 = 55. The **range** is the highest score minus the lowest score.

Range: A measure of dispersion indicating the difference between the highest and lowest values in the data set.

The mean or average score, mode, and median are all often used in conjunction when reporting statistics; however, it might be useful to also know how much variability exists in a sample or a population. Knowing the variance and standard deviation is useful.

Deviation from the Mean. It is easy to calculate how much each score deviates from the mean or average response. In the exam scores listed earlier, the M_1 is 78.5. The highest score was 100, so the deviation from the mean for the highest score is 21.5, since 100 – 78.5 = 21.5. Just knowing what the deviation from the mean is for *one* exam score is not as useful as knowing the average deviation for all the scores. This calculation is also relatively simple. First, list all the exam scores (X). Next, subtract the mean from each score ($X - M_x$). Then, add all these numbers. The sum of this column will always equal zero! This is not a very useful calculation and really provides no useful information. The reason that this occurs is that the positive (+) and negative (–) deviations cancel each other out. To provide a much more useful measure of variability, square (X^2) each deviation $(X - M_x)^2$. The following columns illustrate this for the scores from the hypothetical exam listed earlier:

Variance. The variance is the most common measure of the spread, range, or variability of a group. The symbol for variance is s^2. The formula used to determine the sample variance is:

Scores	$X - M_x$	$(X - M_x)^2$
45	45 − 78.5 = −33.5	−33.52 = 1,122.25
56	56 − 78.5 = −22.5	−22.52 = 616
59	59 − 78.5 = −19.5	−19.52 = 380.25
67	67 − 78.5 = −11.5	−11.52 = 132.25
72	72 − 78.5 = −6.5	−6.52 = 42.25
72	72 − 78.5 = −6.5	−6.52 = 42.25
72	72 − 78.5 = −6.5	−6.52 = 42.25
72	72 − 78.5 = −6.5	−6.52 = 42.25
77	77 − 78.5 = −1.5	−1.52 = 2.25
78	78 − 78.5 = −0.5	−0.52 = 0.25
79	79 − 78.5 = 0.5	0.52 = 0.25
79	79 − 78.5 = 0.5	0.52 = 0.25
86	86 − 78.5 = 7.5	7.52 = 56.25
89	89 − 78.5 = 10.5	10.52 = 110.25
91	91 − 78.5 = 12.5	12.52 = 156.25
92	92 − 78.5 = 13.5	13.52 = 182.25
93	93 − 78.5 = 14.5	14.52 = 210.25
99	99 − 78.5 = 20.5	20.52 = 420.25
99	99 − 78.5 = 20.5	20.52 = 420.25
100	100 − 78.5 = 21.5	21.52 = 462.25
$\Sigma X = 1{,}577$	$\Sigma(X - M_x) = 0$	$(X - M_x)^2 = 4{,}431.75$

$$S^2 = \frac{\Sigma(x - m_x)^2}{N - 1}$$

To calculate the **variance,** square the actual deviations from the mean and add them together. Variance is really the "mean sum of squares." This eliminates the negative (−) signs, since squared (^{2}) numbers will always have a positive (+) value. Next, for a sample, divide this number by the total N of cases minus 1. For a population, divide by the total N for the entire population as shown here:

Variance: A measure of dispersion indicating the average squared deviations of each case from its mean value.

$$\sigma^2 = \frac{\Sigma(x - m_x)^2}{N}$$

Standard Deviation. The variance is a useful statistic, but the main problem is that it provides a number that is in a different scale from the original data. For example, in the exam score illustration, recall that the variance was 4,431.75. This value does not have much use when the highest exam score was only 100. It is actually confusing. In order to make the data easier to interpret, or to put the values in the same context, another step is required, which is called the *standard deviation.* The **standard deviation** (SD) is the square root (√) of the variance. The formula for the standard deviation is as follows:

Standard deviation: A measure of dispersion showing how the scores relate to the mean.

$$S = \frac{\sqrt{\Sigma(x - m_x)^2}}{N}$$

The value created by the deviation is easier to interpret than the variance, since it is in the correct (or same) unit of measurement as the original data. The number obtained represents the average of *all* the individual variations from the mean in the data examined. For the preceding problem, the standard deviation of the scores is 8.397.

All the statistical procedures discussed so far describe or summarize the data collected. For example, in one study, Dantzer and colleagues examined what police chiefs perceived as "necessary criteria and skills for those individuals seeking to become police chiefs" (Dantzer, Lurigio, Magnus, & Sinacore, 1998, p. 71). Because the data collected are nominal and ordinal level data, the most appropriate way to present the study is with the standard measures of central tendency, since it is a research project designed to simply report the opinions of the police chiefs. Another study designed to report opinions is by Briggs and Mason (2008), who describe first responders' perceptions of level of preparedness for natural and terrorist disasters. Quite often, however, researchers also need to determine probabilities or calculate odds. To do this, a frequency distribution and the *normal curve of the data* must be understood; these are covered next.

INTERMEDIATE DATA HANDLING: BIVARIATE AND MULTIVARIATE STATISTICAL ANALYSIS

The first half of this chapter explored elementary data analysis by focusing primarily on univariate statistics and data handling; the chapter now continues with an overview of bivariate and multivariate analysis, but with the intention of fostering a basic understanding of the procedures, as well as the logic behind them. Hopefully, this will help prepare students for their statistics or advanced research methods courses, where they will be able to conduct their own statistical analysis. This is a simple overview, but an important goal is to enhance one's ability to comprehend and better critique the research efforts of others. Because research projects are "built," it is very important to review the work of others (as a reminder, refer to the earlier discussion on the importance of literature reviews); however, without some level of exposure to data analysis, understanding empirical work can be extremely difficult and/or frustrating.

If the researcher wants to move beyond descriptive analysis and explore the statistical associations between two or more variables or to assess cause-and-effect relationships, then bivariate and multivariate analyses need to be conducted. While many research methods students will not actually conduct statistical analysis until they take statistics, an early exposure in research methods can help bridge the gap between the two courses. In other situations, students are required to take only the research methods course, so for those it is even more important to have a basic understanding of what statistics typically involve. Being exposed to statistics also helps students make the connection between different research designs.

BIVARIATE STATISTICS

Bivariate statistical analysis: Explores the statistical association between two variables.

Bivariate statistical analysis is used to assess the relationship between *two variables*. Very often researchers are interested to know whether variables are *statistically correlated* with each other. The question to be assessed is: As one variable increases or decreases, does the other variable do the same? Not only can a test of statistical significance evaluate whether a relationship exists, but through the use of statistical analysis, the strength of the relationship can be evaluated, and it can be determined in what direction the variables move. Variables can move in the same direction (up or down), as well as in the opposite direction (as one variable increases, the other variable decreases, or vice versa). These are referred to as **inverse statistical relationships** (when the variables move in opposite directions). An example of an inverse relationship would be: As self-esteem *increases*, alcohol use *decreases*. In situations where one variable moves and the other variable moves in the same direction, this is referred to as a **positive statistical relationship.** An example of a positive relationship would be: As amount of time spent studying for an exam increases, the grade on the exam also increases.

Inverse statistical relationship: Also called a negative relationship; it suggests that as one variable increases, the other variable decreases, or alternatively, as one variable decreases, the other variable increases. The interaction between the variables causes them to move in opposite directions.

Positive statistical relationship: Suggests that as one variable increases (or decreases), the other variable moves in the same relationship direction.

A researcher could determine whether first responders' perceptions about being prepared for disaster are correlated with the level of funding an agency receives. Specifically, as funding increases for an agency, confidence in dealing with disaster also increases. Alternatively, confidence in being prepared to respond to disaster is statistically correlated to levels of training; as levels of specific training increase, the perception of being prepared to deal with the specific disaster increases as well (see Briggs & Mason, 2008). Bivariate analysis allows the relationship between two variables to be statistically evaluated.

Bivariate statistics show the relationship between an independent variable (X) and dependent variable (Y). As just mentioned, among the things measured are if relationships statistically exist, the actual direction of the relationship, and the statistical strength of the relationship. To help understand these procedures, the means of plotting and showing data are helpful. These procedures typically are predicated on data distributions, or "curves," which are symmetrical or asymmetrical shapes. Knowing the frequency distributions is an important first step. We discussed frequency distributions as they related to univariate analysis earlier, where we also introduced the concept of normal probability curves. Both of these are important concepts for comparing the relationship between two variables.

FREQUENCY DISTRIBUTIONS

The standard practice among statisticians is to create a frequency distribution to better represent and understand the bivariate data. The horizontal axis is the X-axis (e.g., exam scores), while the frequencies are displayed on the Y-axis (how many students made a specific grade). If each score is placed on the chart, and then the points are connected, a curve is created. The pattern of the curve is important for understanding the data.

Normal bell-shaped curve: Based on the normal distribution of the data. If the data are normally distributed, scores will be evenly distributed with few high and low scores and most scores in the middle or average range (called a quartile).

Normal Curve. If the scores recorded on the graph are evenly distributed, a **normal bell-shaped curve** results. This symmetrical bell-shaped curve created from plotting a frequency polygon is called a *normal probability curve*. The intelligence quotient (IQ) curve (first shown in Chapter 3) provides a good example of a normal bell-shaped curve. Because the "average" IQ is 100; the vast majority of people (68%) will have an IQ between 85 and 115. Virtually everyone, 95% of the population, will have an IQ between 70 and 130. After this large grouping, many fewer people will have very high (up to 145) or very low (down to 55) IQ scores (Figure 9.1). From the probability curve plotted in the graph, it can be determined what percentage of the population is likely to have what score. The data in this case are normally distributed.

Skewed Curves. Quite often the scores, arrests, drugs, hours, values, or any other numerical data, when plotted, do not result in a symmetrical "normal" distribution. Consider a few examples: If most research methods students make As and Bs on the exam and very few make Ds and Fs, then a skewed curve will result. The data would be concentrated at one end and are therefore not normally distributed. Criminal justice data will not always be normally distributed; the nature of the subject matter ensures this. For example, if a criminal justice researcher were to plot the age of criminal offending, a skewed curve would result because the data would be heavily concentrated at the junior high school and high school and perhaps even the college years, but not at the middle-age or elderly years. Visually, we would actually see a spike in the curve for a very specific age-group when it comes to criminal offending. It is known that young people commit more crime than the elderly,

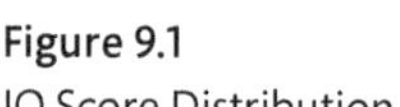

Figure 9.1
IQ Score Distribution

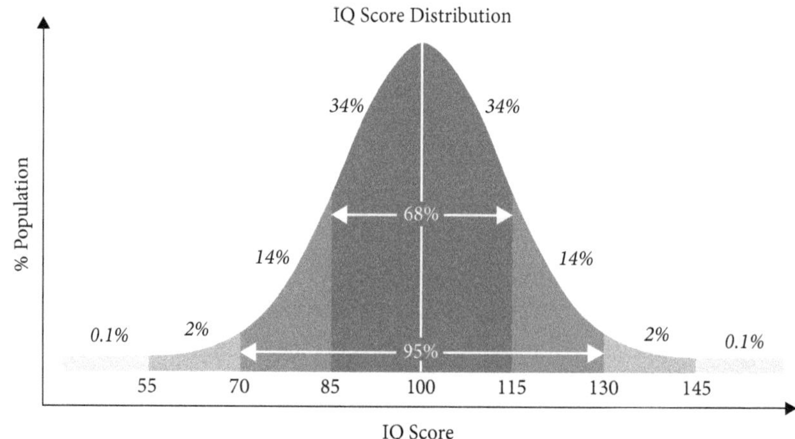

and multivariate statistics allow one to determine all the possible reasons for this: immaturity, opportunity, hormones, underemployment, brain development, peer-pressure, and so forth.

Data Distributions: Curves

There are three types of curves, or frequency distributions. The first is the normal bell-shaped curve discussed previously. In statistics language, this type of a distribution is called a **mesokurtic curve.** *Meso* means "normal" or "average," and *kurtic* is another word for "curve." This type of curve assumes a normal distribution; most scores or people will be in the middle, but some people will score or rank very high or very low. Consider criminal offending: some people never commit a crime, most people commit some crime (e.g., speeding, texting while driving), and a small cohort commits considerable amounts of crime.

Mesokurtic curve: Refers to a normal shaped curve when the data are plotted on a graph.

Another type of distribution is when many, or even most, scores group tightly together, as in the case of plotting the exam grades. If they are plotted on a graph (Figure 9.2), a skewed distribution and curve would result. This type of curve is called a **leptokurtic curve.** In the case of exam scores where most students scored between 80 and 100, these scores would be congregated at the upper end of the graph (with some to the right of the mean); this results in a "tail" being pulled to the left of the normal curve. This type of distribution is called a *negatively skewed curve*. Basically, a negative skew indicates that the tail on the left side of the mean is stretched out farther than the tail on the right side. Alternatively, if many of the scores are low (e.g., few high grades), the data would be congregated to the left of the mean, and the tail would be stretched out to the right, resulting in a positive skew.

Leptokurtic curve: Refers to a skewed distribution where scores are tightly grouped together. When the data are plotted on a graph it appears as a high, thin distribution.

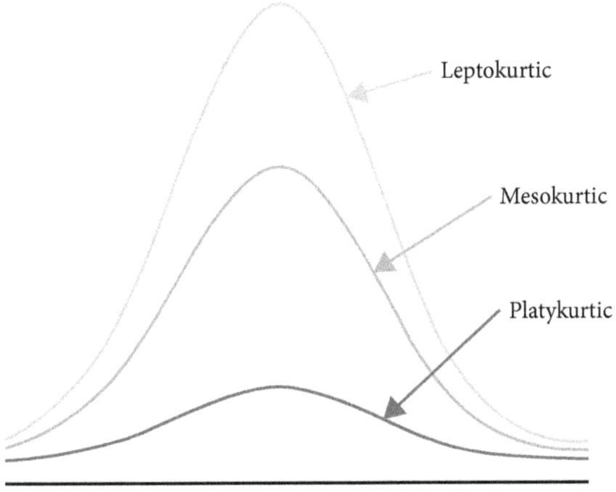

Figure 9.2
Frequency Curves
These illustrative curves were downloaded from http://www.internet-raining.com/Statkit/StatKit.htm (accessed February 2, 2012)

Platykurtic curve: Refers to a flatter curve where the scores are spread out evenly. When the data are plotted on a graph. the line is relatively flat.

The final type of curve results when the scores are spread out relatively evenly. When plotted, this results in a flat curve, which is called a **platykurtic curve.** If the 20 exam scores listed at the beginning of this chapter were actually plotted, a relatively flat curve would result because there is not much variation in the exam scores.

A skewed curve can also result when just one score (or more) pulls the tail either left (negative skew) or right (positive skew) because the value was either a very high or a very low score (Figure 9.3). When a skewed distribution exists, it can greatly influence the mean value. According to Kranzler and Moursund:

> When a distribution is skewed, the mean is the most strongly affected. A few scores far out in the tail of a distribution will "pull" the mean in that direction. The median is somewhat "pulled" in the direction of the tail, and the mode is not "pulled" at all.
>
> *(1999, p. 28)*

The mode is not really impacted, but the mean can change significantly by just one extreme score (outlier). For example, if one wants to know the average age of students in a college freshman course, and there happens to be *one* student who is 80 years old in the class, the mean average for the entire class would be pulled heavily in the direction of the 80-year-old, thus representing the average age as much older than it actually is for a typical college freshman course. This is why it is important to run univariate statistics before more advanced statistical analysis occurs. Outliers need to be addressed so as not to misrepresent the data. A distribution can be represented visually, which helps one to conceptualize the data.

Presentation of Data

Representing data by graphs and plotting the distribution of scores is an effective way to visually assess the data for the issues just mentioned; for example, by plotting the scores, outliers can be identified. Graphs are also an effective way to

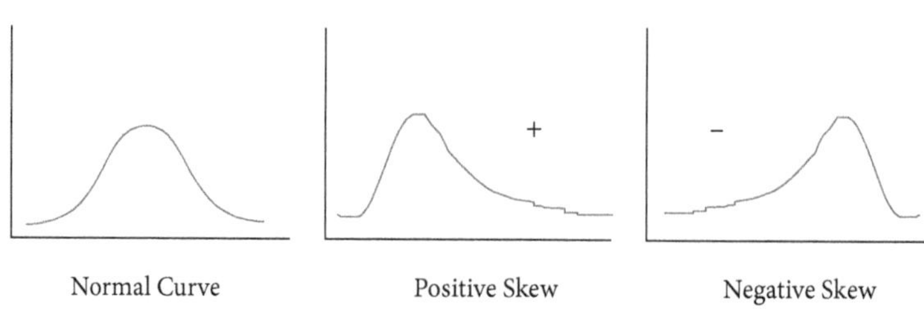

Figure 9.3
Skew of Curves

Retrieved on February 2, 2012, from http://allpsych.com/researchmethods/distributions.html

communicate about the data in a research report. When describing data in a research report, sometimes a picture "captures a thousand words." A simple visual graph is especially useful for presenting data to those who may be apprehensive about or unfamiliar with statistical analysis. To depict data graphically, it is not necessary to use complicated graphs. Usually the basic charts are preferable. Many times a simple bar chart or graph is all that is needed to accurately and succinctly present data and show data patterns. For instance, Vito, Holmes, Keil, and Wilson note:

> We chose to use discriminant (bar charts) for several reasons. First, our dependent variable, the drug test result, is nominal (positive/negative). Second, discriminant function would develop a profile for each type of drug test that is easily interpretable by persons not familiar with statistical analysis.
>
> *(1998, p. 24)*

Several types of graphs can be used, and all reveal considerable information in a concise manner. When creating or reading a chart, it is important to remember the vertical part is normally the Y-axis and shows values of the variable. The X-axis, or horizontal part, displays the categories. A **bar chart** consists of solid bars that are separated by spaces. The distinction between the bars makes this kind of chart useful for displaying nominal level and other discrete types of data (categorical data). A **pie chart** is also good for representing the percentage breakdown of categories of a variable. In a pie chart, each category, or attribute of a variable, is represented as if it were a piece of a pie. Another common type of graph is the **histogram,** which has bars touching one another and is used with continuous level data. When the attributes of a variable are represented by data that is not categorical, histograms are an effective way of presenting this type of data. These types of graphs are especially useful for representing univariate data and plotting probability curves that identify the association between two or more variables. *Scattergrams* are useful graphs for **multivariate analysis,** which is analyzing the effects of multiple independent variables on the dependent variable (more discussion on this later); they are also important for identifying what the data look like, what the form is, how the direction of the data "runs," and what the overall associations between variables are. A scatter plot is a helpful initial step to give a visual picture of the potency of relationships between data points. It is a great way to provide a quick "snapshot" of the data.

The relationships between variables can also be presented graphically in research reports, such as in a cross-tabulation table, and by reporting values such as beta coefficients, which represent the statistical association between variables. Let us begin with a discussion on the use of cross-tabulation.

Bar chart: A graph that depicts the data by utilizing individual bars to represent the variables.

Pie chart: A graph that depicts the data by representing the percentage breakdown as if they are pieces of a pie.

Histogram: A bar graph showing the frequency of *each* value appearing in the distribution of scores.

Multivariate analysis: Involves the statistical testing of multiple variables at one time. It is often useful for helping determine causality. It allows for a statistical examination to determine whether independent variables influence the dependent variable (that which the researcher is trying to explain).

Measures of Association and Tests of Statistical Significance

Cross-tabulation: Allows for statistical examination of two or more nominal or ordinal level variables by displaying the distribution of the attributes of one variable by the attributes of another variable.

Cross-tabulation assists in hypothesis testing by allowing for statistical analysis of relationships between two or more variables. It is especially useful for categorical data and can be portrayed visually by showing how the categories or attributes of variables intersect with the categories of another variable. This type of contingency table or cross-tabulation ("cross-tab") is the simplest and most common means used to compare nominal level and ordinal level data. A cross-tabulation shows the distribution of one variable for each category (e.g., possible values or answer categories) compared with the categories of another variable. One benefit to a cross-tab is the ability to statistically control one or more variables while simultaneously examining the relationship between variables. A simple illustration of a cross-tab is:

		AMOUNT OF ALCOHOL CONSUMED WEEKLY				
		None	1–3 ounces	4–6 ounces	7–9 ounces	> 10 ounces
Gender	Male	12	20	10	2	4
	Female	20	15	12	6	1
	Total	32	35	22	8	5

In this example, we can graphically determine the amount of alcohol consumed in a given week by the categories of gender: male and female. For example, out of the sample, 20 females consumed no alcohol, as did 12 males. The cross-tab is normally used with nominal (e.g., gender) or ordinal or ratio (e.g., ounces consumed) level data, as the example shows.

The cross-tab can show four important associations between two or more variables: (1) whether a relationship exists, (2) the strength of the relationship, as well as the (3) direction and (4) pattern of association. A more complete cross-tab (generated from the use of statistical software) than the one just given would display these properties and could also show percentages, expected values, and other measures of association, which are discussed next.

When comparing variables, it is necessary to "standardize the data" because doing so provides a higher or better level of comparison. For example, standardized data provide the ability to know what *percentage* of females out of the *total sample* does not drink alcohol compared with the percentage of males who do not drink alcohol in order to determine which gender is less likely to consume alcohol. When only raw numbers are used, this cannot be determined. Standardizing the data basically means converting raw frequencies into percentages, which is very important when analyzing the statistical relationship between variables. Alternatively, for example, in this case, if the data are standardized, it could be determined which gender is likely to consume *more* ounces of alcohol. While standardization can easily be computed manually, statistical software allows this to be done easily, and the researcher also can choose which statistics to calculate in the cross-tab tables. It should be remembered that many statistical techniques are offered through statistical software packages, and specific statistics need to be used in certain situations. If this data set included assessments regarding self-esteem, a bivariate analysis could be conducted to see if there are statistical correlations between a person's level of self-esteem and alcohol consumption. It could be hypothesized that as the level of self-esteem rises, alcohol consumption will decrease. Measures of association and tests of statistical significance would need to be conducted to assess this relationship.

The measure of association that is used is determined by how the data are measured as well as what the goal of the research is: to compare variables or compare separate groups? Basically, measures of association are about estimating values on one variable by knowing values on another; recall that statistics are based on probabilities.

When both variables to be compared are on the nominal level (both are simply categories), **lambda** can be used. When lambda is computed, values range from 0 to 1; a perfect statistical association between the variables would be represented by the number 1.00. As mentioned earlier, nominal level data do not offer a lot of statistical options, but lambda allows a score to be given that shows how probable it is that the nominal variables are related, such as gender (male or female) and alcohol use (yes or no).

Lambda: A test of statistical significance for *nominal* level variables.

When a measure of association is desired for *ordinal* level data (categorical data that can be ranked), a common statistical measure of association between the variables is **gamma.** When gamma is computed, values range from −1 to 1. A strong negative association would be represented by a −1; 0 would indicate no relationship; and 1 would be a strong positive correlation between the variables in question. The difference between lambda and gamma is simply the level at which the data were collected. Later, Pearson's correlation (*r*), which is used for interval or ratio variables, is presented.

Gamma: A test of statistical significance for *ordinal* level variables.

To determine whether the association between the variables is not due to chance, a test of statistical significance is required; the most common one is chi-square (χ^2). When comparing *mean* (average) values between two or more separate groups, a statistical test such as the *t* test could be used.

t test: A statistical test used to determine whether the *mean* values between variables or between samples are statistically different from each other.

t Tests. The ***t* test** is a very common statistical test. Its purpose is to determine if the means, or averages, of two groups of scores differ to a statistically significant degree. As with other statistical tests, a set of mathematical procedures will provide a numerical value. The larger the absolute value of *t*, the more likely it is to show a significant difference between the two groups being compared.

There are three different types of *t* tests (one-sample, paired, and independent/dependent). The first is used with one group of subjects, or one sample. The second type is used with two groups that are paired in some way. For example, if a group of prisoners is randomly divided into two groups, and one group (treatment) receives anger management training, and the control (comparison) group does not get the treatment, then a paired *t* test should show the mean difference between the two groups following the anger management intervention. Because the two groups of prisoners were randomly divided, the mean difference prior to the intervention should be the same, or show no statistically significant difference. If the treatment (anger management) has any impact, then a *t* test will show a statistically significant difference. If the two groups being compared have no connection to one another, then an "independent *t* test" would be used. For example, a researcher could assess whether students at X high school differ in their mean scores on end-of-the-year testing compared with the students at Y high school. While there are two separate groups, randomization is not essential in the independent *t* test.

Once a *t* value has been determined, the researcher still needs to know what the value means. To determine if the value obtained is statistically significant, meaning the number is large enough to reflect that the differences between the groups are not just due to chance, the researcher must rely on a chart or table that will show if the value is statistically significant at various levels (e.g., .001, .01, .05), which in statistics means that the result of sampling error is no more than 1 in 1000, 1 in 100, and 5 in 100.

When assessing relationships between variables, it is important to be able to accept with some level of confidence that the differences found between two groups or two variables are not due just to chance or to some other variable not accounted for in the data. While there is always the possibility that mistakes exist in one's ability to know that true differences exist, statistical procedures are helpful in providing some level of assurance. In statistics courses, attention will be given to issues of having mathematical "checks and balances" to help promote this ability. There is always a chance of being wrong by trusting the findings; therefore, important verification steps must be taken. For example, confidence intervals require statistical measures that help identify the margin of error considered acceptable for accepting the results. In the following sections, the discussion on the statistics used to help determine if true relationships exist in the data is provided; we will elaborate on how to reduce the common errors associated with the statistical procedures in order to promote confidence in trusting the statistical outcome.

Chi-Square. The researcher who desires to test hypotheses about categorical data (such as alcohol use and gender, or one's race and attitude toward the police) would likely use a statistical tool called **chi-square.** Typically, chi-square is used to analyze the association between variables. It can be used for either two-variable comparisons or when multiple variables are considered. If, for example, a researcher wants to know if males are more likely than females to have speeding tickets, then a chi-square is an acceptable test. Further, it could be evaluated if the type of car one drives affects the outcome as well. Chi-square allows several independent variables to be analyzed in one table against one dependent variable, and is particularly useful when the cross-tabulation matrix is greater than a 2 × 2. A researcher may have more than two categories on a variable (e.g., gender normally has just two categories, but the breakdown of ounces of alcohol has more than two categories). Likert scale responses are another example of a variable having multiple categories such as "strongly agree," "agree," "disagree," and "strongly disagree."

Chi-square: A test used when assessing the relationship between variables. It determines whether there is true statistical significance in the association between two or more variables.

Chi-square will provide not only a numerical value but also a measure of the *level of confidence*. In other words:

> Even when the association between two variables is consistent with the researcher's hypothesis, it is possible that the association was just due to chance or to the vagaries of sampling. . . . It is conventional in statistics to avoid concluding that an association exists in the population from which the sample was drawn unless the probability that the association was due to chance is less than 5%.
>
> *(Bachman & Schutt, 2011, p. 412)*

Type I error: When the null hypothesis that there is no relationship between the variables was erroneously rejected.

This means that if a researcher is accepting that variables are statistically correlated, the likelihood that there are errors needs to be small. If the chances are small, the null hypothesis that there is no relationship between two variables can be rejected.

Significance levels are reported as *p levels* and help determine the probability of making an error in assuming that variables are truly statistically related. These errors can be of two types. A false positive, or **Type I error,** occurs when the researcher thinks a relationship between variables exists when it really does not. The other type of error, a false positive, or **Type II error,** occurs when the researcher does not think a relationship exists between variables, and there really is a relationship.

Type II error: When the null hypothesis that there is no relationship between the variables should have been rejected but was instead accepted.

The lower the reported value of statistical significance set by the researcher (*p* level), the less likely it is that a Type I error will occur, but the risk of a Type II error increases. The researcher must determine which type of error is most relevant based on the research topic. The competent researcher can then specify, prior to data analysis, which level of statistical significance should be used. A level of statistical significance tells whether the observed difference is due to chance or is a real result between the variables. The common levels of statistical significance are .001, .01, and .05. For example, if the researcher uses a 5% (.05) significance level, he or she will reject the null hypothesis (that there is no relationship between the variables or groups) only if there is less than a 5% chance of making a Type I error. Eck and La Vigne illustrate the importance of this:

> The costs of making type I and type II errors will vary. For example, when evaluating a program to save officers' lives, making a type II error means rejecting a program that will save lives. Making a type I error means accepting a program that will not save lives. Most police managers would see a greater penalty for making a type II error in such a situation. However, when evaluating a relatively expensive and controversial program, most managers would see making a type I error (accepting the program when it offers no benefits) as more serious than making a type II error.
>
> *(1994, p. 133)*

Correlation Coefficients

As mentioned earlier, with interval level data, when the distance between the groups can be measured and when there are numerous attributes to a variable, simple cross-tabulations are not the most appropriate statistical choice. The use of correlation coefficients would be better when analyzing the relationship between variables that are interval level or ratio level of measurement. A correlation is the most frequent type of bivariate statistic, and a correlation coefficient is designated by the small *r*, with values ranging from –1.0 to 1.0. The closer the value is to 1.0, the higher the statistical relationship or correlation between the variables.

Pearson correlation coefficient: A measure of association between two continuous variables that can tell both the strength and the direction of the linear relationship.

Pearson Correlation Coefficient. The **Pearson correlation coefficient** is the most common tool used to measure the relationship (correlation) between interval level or ratio level variables. This procedure is extremely informative, since it reveals the *strength* as well as the *direction* of the relationship between variables. For example, if a criminal justice researcher wanted to measure the relationship between educational level and crimes committed by convicted felons, then the Pearson correlation coefficient would tell precisely the probability of association and the direction of the relationship. One would be able to determine, for example, whether lower education is statistically correlated to increased criminal offending.

Note that a correlation between two variables does not signify a "cause-and-effect" relationship. Correlation only measures the strength of the relationship between variables; it does not indicate whether one variable *causes* another because it does not control for the influence of other variables that could be affecting the relationship. If the goal of the research question is to determine what variables influence another variable, a multiple regression analysis would be preferred. For example, education level alone is not likely the cause of criminal behavior; other variables need to be considered if one desires to better understand criminal behavior. For example, could one's home life, peers, gender, geographic location, job opportunities, or level of self-control influence the probability of offending? To analyze cause and effect, multivariate analysis is needed.

MULTIVARIATE STATISTICS

When the research goal is to determine what effect the independent variables have on the dependent variable, a higher level of analysis is necessary. This involves moving beyond simply looking at one variable (univariate) or analyzing the relationship between two variables (bivariate). *Multivariate* analysis involves assessing the effects of multiple variables on the outcome variable(s) in order to determine cause-and-effect relationships.

Recall from previous discussions that the dependent variable is the variable of focus, or what is trying to be explained. What one thinks explains or causes the change is referred to as the independent variable(s). The dependent variable *depends* on the independent variables. Many times in the field of criminal justice and criminology, researchers are trying to explain why something occurs. For example, a researcher may be interested in explaining recidivism. Why do some inmates continue to commit crimes and return to prison? If the dependent variable is recidivism, what kinds of things influence recidivism? Could it be that the "kind of life" an inmate returns to affects the probability of returning to prison? A researcher can measure these effects and test hypotheses about recidivism. The "kind of life" is a very subjective concept, however. It would need to be operationalized, which means putting concepts (variables) in a form that can be measured statistically.

For example, one could assess the marital status of an ex-convict. A researcher might hypothesize that an inmate who returns to an established home with a spouse may be less likely to return to prison. The level of stability or happiness in the marriage might also need to be gauged in assessing the relationship between marital status and recidivism. Would the researcher also need to assess whether the married partner is involved in crime, as this could be a spurious variable between marital status and recidivism? The characteristics of the partner could be an influencing factor when assessing the relationship between marital status and recidivism. A researcher could hypothesize that if inmates have successful jobs upon release from prison, they will be less likely to recidivate. One could also suggest that if an inmate returns to a high-crime area, then recidivism is more likely; one might also evaluate whether the type of charge the inmate was incarcerated for has an impact on the likelihood of recidivism. Specifically, one might hypothesize that drug offenders are more likely to return to prison than are other types of offenders. If inmates return to drug use upon release, the probability is greater that they will return to prison. This prompts a researcher to think about the inmates' involvement with treatment or rehabilitation programs. Does the involvement in such programs reduce the likelihood of recidivating? The list could go on, but we hope it is clear what the goal is in multivariate analysis: using multiple independent variables to explain variance in the dependent variable. The most common way to assess the impact of independent variables on the dependent variable is through a statistical technique called *regression analysis*.

Regression analysis: A statistical procedure designed to determine whether the values of the dependent variable can be "predicted" by knowing the values of the independent variable(s). It is a measure of association (existence, strength, and direction) between multiple variables. There are many types, including Logit and Negative Binomial, although the most common is Ordinary Least Squares (OLS).

Regression Analysis

In **regression analysis** the goal is to determine if "Y is a function of X," which suggests that the values of Y can be understood in terms of how the values of X change. Basically, regression is about evaluating cause and effect. There are several types of regression, but stated briefly, "Regression analysis is a technique for establishing the regression equation representing the geometric line that comes closest to the distribution points" (Maxfield & Babbie, 2008, p. 417). If two variables have a perfect (1.0) positive relationship and the values or scores are plotted on a graph, then the resulting line would be straight and would run from the lower left (lowest value and fewest occurrences) to the upper right (highest values and greatest number of occurrences). The line that is created reveals a linear relationship where all the data points fall on a straight line, with a greater or lesser slope to the axes. This regression line is a "line that is the best fit to the points in a scatter plot, computed by ordinary least squares regression" (Bohrnstedt & Knoke, 1988, p. 259). Again, graphs are helpful; in this case, plotting the points on a regression line reveals how close the cases follow that line—the straighter and closer the better. Basically, this method of statistical analysis assesses if the independent variable(s) influence the outcome variable (the dependent variable), not just by chance but by statistical probability. Ultimately, we are trying to determine the *cause* of things, like crime, drug use, binge drinking, violence, pedophilia, successful marriages, good grades, job satisfaction, delinquency, successful parenting, and more. The possibilities are endless.

The Importance of the Planning Process

How research projects are designed in the early stages determines what statistical methods can be performed later. The reliability and validity of the outcome of the study are contingent upon early decisions. It is important to understand why such care needs to be given in the construction, development, and details of research projects. Those early decisions not only will determine what statistical procedures can be conducted once the data have been gathered, but also will dictate how much the researcher can trust the outcome of the statistical data analysis. Every decision is important for the quality and integrity of the study.

Early decisions about who to study, how to sample the population, what variables should be included, and how variables are operationalized are all important. The data collection and entry stage are as important as the actual analysis. Diligence needs to exist at every stage of the research project. Great care should be given to ensuring that the data are entered into the statistical analysis program as accurately and ethically as possible. During analysis, it is also a good time to reflect on all ethical issues and to avoid becoming so headstrong about finding statistical support that opposing evidence is overlooked.

Another reason for research methods students to be aware of the different types of data analysis is because it can help students understand and appreciate the empirical work they read when they utilize peer-reviewed journal articles. As mentioned elsewhere in this book, it is important to understand what work already exists on a topic at the start of any research venture. It can be very frustrating to find quality research but not be able to decipher what it means. This can be true with both quantitative and qualitative data. Hopefully, this elementary discussion on data analysis has fostered a better understanding of what the objective is in quantitative research, and also hopefully provides a basic understanding of what will be forthcoming in statistic courses.

SUMMARY

For those in their first research methods course, this chapter may seem overwhelming. There is mixed opinion on whether a statistical-based chapter should even appear in a research methods text. Some research methods instructors will appreciate the focus, and others will contend it is best left for the statistics courses. It is our opinion that the better the connection between research methods and statistical data analysis procedures, the better the opportunity for quality research projects and the better the chance of student comprehension. Do not be worried if everything presented in this chapter does not *automatically* resonate, it may take some time. You should appreciate that mathematical procedures are available to help contribute to scientific inquiry, and be aware that early decisions in the research process will determine the ability to conduct advance statistics analysis after the data have been collected. Your department may offer two (or more) separate courses, but the two topics are "joined at the hip."

The next chapter on qualitative analysis will also entail some of the basic statistical procedures presented in this chapter. However, it will focus more on those employed by qualitative researchers and presents many alternative ways of analyzing research data.

KEY TERMS

- Bar chart
- Bivariate statistical analysis
- Chi-square
- Cross-tabulation
- Continuous data
- Discrete data
- Gamma
- Histogram
- Inverse statistical relationships
- Interval level data
- Lambda
- Leptokurtic curve
- Mean
- Measures of central tendency (MOCT)
- Median
- Mesokurtic curve
- Multivariate analysis
- Mode
- Normal bell-shaped curve
- Nominal level data
- Ordinal level data
- Pearson correlation coefficient
- Pie chart
- Platykurtic curve
- Positive statistical relationships
- Range
- Ratio level data
- Regression analysis
- Standard deviation
- Statistics
- *t* test
- Type I error
- Type II error
- Variance

CRITICAL THINKING EXERCISES

1. Describe the strengths of quantitative research when it comes to data analysis.
2. List and define the four levels of measurement and why are they important to discuss in a chapter focused on data analysis.
3. What are measures of central tendency? List and describe four.
4. Describe how outliers affect the distribution of the data and why they should be addressed.
5. Identify an empirical article and focus on making sense of the data analysis section. What are some of the basic procedures that you recognize?
6. What is meant by tests of statistical significance? How do these tests vary depending on the level of measurement of the variable? Be specific.
7. What does the term *inverse relationship* mean? Be specific and provide three examples.
8. In order to assess causality, three important criteria must be met. Please list and describe each of these.
9. Describe what Type I and Type II errors are and why they occur.
10. Identify an empirical article and focus on making sense of the data analysis section. What are some of the basic procedures that you recognize?
11. If you are interested in understanding drug use, you could conduct a study on causality (multivariate analysis). If the dependent variable is "cocaine use," what independent variables do you think "predict"/influence the likelihood of being a cocaine user? List at least five independent variables. Then, write these five independent variables in a question format as if they were going to be administered in a questionnaire. Refer to chapter 6 in this book on survey research if needed.
12. What is a regression analysis? Why is it useful?
13. When using regression analyses, what must one guard against?

CHAPTER 10

Qualitative Data Analysis

CHAPTER OBJECTIVES

After reading this chapter students should:

- Better understand causality.
- Understand why all researchers do not value causality equally.
- Know the traditional and contemporary means of qualitative data analysis.
- Appreciate the tension that may exist between traditional and recent methods of analysis.
- Understand why some qualitative researchers employ statistics.
- Recognize qualitative software packages.
- Be able to identify a priori and convergent analytical differences.
- Design a mixed methods strategy for data analyses.

Chapter 9 explored elementary and intermediate data analysis by focusing primarily on statistics and data handling for quantitative research designs, as well as the logic behind it. This chapter provides an overview of the analytical process with qualitative data. In keeping with the core research requirement that biases be made explicit, we acknowledge that this chapter was a learning experience for us; we are each much more familiar with conventional statistical analysis. The chapter begins with a review of the important topic of causality, which was first introduced in chapter 1. The idea of causality is an effective means to illustrate some core differences between quantitative and qualitative analysis. These differences present a schism that some argue is insurmountable, as the discussion of causality illustrates.

Causality: Specifying the cause for why things occur. Three criteria must be met to establish a relationship: covariance, temporal sequencing and no additional influencing variables.

Historically, qualitative data analyses did not rely much on statistics, and even today **causality** is of little interest to many qualitative researchers. While reviewing this chapter Polizzi, a clinical psychologists commented (correctly) that, "Causality is simply not part of this conversation and if it is, the approach is either not truly qualitative or it reflects a type of apologist stance. Qualitative research is not interested in attempting to legitimate its existence relative to quantitative methodology and theory. As a subjective/constructionist perspective, such constructs as causality and validity do not have the same meaning and therefore can't be employed as if these are objective constructs that carry no specific value-laden philosophical content" (personal correspondence, April 18, 2017). On the other hand, quantitative researchers are acutely concerned with causality and in fact most statistical techniques (e.g., regression analysis) are predicated on this underlying assumption. Establishing causality is but one of the differences between the two approaches. Polizzi noted, "there is a wide gap between quantitative and qualitative research methodologies but there also exists the unstated question that is almost never asked: how do we address the ontological gaps between these two methodological approaches? . . . but it may not be resolvable" (personal correspondence, April 18, 2017). However this disconnect has been recognized and some researchers have sought to bridge the divide between methodologies. **Ethnostatistics** was one of the first such efforts. According to Van Maanen, Manning and Miller (1988, pp. 5–6 in Gephart), "ethnostatistics is another long line of attempts to bridge the gap between qualitative and quantitative research. It is, perhaps, a more sophisticated attempt than many because it suggests that this gap can be narrowed only when the methods developed by members of one camp are made use of by members of the other." Ethnostatistics has evolved considerably since then, but a schism, or gap, still remains between quantitative and qualitative researchers, a gap that in the view of some (e.g., Polizzi) is unresolvable. However, bridging this gap has become an increasing trend, predicated on the availability of massive computing strength and improved software for qualitative data handling. The result is that, for better or worse, increasingly statistics are used in qualitative studies. For these reasons, this chapter is divided into two sections, initially the more traditional means of analysis are presented (which must be understood first), followed by the more recent use of statistical methods. First, however, the vital though controversial role of causality must be understood from each perspective.

Ethnostatistics: Studies the social phenomenon of statistics as a unit of analysis in its own right. The focus of understanding is on the when, why and how statistics are used as a resource by people and institutions.

CRITIQUE OF CAUSALITY

The previous chapter concluded with multivariate analysis. Multivariate analysis is predicated on the assumption of causality. Recall the goal is to determine what factors *cause* a particular outcome. One can rely on a statistical analysis to help assess

Association: Statistical test to determine if two or more variables are truly associated. The link between variables can move in the same direction (positive) or opposite directions (negative).

Temporal Order: One of the fundamental requirements for determining causality; it means the cause must precede the effect.

Spuriousness: When the relationship between dependent and independent variables is really due to some variable that is not known or accounted for in the study.

this, or one can utilize a more personalized subjective technique—as qualitative researchers advocate. For causality to be established from a statistical perspective, three conditions or criteria must be met. One could not really infer causation if any one of the three is absent. The easiest way to remember these is to focus on the terms: ***association***, ***temporal order***, and ***spuriousness***. If a researcher intends to run multivariate analyses, these factors must be considered at the very initial stages of the research design. This is another reason it is important to have a basic understanding of statistics. If a researcher desires to infer causality, the factors connected to statistical procedures have to be considered early in the research process to ensure a better chance of meeting the criteria of causality. If conducting a qualitative study, this is much less important and often of no importance. Causality might still be important and can be rigorously assessed, however it is often difficult to plan and strategize for it prior to the study. This is because with qualitative research one may not even know which variables will be important until the study is well underway. For example, during a 3-year study of community policing, it became apparent that there were very distinct differences between male and female police officers. After reviewing reams of field notes these differences (themes) became a focus of the study (Lanier, 1996). Causal relationships therefore could not have been predicted in advance since the focus was community policing, not gender differences.

Stated simplistically, in order for quantitative researchers to assess causality, specific criteria must be met. There must be a statistical association between the variables, the cause must precede the effect in time, and the relationship between the variables cannot really be due to some other variable influencing the relationship between X and Y. Importantly, other factors must be accounted for and taken into consideration. Conversely, causality is not even a subject for reflection by many qualitative scholars.

There are thus differences between quantitative and qualitative studies with regards to establishing and/or considering causality. First, there are philosophical differences between the methods that revolve around causality. These differences are so pronounced that some deem them unresolvable. For example, as Polizzi observed, "there is no way to narrow the gap you observe without first exploring the ontological approaches from which these two methods emerge. Causality assumes a Newtonian logic—that is, the ability to trace a 'backward trajectory' by which to determine cause or first mover. The qualitative approach is concerned with the 'in-between' of subjective perspective and world and therefore really has no backward trajectory to legitimately trace" (personal correspondence, April 18, 2017). One approach thus is interested in causes while the other in consequences or effects. So, by combining both in one study—mixed methods- one may be able to ascertain cause and effect.

Second, with a quantitative study the researcher should strategize prior to data collection on how to best ascertain causality. However, due to the more flexible nature of qualitative research, causality is not considered until the final stages of a study. Third, beginning with Durkheim's seminal study of suicide (1951), social science researchers have displayed a preference for statistics. In fact, Van Maanen (1979) went so far as to state that "statistical procedure and quantitative methods held an almost monopolistic grip on social science until recent years" (cited in Gephart, 1988, p. 9). However qualitative researchers have used methods other than data analysis to determine casual relationships (as shown next). This tension between analytical methodologies persists. Fourth, one's understanding of the nature of reality dictates specifics methods. W. I. Thomas (1923) first observed that if subjects define a situation as real, or as reality, that situation is *real* in its consequences. For example, if a student has a fear of the dark and the power suddenly goes off in the classroom the student may experience physical manifestations of fear. Logically, the student knows that no monsters are lurking in the shadows or under the desk, but this rational knowledge cannot offset the increased heart rate and respiration that accompanies the ensuing panic attack due to terror caused by the darkness. The measurement of this reaction would be quite different between qualitative and quantitative researchers! The qualitative researcher would likely engage in thick descriptions using artful words to convey the senses of black, foreboding doom. For example,

> The fear of the dark is the flame
> at the end of a match: one scratch,
> and it flares.
> Then a voice calls in the night.
> And you go to it.
> Wherever earth is in shadow,
> these fears burn like fires.
> This one is yours.
> You tend it. Feed it a stick.
> The flame crouches to eat the wood . . .
>
> *("The Fear of the Dark" by Nan Cohen, 2013)*

Conversely, the quantitative researcher would likely measure heart rate and breathing frequency in statistical terms: "The subject's heart rate increased from 80 beats per minute to 120 per minute when the lights were extinguished. This represents a 25% increase at a .05 level of significance. The respirations went from

15 breaths per minute to 30, or a 50% increase at .005." The quantitative researcher would likely then present the data in a chart:

SUBJECT 1

	Lights On	Lights Off	% Change
Heart rate	80	120	25*
Respirations	15	30	50**

*POC .05.
** POC .005.

Which analytical method would best convey the measure of fear? The feeling of fear? Which is most useful? What are the causality issues—the cause of the fear or the light being extinguished? What caused the underlying fear initially may interest a quantitative researcher while the effects of the fear might interest qualitative researchers. These differences are pronounced and are explained in greater detail next as we present traditional followed by contemporary qualitative analysis and as shown in insert 10. It is these types of incongruent underlying assumptions that lead some to question the possibility of mixed methods research.

INSERT 10.1

The (Insurmountable?) Divide between Qualitative and Quantitative Methodologies

David Polizzi, PhD, MA, LCAC
Indiana State University

The debate concerning quantitative and qualitative methodologies has been an ongoing conversation in the social sciences for over fifty years. In fact, if one was were to attempt to situate this conversation within its proper philosophical context, it would not be unreasonable to begin in the late 1600s and early 1700s with Rene Descartes and Giambattisa Vico. However, for our current discussion, it is probably more helpful to begin with something a little more contemporary. Robert Agnew's text, *Toward a Unified Criminology: Integrating Assumptions about Crime, People, and Society*, provides an appropriate starting point from which to explore this debate.

In this text, Agnew attempts to resolve perhaps the most vexing issue facing the social science research today: how to undo the divided nature of theory and methodology? The central culprits preventing the resolution of this divide are generally configured around the nature of reality, the nature of human beings, and the nature of society. Agnew correctly observes that until some agreement can be reached concerning the way in which these questions should be answered, the divide will likely remain (Agnew, 2011; Polizzi, 2016). So what does this so-called theoretical divide have to do with methodologies, research and theories; well actually, everything!

The issue concerning whether a graduate student or academic researcher uses a qualitative or quantitative research model is not solely determined by their fear or love of numbers or a "legitimate" application of "science"; rather, it also reflects the way in which they understand what it means to be human along with how that humanity takes up the reality of a social world. When a researcher employs a certain methodology, by which to study a specific topic or phenomenon, they are also employing a specific philosophical stance, which not only informs the methodology in question, but will likely determine the very content that they will examine and seek to explain. Like it or not, all social scientists are also philosophers, and as philosophers (Ph.D. actually stands for Doctor of Philosophy), the perspectives which we employ to establish what we know—epistemology—will also be greatly influenced by the philosophical stance concerning the general characteristics of that which we will be studying—ontology.

In attempting to answer the question concerning the nature of reality, the individual, and society, Agnew first seeks to establish the ontological frame of reference to be employed by the researcher or theoretical perspective that is attempting to say something about (in his examples) crime or criminal behavior. For example, if we determine that the basic characteristics of being human are defined by such constructs as rationality, free will, self-interest, or social concern, the methodology that we employ to study criminal behavior or crime will undoubtedly reflect these ontological assumptions and will privilege content that reflects the same. If, on the other hand, an ontological point of view is configured by a stance that views human being and social world as an inseparable relationality, the research methodology employed will reflect that position. When applied to either a quantitative or qualitative methodology approach these differences, perhaps unresolvable, clearly come into focus.

When attempting to identify the basic differences between qualitative and quantitative methodologies, two basic characteristics emerge: quantitative approaches to this topic are concerned with identifying generalities either within or between data sets, providing a degree of statistical significance to the findings of a given study, whereas qualitative methodology, is focused upon the unique perspective of a small group of research subjects. Whereas quantitative studies may have an enormous "n"—the actual number of items or individuals in a given study—and as a result are able to identify statistical generalities that can be applied to similar populations not specifically involved with a given study. Qualitative studies, on the other hand, may employ the use of

continued

Insert 10.1 *continued*

a single case study subject or include a very small number of individuals to study a specific topic or experience. Take for example the topic of heroin addiction.

When contextualized within the framework of a qualitative research study, the research topic, heroin addiction, is viewed from a more specifically subjective point of view. As I approach to study this experience, my focus is on the specific individual or small group of individuals, who have volunteered to take part in this study. My research question may simply be, "Please describe for me in as much detail as possible your experience of heroin use." From the responses from this initial reflection, additional questions may be asked, inviting the subject to further clarify a passage or set of thoughts that do not appear sufficiently clear to the researcher. As this process moves forward, the researcher and subject attempt to clarify as clearly as possible the depth of meaning the subject gives to this experience. As a result, it is extremely important, if one is to remain faithful to the qualitative perspective, for the researcher not to have a specific agenda or direction that he or she would like the discussion to follow. If I am truly interested in the individual experience of heroin addiction, then it is imperative that I allow the individual to pursue the direction of this narrative, as they will, without my imposition on that result.

Now it may be argued that such a pristine intention is disingenuous. The very fact that subjects are being recruited and asked to answer the researcher's question, already reveals a type of directive stance that is impossible to escape. Though this observation is perhaps generally true, if the researcher remains aware of this potential influence, it will be greatly reduced and acknowledged. Though the researcher is offering a general and open-ended research question, the process which it evokes is attempting to make sense of the experience of the client. This final observation leads us to another important question: How can this type of research be generalized? The short answer to this question is that it can't. Though this answer may be unsatisfactory to many reading this, it is one of the most important distinguishing factors between qualitative and quantitative research methodology.

Let's return to the experience of heroin addiction. When someone explores that experience from a qualitative perspective, it is exclusively focused on the understanding of that experience from the perspective of the individual subject or subjects. The conceptualization of heroin addiction in the aggregate, is simply not relevant to this type of research. Given that the fundamental starting point for qualitative research begins within the confines of subjective experience, only that narrative account becomes relevant to the study of that phenomenon. Though a number of generalities undoubtedly exist, they are not necessarily specific to this individual. When we stay overly fixated on the general qualities of a given experience, we lose all the subtle meanings that are perhaps central to how this individual has constructed their experience.

When we choose a specific research methodology, we are really deciding upon whether or not these results will reveal a specific set of generalities relative to a specific topic or provide a small number of specific narrative accounts of a given experience for a given individual. However we choose, two specific realities are simply unavoidable: either we conclude with a generalizable, but not specific, research finding or, we conclude with a very specific research finding that may be very beneficial to the participating subjects, but cannot provide any general understanding of the experience under study. As a result, there will certainly be instances when a more quantitative approach is more appropriate, due to the size of the number of participants and the specifics of the question or topic. On the other hand, because certain phenomena or experiences are so laden with immeasurable latency that a qualitative approach will be able to provide a greater depth of insight concerning the question being studied. If qualitative methodology is not concerned with the generalizability of its findings, how else does this perspective differ from more traditional research?

Take, for example, the construct of causality, as Lanier and Briggs (2017) present in this chapter. In its most general formulation, causality implies a first mover, a specific action or circumstance that results in a given behavior such as crime. From a qualitative perspective, subjective meaning replaces causality; the focus is less upon the why of some certain experience or result and more focused on the meaning given to it by the subject. An example may help to further clarify this point. I recall a client describing for me during his intake interview the specifics of his criminal conviction. When asked to describe the event, he stated, "Dave, I really should have killed him for disrespecting me, but I didn't. What I did was hit him with a hammer, and broke both of his knee caps."

The reason that I am using the preceding narrative account in a discussion concerning causality is to better clarify how that construct may be viewed from a more qualitative perspective. Though it could be observed that the cause of the client's violent action was a reaction to the experience of being disrespected, that observation would only be generally correct. The relationship between feeling disrespected and acting violently to address the "strain" evoked by that experience really does not tell us a great deal about how this process unfolds for this specific individual. In fact, his statement reveals that in this specific experience, he actually believed that a more severe response was warranted but had decided to act in a more "restrained" way. It is important to note that the client genuinely believed that his act of "restraint" was something to take pride in because his victim really "deserved" a more severe response. What does this brief account reveal qualitatively about the relationship between disrespect and violence?

As was stated previously, a general structure can be recognized between the experience of disrespect and the subsequent violent response employed by the individual to address the situation. However, as the client's statement reveals, the meaning of disrespect, and the response by which to resolve this experience, has a much more subtle context. Though the general relationship between disrespect and violence remains intact, the experience of disrespect does not

continued

Insert 10.1 *continued*

always require the same degree or severity of violence. Qualitatively, this distinction reveals that for this individual, the experience of disrespect is more subjectively fluid and is therefore not overly determined by a specific result. Such a subtle distinction would be important to follow with the subject.

Though it is important to stay with the narrative presented by the subject, it would be legitimate to ask him to reflect on other experiences of disrespect where he perhaps did not act violently. For example, it would be appropriate to ask him to describe what being disrespected means for him and how he normally resolves these situations. Does the experience of disrespect require some type of violent response regardless of context, or does context have some influence concerning how he will resolve the situation? By taking up the topic in this way, we begin to recognize the contours of this relationship from the meaning and perspective provided by the subject. Another example of the importance of subjective meaning within the context of qualitative inquiry can be observed in the following account.

A client entered his intake interview with a report he received from a hospital, which described him as a "belligerent drunk" after an altercation in their emergency room. He was very upset by this language and felt that it was very unprofessional of the hospital to describe him this way in an official report. The intake began by him describing the events of the situation outlined in the report. He reported that he was taken to the emergency room intoxicated and a violent altercation ensued during the evaluation process. Though he objected to the description of him in the hospital report, he seemed to confirm the basic facts of the situation: he was drunk and later became belligerent with hospital staff. When he was asked during the intake if he was drunk at the time, he reported, yes. When asked if he was involved in a violent confrontation with hospital staff, he also replied that he was. However, when I then replied, "So you were drunk and belligerent," he quickly became annoyed and said, "No, Dave, that's not right!"

Central to this experience for the client was the meaning he gave to the phrase "belligerent drunk." Much like the brief account discussed earlier, the fact of drunkenness and belligerence were not only present but were actually reiterated by the subject. However, that general fact really took us no closer to the subjective meaning of that experience for this individual. In fact, if I were to stay with the dictionary meaning of these two words, the actual meaning of this situation would have been left unstated. So although we could perhaps conclude that drunkenness greatly contributed to the violence that followed, these two signifiers are really pointing to something else for this client.

When I stated to the client my confusion, he clarified the significance of his upset in the following way. Though he never denied being drunk—and actually admitted being an alcoholic—and never denied that he was involved in the altercation at the hospital—he took great exception when he was described in the official report as being a drunk. For this client, being a drunk meant that he was someone who panhandled for cash to buy his liquor, was often unclean and smelled badly, wore dirty clothing and slept on street benches because he did not have a place to stay, and this description did not fit him. In fact, though on welfare, he was always sure to wear clean clothes, which he had purchased at Goodwill, had his own apartment and was always well groomed.

In each of the preceding accounts, a more subtle set of lived-meanings emerges when these narratives are taken up from a qualitative point of view. General observations can certainly be recognized in both brief narratives, but the actual subjective meaning of these experiences would not be clearly recognized. Any attempt to make any clear causal connection between experience and individual response would be incomplete at best, and likely miss the most important nuances of these situations. If, however, this type of research is uninterested in generalizable data, how can we be certain about the results that this type of research methodology provides?

One of the more important aspects of traditional quantitative research is the ability of others to replicate the findings of a completed study. For qualitative research methodology, replication takes on a different significance. Given that most qualitative research employs some type of subjective narrative account of a given experience or situation by which to study that phenomenon, it is often necessary to include those narratives, interviews, or written reflections along with the researcher's findings. The inclusion of such data allows the reader to follow the thinking of the researcher by reading the actual subjective accounts obtained from the study. The actual conclusions provided by the researcher can then be examined to determine how accurately they reflect the perspective offered by the participating subject(s).

However, it is important to keep in mind that this strategy may also reveal other possibilities that could have been pursued by the researcher but were not. Such a conclusion does not reflect the flawed nature of the study; rather, it clearly reveals the subjective quality of this process, which by definition must also include the specific ways in which the researcher approaches this material. As a result, the "structure" of this type of methodological approach is both subjective and relational to the topic under study and rejects the "subject/object dichotomy" often configuring more traditional research findings. Though it is certainly reasonable to observe that any form of research is in the end a type of subjective speculation, the approach which underlies that speculative process will determine the specific ways in which the methodological context of that speculation will be understood. This leads to our final question.

As was mentioned previously, one of the most difficult questions that one confronts when discussing the differences between qualitative and quantitative method is the ontological framework from which these two perspectives emerge. Perhaps stated more simply, what are the characteristics of a given subject that would become something else if these characteristics were not present? For example, how would we talk about human beings who do not have bodies?

continued

Insert 10.1 *continued*

How would we study the migration of birds that don't fly? I think you get the idea. Ontology or ontological characteristics of a given organism are simply those attributes or physical forms that are required or fundamental to that animal or situation. It would make little sense to attempt to study the migratory flight path of human beings, for the simple reason that we do not have wings—and airplanes don't count.

Ontology, then, becomes the philosophical context from which research methodology emerges. For example, qualitative research is driven by an ontological frame of reference that privileges a subjective point of view concerning what things mean. The truth is not something to uncover or something that is ready-made; rather, the truth emerges from the in-between of subjective perspective and social world. Such an understanding of the truth remains fluid and never complete. Think of any experience that you have had where there was some degree of anticipation or expectation before it actually occurred. Now think of how you felt the next day. Was your understanding of the anticipated event the same as the meaning you gave it the next day? Truth then may be considered relative and transitory.

The preceding comparison offered does take us in a slightly different direction, but in the end it attempts to resolve the same concern. If your expectation is not actually experienced, how is that event understood? Does the difference reflect a type of personal movement that allows you to recognize this new possibility in some way, is the new experience simply rejected because it does not reflect your anticipated causality, or does the new experience allow you to recognize something changing in you that has helped to construct this anticipated situation into something unexpected?

The anticipation of this experience becomes a type of research topic that actually tests your hypothesis concerning what this anticipated event means for you. Imagine the anticipation you had concerning a first date with someone you had recently met. Related to this anticipation are those past relationships that helped to create the person you currently are, or at least the person you believe yourself to be. Is your anticipation weakened by the belief that this too will result in another failed relationship that will prove how unlovable you truly are, or will this be the person you have always hoped to meet but never did, or something in-between? If you construct yourself as someone who will never be happy or loved, that will likely be the result. In a manner of speaking, you have ontologized unhappiness as one of the fundamental characteristics that defines you. You have predetermined what this experience must mean. However, if you stay open to this new experience and the possibility that it may offer, something else becomes possible. Such a stance does not change the past, but neither does it hold you captive to it.

What this example has attempted to illustrate is the way in which ontology greatly influences what we know. If what I know is predicated upon an unchanging set of beliefs or assumptions about the world, the world and my beliefs never change. If I accept, for example, the phrase, "once a criminal always a criminal," I have rejected outright any possibility that I will ever allow this individual to be seen as anything but a criminal. Though there may be some variance in meaning, in the end such possibility will be understood as a possibility exclusively for the ontologically criminal.

The resolution of the ontological differences within these competing methodologies is likely not possible. Whereas the quantitative perspective remains indebted to Descartes and Newton and Russell, qualitative analysis remains tied to Vico, the phenomenological tradition, American pragmatism, social construction, and the Continental philosophical tradition. Because each approach and methodology starts from a very different point of reference, and tends to reject the fundamental aspects of its competitors' philosophical perspectives, many social sciences will likely remain divided on methodologies. Though certain attempts at mixed methods have emerged over the last twenty or so years, these fundamental ontological concerns really have not been addressed. Superficial attempts at healing this divide may be offered, but they will not be successful without sufficiently answering the more difficult questions that lie just below the surface of this discussion.

References

Agnew, R. (2011). *Toward a unified criminology: Integrating assumptions about crime, people, and society.* New York, NY: New York University Press.

Polizzi, D. (2016). *A philosophy of the social construction of crime.* Bristol, UK: Policy Press.

TRADITIONAL QUALITATIVE ANALYSIS

Qualitative analysis is actually more diverse and complicated than statistical analysis. For one thing, there are many forms of qualitative research (e.g., oral history, ethnography, interviews, participant observation, etc.), and each may have a preferred method of analysis. For example, Gubrium argues, "While it is usually distinguished from a positivist approach, qualitative sociology is nonetheless not a unitary enterprise. . . . Three orientations . . .—structural, articulative and practical—show how analytic focus provides different visions of field reality" (1988, p. 23). However, all qualitative analytical schemes share some common features. This section outlines those commonalties for selected methodologies (yet are not all covered due to space considerations).

In very general terms qualitative analysis is concerned with identifying consistent themes and patterns that emerge from the data (regardless of the collection method). But qualitative analysis is also concerned with context, meaning, ritual, and sensing. The identified themes and other analytical sources are then compared between research subjects and situations to see if they share commonalities. From this emerges theory testing or theory generation. How these themes and contextual meanings are identified varies between the types of qualitative methods employed, as demonstrated next.

Oral histories: Precedes other forms of recorded history, using information passed verbally from one generation to the next.

Oral Histories. **Oral histories** are the oldest research method still employed. This method of knowledge transmission is displayed through folk tales, family histories, religious ceremonies, and other means still utilized daily, without recognizing their history. Some of these historical mechanisms are not even oral but physical. For example, in Western cultures, typically hand shakes correlate when greeting someone. Parents or guardians, however, should explain the meaning behind a handshake orally. Our experience has been that many students today, and presumably their parents and guardians, do not understand why we shake hands. In class we use this explanation to introduce oral histories. The analysis of oral histories is probably best conducted by **linguistics**. A deep understanding of old fables, songs, and nursery rhymes thus comprises a type of analysis. For example, the popular children's song "Ring around the Rosy" goes:

Linguistics: The scientific study of language.

> Ring around the rosy
> Pocket full of posies
> Ashes, ashes,
> We all fall down.

The specific meaning of this nursery rhyme is lost to history, but some scholars attribute it to the black plague that devastated England in 1665. In this analysis, "posies" are herbs that were carried by Brits in an effort to ward off the plague; "ashes" refers to the cremation of the bodies of victims, and "falling down" signified death. The meaning of this tune would present an interesting early public health research topic. However, there are other scholars who reject this interpretation and instead attribute it to early pagan rituals. The important point is that the search for the origin and meaning of the nursery rhyme is a type of qualitative analysis of an oral history. Clearly this analysis may interest researchers from varied academic disciplines such as public health, linguistics, English, or sociology.

Ethnography: Research whereby the data collector immerses him- or herself in the study.

Ethnography. After oral histories, the second oldest type of qualitative research is **ethnography**. According to Gephart, "Ethnography is the use of direct observation and extended field research to produce a thick, naturalistic description of a people and their culture. Ethnography seeks to uncover the symbols and categories members of a given culture use to interpret their world, and ethnography thus preserves the integrity and inherent properties of cultural phenomenon" (1988, p. 16). The key phrase is "thick, naturalistic description." In other words, the researcher will immerse himself or herself as deeply as possible into the group under examination. Initially cultural anthropologists developed this technique. The more a researcher can "play a role" or immerse himself or herself in the culture or group being studied, the better the resulting analysis, interpretation, and understanding will be. One classic example of an early ethnography is Howard Becker's *Outsiders* (1963).

Ethnography generally relies extensively on note taking. Over time the methods of note taking have evolved along with technological innovations. Where once paper and pencil were used to fill volumes of notebooks, today laptop computers and cell phones are much more likely to be used to compile the massive amounts of data typically collected during an ethnographic study. However, due to the nature of the methodology, taking immediate notes is sometimes not feasible or safe. For example, if one were mountain climbing, pulling out a pen and paper would be ill advised. But good researchers will record their observations and experiences as soon as possible after the event. This enhances accuracy and reduces faulty memory. It is critical to record events exactly as they occur, without bias or interpretations (at this point). Regardless of how the data are captured, the analytical process remains little changed. Once the data are first captured, the researcher—toward the end of the study—will seek to identify common themes or patterns. This is where the researchers' interpretations are applied. Depending on the size of the accumulated data set, a computer may assist with this process. Modern software is constantly improving in its ability to process, synchronize, and analyze qualitative data. However, ultimately it left to the researcher to recognize, categorize, and analyze the recurrent themes. From these themes and observations, theory is then generated, tested, and may then become part of the social science knowledge base.

Interviews. Another traditional means of qualitative data collection and analysis derives from the use of interviews. Darrell Steffensmeier (1986) interviewed "Sam" and provided a rich, thick, and complete analysis of the experiences, practices, methods, and motivations of a dealer in stolen property—a "fence." Steffensmeier also conducted one of the first mixed methods studies (although it was not called that then) since he corroborated the interview data provided by "Sam" with court records, newspaper articles, and other sources such as fellow criminals and law enforcement officers. Interview data can be analyzed in a variety of ways Loehnert (2010). Some, like Loehnert, go the route of quantification followed by traditional statistical analysis. Historically and contemporarily, interview data as analyzed by qualitative scholars is still subjected to the traditional analytical goal of theme identification and theory development. Interviews can come in many forms in qualitative research, but a typical characteristic of each is that the words of the spoken (those being studied) are typically maintained as they are written. An example of this is in use of Stand Point Theory or First Person Statements.

First Person Statement: Writing or speaking from the research subject's point of view.

First Person Statements. Related to qualitative interviews is the use of **first person statements.** A qualitative researcher may collect data written by the research subjects themselves (such as solo papers, letters, or diaries) which are not diluted, tainted, or revised by the researchers. Despite the obvious lack of objectivity and generalizability, these types of studies nonetheless have considerable merit. Petersen and Truzzi (1972) long ago compiled over 30 "stories" of virtually every type of criminal. The strengths of this Non-Analysis (our term) of first person statements are (1) they show the firsthand and life history experiences of criminals in their own vernacular without editorial (i.e., scientific) comment, (2) first person statements better expose the lifestyle of criminals, (3) causality is better understood, and (4) this type of (non)analysis adds "humanity and compassion to the field of scientific criminology because they help the reader identify with the criminal" (1972, p. ix). The analysis of this type of qualitative research is purposefully absent. It is left to the consumer or reader of the "research" to draw their own conclusions and identify themes. For this reason, perhaps, it is a less commonly employed study strategy. A much more commonly utilized research methodology is participant observation.

Participant Observation: A form of data collection in qualitative analysis, whereby the researcher comes to better understand the group, the culture or other phenomena of interest by sharing in its activities and participating in related events.

Participant Observation. **Participant observation** is the strategy where the researcher actively engages in the phenomenon being studied. Obviously, gender, age, race/ethnicity, and any possible combination of these demographic characteristics will limit the degree of participation. For example, a participant observation of pipeline welders would dictate a certain skill set (being able to weld) and physical ability (since climbing high in adverse conditions requires strength and stamina).

Once the participant observer enters the field, he or she must decide to what degree they desire to participate—bearing in mind that the greater the degree of participation the greater the understanding, however the greater the level of participation the more the researcher is likely to alter or influence the research data. Copious note taking and recording of seemingly insignificant events remains a fundamental feature of data collection on participant observation studies. Obviously, many events must be recorded after the fact—for example, after a day's work on the pipeline. The insignificant events, just mentioned, may later prove to be a fundamental part of the theory development.

Source: Berkut_34

There are many means of recording and storing the observations collected during a participant observation study. Diaries, video and audio recordings, and simply scribbled notes can all be used. Technological advances (e.g., the enormous computing and storage capacity of cell phones) have greatly altered the data collection and storage options. Once collected, the data must still be organized and analyzed. This once required many laborious hours spent reading, correlating, and organizing. Today, many qualitative researchers rely on software to recognize, categorize, and identify topics and trends worthy of further pursuit. The good researcher will, however, still be responsible for creating or recognizing theory to explain the data. Historically, when one conceptualized qualitative data analysis the use of software and technology was not a defining characteristic; that is not the case today.

Qualitative Mixed Methods. Adding to the complexity is the fact that one hallmark of good qualitative research is the use of multiple qualitative strategies in one study. Stanley Cohen (1972/2002), in his seminal study of "Folk Devils and Moral Panics" in a refutation to basic quantitative strategies, relied on this strategy:

> Using criteria determined by my theoretical interests rather than by how concepts can best be "operationalized," I decided to study reaction at three levels, in each case using a range of sources. The first was the initial on-the-spot reaction, which I studied mainly through observation, participant observation and the type of informal interviewing used in community studies. The second was the organized reaction of the system of social control, information about which I obtained from

> observation, interviews and the analysis of published material. The third level was the transmission and diffusion of the reaction in the mass media.
>
> *(Cohen, 2002, p. 19)*

From this description it is clear that document analysis, interviews, participant observation, and content analysis were all utilized. Each of these methodologies could rely on different analytical strategies, or they could be presented complimentarily in one style relying on labeling theory, cultural politics, and critical sociology (2002, p. xxvii), as Cohen did. These later became subsumed under the social constructionist paradigm. In this analysis problems are deemed to be socially constructed, and consequently context, theme, and linguistics are the topics (variables in positivistic terms) of interest. Cohen correctly notes that, "the idea that social problems are socially constructed does not question their existence nor dismiss issues of causation, prevention and control" (2002, p. xiii). The issue to him was proportionality: what affect the crime had, the media's influence, and the ensuing moral panic. Measurement was thus implicit; it was not an identifiable part of the qualitative analysis.

Meta Analysis: A research approach of combining qualitative and quantitative data from several studies to develop a single conclusion that has greater statistical value.

Scholars have conducted research on the rigor associated with qualitative research. Recently Hays, Wood, Dahl, and Kirk-Jenkins (2016) conducted what in quantitative terms would be considered a **meta analysis** when they examined 15 years of qualitative research (68 articles from 1999–2014). They sought to "provide longitudinal context of research quality" and concluded that thick description, triangulation and reflexivity were the most common research strategies while the least commonly employed were peer debriefing, external audit, and substantive validation. There are also an increasing number of journals that are solely devoted to qualitative research and/or theory. Among the best, by academic discipline, are the *Journal of Philosophical and Theoretical Criminology, Qualitative Sociology, Qualitative Research* (multi disciplinary), and *Qualitative Health Research*. While with the exception of *Qualitative Research* these are generally discipline specific, we suggest that mixed discipline research teams allow for the potential for a stronger research design.

Likewise, since we advocate mixed methods research, it is vital to outline how the analysis should occur. It is first important to recognize that the two methods and subsequent analysis serve very different functions. Curry and Nunez-Smith succinctly laid this out:

> Qualitative inquiry can inform the development or enhancement of quantitative instruments or interventions, generate hypotheses for testing in the quantitative component, or help to explain unexpected or incomplete findings from the quantitative analyses. Quantitative inquiry can test hypotheses that are grounded in the qualitative data or generate questions to be explained with qualitative data.

> Fundamentally, each type of data addresses an aspect of the research question that the other cannot, such that the findings are "mutually illuminating."
>
> *(2015, p. 230)*

This chapter will conclude with a discussion of combining qualitiative and quantitative (mixed methods) analysis. First, however, a review of analytical strategies of contemporary qualitative researchers is beneficial.

CONTEMPORARY STATISTICAL QUALITATIVE ANALYSIS

Ethnostatistics was one of the first contemporary efforts to blend qualitative data with statistical manipulations. Van Maanen, Manning, and Miller noted:

> Ethnostatistics involves one or more of the following research activities: (1) conducting ethnographic studies of groups that routinely produce statistics, (2) testing the technical and operational assumptions that are involved in the production of statistics, and (3) examining the use of statistics as a rhetorical device in various kinds of research publications
>
> *(1988, pp. 5–6, cited in Gephart, 1988).*

In other words, in this connotation, the use of statistics is the research topic!

Since then, it has become increasingly common for scholars to take questionnaire and interview data that is open ended and analyze it. Loehnert attempts to show "how data of qualitative category type, often gathered via questionnaires and surveys, can be transformed into appropriate numerical values to enable the full spectrum of quantitative mathematical-statistical analysis methodology" (2010, p. 1). It should be mentioned however, that some qualitative scholars do not consider this qualitative research at all; nonetheless it is published as such by others.

There are many effective software programs that qualitative researchers can rely on. Just as software programs such the Statistical Package for the Social Sciences (SPSS) and Statistical Analytics Software (SAS) for the past 40 years revolutionized how quantitative research is analyzed, these new qualitative packages also show great potential and have increased the ability to analyze qualitative data. There are even websites (e.g., http://www.predictiveanalyticstoday.com/top-qualitative-data-analysis-software/) that rank the many different available programs. The website http://www.predictiveanalyticstoday.com recently ranked QDA Miner, ATLAS.ti, HyperRESEARCH, MAXQDA, and NVivo as being the top programs. Quirkos is yet another popular program. Clearly this is a huge growth area within qualitative research. While only a very few (relatively speaking) software packages have dominated quantitative research, in large part due to their earlier development and historical dominance, a plethora of qualitative analytics packages exist and no clear-cut programs dominate the field (such as SPSS and SAS do for quantitative analysis). Qualitative data software is used for "transcription analysis, coding and text interpretation, recursive abstraction, content analysis, discourse analysis and grounded theory methodology" (http://www.predictiveanalyticstoday.com/top-qualitative-data-analysis-software/). There are specific programs that specialize in certain types of analysis. For example, QDA Miner is designed primarily for mixed methods qualitative analysis. Another popular program, NVivo, is designed to analyze text-based (books, articles, etc.) and multimedia data sources for both large and small data sets. It can "test theories, identify trends and cross-examination information" (http://www.predictiveanalyticstoday.com/top-qualitative-data-analysis-software).

One general characteristic that most of these programs share is a capacity for storing and categorizing large amounts of data, data which may appear to be unrelated to one another but which can be made congruent. The software used by qualitative researchers greatly simplifies the coding and identification of important words. At a basic level, just consider how word searches and spell checking has simplified all writing that relies on software (e.g., Microsoft Word).

Traditional qualitative researchers (one of us included) seriously question the ability of software to accomplish tasks such as theory development. But regardless of some skepticism this is clearly the future of qualitative research. This however, is one of the very reasons that this book was created to show the pros and cons of both quantitative and qualitative research methods, as well as to offer up the potential benefits of combining the two.

MIXED METHODS ANALYSIS

In mixed methods research qualitative and quantitative data can be, and often are, analyzed independently; however, each method should influence the analysis of the other. In other words, a constant conversation must exist that aims to strengthen the overall study conclusions. As a means of a brief review consider the words of health sciences scholars Curry and Nunez-Smith: "Qualitative analysis is a systematic and iterative process of analysing textual data inductively, generating conceptual categories or recurrent themes to describe or explain phenomena . . . Quantiative analysis uses statistical approaches with numeric data to produce measures of statistical significance and association between variables (2015, p. 231).

One key issue is *when* the data analysis strategy should be developed, either a priori or emergently. These are two very different approaches. With a convergent mixed methods research design both the quantitative and qualitative analysis are described in the initial study development or proposal, hence this is called "a priori." Conversely, with a sequential or multiphase research strategy, data analysis is not defined until the actual data collection is underway (Curry & Nunez-Smith, 2015, p. 231). This "emergent" approach will create IRB challenges for some, if not many, researchers.

There are several factors that must be considered with mixed methods analysis. First, the analysis plan must be aligned with the study goals and design. Second, various study components must be prioritized. Will the qualitative and quantitative approaches have equal weight or will one be prioritized over the other? Finally, the astute mixed methods researcher will determine points of data integration. Will the data remain independent until the research results are tabulated or will the data be integrated as the study progresses (as in sequential designs)? See Curry and Nunez-Smith (2015) for more on this.

This chapter has provided a brief overview of qualitative data analysis methods, analytical tools, and strategies. Just recognize that regardless of software or technique the overall objective should be to identify themes, patterns, and anomalies to help develop or test theory. This theory can be original or existing (Lanier, Henry, & Anastasia, 2015).

KEY TERMS

Association
Causality
Ethnostatistics
Ethnography
First Person Statement
linguistics
Meta-analysis
Oral histories
Participant Observation
Spuriousness
Temporal Order

CRITICAL THINKING EXERCISES

1. In order to assess causality, three important criteria must be met. Please list and describe each of these.
2. What philosophical differences exist between qualitative and quantitative researchers?
3. How do these differences impact the issue of causality?
4. Does qualitative analysis differ from quantitative analysis? What do you think about combining the two? Why?
5. What is the common means of evaluating field data?
6. What are the more common types of qualitative research? Least common?
7. What is the ultimate goal of qualitative analysis?

CHAPTER 11

Beyond Research: An Aid to Writing Success

CHAPTER OBJECTIVES

After reading this chapter students should:

- Be able to specify what plagiarism is and how to avoid it.
- Understand and incorporate the referencing guidelines for the social sciences.
- Implement the foundations for more successful writing.
- Recall and integrate the keys to successfully constructing sentences.
- Be reminded and have a resource guide for the proper use of common grammatical rules used in sentence structure.
- Be able to construct paragraphs and organize written work to provide the best flow and organization.
- Appraise why slang, value-laden words, emotional terminology, and "flowery" statements can reduce the quality and professionalism of research manuscripts.
- Select appropriate word choice for written work.
- Have more confidence in formally presenting both verbal and written communication.
- Understand why first and second person should be avoided in most research manuscripts.

Chapter organization in a textbook is fairly subjective. This chapter on "tips for successful writing" might come at the beginning, middle, or end; or it could simply be included as an appendix as a source of reference. For the authors of this text, their many years of teaching have proven to them that not all students know how to cite properly nor do they have the background and experience in being strong, effective writers, so one whole chapter has been dedicated to that objective.

It is hoped that students at the college level have realized that conducting research is far more than just pulling together a literature review on a specific topic, and students also understand that *how* the research is presented is extremely important. A research design and project could be exemplary in many regards, but if it is not written in a professional, sound manner it will not be taken seriously. It is important to understand how to conduct a research project from start to finish; however, to be a successful researcher, effective citing and writing skills are also needed. "Selling" a point in academic work (research included) is about the content as well as the structure and professional presentation. Importantly, the research manuscript or report needs to be written in a manner that adheres to professional referencing guidelines and follows basic writing requirements. Spelling and grammar check have been great technological advancements, but the software does not identify all errors (just ask the editors of this text!), and unless the document has been vetted through Turnitin.com, Safeassign, or some other author originality check, the software does not flag plagiarism. Students need to be very proactive to make sure they are properly citing work.

One of the very first steps in a research project is to identify what is already known on the topic. By doing this, researchers are empowered with knowledge, questions to ask, and options to include in their own work; however, they need to incorporate others' research in a professional, organized, and meaningful way. Writers must always give credit for what is utilized from others' work; if that rule is violated, it is considered plagiarism. Plagiarism is not always intentional; sometimes students have just not learned accurate referencing and citing protocol (or do not understand its necessity). These students are not purchasing papers nor copying classmates' work; they are simply not following correct citation procedures. However, just as "ignorance of the law" is no excuse for breaking the law, students are *expected* to know how to correctly reference and can be held accountable when they fail to do so. In the research domain, plagiarism is considered a serious offense. Individuals can be legally liable, suspended from school, dismissed from the course, or fail the assignment. The good news is that plagiarism can be easily avoided. The next section explains how.

PLAGIARISM

Plagiarism: Intentional or unintentional failure to "give credit where credit is due" when utilizing the work of others.

Avoiding Plagiarism

Plagiarism is claiming others' ideas, work, or words as one's own. A good researcher will always incorporate others' work into his or her own research; this is an important foundation of the research process. In fact, reviewing the literature generated by prior research is essential; however, proper credit must be extended to every single source utilized (borrowed).

While there are several forms of plagiarism, perhaps the most flagrant is copying another person's paper. This type of cheating can occur among classmates, or papers can be purchased or copied online. It is quite ironic, however, that some of the same online venues that sell research papers also sell the software required to detect this occurrence. Professors easily have the ability to detect when plagiarism occurs in a student paper. Many will take the time to investigate it and mete out the justice that thievery merits. Purchasing a paper is a bad practice from a commonsense perspective, but, more important, it never fosters true academic pursuit. Cheating and stealing (since plagiarism is a form of theft) are contrary to the very concepts of justice and ethics that should be at the center of social science research. Research finds that typically university students do not view plagiarism as a serious offense. Kraus (as cited in Power, 2009) states that students viewed plagiarism as a "quaint" concern of their professors, "something in the order of jaywalking or sneaking a grape while shopping for produce" (p. 82). Briggs, Sefiha, Burgason, and Smith (2018) find that students vary in their views on plagiarism with some viewing it as a serious offense, some viewing it as not even a form of deviance, and others viewing it as a form of misconduct but one that can easily be rationalized.

Paraphrasing: The proper way to borrow the work of others. The referenced work should be put in the borrowing author's own words and then properly cited.

Quoting: Used more extensively in qualitative research projects. Otherwise quoting should be reserved for those statements that cannot be paraphrased and still retain the actual meaning. When following APA guidelines, if a quotation is utilized, the page number must be included along with the author and date in the in-text citation.

With the advent of the computer, and the internet, it is easy to locate information, material, statistics, research manuscripts, and so on. It is even possible (and very easy to do with current technology) to "cut and paste" directly from the work of others and include the material in one's own work. This is a risky practice, as work must either be paraphrased and referenced *or* quoted and referenced with complete in-text citations (including page numbers or paragraph numbers if quoting). The practice of cutting and pasting existing work could unintentionally result in plagiarism. The best practice is to put the work in "your own words" (to paraphrase it) and simply cite the source where the borrowed material originates. It is important to understand the concept of **paraphrasing.** It does not mean simply changing a word or two of the borrowed work; the material must be completely paraphrased. If instead the work is quoted, there are specific rules to follow for that. It is important to note however, that the American Psychological Association (APA) guidelines suggest to avoid quoting unless the original words cannot be amended or the meaning would be sacrificed (*Publication Manual for the American Psychological Association*, 2018.

Quoting is one way to include the work of others. When this strategy is used, quotation marks are placed around the words or sentences borrowed, and the author, date, and page number are included in the in-text citation. If it is a source that does not include page numbers, then the paragraph number should be substituted.

Typically, quoting should be reserved for verbiage that is so uniquely expressed that it cannot be paraphrased and still capture, or appropriately accentuate, the underlying thought. While quoting has been used in this text, it is done as a deliberate attempt to capture the true essence of qualitative research. It is a unique feature of qualitative work to replicate the words of others as they are originally spoken or written in the data collection process. This is different from citing someone else's research. Again, paraphrasing (and citing the work of others in text) is the typical approach—and not quoting.

Sometimes a student who is concerned about avoiding plagiarism will reference *every* sentence. This is unnecessary and distracting. Remember that it is acceptable to introduce a paragraph with "According to [author (date)]," and then the referenced work can follow. When a "train of thought" changes, the citation would need to be repeated (or a new reference included), but every sentence does not need to be referenced if it is on the same topic with the same author(s) in the same paragraph. If the paragraph is unusually long, it may be necessary to reference the citation more than once to remind the reader where the work originates. This also holds true when the borrowed work is simply injected into the paragraph and the citation comes at the end instead of the beginning.

Speaking of paragraphs, it is also necessary to consider the length. There should be no one- or two-sentence paragraphs, and rarely should one paragraph extend beyond a single page. In addition, an unwritten rule, but a good practice to follow, is to include at *least* one documented source in every paragraph of a literature review. A *single* source should not be the total focus of an entire literature review; a good review shows variability between sources, thereby demonstrating a thorough knowledge of the relevant literature. It is a good idea to verify if there is at least one source in each paragraph as a way of double-checking that plagiarism has not occurred in the literature review. For a detailed explanation of how to write a literature review and what should be included, see chapter 2. The next section of this chapter focuses on the specific mechanics of writing and referencing.

Publication Manual of the American Psychological Association (APA): One common referencing guideline for the social sciences; others include Turabian Reference Guide, Modern Language Association (MLA), and American Sociological Association (ASA).

PUBLICATION MANUAL OF THE AMERICAN PSYCHOLOGICAL ASSOCIATION (APA)

Students in the social sciences will likely rely on the ***Publication Manual of the American Psychological Association* (APA).** It is a good idea to purchase a copy of the manual, which outlines how to correctly format a paper and cite others' work and includes other tips to enhance a written product and the skill in conducting research. The authors of this research methods text considered providing an example of a research manuscript in this chapter; however, the APA manual also includes several examples itself. The APA style manual is updated periodically and is readily available, just be sure to purchase the most recent version. Students can also find referencing guidelines, answers to particular questions, and examples of proper referencing readily online. Be sure to use only trusted sites, however; for example, the APA has an online resource available, and Purdue Owl has become a popular reference among students. Another strategy (albeit less desirable) is to simply acquire a published paper written in APA style and "replicate" how that paper is formatted (do not assume it is devoid of mistakes, however). Some journals do have slight stylistic variations on APA style for their own journals, so unless a work is being published in a specific journal, the best approach is to utilize the APA manual itself.

Some students may be more familiar with another formatting style such as MLA; however, APA is typically utilized in the social sciences. The most logical way to think about citing via APA is that the *author* and *date* should appear next to what has been borrowed. There are variations on exactly how this can be accomplished, but the point is that the citation must be included *before* or *after* the work that has been borrowed.

Here is a brief example of APA in-text citing:

In order to deter crime, the punishment must be swift, severe, and certain (Wilson, 1983).

Note that the period comes at the end of the sentence, after the parentheses and not before them.

Incorrect = .(author, date)
Correct = (author, date).

Another easy way to reference someone is to put the citation at the beginning of the sentence.

According to Wilson (1983), in order for deterrence to be effective, the punishment must be swift, severe, and certain.

Because there are a variety of venues that can be used to find research that one would want to cite, the APA manual is important to have because it shows how different types of publications and online resources should be cited (e.g., a peer-reviewed journal article is cited differently than a government website, different than a book, and different than personal correspondence). Learning APA can initially seem daunting to a student, but having the manual enables one to avoid memorizing any stylistic protocol; just learn to use the table of contents to locate examples, until APA becomes routinized.

The APA guide guards against plagiarism by explaining what it is and how to avoid it. The key to remember is that if a statement is not something everyone knows (general common knowledge, such as that the sun can burn skin), then it needs to be verified with a reference. This means that periodically writers have to take the time to locate verification for information they might already know. In other words, one cannot make "swooping" statements without supporting them with a cited reliable source. When researchers publish their work, they often spend a great deal of time finding the sources to document something they might have read years ago. It can be a burdensome process, but it is necessary. The other thing to remember is that anything that is read and utilized in one's own work must properly extend credit to that original source.

Once the basics of knowing how to incorporate others' research into one's own work have been mastered, the actual mechanics of writing the manuscript need to be the focus. Correct writing ultimately rests with the researcher. Not only are there correct ways to spell words and construct sentences, but there are simple little things that can be done to increase the professional quality of the work. By taking the time to incorporate the following "tips," the writing process will be much more enjoyable and successful.

EFFECTIVE WRITING PRACTICES

Strong paragraphs are important. Thinking about the whole written project can be overwhelming, but taking one paragraph at a time is easy. When developing a paragraph, the first sentence should introduce the content of that paragraph, and each following sentence should support the direction or point of the first sentence; when the subject or topic changes, a new paragraph should be started. It is a good idea to make sure that every sentence in the paragraph deals with the primary subject of that paragraph. If words or sentences do not fit the *specific* topic of the paragraph, then place them in a more appropriate paragraph or just eliminate the work that is off topic. This will greatly help the flow and organization of a manuscript.

Avoid First and Second Person

Try to minimize or completely avoid using first and second person (I, we, and you). It is a very hard habit to break, but once accomplished, academic writing will become even stronger and more professional. This means that academic work (research papers, journal articles, and such) should be written in "third person." Providing directions or material in a textbook is often an exception (like this book) because it is used as a writing technique to connect with the reader and makes it easier to read the text. Nonetheless, even these venues could eliminate first- and second-person usage.

In academic work, writing in third person is desired; assume, if majoring in the social sciences, like criminal justice, this is what the professor prefers. One could have a college assignment in which the student is *actually asked* to use first or second person (perhaps in an English class). There are also situations, especially in qualitative work, when first person is warranted. For example, in the theoretical approach called "standpoint epistemology," the writer shares personal experiences from the first-person perspective. In the data collection process of qualitative work, the researcher will typically use the words of the subject as they are stated. If the subject used "I," for example, it would be included as such. Usually, though, in typical academic writing, use of first person should be avoided. The reader of a research paper will know, without having to be told, which are the writer's own thoughts. If any material is not your unique work or thoughts, citations are provided to demonstrate that someone else's work is being borrowed. In other words, in academic writing avoid statements like "I think," "I believe," "I feel," "I would," or "you should," "you are," "you will," "we have, "we are," and so on. Simply state what you think! Unless references are included the reader will know it is your opinion.

Writing in third person can be an especially difficult habit to break for some career professionals such as police officers because they often write police reports in first person. For example, an officer may give his or her account of an investigation ("I asked the witness questions and this is what they said"). Keep in mind that academic writing is different. Using "I" and "you" can actually reduce the professional quality of the work. Even in the example just given, the officer could say, "The witness was questioned; this is what was said." It makes the work even more professional.

Here is another example:

The research topic is prisonization, and someone might say. . . .
"I think that when you enter a prison, you will be really scared."
A more professional way to write would be. . . .
"When a person enters prison, fear is likely."

Notice the elimination of "I" and "you" and the elimination of unnecessary words in the second example. The second example is stronger and more professional, and was a simple correction.

Become watchful for the use of first and second person; once it is identified, rewrite the sentence. All work can be written without using "I," "we," or "you"; it just takes a little practice. Many times when writing in third person, authors turn to *passive voice* in order to avoid the use of first person. The use of passive voice is something that some professors and publishers are keenly aware of and disapprove of, while it is rarely noticed by others. The general rule is to write in ***active voice***. Simply paying more attention to verb usage will help correct problems in this area. Verb tense is discussed later in this chapter.

Active voice: Describes writing tense in academic writing. It is best to write academic manuscripts in active voice.

BECOMING A MORE PROFESSIONAL WRITER

For many students, writing is not their favorite thing to do; however, the task can be much less burdensome by following some basic principles and trying to avoid having a negative attitude about written projects. It is also very important to avoid procrastination, as papers need to be edited. Several versions are typically required in order to eliminate errors.

Manuscript Organization

First, all the sentences need to be logically sequenced and neatly structured, but the overall content of the entire paper also needs to flow logically. A common problem with manuscripts is that they are often "jumpy" and disorganized. By organizing paragraphs to have only one main topic, the overall flow of the paper will be improved.

Here is a personal example. A professor once wrote, "I am getting dizzy just trying to read your paper." It hurt my feelings, but was in fact an accurate description of what I had written. The problem is that I really did not know how to fix it! Many years later, I learned that the "one thought" per paragraph approach is a great way to solve this problem. The first sentence in the paragraph identifies the direction for the inclusion of the other words and sentences in that paragraph. Make sure each additional sentence fits well with the prior one. In other words, later sentences should not follow a totally different "train of thought." When a new "train of thought"/subject is introduced, simply start a new paragraph and do the same over again. A common mistake occurs when the sentences of the paragraph and the research included in that paragraph do not really connect. Some students rapidly select a citation in order to include references in their work, even if the references do not properly fit the focus of the paper. Make sure to demonstrate the relatedness of every inclusion. Also, make sure that everything that is introduced is actually developed. Avoid "leaving the reader hanging," so to speak, which is a common mistake. (By the way, is anyone noticing the usage of *slang* included in quotations?) This is discussed soon.

Headings and subheadings: Organizational tools for structuring a manuscript.

Transition sentences: Can help move the reader's attention from one paragraph to the next.

Headings and subheadings can guide the writer's organization. Headings are a simple way to stay focused because they remind the author of what should be included in what sections. Sometimes **transition sentences** between paragraphs and between subsections can add clarity to the manuscript; however, avoid being too elementary in using transition sentences. In other words, try to avoid simply writing something like "This next section is going to talk about. . . ." *Mildly* leading one paragraph into another is preferable. For example, if one paragraph describes the large caseloads of prosecutors, the last sentence of that paragraph could say something like, "Another agency within the criminal justice system with a typically large caseload is probation." Then, start the next paragraph focusing on the subject of large caseloads of probation officers.

Sentence Structure

Some people assume that the longest or most complex sentence sounds and looks the best. This is not necessarily true, however. The best sentence is a fairly simple one, with the subject, verb, and object in that order. A general rule is to avoid really short sentences or really long ones. For those who do not know all the English grammar rules, it is safer to write *correct* simpler sentences than to risk being wrong. Other professors may disagree with the advice to write in short sentences because it *is* certainly best to know *all* the rules. Nevertheless, many students do not, so keeping to the basics might be a good start until the rules are mastered; in any event, do not neglect the *basics*.

Always start a sentence with a capital letter, include a subject and verb (make sure the *subject and verb are in agreement,* which means a plural subject gets a plural verb, and a singular subject gets a singular verb), and end the sentence with proper punctuation. It is surprising how often students will complete class assignments without even covering these fundamentals. A professor should never have to remind college students to use complete sentences. Even when addressing short answers on exams, writing in complete sentences is preferred.

The best writing *varies its pace*. After a long sentence, or especially after two in a row, use a short sentence to "give the reader a break" (slang again!). If a sentence is longer than two lines or has more than two commas, it is probably too long to be understood easily. Trying to impress the reader with big words or long sentences may actually detract from the clarity. Also avoid adding "flowery" words in an attempt to impress the reader. Sometimes this can actually weaken instead of strengthen the work. In academic writing, just say what is actually meant. Be direct; "save a tree." Avoid detracting from a sentence by adding too many words. Being verbose does not impress the reader, and the point is often lost in all the rhetoric. Also, consider whether one word will substitute for multiple words. There is no need to include extra verbiage in an attempt to sound more intellectual. Short sentences can be powerful. Write strongly and confidently, but avoid doing it by including value-laden statements.

Value-laden terminology is emotionally charged or biased. For example, if a researcher is interested in the harmful effects of snorting bath salts and refers to a person who experiments with these products as "stupid," the researcher has interjected biased wording. Rather than saying that "the stupid person who experiments with snorting bath salts may experience x, y, z," just omit the personal injected word "stupid," and include the citations for the associated side effects of using the synthetic drug.

Value-laden terminology: Terminology that infers judgment, can bias the reader, and should be avoided in research papers.

Sometimes researchers try to add these words to convince the reader of something. A good literature review and presentation of research should do that instead. Let the data "speak for themselves." In the preceding example, the researcher should not say that the potential risks of snorting bath salts are ridiculous but instead could simply list (and reference) what those potential risks are.

It is also important to avoid verbiage that weakens the content. When the writer breaks the habit of using first person, this should help. For example, when writing a paper on house arrest, do not say, "I think maybe sometimes I would give house arrest a shot as an alternative to prison because it could save us taxpayers a bunch of ridiculous bucks and stop wasting my hard-earned cash." Just say, "House arrest is an acceptable alternative to prison that may reduce cost to taxpayers." Then, of course, this statement should be backed up with research.

Notice how it helps the sentence to eliminate first person and weak wording like "maybe" and "sometimes." Flowery "emotion" words do not necessarily add value either. Be aware when emotion words are used, words like "pathetic" or "ridiculous." It is also important to eliminate slang such as the word "bucks."

Using slang is also a common way of weakening the content of the research project. It is important to remember that a student should write more formally than they speak. Often spoken language utilizes slang, informality, and abbreviations. This does not mean writing has to be "highbrow," but it should be professional. Again, by avoiding **slang terminology** in academic work, writers have made some progress. For example, when writing about the legalization of marijuana, use the word *marijuana* and not "blunt," "pot," or "weed." It is surprising how often writers use slang in written work, and most do not even realize it. The best way to correct this habit is

Slang terminology: Words substituted for formal terminology; they should be avoided in academic writing.

to simply state exactly what is meant. If the use of slang is needed for some reason, then put it in quotation marks, as is done frequently in this chapter. Several times in this chapter, for example, colloquial terms are used in an attempt to give a better visualization to help these writing suggestions "stick," and to point out what slang terms are. This would not be a desirable method in research projects and research reports, however. Slang statements, colloquial terms, and clichés are basically the same thing; clichés are often a bit more "cheesy."

There are "loads" of examples of clichés and slang statements (like "cheesy" and "loads"), but some of the common ones are statements like: "throw them in the slammer," "save a tree," "throw the book at them," "open a can of whoop-ass," "flying down the road," "the person was wasted/stoned," and the list goes on.

While in verbal communication, Americans are much more relaxed and often utilize slang, a more professional approach is preferred in academic writing. For example:

Do not write: "throw them in the slammer."
Do write: "put them in jail" or "incarcerate them."
Do not write: "the offender was wasted."
Do write: "the offender was very intoxicated."

There is one exception to this rule. In qualitative work when collected data are being presented, it is very important to state *exactly* what the subject said or wrote, so this is an exception to the just mentioned discussion on substituting a formal word for slang. To maintain the richness of the data, words should not be changed from their original form from a respondents' own words; however, the researcher would want to utilize quotation marks or somehow let the reader know that the verbiage is raw data and not the researcher's contribution.

Writing Style

Another difficult habit to eliminate in formal writing is to avoid using contractions such as "can't" or "won't." They are correct, but they are too informal in professional research manuscripts. Write the words out in full, such as "cannot" or "will not." It may seem strange to do this because most are comfortable with the shorter versions of a word, but contractions do lower the professional quality, especially for academic work. Even though the authors and editors of this chapter are cognitive of avoiding contractions, they still accidently occur; contractions have become a very common form of abbreviations. They are often used in this text to make the readers feel more relaxed and less intimidated by the new material.

While most **abbreviations** should be avoided, it is acceptable to use them when repeatedly referring to a term such as an organization's name, but the text needs to make clear what the letters mean. Give the complete name the first time it is used; after that it can be abbreviated. Here is an example:

The Federal Bureau of Investigation (FBI) is a branch of government responsible for all federal crimes not under the jurisdiction of another federal law enforcement agency (then FBI can be used in the rest of the text after it has been introduced formally).

Also do not start sentences with a **numeric.** In the rare situation that a sentence begins with a number, write out the words and do not use the numeric form. Here is an example:

Do not start a sentence: "33% of the sample support the death penalty."
Do write: "Of those surveyed, 33% support the death penalty." Or . . .
Do write: "Thirty-three percent of those surveyed support the death penalty."

Some style guides recommend avoiding beginning or ending sentences with words such as "however," "though," "for example," or "for instance" (this can be difficult to do!). Also, avoid ending a sentence with a **preposition.** One of the authors of this book remembers learning what a preposition is by memorizing the statement that a preposition is "anywhere a mouse can go"; while there are some exceptions, these are words like "up," "down," "over," "in," "out," and "at."

Here is an example to avoid:

Do not write: "Where is he *at*?"
Do write: "Where is he?"

Abbreviations: Using the first letters of the words in a name instead of the full name. This is acceptable as long as the entire name is spelled out the first time—for example, "Republic of South Africa (RSA)," and then "RSA" for later occurrences of the name.

Numeric: A mathematical symbol, which should be avoided as the first word in a sentence; the number should always be expressed in word form if it is the first word in the sentence. "Ten people played in 10 minutes."

Preposition: Word that typically indicates a location. A preposition should not be used as the last word in a sentence.

Word Choice

As already discussed, a writer should avoid choosing "emotion"-laden words to validate an argument or position in the paper. It is much better to use a neutral tone and let the incorporated data or research (i.e., the references) make the point. In other words, try to make the point with the research and references instead of by using emotionally charged words to influence people's opinions. It is the facts gathered that should do that (if done properly). An English literature or poetry class may encourage students to use expressive or value-laden language to make their writing more descriptive. This is not the norm in academic work. Doing this could suggest bias in research. For example:

Do not write: "It is absolutely pathetic to use meth because it totally fries your brain and you end up dumb as a doorknob." (Note the value-laden words, the slang words, the use of second person, and the unnecessary words.)
Do write: "The use of methamphetamines can lead to addiction and mental deficiency." (This is something that would need to be verified with a reference.)

Also, avoid using the same word redundantly. Writers especially would not want to use the same word twice in one sentence or multiple times in a paragraph. Fortunately, online thesauruses are readily available. To use one, highlight the word, right click, and select an appropriate synonym from the options provided. When "wordsmithing," avoid selecting words just to try to impress the reader. Simply utilize the most appropriate wording.

A good rule is to avoid starting sentences with "that," "this," or "it" (this is a hard habit to "break"). Also, reduce the use of "that" within the sentence. Some writers misuse this word often. Keep in mind these tips: check when the word "that" is used in the sentence, and evaluate whether it can be removed without jeopardizing the meaning. If it can be removed without jeopardizing the sentence, do so. Remember, "that" does not equal "which," "this," "who," "if," or "whom."

Do not write: "Keith Bell is a person that likes cars."
Do write: "Keith Bell is a person who likes cars" (Keith Bell is not an object but a person).
Do not write: "He is unsure that the puzzle is difficult."
Do write: "He is unsure if the puzzle is difficult."

There are words that sound the same but mean entirely different things (e.g., "the *write* way to *right*"—note the inversion of the terms). It is important to pay attention and choose the correct word. The following tips are provided to help distinguish the difference. (More of these and also rules for comma usage can be found in Rozakis, 2000, or any good reference on writing.)

Accept vs. except: I will **accept** any papers, **except** after one week. Think of "ex" as an "exception."
Advise vs. advice: I should **advise** her not to trust my **advice**. Note that one has a "c" in it and think about "calling" someone for advice.

Breath vs. breathe: Take a deep **breath**, and **breathe** deeply. (**Breath** is a noun; **breathe** is an active verb.)
Choose vs. chose: I will **choose** Cody on my team today because I **chose** his sister, Alex, yesterday. Think about double vowels for current or future time. There is only one "o" for the past-tense verb.
Cite vs. sight vs. site: He will **cite** his resources using APA. She gets sick at the **sight** of blood. The building **site** is ready for the construction team.
Effect vs. affect: The storm had a devastating **effect** on the house, but it is not likely to **affect** the scheduled ballgame. (**Effect** is usually used as a noun; **affect** is almost always used as a verb.) Think of **affect** as being "active" (action verb).
Here vs. hear: Hear is what is done with **ears. Here** is a location.
Its vs. It's: The cat chased **its** own tail. This does not mean **it's** a crazy animal. (**It's** = "it is" or "it has"; **its** = possessive.). Recall, however, what was just mentioned about avoiding conjunctions.
Lay vs. lie: A person can **lay** an object down on the table, but a person **lies** down on a bed to go to sleep.
Led vs. lead: I **led** the camp songs yesterday; today it is Kent's turn to **lead** the group.
Lose vs. loose: I do not want to **lose** my pants because my belt is **loose**. (Think of the statement "**loose** as a goose." Notice the double "o.")
Principal vs. principle: The **principal** at my high school had one guiding **principle:** "Do not speak unless spoken to in class." Remember the word "pal" is included in **principal**, which makes us think of person.
Their vs. there vs. they're: The word **there** has "here" in it, which means location. **There** it is. **Their** has an "i" in it—think of it as being connected to an individual. A car hit **their** dog, and **they're** really sad (**their** = possessive; **there** = adverb showing location; **they're** = "they are").
Two vs. to vs. too: Only **two** people have agreed **to** sign up for extra credit. The other research methods professor is offering extra credit **too** ("also" actually works better than **too** in most cases). Just remember the extra "o" on **too** means "in addition," especially if it comes at the end of the sentence.
You're vs. your: You're going to make a good grade on **your** test if you study **your** notes. **You're** = you are; **your** = possession.

There are other words that we often confuse, such as the following:

Between vs. among: "**Between** the two of us, I do not think there are many **among** us who will pass the test." (**Between** is used when discussing only two subjects; **among** is used with at least three subjects.)
Have vs. of: Many people confuse the two.

Examples:

> **Do not write: "She could of completed the punishment."**
> **Do write: "She could have completed the punishment."**
> **Fewer vs. less: "He is carrying fewer burdens because he has less time to think about them." (Use fewer with items that can be counted [burdens].)**
> **Well vs. good: "He sang well. He was a good singer." ("Well" describes how something happened, and it is an adverb, which describes the verb. Good modifies a noun and is an adjective, which describes the noun.)**

The easiest way to double-check which wording is correct (**I** or **me**) is to take out the other person and see which one still makes sense in the sentence.

> **"They moved my sister and me in the fourth grade." Or is it "They moved my sister and I in fourth grade"? Take out "my sister" and ask which one works (They moved me in the fourth grade *or* They moved I in the fourth grade.)**

How about this one:

> **"My friend and me went to the store." *Or* "My friend and I went to the store." Take out "my friend" and ask which one makes sense (Me went to the store *or* I went to the store).**

Finally, another general rule is that the other person always comes *first*. Think of it as being polite, and place yourself last (much like opening the door for someone; you are the last one to enter when being polite). It is not "me and my sister" but "my sister and me."

Misplaced Modifiers

Proper sentence structure is about word ordering. The modifier, which is a word that describes (or modifies) the noun (Gordon, 1993), should come immediately in front of or immediately following the noun that it is describing. Modifiers are misplaced when they are not in the right word order.

> **Do not write: "Walking down the road, the dust got in her eyes."**
> "She" is the one walking down the road, not the dust; therefore, the order is incorrect.
> **Do write: "Walking down the road, she got dust in her eyes."**

> **"Upon getting in the car, the loud music offended Sue."**
> Sue is the one getting in the car (not the loud music).
> **"Upon getting in the car, Sue was offended by the loud music."**

Comma Splices and Run-On Sentences

A comma splice is when only a comma separates two complete clauses (independent sentences), when they should actually be separated by a conjunction, a semicolon, or a period (Rozakis, 2000).

The professor makes students read the chapters students always have to take quizzes on the reading material.
A run-on sentence happens when two independent clauses are not joined by anything.

How to fix:

The professor makes students read the chapters; students always have to take quizzes on the reading material.
The professor makes students read the chapters, and students always have to take quizzes on the material.
The professor makes students read the chapters. Students always have to take quizzes on the reading material.

If a comma is used to join two independent clauses, then a conjunction like "and" needs to join the two, and a comma is provided before the conjunction.

Other Comma Use Issues

It is worth the investment to purchase a writing guide in order to have immediate access to rules at all times. For example, *The Complete Idiot's Guide to Writing Well* (Rozakis, 2000) and *The Complete Idiot's Guide to Grammar and Style* (2003) were used to verify some of the comma splice rules in this chapter.

Use a comma when the information interrupts the flow of the sentence and is not crucial to the sentence structure.

The man in charge, Mr. Ayers, is always happy.
Research Methods, which is normally boring, was exciting this week.
In other words, if the phrase can be removed and the sentence still makes sense, put commas around it.

If someone (or something) is sufficiently introduced, the identifiers after it are considered unnecessary and should be surrounded by commas.

The driver, who is short, received injuries in an auto accident because she sits too close to the steering wheel.

Alternatively, commas would not be included if the introduction is too general.

The child who is short was unharmed in the wreck.

Use a comma to separate a statement from a question.

A person guilty of murder should go to prison, right?

Use a comma when there are two conflicting statements in a sentence.

The police officer was the first to the crime scene, not the media.

Use a comma when connecting items in a series of three or more:

Final exams are required in history, math, research methods, and science.

Some say there is no need for a comma after the next-to-last item; some say a comma should be used. Journals vary on this preference.

Use a comma when the sentence includes introductory words:

This is especially true for words like "since," "however," "once," and "nevertheless."

Once the anthropologist arrived, the officers helped exhume the clandestine grave.
Now that the honeymoon is over, the couple has started to argue.
After the president is elected, he will work on international relations.

Use a comma when two or more clauses are complete sentences and are joined by a conjunction ("for," "but," "or," "and," "nor," "yet," and "so"); consider a comma if the words link two complete sentences.

The offender seems like a nice person, but in reality, he is evil.
His wife divorced him while in prison, so he has no home to return to when released.

Use a comma after or before a direct quote:

"Do not hesitate to ask me questions," the professor told her class.

The offender repeated himself in court, "I am not guilty," but the jury did not believe him.

Use a comma to separate two adjectives if the word "and" could be inserted between them.

Kent is a nice, attractive man.

Note, the word "and" could be inserted, so the comma is substituted in its place. Do not use a comma between the adjectives when the word "and" does not work.

The department bought an expensive search and rescue boat.

We do not say expensive "and" search and rescue boat, so no comma. Note that when two adjectives are used together in a sentence and the first one ends in "ly," a comma will usually follow it.

The district attorney was a lovely, intelligent woman.

This is a hard one because sometimes it is difficult to know if the word ending in "ly" is an adjective. Grammerbook.com provides a tip suggesting one way to test whether an "ly" word is an adjective is to determine if the word can be used alone with the noun; if it can, then use the comma. In other words, if the "ly" word can be used next to the noun, then use a comma. If not, omit the comma.

One cannot read in dimly lit rooms.

"Dimly" cannot be used alone with "rooms" ("One cannot read in dimly rooms"); therefore, omit the comma.

Use a comma when words such as "however," "for instance," "namely," "therefore," or "nevertheless" interrupt the sentence and when such words begin a sentence.

Ironically, the student was rude in class, and therefore, she was asked to leave.
Nevertheless, the grades indicate that the students did not study.

Use a comma to separate the day of the month from the year; however, if any part of the date is omitted, leave out the comma.

His birthday is July 10, 1995.
She met her future husband in June 2008 at the golf course.

WRITING TIP SUMMATION

The right way to write entails more than spelling, grammar, and comma usage. Well-written projects introduce a problem or issue to the reader by establishing some facts in the introductory section that convince the reader of the need for research attention. These are not unsubstantiated, "sweeping" comments but are supported by credible sources; neither are they value-laden words that introduce bias and elementary forms of writing a manuscript. The reason biased wording should be avoided is because a true scientist is objective—letting the research and the data present the facts. The right way to write is about getting the point across in a coherent, organized, and systematic order. A successful research project has a sequence of logical events. Always make sure that the manuscript is organized and reads smoothly. One of the best tools is to read the work out loud. It is strange that sometimes what one thinks one is writing is not what he or she is trying to say at all, and speaking the words out loud can assist greatly in the overall writing process. It is a great tool for proofreading.

One of the biggest mistakes many writers make (or just do not bother to do) is proofread their work. As just mentioned, often what writers think they are saying is not what they actually write. One reason this happens is because when people are in the middle of a project, and have read it many times, they are too close to the work to identify mistakes. It is always a good idea to put the finished project away for a couple of days, then return to it and read it (and read it out loud). During this process, think about what a reviewer or professor would say about the writing. It is also a good idea to have someone else proofread the work. Even the work of the best professional writers is edited multiple times (just remember to number the edited manuscripts when saving the file on the computer so the right version will be used each time, e.g., "Ch. 11(3)" follows "Ch. 11(2)").

This brings up the importance of saving the work periodically and backing it up in several locations. Avoid being one of those victims who learns this habit the hard way. Usually all it takes is losing a report or data one time to learn the importance of periodically saving the work in multiple locations. It is also a good idea to print the manuscript and proofread the actual hard copy. It is easier to observe any mistakes this way. A paper is *never* perfect the first time it is written. Having someone else proofread it is also a great idea.

One reason some people dread having to write is because it is hard to get started for fear of making mistakes. Just remember that no one's work is perfect the first time. If one can learn to be an effective proofreader, then the apprehension about getting started can be minimized. *Just write* a draft and do not worry too much about the errors the first time it is written. Then, with each improved revision, be more meticulous about identifying mistakes. It is most important to *just get started*. Sometimes the writer needs to quickly get his or her thoughts on paper before the idea passes, so do not worry about the technicalities, just write! Also, when conducting research on the chosen topic, ideas will emerge to help direct the research project. This informed knowledge should help give confidence and is one reason that a comprehensive literature review is important. Students who are apprehensive or wait until the last minute to start, or who neglect the important proofreading process, will likely have a deficient product.

Please avoid interpreting some of the suggestions in this chapter as concrete rules (though some are); rather, view them as suggestions from someone who has made many mistakes (some are still likely in this book). Nevertheless, if students understand the basic mechanics of writing, they can alleviate some of their fears, and perhaps the task will not be so burdensome or dreaded. For a quick review of writing tips, refer to Table 11.1.

TABLE 11.1 *Suggested Tips for Writing*

Good researchers find out what has already been done on the subject and include the related and important material in their research.
Avoid plagiarism in all forms; simply paraphrase and then cite.
Provide in-text citations following APA guidelines. Note, the author and date are included in parentheses, and the sentence ends after the citation, not before it.
Almost every paragraph in a literature review should have at least one reference. Make sure each sentence in a paragraph deals with the specific topic of that unit. When the topic changes, start a new paragraph. This will also help with the structure and flow of the entire paper. Make sure each paragraph fits the overall topic of the manuscript. Also, keep paragraphs to appropriate lengths.
It is important to learn the APA guidelines; writing will become easier, research will be better, and grades will likely be reflective.
Make sure that every reference included in the paper is also included in the bibliography.
Avoid slang, avoid abbreviations, use active voice, be direct, avoid rambling, check subject-verb agreement, and group like thoughts together.
Maintain flow and organization.
Before submitting the research paper, double-check the following: • Is every word necessary for the sentence? • Is every sentence necessary for the paragraph? • Is every topic necessary for the paper? • Are there words included that do not add value or are distracting to the meaning of the sentence? If so, remove them.

KEY TERMS

Abbreviations
Active voice
Headings and subheadings
Numeric
Paraphrasing
Plagiarism
Preposition
Publication Manual of the American Psychological Association (APA)
Quoting
Slang terminology
Transition sentences
Value-laden terminology

CRITICAL THINKING EXERCISES

1. Identify at least three forms of plagiarism and provide a discussion on how to prevent it.
2. What does *APA* refer to? Identify how to provide in-text citations following APA guidelines and provide a discussion on why this practice is necessary.
3. If a researcher wants to give his or her opinion on something, how can this be done while still avoiding first-person usage in written manuscripts? Please provide examples. Write three statements that start with "I think . . ." and then rewrite the same sentences in third person.
4. Write an introductory paragraph on the use of incarceration in America. The research question is whether incarceration is used too much or not enough. In your response to this question, include what you think about the issue by saying, "I think," and then give your opinion. Also include value-laden language, slang, and emotionally charged words to convince the reader that your opinion is correct. After completing the paragraph, begin the editing process. Rewrite the paragraph by eliminating first person, value-laden language, slang, and emotionally charged words. Notice how the edited paragraph sounds and looks more professional. If you have made swooping statements, consider locating a reference to back up your point and help validate the position. What kind of outside resource would be beneficial in this situation? Provide an example.
5. Please provide at least five rules for comma usage and write an *original* sentence utilizing each rule.
6. Choose a research topic such as "pedophilia" or "pedophile." Search for research via the World Wide Web, select the first 10 "hits," and then note the author, publication source, and use of referencing format for works cited. Do this for each of the 10 sources of information. Do these sources even have works cited, noted author, or publication information? Now search the same topic using your college or university library. Locate the tool that allows you

to select only "peer-reviewed" journal articles. Repeat the process of noting author, publication source, and use of referencing format for works cited. Be prepared to discuss the difference between simply googling the internet and locating academic rersources through your college/university library (whose fees are paid for as part of your tuition). Which method is best and why? Which referencing style was most common in the academic journals; why? When you find an article that uses APA style, study how others' work is borrowed. Compare it to the APA publication manual for accuracy.

Glossary

Abbreviations: Using the first letters of the words in a name instead of the full name. This is acceptable as long as the entire name is spelled out the first time: Republic of South Africa (RSA) and RSA for later occurrences of the name.

Abstract: Typically a 100- to 200-word summation of the research project that comes at the beginning of the manuscript. A good abstract will explain each major part of the study (e.g., literature review, problem statement, methods, and findings).

Active voice: Active voice (e.g., "present tense") describes verb usage in writing. It is best to write academic manuscripts in active voice.

Alternate-forms reliability: The process of creating variation in the way a concept or item is measured in order to assess the consistency of the measure.

***Publication Manual of the American Psychological Association* (APA):** One common referencing guideline for the social sciences; others include Modern Language Association (MLA) and the American Sociological Association (ASA).

Analysis and reporting: The process of making sense of the research data and reporting the findings to others.

Anonymity: The status of not being identified. Research participants have the right for their identities not to be revealed.

Applied research: A type of research with a specific goal in mind, typically directed at program evaluation or policy analysis.

Association: Statistical test to determine if two or more variables are truly associated. The link between variables can move in the same direction (positive) or opposite directions (negative).

Bar chart: A graph that depicts the data by utilizing individual bars to represent the variables.

Basic research: A type of research driven by the curiosity of the researcher, typically designed to expand knowledge in general, often with no specific goal in mind.

Bell-shaped curve: A normal distribution of data.

Belmont Report: One of the first comprehensive guides and recommendations for protecting subjects of research.

Biased terminology: Words that can influence the research subject in a particular direction.

Bivariate analysis: Demonstrates the relationship between two variables of interest. A researcher would determine, "As one variable changes, does the other variable change with it?"

Causality: Specifying the cause for why things occur. Three criteria must be met to establish a relationship: covariance, temporal sequencing and no additional influencing variables.

Chi-square: A test used when assessing the relationship between variables. It determines whether there is true statistical significance in the association.

Classic experimental design: Designed with random assignment of groups, with measures taken to ensure that the experimental and control groups are similar. The experimental group receives a pretest and posttest and is compared with the control group.

Closed-ended questions: Survey questions that provide the answer options for a respondent to select.

Coding: The process of transforming the attributes of a variable into representative numbers so that statistical analysis can be generated. It also involves giving names and labels to the social constructs (variables) in the study.

Compensatory rivalry: When control group participants learn of potential benefits of the experimental group's "treatment" or stimuli and then alter their own behavior based on that information; they may "compensate" and perform in an atypical manner.

Composite measure: A collection of questions to better measure a research concept (commonly called a scale).

Concomitant variation: A way to say there is a true relationship between variables: as one variable changes so does another.

Confederates: Members of the research group who provide an even richer insight to the topic of study and often assist with aspects of the study.

Confidentiality: The process of knowing the identity of a research subject but keeping it private. It involves taking necessary steps to protect participants' identities from others.

Confounding interactions: When more than one threat to validity interacts with another threat (both occur at the same time); it is not uncommon to have two or more threats in a study.

Construct validity: Determines if the instrument measures the intended concept accurately.

Content analysis: Examines existing books, letters, websites, documents, and other sources of data (e.g., graffiti) in order to identify commonalities or themes.

Content validity: Deals with how well the measure covers the breadth of the concept.

Contingency questions: Questions that should be answered only by those meeting or fulfilling a particular condition or requirement.

Continuous data: Variables that can have a nonspecific (infinite) number of values, meaning the numbers can always be broken down further, for example, possible numbers indicating the weight of marijuana between 120 pounds and 121 pounds (120.1, 120.2, 120.3, etc.).

Control group: The group in an experiment that does not receive any treatment (stimulus) and is compared with the group that does (experimental group).

Convenience sampling: Samples that are chosen simply because subjects are accessible to the researcher. Also called an *accidental sample* because the researcher studies whoever is readily available.

Criterion validity: Utilizes a well-established measure (criterion) to compare to an alternative measure, which together can provide more predictability.

Cronbach's alpha: A statistical procedure to measure the strength of a particular scale or index (e.g., how good is the measure?).

Cross-tabulation: Allows for statistical examination of two or more nominal or ordinal level variables by displaying the distribution of the attributes of one variable by the attributes of another variable.

Cut and paste: A form of plagiarism in which the borrowed work is not properly paraphrased but simply transported from one document to another. Even if the work is cited, this practice still constitutes plagiarism.

Deceiving subjects: The practice of tricking or misleading a subject for the purpose of research.

Deductive reasoning: Logic that begins with a theory and then tests that theory.

Dependent variable (DV)(Y): The variable that the researcher is trying to explain in a research project and is thought to be caused by independent variables.

Descriptive research: "Describe"; method of research focused on describing (counting or documenting) the details of the social issue under consideration.

Diffusion of treatment: Can occur if a respondent learns too much information about the study or experiment and it influences his or her response to the study.

Discrete data: Variables that are limited to a specific (finite) number of cases. They are expressed as whole numbers without decimal places. Number of arrests would be an example (1, 2, 3, 4).

Double-barreled questions: Questions that inadvertently ask two questions in one.

Double-blind experiment: Excludes the participants and the researcher from knowing which groups of respondents belong to the control and which belong to the experimental group; this reduces many threats.

Dramaturgy: A research methodology in which the researcher scripts, or plays a role, based on the subjects' reactions and the research setting.

Ecological fallacy: Making a judgment or assertion about an individual (specific person) based on group data or group-level characteristics (e.g., all professors must be smart).

Epistemology: A branch of philosophy that focuses on understanding how we know what we know.

Ethical standards: Guidelines developed to lead and direct research so that little or no harm occurs to research subjects (and researchers).

Ethnography: Research whereby the data collector immerses him- or herself in the study.

Ethnostatistics: Studies the social phenomenon of statistics as a unit of analysis in its own right. The focus of understanding is on the when, why and how statistics are used as a resource by people and institutions.

Evaluation research: "Evaluate"; a method of research focused on assessing a program, problem, or policy.

Ex post facto hypothesizing: Creating hypotheses to predict relationships after they have already been observed or measured.

Exhaustive: Means every possible answer or response is provided for the respondent to select from.

Exogenous variables: Those factors external to the study that influence the relationship between the variables being examined.

Experimental group: The portion of respondents in the sample who receive the stimulus (treatment) in order to compare with the control group.

Experimental mortality: A research threat when original participants in a study drop out, die, or are otherwise missing from the research before the study is complete.

Experimental design: A research design that assesses the relationship between dependent and independent variables by utilizing a statistical comparison between groups, with one receiving the "experimental intervention" and one not. For true experimental research, the subjects are randomly assigned to these two groups and then compared.

Experimenter expectancy: A threat to research when the researcher makes too much information known to the respondents about the study that can bias or influence the participants' behavior or opinions.

Explanatory research: "Explain"; a method of research focused on explaining *why* the specific social issue or problem exists.

Exploratory research: "Explore"; a method of research used when a problem is not yet clearly defined; involves developing an initial understanding of the issue under consideration.

External validity: The ability of a specific study outcome to be generalizable to a larger population or setting.

Extreme methods: Creative, but often risky, data collection processes.

Factorial designs: Designed to assess more than one treatment or different levels of the same treatment in a single study.

Field research/fieldwork: Observing behavior in its natural environment through direct personal observation by the researcher.

First person statement: Writing or speaking from the research subject's point of view.

Fluid research: A research approach providing flexibility (not viewing the process of research as a set concrete formula) and the ability to adapt to changing circumstance, including taking advantage of new research opportunities that may present themselves during a study.

Focus group interviews: Interviews with small groups in order to explore in greater detail issues or questions raised in the study.

Formal or structured interview: A type of interview that is preplanned, with questions that are structured in advance, and does not allow deviation from set scripts. The exact same questions, in the same order, are asked of all respondents.

Gamma: A test of statistical significance for *ordinal* level variables.

Gatekeeper: A member of the research group who enables the researcher's access to the group of interest.

Google Scholar: An Internet search option providing access to more scholarly work than typical Internet searches.

Halo effect: A threat when a researcher's judgment, opinion, or personal bias about research subjects or the topic influences the outcome of the study.

Hawthorne effect: A label given when respondents know they are being studied and somehow alter their normal or typical behavior or opinion.

Headings and subheadings: Organizational tools for structuring a manuscript.

Hired-hand research: Research conducted by someone *outside* the organization seeking the information but hired directly by that organization.

Histogram: A bar graph showing the frequency of *each* value appearing in the distribution of scores.

Historical research: Attempts to contribute to science by understanding the past.

History: In a research study it is when external events that occur may influence the study findings.

Hypothesis: Is based on an informed, educated guess about the relationship between variables in a study.

Independent variable (IV)(X): What is thought to cause change in an outcome variable. IVs are hypothesized to influence the dependent variable (DV); as the IV increases or decreases, so does the (DV).

Inductive reasoning: Logic that begins with data (a problem) and then tries to develop a theory or explanation.

Informed consent: Informing potential subjects about research participation (benefits and risks) and securing consent before the study begins.

In-house research: Research conducted by someone *within* the organization seeking the information.

Institutional review boards (IRBs): Bureaucracies, often in universities and government agencies, created to oversee that ethical standards are ensured and necessary steps are taken to reduce the risk to research participants.

Instrumentation: A threat to the quality of a study when changes are made to the testing instrument (e.g., between the pretest and posttest).

Intercoder reliability: A research threat when inconsistencies exist in the data collection stage or the data entry stage.

Interitem reliability: The process of measuring concepts/items in multiple ways to help ensure reliability of the measure.

Interlibrary loan: The process of "borrowing" research studies or books that may not be available at one's own university library.

Internal validity: Addresses whether two variables are in fact related. If they are related, then when one variable changes (increases or decreases), so does the other.

Interval level data: Mutually exclusive, exhaustive, rank-ordered data that have a known distance between the numbers; the third level of measurement.

Interview: Interaction between researcher and subject in order to elicit information. Often occurs face-to-face but can be by Skype, videoconference, phone call, or other methods. It is a method of gathering data that is typically more common in qualitative research which allows the researcher and respondent to come together in a conversational setting.

Intraobserver reliability: When two separate researchers at different times observe the same results or behavior.

Inverse relationships: Also called negative relationships; suggest that as one variable increases, the other variable decreases, or alternatively, as one variable decreases, the other variable increases. The relationship between the variables moves in the opposite direction.

Lambda: A test of statistical significance for *nominal* level variables.

Leptokurtic curve: Refers to a skewed distribution where most scores are tightly grouped together-when the data are plotted.

Likert scale: A type of closed-ended question whereby the responses are "rankable," such as: strongly agree, agree, unsure, disagree, and strongly disagree.

Linguistics: The scientific study of language.

Literature review: The process of gathering and evaluating existing research that can help inform research projects.

Maturation: The changes to a respondent (e.g., age, maturity) during the course of a study that can influence the findings.

Mean: Commonly known as the *average*. It is calculated by dividing the sum of the scores by the number of scores.

Measures of central tendency: A typical description of a data set, based on how the numbers compare mathematically to each other including the mean, median, mode, and standard deviation.

Median: The midpoint in a data set. It is the value in the data set that divides the scores into two equal halves.

Mesokurtic curve: Refers to a normal curve when the data are plotted.

Meta analysis: A research approach of combining qualitative and quantitative data from several studies to develop a single conclusion that has greater statistical value.

Mixed methods research: Combines qualitative and quantitative research techniques into one study or a series of studies.

Mode: The number, or numbers, that occurs most often in a data set (and along with frequency and percentages is the only thing that can be presented for nominal level data).

Moderator: A person who leads discussion, often in focus groups.

Mortality: A research threat when original participants in a study drop out, die, or are otherwise missing from the research before the study is complete.

Multistage stratified random sampling: Allows categories in the stratified sample to be further subdivided to ensure equal representation of subjects who otherwise might not be selected for participation.

Multivariate analysis: Involves the statistical testing of multiple variables at one time. It is especially useful for determining causality. It allows for a statistical examination to determine if independent variables influence the dependent variable (that which the researcher is trying to explain).

Mutually exclusive: A particularly important aspect of closed-ended questions whereby the options provided do not overlap with one another; in other words, there is only one correct response.

No harm to participants: Researchers need to take necessary steps to reduce the possibility of harm to their research participants. While harm can come as a direct result of participation in research, the subject should be made aware of the potential risk and knowingly agree to participate in the research event.

Nominal level data: Data that are divided into mutually exclusive, specific (named) groups and are exhaustive (all groups are included); the most basic level of data collection.

Nonprobability sampling: Does not involve processes of random selection when selecting the sample; often used in qualitative studies, or when a random sample is not possible or desired.

Normal bell curve: Based on the normal distribution of the data. If the data are normally distributed, scores will evenly distributed with few high and low scores and most scores in the middle or average range (called a quartile).

Null hypothesis: Is based on the logic that there is *no* relationship between the variables in a study.

Numeric: A mathematical symbol, which should be avoided as the first word in a sentence; the number should always be expressed in word form if it is the first word in the sentence. "Ten men played in 10 minutes."

Nuremberg Code: Evaluated the ethical issues of experiments in World War II and helped develop legal statutes to protect human subjects.

Objectivity: The ability of the researcher to remain "neutral" and avoid allowing any influencing factors to taint the study or the conclusions reached.

One-shot case study: When one group is studied at one point in time after the "intervention" has been given.

Open-ended questions: Survey questions that do not provide predetermined options but that prompt respondents to answer the questions as they wish.

Operationalization (operationalize): The process of taking abstract concepts and converting them into measurable variables.

Oral histories: Precedes other forms of recorded history, using information passed verbally from one generation to the next.

Ordinal level data: Mutually exclusive, exhaustive data that have a rank order, but an exact measurement cannot be taken *between* the data points, the second level of measurement.

Outlier(s): The extreme scores that influence a normal distribution of data (e.g., bell-shaped curve).

Paraphrasing: The proper way to borrow the work of others. The referenced work should be put in the borrowing author's own words and then properly cited.

Participant observation: A form of data collection in qualitative analysis, whereby the researcher comes to better understand the group, the culture or other phenomena of interest by sharing in its activities and participating in related events.

Parsimony: Reducing many possible explanations to the one, or fewest, which make the most sense and are the simplest.

Pearson correlation coefficient: A measure of association between two continuous variables that can tell both the strength and the direction of the linear relationship.

Peer-reviewed article: Research that has been evaluated by selected experts (reviewers) before it is allowed to be published in an academic journal; normally the study authors are not identified, so it is often called a "blind peer-review process."

Pie chart: A graph that depicts the data by representing the percentage breakdown as if they are a piece of pie.

Placebo effect: When a respondent is given a "make-believe" treatment or stimulus and believes the effects are real.

Plagiarism: Involves intentional or unintentional failure to "give credit where credit is due" when utilizing the work of others.

Platykurtic curve: Refers to a flatter curve where the scores are spread out evenly-when the data are plotted.

Positive relationships: Suggest that as one variable increases (or decreases), the other variable moves in the same direction.

Positivism: Knowledge acquired through direct observation or experimental observation.

Positivist: A philosophical approach to knowledge that promotes strict adherence to scientific standards and the avoidance of speculation.

Postmodernism: Promotes the questioning of modern thought and assumptions, noting we should not just assume "fact to be fact."

Postpositivism: A school of thought that values qualitative over quantitative data because it raises doubts about true objectivity being possible in science.

Poststructuralism: Promotes a new set of protocols, not based on positivism, which pertain specifically to qualitative research.

Posttest: Measures the dependent variable *after* the experimental treatment. The pretest and posttest are identical assessments, with one being given before the "intervention" and one given after.

Preposition: Word that typically indicates a location. A preposition should not be used as the last word in a sentence.

Pretest: Measures the dependent variable *before* the experimental treatment is administered.

Probability sampling: Utilizes random selection of the population to help ensure equal chance of representation in the sample.

Purposeful sample: Occurs when subjects are specifically chosen for participation. For example, a researcher may want to study police discretion for a specific group of police officers.

Qualitative research: Provides an *in-depth personal experience* or understanding of social issues in order to contribute to science.

Quantitative research: A method of research focused on large samples and utilizing statistical procedures to assist in making sense of the data collected.

Quasi-experimental design: A research design with the ability to compare a group that receives the treatment (experiment) with one that does not (control); however, there is no random selection to group membership.

Questionnaire: A form of obtaining information (data) by providing a series of questions given to respondents with pen and paper, online, in person, or over the telephone.

Quota sampling: Sampling procedures in which an effort is made to keep selecting participants until a certain quota (representation of specific characteristics) is reached.

Quoting: Used more commonly in qualitative research projects. Otherwise, quoting should be reserved for those rare statements that cannot be paraphrased and still retain the actual meaning. When following APA guidelines, if a quotation is utilized, the page number should be included along with the author and date in the in-text citation.

Random digit dialing: A process of selecting participants for telephone surveys/interviews by generating the numbers at random. Computers can be used to do this.

Randomization: A process to allow "participants" equal chance of representation from the total population to be included in the sample; the sampling process has very specific requirements.

Range: A measure of dispersion indicating the difference between the highest and lowest values in the data set.

Ratio level data: Mutually exclusive, exhaustive, rank-ordered with known distances between data points but also with a *true* zero point; the fourth, or highest, level of data.

Reactivity: When respondents change their behavior because they know they are being studied.

Refereed research: The same as "peer-reviewed." The work is evaluated by reviewers before being published.

Regression analysis: Also referred to as *multivariate analysis*. An analysis that is focused on causality. It is designed to determine whether the values of the dependent variable can be "predicted" by knowing the values of the independent variable(s).

Reify: To treat something abstract as if it were concrete, or to treat something as being real when it is in fact not real.

Reliability: In research methods, the ability to have confidence that similar results, responses, and conclusions would be reached if the study were repeated. It is the ability to consistently reproduce the same results under similar research conditions.

Replication: The practice of duplicating existing studies in order to validate or refute previous research findings.

Research ethics: Principles designed to govern the practices of researchers and to assure accountability.

Response rate: The number of individuals who actually participated in the study out of the total number of participants desired. A researcher would divide the total who actually participated by the total number desired to determine the actual response rate.

Rival causal factors: Determines if all the factors influencing the relationship between independent and dependent variables are considered.

Sample: A subgroup of the total population.

Sampling: A strategy or set of strategies that permit the researcher to select a portion of the total population to be studied, as opposed to studying the entire group.

Sampling error: Occurs when the chosen sample does not exactly represent the total population. It is the amount of difference between the sample selected and the actual population.

Science: a rigorous process used to provide a reliable method or means of knowing things.

Secondary data: Involve research utilizing data that have already been collected by others.

Secondary data analysis: The use of data that have been previously collected.

Selection bias: Occurs in the sampling process when selection to a research group or assignment to research groups, experimental or control, is poorly done and compatibility is lacking.

Semiformal or semistructured interview: Affords some flexibility to explore issues that develop and allows more open, flowing communication but still relies on preconceived questions and areas to explore.

Semiotics: The study of signs and symbols (including words and language) as forms of communicative behavior.

Simple random sample: The most basic probability sample; ensures that everyone in the study population has an equal chance of selection.

Skip patterns: Involve allowing (and directing) respondents to skip a question, or series of questions, if the questions are not applicable to them.

Slang terminology: Words substituted for formal terminology; they should be avoided in academic writing.

Snowball sample: Often occurs when the desired sample characteristics are rare or secretive (often used in deviance studies). The researcher will begin with one participant who meets the characteristics required by the study and then asks the subject to recommend more participants. The sample starts with one, and snowballs from there based on the initial subject identifying more participants.

Social sciences: The study of human behavior, including the fields of criminology, sociology, political science, psychology, and others.

Social Sciences Citation Index (SSCI): A research tool showing how many times particular research has been referenced in the literature.

Solomon four-group design: Is when the study is designed with two experimental and two control groups, and one group receives the pretest and the other does not. Subjects are randomly assigned to the groups, making the study a true experimental design.

Spuriousness: When the relationship between dependent and independent variables is really due to some variable that is not known or accounted for in the study.

Standard deviation: A measure of dispersion showing how the scores relate to the mean.

Standpoint epistemology: Learning about the perspective of another from the unique experience of the actual person(s) being studied: "walk a mile in my shoes."

Static group comparison: When two groups are studied at one point in time; one receives the "intervention," and the other does not. The differences between the groups are then analyzed.

Statistical conclusion validity: The attempt to statistically account for all the variables that could be influencing the variable of interest (dependent variable).

Statistical regression: When statistical outliers move closer to the average response; also known as regression to the mean.

Statistics: The use of mathematical techniques to analyze population characteristics through sampling strategies in an attempt to provide a rational means of understanding the social world based on probabilities. It is basically to tool to help validate research findings.

Stratified random sampling: Divides the population into specific strata or group characteristics and then draws a random sample from each category. This is especially helpful if there is a specific characteristic that might not have an equal chance of being selected otherwise, such as females in leadership roles in law enforcement.

Survey research: A method of collecting data, typically through personal interviews or questionnaires.

Systematic sampling: A method of selecting a sample from the population by using an arbitrary starting point and then following the specific pattern until a sufficient sample is drawn. For example, every Nth subject is selected for participation.

Table of random numbers: A table or chart used to select random samples. Today online random number generators are available to promote randomization in the selection process.

Temporal sequencing/temporal order: One of the fundamental requirements for determining causality; it means the cause must precede the effect.

Testing effect: Typically occurs in pretesting and posttesting studies when the familiarity of the test instrument influences the outcome of the posttest.

Test-retest reliability: Is when two separate researchers generate the same outcome of the same measure—or the same measure produces the same results with multiple testing (e.g., testing instrument).

Theories: Propositions developed to help make sense of reality. The researcher would need to ask, "Are the propositions (logical guesses about reality) testable?" If logical explanations about reality cannot be tested (falsifiable), they are not recognized as true theories.

Third-party research: Research conducted by an *outside* researcher typically not paid by the organization seeking the information.

Time series designs: Research studies conducted over an extended period of time.

Transition sentences: Help move the reader's attention from one paragraph to the next.

Triangulation: Using multiple research methodologies in one study.

***t* Test:** A statistical test used to determine whether the *mean* values between variables or between samples are statistically different from each other.

Two-group posttest-only design: A classic experimental design, but with no pretest given, only the posttest; unlike in the static group design, respondents are randomly assigned to groups.

Type I error: When the null hypothesis that there is no relationship between the variables was erroneously rejected.

Type II error: When the null hypothesis that there is no relationship between the variables should have been rejected but was instead accepted.

Univariate analysis: Provides a statistical summary of each individual variable in the study. Basically, it involves describing one variable at a time in order to illustrate the total variables in the analysis.

Unstructured or informal interview: Interviews that are more free-flowing and not constrained by preconceived questions. Often used with exploratory research.

Validity: In research methods, the ability to measure what is actually intended. Researchers must ask the question, "Am I really measuring what I think I am measuring?"

Value-laden terminology: Words that convey a personal opinion on the part of the researcher, which may sway the respondent's answers. Such terminology should also be avoided in research papers.

Variance: A measure of dispersion indicating the average squared deviations of each case from its mean value.

***Verstehen*:** A German term meaning a deeper understanding of the social world.

Voluntary participation: Means that every participant has the right to refuse to be a part of a research study. Participants must agree to participate.

References

A Research Guide to the Federal Register and the Code of Federal Regulations. Law Librarians' Society of Washington, D.C

Auerbach, C.F. & Silverstein, L.B. (2003). Qualitative data: An introduction to coding and analysis. New York University, New York.

Becker, H. (1963). Outsiders: Studies in the sociology of deviance. The Free Press. New York, NY.

Belmont Report (1979). Ethical Principles and Guidelines for the Protection of Human Subjects of Research (National Commission for the Protection of Human Subjects of Biomedical and Behavioral Research. Washington DC. U.S. Department of Health and Human Services, 1979).

Berman, Steve, (2016). The Media is Spinning a False narrative. *http://theresurgent.com/the-media-is-spinning-a-false-narrative/*

Briggs, L., Sefiha, O., Burgason, K. & Smith, B. (2018). But is it really cheating? Evolving expectations of online academic dishonesty in Brown, S. and Sefhia, O. (2018). Routledge Handbook on Deviance. Routledge, Taylor & Francis Group.

Clark, V. P & Ivankova, N. V. (2016). Mixed Methods Research: A Guide to the Field. Sage, Los Angeles, CA.

Cohen, Nan (2013). The Fear of the Dark. Poetry reading February 26. http://www.slate.com/articles/arts/poem/2013/02/_the_fear_of_the_dark_by_nan_cohen.html

Cohen, S. (1972/2002). Folk devils and moral panics: The creation of Mods and Rockers. Routledge, Taylor and Francis Group. London and New York.

Curry, Leslie & Nunez-Smith, Marcella (2015). Mixed Methods in Health Sciences Research. Los Angeles, CA: Sage.

Department of Health, Education and Welfare (1972). A common thread of service: A historical guide to HEW. DHEW Publication No. (OS) 73–45.

DiClemente, Ralph J., Lanier, M., Horan, P.F., & Lodico, M.* (1991) "Comparison of AIDS Knowledge, Attitudes and Behaviors among Incarcerated Adolescents and a Public School Sample in San Francisco." The American Journal of Public Health, 81, 5, 628–630.

"Dramaturgy." Boundless Sociology Boundless, Retrieved 9 Jun. 2017 from https://www.boundless.com/sociology/textbooks/boundless-sociology-textbook/social-interaction-5/understanding-social-interaction-50/dramaturgy-316-10348/

Durkheim, Emile (1951). Suicide. New York, NY: The Free Press.

Editors. (1976). Editorial: Berkeley's School of Criminology, 1950–1976. Crime and Social Justice 6: 1–3. Copyright © 1976 by Social Justice

Einhorn, C. (2015) A project to turn corpses into compost. New York Times, April 13, 2015.

Gephart, Robert (1988). Ethnostatistics: Qualitative Foundations for Quantitative Research. Newbury Park CA: Sage.

Gubrium, Jaber (1988). Analyzing Field Reality. Newbury Park, CA: Sage.

Hamburger, P. (2005). The new censorship: Institutional Review Boards. University of Chicago, Public Law Working Paper No. 95. Columbia University - Law School. Available at SSRN: https://ssrn.com/abstract=721363 or http://dx.doi.org/10.2139/ssrn.721363

Hatfield E., Bensman, L.; & Rapson, R. (2012). A brief history of social Scientists' attempts to measure passionate love. Journal of Social and Personal Relationships 29(2) 143–164.

Hays, Danica, Wood, C., Dahl, H., & Kirk-Jenkins, A. (2016). Methodological Rigor in Journal of Counseling & Development Qualitative Research Articles: A 15-Year Review. Journal of Counseling and Development, 94, (2): 172–183.

Hinduja, S. & Patchin, J. W. (2015). Bullying Beyond the Schoolyard: Preventing and Responding to Cyber bullying. Thousand Oaks, CA: Sage Publications (Corwin Press). 2nd Edition. ISBN: 1483349934

http://www.industrytap.com/knowledge-doubling-every-12-months-soon-to-be-every-12-hours/3950

https://www.apha.org/~/media/files/pdf/membergroups/ethics_brochure.ashx

Johnson, R. B., & Onwuegbuzie, A. J. (2004). Mixed methods research: A research paradigm whose time has come. Educational Researcher, 33(7), 14–26. DOI: 10.1177/0265407511431055

Jones, J. (1981). Bad blood: The Tuskegee syphilis experiment: A tragedy of race and medicine. New York, NY: Free Press.

Koesterr, R. (2008). Lost person behavior: A search and rescue guide for where to look-for land, air and water. dbS Productions, Charlottesville, Virginia.

Lacey, Hugh (2016). Science, respect for nature, and human well being: Democratic values and the responsibilities of scientists today. Foundations of Science, 21, 1, 51–67.

Lanier M.; Henry S., & M. Anastasai (2015) Essential Criminology. 4th ed. Westview Press.

Lanier, Mark & McKenzie, D. (2017). Multi State Comparison of Human Trafficking. International Organization of Social Sciences and Behavioral Research, New Orleans, LA. March 22.

Lanier, Mark M. (1996) An Evolutionary Typology of Women Police Officers. Women and Criminal Justice, 8, 2, 35–57.

Lanier, Mark M., Pack, R. P. Pack* & T. Akers (2010) Epidemiological Criminology: Drug Use among African American Gang Members. Journal of Correctional Health Care, 16, 1, 6–16.

Loehnert, Stefan (2010). About Statistical Analysis of Qualitative Data. International Journal of Quality, Statistics, and Reliability, vol. 2010 849043.

McKenzie, Daniel (2017). An Analysis of Human Trafficking in Alabama. Masters Thesis. Tuscaloosa, Alabama: University of Alabama.

Nastasi, Bonnie & Hitchcock, J.H. (2016). Mixed Methods Research and Culture-Specific Interventions. Los Angeles: Sage.

National Commission on Aids: Annual Report to the President and the Congress, August 1990. *Forgotten Books*. FB &c Ltd, Dalton House, 60 Windsor Avenue, London

Neuman, W. L. (2011). Social research methods: qualitative and quantitative approaches. 7th edition. Allyn and Bacon: Boston, MA.

Operationalizing Love see DOI: 10.1177/0265407511431055

Patchin, J. W. & Hinduja, S. (2016). Bullying Today: Bullet points and Best Practices. Thousand Oaks, CA: Sage Publications (Corwin Press). ISBN: 978-1-5063-3597-1.

Petersen, D. & Marcello.P. (1972). Criminal life. Englewood Cliffs: Prentice Hall

Plowright, D. (2011). Using mixed methods: Frameworks of an integrated methodology. London: Sage.

Power, L. (2009). University students perceptions of plagiarism. The Journal of Higher Education. 80(6): 643–62.

Publication Manual for the American Psychological Association, 6th Edition. American Psychological Association. Washington, D.C.

Sheehan, N. (1989). A bright shining lie: John Paul Vann and America in Vietnam. New York, Vintage.

Steffensmeier, D. (1986). The fence: In the shadow of two worlds. Rowman and Littlefield. Totowa, New Jersey.

Thomas, W.I. (1923). The unadjusted girl. Boston: Little, Brown and Co.

Urban Death Project https://www.recompose.life

Index

Note: Page references followed by a "*t*" indicate table; "*f*" indicate figure.

abbreviations, defined, 313
abstract, defined, 53
Academy of Criminal Justice Sciences (ACJS), 58
accidental sample, 246
accuracy, 92
accurate data
  qualitative research, 74
  quantitative research, 72–73
ACJS. *See* Academy of Criminal Justice Sciences
active voice, defined, 309
Add Health database, 185
Agnew, Robert, 286–87
alternate-forms reliability, 97
American Psychological Association (APA)
  plagiarism and, 307
  Publication Manual of the American Psychological Association, 305–7
  quoting guidelines, 304
American Public Health Association (APHA), 59
American Society of Criminology (ASC), 58
American Sociological Association (ASA), 305
  ethical standards, 59
  Tearoom Trade study and, 80
analysis. *See also* multivariate analysis; qualitative data analysis; quantitative data analysis; statistical analysis
  bivariate, 52, 254, 260
  coding, 73
  content, 141–46
  defined, 72
  ethics, 72–75
  massaging data, 74–75
  mixed methods, 300–301
  qualitative data, 74–75
  quantitative data, 51, 72–74
  regression, 278–79
  secondary data, 184–87, 229
  univariate, 51–52, 260–66
anonymity, 68–70
  defined, 68
APA. *See* American Psychological Association
APHA. *See* American Public Health Association
applied research, 19–20
  defined, 19
  quantitative research, 204
approximation, 91
area probability sampling, 243
ASA. *See* American Sociological Association
ASC. *See* American Society of Criminology
association, 284
  measures of, 272–76
assumptions
  quantitative data analysis, 253
  theoretical, 34
ATLAS.ti, 299
at-risk populations
  no harm to participants and, 64–65
  research on, 63
Auerbach, Carl F., 161–63
availability sample, 246

Bachman, Ronet D., 126
Baggerly, Keith, 79–80
bar chart, 271
baseline
  data, 73
  measures, 206
basic research, 19–20
Beecher, Henry, 117
bell-shaped curve, 108*f*
  defined, 108
  normal, 268
Belmont Report, 62
Berman, Steve, 213
best approach, 19
best practices of research, 6
Bezuidenhout, Christiaan, 170–75
bias, 29–30, 188
  researcher, 132
  sampling, 247
  selection, 112, 178
biased terminology, defined, 195
biomedical methods, 62
bivariate analysis, 254, 260
  defined, 52
bivariate statistical analysis, 266–67
  defined, 266
BP Deepwater Horizon, 10–11, 10*f*
Brent, John J., 209–10, 224
A Bright Shining Lie (Sheehan), 133
Buxton, Peter, 84

Campbell, Donald, 91, 97
Carnegie Classification, 240–42
  location and, 241
  size and, 241
  type and, 241
Casadevall-Keller, Mary Lou, 4
case studies, 46
  one-shot, 176–78, 176*t*
causality, 260
  concomitant variation, 23–24
  construct of, 289
  criteria of, 23–24
  critique of, 283–86
  defined, 23
  direction of change and, 24
  establishing, 283
  mixed methods research and, 284
  qualitative data analysis and, 282–86

causality (*continued*)
quantitative data analysis and, 283–86
rival causal factors and, 23–24
spuriousness and, 25
temporal sequencing and, 23–24
cause and effect, 254
charts, bar and pie, 271
Child and Young Adult Supplement of the National Longitudinal Study of Youth (NLSY79), 229–30
chi-square, 275
classic experimental design, defined, 179
clean data, 50–51, 72
climate data, 46
clinical trials, 62
closed-ended questions, 47, 193
cluster sample, 243
multistage, 244
Code of Federal Regulations, 63
coding, 49–51, 163–65, 260
defined, 49, 73
intercoder reliability, 97
questionnaire results, 189
of variables, 161
coercion
financial, 67
voluntary participation and, 66–67
Cohen, Stanley, 297–98
community policing, 105–6, 211
compensatory rivalry, 114–15, 180
defined, 114
composite measures, 165–66
defined, 94
of love, 166
conclusion, 52–53
statistical conclusion validity, 98
concomitant variation, 23–24
defined, 24
confederates, defined, 133
confidence intervals, 274–75
confidentiality, 68–70
defined, 69
confounding interactions, defined, 116
construct validity, 118–19
defined, 118
content analysis, 141–46
criminal justice research, 141–45
defined, 141
content validity, defined, 119
contingency questions, defined, 195
continuous data, 258
control group, defined, 46, 169
convenience sample, 246–47
defined, 246
Cook, Thomas, 91, 97
Coombes, Kevin, 79–80
copycat behavior, 215–20
correlation coefficients, 276–77
credible research, 35–36, 38–39
Creswell, John W., 210, 233–24
crime
copycat behavior, 215–20
research challenges, 63
technology and, 9
UCR, 185–86
Criminal Career and Life Course Study, 182
criminal justice research
content analysis, 141–45
ethics and, 58–59
historical analysis in, 140–41
Kansas City Preventive Patrol Experiment, 60, 85–87
mixed methods, 221
organizations, 58–59
criminology research
ethics and, 58–59
organizations, 58–59
criterion validity, 118
Cronbach's alpha, 92
defined, 95
cross-tabulation, 272
Cubellis, Louis J., 211
Curry, Leslie, 298–99
curve
bell-shaped, 108, 108*f*, 268
frequency distributions, 269–70, 269*f*
knowledge doubling, 8*f*
leptokurtic, 169, 269*f*
mesokurtic, 269, 269*f*
normal, 266, 268
platykurtic, 269*f*, 270
skewed, 268–70, 270*f*
cyberbullying, 9
cyberspace, privacy and, 69. *See also* internet

data
accurate, 72–74
baseline, 73
clean, 50–51, 72
climate, 46
continuous, 258
discrete, 258
field research, 127–28
frequency distributions, 270–71
interval level, 259
ISRID, 229
massaging, 74–75
nominal level, 258
ordinal level, 259
participant observation, 297
qualitative research, 74
quantitative research, 72–73, 160
ratio level, 259–60
reduction, 128
secondary, 46, 184–87, 229
self-report, 186–87
sources, 185
standardized, 272–73
UCR, 185–86
data analysis, 51–52, 128. *See also* qualitative data analysis; quantitative data analysis
components, 129*f*
secondary, 184–87
data collection, 49–51
mixed methods research, 223
qualitative research, 17, 128, 152–57
quantitative research, 17, 128
researcher and influencing, 76
deceiving subjects, 70–72
"Deception at Duke" (*60 Minutes* new report), 78–80
deductive reasoning, 4, 12
Department of Health, Education, and Welfare (DHEW), 77
dependent variable (DV), 33, 277
example, 34
descriptive research, 21–25
defined, 22
descriptive statistics, 260–66
deviation from mean, 263–64
DHEW. *See* Department of Health, Education, and Welfare
diffusion of treatment, defined, 114
discipline-specific theory, 30
discrete data, 258
domain names, 39
domestic abuse, 63
double-barreled questions, 194
double-blind experiment, 117

dramaturgy, 148–49
  defined, 148
Duke University study, 78–80
DV. *See* dependent variable

ecological fallacy, 229
Ellsberg, Mary Carroll, 63–65
emotion words, 196
epistemology, 3
  standpoint, 146–48, 308
Erikson, Kai, 71–72
ethical guidelines
  analysis and reporting, 72–75
  anonymity and confidentiality, 68–70
  deceiving subjects, 70–72
  informed consent, 66–68
  no harm to participants, 64–66
  voluntary participation, 66–68
ethically questionable studies
  Duke University, 78–80
  Kansas City Preventive Patrol Experiment, 85–87
  Tearoom Trade, 80–83
  Tuskegee Syphilis Study, 83–85
ethical principles, 58–59
  in Belmont Report, 62
ethical requirements, 58
ethical standards
  APHA, 59
  ASA, 59
  defined, 58
ethics, 48, 56–88
  analysis and reporting, 72–75
  anonymity, 68–70
  confidentiality, 68–70
  criminal justice and criminology, 58–59
  deceiving subjects, 70–72
  defined, 57
  ethically questionable studies, 78–87
  experimental design, 180
  of funded research, 77–78
  guidelines, 64–75
  HRPP, 59–60
  informed consent, 66–68
  IRB, 60–63
  mixed methods, 76
  no harm to participants, 64–66
  qualitative research, 156
  researchers and, 76
  voluntary participation, 66–68
ethnography, 67–68
  confederates, 133
  examples of, 133–34
  extreme methods and, 131
  gatekeeper, 133
  IRB and, 131
  limitations of, 132
  qualitative data analysis, 294–95
  qualitative research, 130–35
  researcher, 131–32
  strategy, 130–31
ethnostatistics, 299
evaluation
  peer review, 154
  program, 220–22
evaluation research, 21–25
  defined, 22
exhaustive, defined, 194
exogenous variable, 33, 169–70
  defined, 98, 170
experience
  human, 18
  personal, 202–3
experiment
  double-blind, 117
  Kansas City Preventive Patrol Experiment, 85–87
  Nazi, 61, 77, 239
experimental design
  classic, 179, 179*t*
  defined, 167
  ethics, 180
  factorial designs, 183–84
  pre-, 175–79
  quasi-, 167
  randomization in, 167–68
  Solomon four-group design, 181
  time series designs, 182
  two-group posttest-only design, 180–81
experimental group, defined, 45–46
experimental mortality, 177
  defined, 113
experimental research, 168–70
  defined, 45
experimenter expectancy, defined, 115
explanatory research, 21–25
  defined, 23
exploratory research, 21–25
  defined, 21
ex post facto hypothesizing, 120
external validity, 97–98, 116–18
  defined, 98
  Hawthorne effect and, 116
  reactivity and, 116
  threats to, 115
extreme methods, defined, 131
Extreme Methods: Innovative Approaches to Social Science Research (Miller, Tewksbury), 131

factorial designs, 183–84
  defined, 184
Family Educational Rights and Privacy Act (FERPA), 59
Fetterman, David, 132
field research, 124–25, 127–29, 156
  data management and, 127–28
  data reduction and, 128
  defined, 45
fieldwork, 127–29
  defined, 127
  researcher, 76
finding research, 35–41
first person statements, 296
fishing around, 73
flexibility
  fluid research and, 90
  of focus group interviews, 135
  of mixed methods, 202
  qualitative research and, 122
fluid research, 5–6
  defined, 28
  flexibility and, 90
  mixed methods, 202
focus group interviews
  benefits of, 135
  defined, 135
  guided interviews, 136
  moderator, 135
  question design, 136
  role play, 136–39
Folger Institute, 141
formal or structured interview, defined, 205
Forrest, Walter, 229–30
frequency distributions, 261–62, 267–77
  correlation coefficients, 276–77
  curves, 269–70, 269*f*
  normal curve, 268
  presentation of data, 270–71
  skewed curve, 268–69, 269–70, 270*f*

funded research, 77–78
Gailey, Jeannine, 69–70
Galileo, 7
gamma, defined, 273
gatekeeper, 133
gathering information, 15–16
Geertz, Clifford, 124
generalizability, 288–89
  of study findings, 98
generalization, defined, 168
Google Trends, 217, 219
grammerbook.com, 319
Greene, Brian, 220–21
grounded theory, 150–51, 163
  defined, 150
gun violence, 182–83

"Haitian Fathers Study," 161–63
Hale, Danna, 244
halo effect, 115
Hamburger, Philip, 87
Hawthorne effect, 116
Hay, Carter, 229–30
headings and subheadings, defined, 310
health. *See also* public health
  APHA, 59
  DHEW, 77
  records, 46
  technology and, 11
Heise, Lori, 63–65
Hells Angels, 71, 149
Hinduja, Sameer, 9
hired-hand research, 20–21
  defined, 20
histogram, 271
historical research
  criminal justice research and, 140–41
  defined, 139
historiography, 139–41
history
  defined, 99
  life history studies, 46
  oral, 139, 294
  quantitative data analysis, 255–56
  of science, 6–9
  validity and, 99
HIV/AIDS, 69–70, 136, 202
homosexuality, Tearoom Trade study, 80–83
how intent is focused, 16
HRPP. *See* Human Research Protection Program
human experience, 18
Human Research Protection Program (HRPP), 59–60
human trafficking, 142–45
Humphreys, Laud, 80–83
Hurricane Katrina, 100–104, 236
  academia's response to, 102
  aftermath, 103–4
HyperRESEARCH, 299
hypotheses, 16, 162
  advantages of, 172
  defined, 32, 170
  ex post facto hypothesizing, 120
  formulating, 170–75
  functions of, 171
  good, characteristics of, 173–74
  null, 32–34
  research, 34
  suitable, 172–73
  testing, 34, 174–75
  types of, 171
hypothesis-generating research, 161, 163
hypothesis-testing research, 161, 163

idolization phenomenon, 218–19
impartiality, 29
independent variable (IV), 33, 278
  example, 34
inductive reasoning, 12
infectious disease, 31, 31*f*
informed consent, 66–68
  defined, 66
  process diagram, 68*f*
in-house research, 20–21
  defined, 20
institutional review board (IRB), 47, 59–63
  approval process, 60–61
  ethnography and, 131
  formation of, 77
  funded research and, 78
  mixed methods research approval, 223
  necessity for, 61–62
  no harm to participants and, 61
  participant protection and, 61–67
  qualitative research and, 61
  rigid research design and, 202
  role of, 76–78, 87
  stratified random sampling, 238–43
  universities and, 238–43
instrumentation, 107–8, 178
  defined, 107
integrity, 90
intercoder reliability, defined, 97
interitem reliability, 97
interlibrary loan, 37
internal validity, 97–98
  defined, 98
  selection bias and, 112
  threats to, 99, 115, 178
International Search and Rescue Incident Data (ISRID), 229
internet
  credible research and, 39–40
  cyberbullying, 9
  domain names, 39
  Google Trends, 217, 219
  grammerbook.com, 319
  peer-reviewed research and, 38
  privacy and, 69
  qualitative research and, 146
  search, 36
  Wikipedia, 39
  Yahoo, subject directory, 38
interpretive understanding. *See verstehen*
interval level data, 259
interval level measure, 259
interval scale measurement, 50
intervening variable, 33
interview, 295–96
  defined, 204
  formal or structured, 205
  semiformal or semistructured, 205
  unstructured or informal, 205–6
intraobserver reliability, 96
inverse statistical relationships, 267
IRB. *See* institutional review board
ISRID. *See* International Search and Rescue Incident Data
IV. *See* independent variable
Ivie, Christine, 142–45

Kansas City Preventive Patrol Experiment, 60, 85–87
Kaufman, Joanne, 185
Keller, Dana K., 4
Kiene, H., 117
Kienle, G. S., 117
knowledge doubling curve, 8*f*
Kranzler, Gerald D., 270
Kraska, Peter B., 131, 209–11, 224

laboratory science methods, 62
lambda, defined, 273
language. *See also* terminology
  MLA, 305
  questionnaires and, 191
  of statistics, 257
  variables and, 93
leptokurtic curve, 269, 269*f*
library
  holdings, 37
  interlibrary loan, 37
  search, 36
  university, 37–38
life history studies, 46
Likert scale, 166, 193
literature review, 28–29, 35, 41–43, 303
  defined, 41
  qualitative research, 42
  quantitative research, 42
litigation, 77
longitudinal panel designs, 187

Manning, Peter, 128, 149
manuscript organization, 309–10
massaging data, 74–75
maturation, 178
  defined, 105
  validity and, 105–6
MAXQDA, 299
MBTI. *See* Myers-Briggs Type Indicator
mean
  defined, 262
  deviation from, 263–64
  regression to, 109–11
measures
  of association, 272–76
  composite, 94, 165–66
measures of central tendency (MOCT), 262–66
  deviation from mean, 263–64
  standard deviation, 265–66
  variability, 263
  variance, 264–65
measuring instrument, 206
median, defined, 263
mesokurtic curve, 269, 269*f*
methodological revolution, 2
methodology, 4, 6. *See also* research design
  selecting, 160
Miller, J. Mitchell, 131, 158
mixed methods analysis
  a priori development, 300–301
  software, 300
mixed methods research, 12–19, 201–26
  approach, critical summary of, 224–25
  benefits of, 207–11
  causality and, 284
  conducting, 212
  constraining factors, 202
  convergent, 300–301
  copycat behavior and, 215–20
  criminal justice, 221
  critics of, 224
  data collection, 223
  defined, 14, 203
  design or strategy, 223
  ethics, 76
  flexibility of, 202
  fluidity, 202
  HRPP and, 59
  illustrations of, 212–20
  interview and, 204–6
  IRB approval, 223
  matrix, 15*t*
  for program evaluation, 220–22
  proponents of, 209–10
  qualitative, 297–99
  research team, 222–23
  steps, 222–24
  weighing decision, 212
MLA. *See* Modern Language Association
MOCT. *See* measures of central tendency
mode, defined, 263
moderator, defined, 135
Modern Language Association (MLA), 305
Morici, Doreen, 136
mortality, 112
  experimental, 113, 177
Moursund, Janet P., 270
multidisciplinary research methods, 2
multistage stratified random sampling, 244–45
multivariate analysis, 260
  defined, 52, 271
  planning process and, importance of, 279
multivariate statistics, 277–79
  regression analysis, 278–79
mutually exclusive, defined, 194
Myers-Briggs Type Indicator (MBTI), 107

National Cancer Institute, 80
National Center for Community Policing, 105–6
National Collegiate Athletic Association (NCAA), 58
National Longitudinal Survey of Youth (NLSY), 187
National Youth Survey (NYS), 187
Nazi experiments, 61, 77, 239
NCAA. *See* National Collegiate Athletic Association
negatively skewed curve, 269
neutrality, in science, 29
Nevins, Joseph, 79–80
Newsome, Sabrina, 227
NGOs. *See* nongovernmental organizations
NLSY. *See* National Longitudinal Survey of Youth
NLSY79. *See* Child and Young Adult Supplement of the National Longitudinal Study of Youth
no harm to participants, 62–66
  defined, 64
  IRB and, 61
nominal level data, 258–59
nominal scale measurement, 49–50
nongovernmental organizations (NGOs), 63
nonprobability sampling, 245–51
  convenience sample, 246–47
  defined, 230
  probability compared with, 231
  purposeful sampling, 248–49
  quota sample, 247–48
  snowball sample and, 249–51
normal bell-shaped curve, 268*f*
  defined, 268
normal curve, 266, 268
null hypothesis
  defined, 32–33
  example, 34
numeric, defined, 313
Nunez-Smith, Marcella, 298–99

Nuremberg Code, 77
NVivo, 163, 299–300
NYS. *See* National Youth Survey

objectivity, 163
  defined, 21, 29
  importance of, 29
  of quantitative research, 203
observation, participant, 296–97
one-group pretest/posttest design, 177, 177*t*
one-shot case study, 176–78, 176*t*
  defined, 176
ontology, 291–93
open-ended questions, 47, 192
  focus group interviews, 136
operationalization, 4, 94, 150, 163–65
  defined, 43, 92
  of variables, 161, 164
operationalize, defined, 165
oral histories, 294
  defined, 139
ordinal level data, 259
ordinal scale measurement, 50
outliers, defined, 108
oversampling, 113, 230

Paoline, Eugene, 207–9
paraphrasing, 304
parsimony, 193
participant observation, 296–97
  data, 297
participants
  deceiving subjects, 70–72
  informed consent, 66–68
  IRB and protection of, 61–67
  no harm to, 62–66
  potential harm, 64–65
  randomly selected, 167
  selecting, 227–28
  voluntary participation, 66–68, 176
  vulnerability of, 67
Pearson correlation coefficient, 276–77
  defined, 276
peer-reviewed article, 36
peer-reviewed research
  defined, 36
  internet and, 38
peer review evaluation, 154, 158
perfect study, 57, 166
personal experience, 202–3
PHS. *See* Public Health Service, U.S.
physical science, 163
pie chart, 271
placebo effect, 117
plagiarism, 48, 75
  APA and, 307
  avoiding, 303–5
  defined, 303
  forms of, 304
  paraphrasing and, 304
  quoting, 304–5
Plano Clark, Vicki L., 210, 223–24
platykurtic curve, 269*f*
  defined, 270
police
  community, 105–6, 211
  Kansas City Preventive Patrol Experiment, 60, 85–87
  National Center for Community Policing, 105–6
  racial profiling, 238
  use of force, 104–5, 207–9
Police Foundation, 85
politics
  program evaluation and, 220–21
  science and, 220–21
  voting trends, 46
Polizzi, David, 282–84, 286–93
population
  at-risk, 63–65
  validity, 117–18
positive statistical relationships, 267
positivism, 4, 6, 204
  qualitative research and, 18
  quantitative research and, 18
postmodernism, 148
posttest, 169
posttest design, 180–81
  one-group, 177
Potti, Anil, 79–80
preexisting questionnaire, 197–98
pre-experimental designs, 175–79
  one-shot case study, 176–78
  static group comparison, 178–79
preposition, defined, 313
pretest, 168
pretest design, one-group, 177
privacy, cyberspace and, 69
probability sampling, 47, 228, 230–45
  area, 243
  cluster sample, 243
  defined, 231
  nonprobability compared with, 231
  randomization, 232–45
program evaluation
  mixed methods research for, 220–22
  politics and, 220–21
program reviews, 34
Prohaska, Ariane, 69–70
psychometrics, 107
Publication Manual of the American Psychological Association (APA), 305–7
public health
  APHA, 59
  Duke University study, 78–80
  Tuskegee Syphilis Study, 61–62, 83–85
Public Health Service, U.S. (PHS), 83
Pulse Night Club shooting, 212–14
Punch, Maurice, 69, 155
purposeful sampling
  defined, 248
  qualitative research and, 249

QDA Miner, 299–300
qualitative data analysis, 128, 129*f*, 282–301
  causality and, 282–86
  characteristics, 287–88
  contemporary, 299–300
  ethnography, 294–95
  first person statements, 296
  forms of, 293
  interviews, 295–96
  mixed methods, 297–99
  oral histories, 294
  participant observation, 296–97
  quantitative compared with, 283, 286–93
  traditional, 293–99
qualitative research, 12–19
  academic, 125
  accurate data, 74
  analysis and reporting, 74–75
  characteristics of, 203–4
  content analysis, 141–46
  data collection, 17, 128, 152–57
  defined, 13, 202
  dramaturgy, 148–49

ethics, 156
ethnography, 130–35
field research, 127–29, 156
flexibility and, 122
focus group interviews, 135–39
grounded theory, 150–51
historical synopsis of, 123–26
historiography, 139–41
internet and, 146
interpretation of, 126
IRB approval and, 61
journals, 298
literature, 15
literature review, 42
methods, 123
modification, 156
oral traditions, 139–41
positivism and, 18
purposeful sampling and, 249
quantitative contrasted with, 13–14, 16–18, 126, 203, 203*t*
questionnaires, 204–5
researcher, 17, 124–25, 155–56
research team, 156
rigor associated with, 298
semiotics, 149–50
social sciences and application of, 125
software program, 299–300
standpoint epistemology, 146–48
strategies, 122–58
subjectivity of, 203
tools, 126
triangulation, 151
types, 129–51
validity and, 122, 202
voluntary participation in, 67–68
quantitative data analysis, 253–81
assumptions, 253
basic, 255–60
bivariate statistical analysis, 266–67
causality and, 283–86
characteristics, 287–88
correlation coefficients, 276–77
elementary, 253
frequency distributions, 267–77
history, 255–56
intermediate, 266
levels of measurement, 258–59
measures of association, 272–76
multivariate statistics, 277–79
order of operations, 256–57
qualitative compared with, 283, 286–93
symbolic representations, 257–58
tests of statistical significance, 272–76
quantitative research, 12–19
accurate data, 72–73
analysis and reporting, 51, 72–74
applied research, 204
characteristics of, 203–4
data, 72–73, 160
data collection, 17, 128
defined, 12, 202
focus on, 161–62
literature review, 42
objectivity of, 203
positivism and, 18, 204
qualitative contrasted with, 13–14, 16–18, 126, 203, 203*t*
questionnaires, 204
reliability and, 122
replication, 291
researchers, 17
social sciences and, 160
statistical analysis and, 202
quasi-experimental design, 167
questionnaire, 16
coding of results, 189
defined, 190
deploying, 198
disadvantages, 191
language and, 191
preexisting, 197–98
qualitative research, 204–5
quantitative research, 204
questions and associated problems, 192–99
response rate, 191
results, 189, 193
questions
closed-ended, 193
contingency, 195
creating survey, 197
double-barreled, 194
exhaustive, 194
open-ended, 47, 136, 192
questionnaire, 192–99
research, 32–35
specificity of, 198
survey research, 192–99
Quetelet, Adolphe, 255
Quirkos, 299
quota sampling, 247–48
defined, 247
quoting, 304–5
defined, 304

racial profiling, 238
random digit dialing, 236–37
defined, 236
randomization, 232–45
defined, 232
in experimental design, 167–68
random digit dialing, 236–37
sample selection, 234
simple random sample, 235
steps to, 232
stratified random sampling, 237–39, 243–44
table of random numbers, 233
range, 263
ratio level data, 259–60
reactivity
defined, 116
placebo effect and, 117
reasoning
deductive, 4, 12
inductive, 12
recidivism, 277–78
record studies, 46
refereed research, 36
regression, statistical, 108–11
regression analysis, 278–79
defined, 278
regression to mean, 109–11
reify, 119–20
defined, 119
reliability, 89–121
alternate-forms, 97
ascertaining, 107
defined, 44, 94
determining, 96–97
intercoder, 97
interitem, 97
intraobserver, 96
quantitative research and, 122
test-retest, 96
validity and, 91–97, 96*f*
religion, 7–8, 194
replication, 75, 80
defined, 30
quantitative research, 291

reporting
  coding, 73
  defined, 72
  massaging data, 74–75
  qualitative data, 74–75
  quantitative data, 51, 72–74
  results, 52
  self-report data, 186–87
representative sample, 228, 236
research
  basic, 19–20
  best practices, 6
  finding, 35–41
  hypothesis, 34
  problem, example of, 33
  process, 28
  stages, 27–55
research design, 43–48, 159–200
  choosing, 166–68
  composite measures, 165–66
  experimental, 167, 179–84
  experimental research, 168–70
  mixed methods, 223
  one-group pretest/posttest design, 177
  operationalization and coding, 163–65
  pre-experimental, 175–79
  quasi-experimental, 167
  rigid, 202
  scenario methodology, 187–89
  secondary data analysis, 184–87
  types, 45–47
researcher
  bias, 132
  data collection influenced by, 76
  ethical behavior by, 61
  ethics and, 76
  ethnography, 131–32
  fieldwork, 76
  harm to, 65–66
  moral and ethical obligations, 63
  personality of, 152
  qualitative research, 17, 124–25, 155–56
  quantitative research, 17
  role play, 136–39
  writing, 302–23
research question, 32–35, 160
  example of, 33–34
research team
  mixed methods, 222–23
  qualitative, 156
research topic, 160, 303
  narrow, 32
  selecting, 28–32
response rate, 247
  defined, 47
  questionnaire, 191
results
  questionnaire, 189, 193
  reporting, 52
rival causal factors
  defined, 24
  elimination of, 23–24
rivalry, compensatory, 114–15, 180
role play, 136–39
Rosendale Fund, 83
routine activities theory, 9

sample, 47–48
  accidental, 246
  availability, 246
  cluster, 243–44
  convenience, 246–47
  defined, 47
  methods, 48*f*
  representative, 228, 236
  selection, randomization, 234
  simple random, 235
  snowball, 249–51
sampling
  bias, 247
  convenience, 246–47
  defined, 228
  frame, 230
  nonprobability, 230, 245–51
  oversampling, 113, 230
  probability, 228, 230–45
  purposeful, 248–49
  quota, 247–48
  stratified random, 237–39, 243–44
  systematic, 240, 245
sampling error, 236
  defined, 229
sampling strategies, 227–52
  best, 251
  nonprobability sampling, 245–51
  probability sampling, 230–45
SAS. *See* Statistical Analytics Software
scale, 94, 166, 206
  accuracy, 92
  measurements, 49–50
scattergrams, 271
scenario methodology, 187–89
  disadvantages, 188–89
school shootings, 215–20
  idolization phenomenon, 218–19
Schutt, Russell K., 125–26
science. *See also* social sciences
  acquiring and validating knowledge through, 3–4
  consequences of, 10–11
  defined, 9
  history of, 6–9
  neutrality in, 29
  physical, 163
  politics and, 220–21
  religion and, 7–8
  research, 3
  technology and, 9
  theories and, 32
  values in, 29
scientific method, 18
  theories in, 32
secondary data, 185
  defined, 46
  self-report data, 186–87
secondary data analysis, 184–87, 229
  defined, 184
selection bias, 112, 178
self-report data, 186–87
semiformal or semistructured interview, 205
semiotics, 149–50
  defined, 149
sentence structure, writing and, 310–12
September 11 terrorist attacks, 132
Sheehan, Neal, 133
significance
  levels, 275–76
  tests of statistical, 272–76
Silverstein, Louise B., 161–63
simple interrupted time series design, 182*t*
simple random sample, 235
skewed curve, 268–70, 270*f*
  negatively, 269
skip patterns, 195
slang terminology, 196, 311–12
  defined, 311

SNA. *See* social network analysis; Social Network Analysis
snowball sample, 249–51
Social Network Analysis (SNA), 214–16
social problems
 interconnectedness of, 2
 as social construct, 298
Social Science Citation Index (SSCI), 41
social sciences
 literature, 38
 qualitative research applied to, 125
 quantitative research and, 160
 questionnaires and, 190
 referencing guidelines for, 305
 research methods in, 2, 8
 statistics and, 285
software
 mixed methods analysis, 300
 qualitative research, 299–300
 SAS, 299
Solomon four-group design, 181
SPSS. *See* Statistical Package for the Social Sciences
spuriousness, 284
 defined, 25
SSCI. *See* Social Science Citation Index
standard deviation, 265–66
 defined, 265
standardized data, 272–73
standpoint epistemology, 146–48, 308
 defined, 146
Stand Point Theory, 296
Stanley, Julian, 97
static group comparison, 177–79, 178*t*
 defined, 178
statistical analysis. *See also* regression analysis
 bivariate, 266–67
 packages, 17
 quantitative research and, 202
Statistical Analytics Software (SAS), 299
statistical conclusion validity, 98
Statistical Package for the Social Sciences (SPSS), 73, 299
statistical regression, 108–9
 defined, 108
 problem of, 110–11
statistics, 17, 255–56
 chi-square, 275
 defined, 255
 language of, 257
 order of operations, 256–57
 social sciences and, 285
 symbolic representations, 257–58
 tests of statistical significance, 272–76
 t test, 274
Steffensmeier, Darrell, 295
stratified random sampling
 Carnegie Classification, 240–42
 defined, 237
 IRBs and universities, 238–43
 multistage, 244–45
studies
 case, 46, 176–78
 Duke University, 78–80
 ethically questionable, 78–87
 generalizable findings, 98
 Kansas City Preventive Patrol Experiment, 85–87
 life history, 46
 NLSY79, 229–30
 perfect, quest for, 57
 record, 46
 Tearoom Trade, 80–83
 Tuskegee Syphilis Study, 61–62, 83–85
subjectivity, 203
survey research, 14, 159–200
 defined, 46, 189
 questionnaires, 190–92
 questions and associated problems, 192–99
 themes, 206–7
syphilis, 84
systematic sampling, 240, 245

table of random numbers, 233–34, 234*t*
 defined, 233
The Tao of Research (Keller, Casadevall-Keller), 4
Tearoom Trade study, 80–83
technology
 crime and, 9
 health and, 11
 science and, 9
temporal order, 284
temporal sequencing, 23–24
 defined, 24
terminology
 abbreviations, 313
 biased, 195
 slang, 196, 311–12
 value-laden, 196, 311, 313–14
Terrill, William, 207–9
testing effect, 106–7, 180
 defined, 106
test-retest reliability, 96
tests of statistical significance, 272–76
 chi-square, 275
 t test, 274–75
Tewksbury, Richard, 123, 124, 158
 on content analysis, 142
 Extreme Methods: Innovative Approaches to Social Science Research, 131
theoretical assumption, 34
theory
 credible, 31
 defined, 30
 discipline-specific, 30
 grounded, 150–51, 163
 routine activities, 9
 science and, 32
 Stand Point Theory, 296
 verified, 31–32
thick description, 124, 285
third-party research, 20–21
 defined, 20
Thomas, W. I., 285
Thompson, Hunter S., 71, 149
threats
 defined, 90
 to external validity, 115
 to internal validity, 99, 115, 178
 validity, 99, 104–16
time series designs, 182
Toward a Unified Criminology: Integrating Assumptions about Crime, People, and Society (Agnew), 286–87
transition sentences, defined, 310
triangulation, defined, 151
true zero point, 259–60
t test, 274–75
Turabian Reference Guide, 305
Tuskegee Institute, 83
Tuskegee Syphilis Study, 61–62, 83–85

two-group posttest-only design, 180–81
  defined, 181
type I error, 275–76
  defined, 275
type II error, 275–76
  defined, 275

UCR. *See* Uniform Crime Report
unfunded research, 77
Uniform Crime Report (UCR), 185–86
univariate analysis, 260–66
  defined, 51–52
universities
  Duke University study, 78–80
  FERPA guidelines, 59
  funded research, 77–78
  libraries, 37–38
unstructured or informal interview, 205–6
  defined, 205

validity, 89–121
  ascertaining, 107
  construct, 118–19
  content, 119
  criterion, 118
  defined, 44, 91
  external, 97–98, 116–18
  history and, 99
  instrumentation and, 107–8
  internal, 97–98, 112, 115, 178
  maturation and, 105–6
  of placebo effects, 117
  population, 117–18
  qualitative research and, 122, 202
  randomization and, 167–68
  reliability and, 91–97, 96*f*
  selection bias and, 112
  statistical conclusion, 98
  statistical regression and, 108–9
  testing effect and, 106–7
  threats, specific, 99, 104–16
  types, 97–119
value-laden terminology, 313–14
  defined, 196, 311
values, in science, 29
variability, 263
variables
  coding of, 161
  exogenous, 33, 98, 170
  intervening, 33
  IV, 33–34, 278
  language and, 93
  level of measurement of, 49–50
  operationalization of, 161, 164
variance, 264–65
  defined, 265
verstehen (interpretive understanding), 123–24
  defined, 123
Vietnam War, 152–53
voluntary participation, 176
  coercion and, 66–67
  defined, 66
  in qualitative research, 67–68
voting trends, 46

Weber, Max, 61, 123
Werther effect, 215
Wikipedia, 39
writing, 302–23
  active voice, 309
  comma splices and run-on sentences, 317
  comma use issues, 317–19
  effective practices, 307–9
  first and second person, 307–9
  headings and subheadings, 310
  in-text citing, 306
  manuscript organization and, 309–10
  misplaced modifiers, 316
  paragraphs, 305, 307
  plagiarism, 48, 75, 303–5, 307
  professional, 309–19
  proofreading, 320
  Publication Manual of the American Psychological Association, 305–7
  saving work, 320
  sentence structure and, 310–12
  style, 312–13
  third person, 308
  tips, summation of, 320–21, 321*t*
  word choice, 313–16
  word meanings, 314–16

Yahoo, subject directory, 38

CPSIA information can be obtained
at www.ICGtesting.com
Printed in the USA
BVHW060609090922
646599BV00001B/2